Walter Ruttmann and th

Walter Ruttmann and the Cinema of Multiplicity

Avant-Garde – Advertising – Modernity

Michael Cowan

Amsterdam University Press

Cover illustration: Stills from Ruttmann. Above: SPIEL DER WELLEN (1925); below: DEUTSCHE WAFFENSCHMIEDEN (1940)

Cover design: Kok Korpershoek, Amsterdam
Lay-out: JAPES, Amsterdam

Amsterdam University Press English-language titles are distributed in the US and Canada by the University of Chicago Press.

ISBN 978 90 8964 585 2
e-ISBN 978 90 4852 189 0 (pdf)
e-ISBN 978 90 4852 190 6 (ePub)
NUR 670

Acknowledgments

My first thanks here goes out to Thomas Elsaesser for supporting this project and helping it to find a home in the "Film Culture in Transition" series at Amsterdam University Press. I could hardly think of better intellectual company for this book. Both Elsaesser and Malte Hagener have inspired and shaped my thinking on the avant-garde, sponsored film and Ruttmann, and I thank them both for their feedback and for opening intellectual doors for me and many others. At Amsterdam, I would also like to thank my editors Chantal Nicolaes and Jeroen Sondervan for their guidance and professionality, as well as the manuscript evaluators, whose thoughtful feedback certainly helped this to become a better text.

While working on this project over the past several years, I have drawn intellectual sustenance from an amazing group of scholars in Montreal. I am particularly grateful to Charles Acland, Eugenio Bolongaro, Luca Caminati, Philippe Despoix, Nicholas Dew, Victor Fan, Marion Froger, Yuriko Furuhata, André Habib, Lynn Kozak, Thomas Lamarre, Martin Lefebvre, Silvestra Mariniello, Rosanna Maule, Derek Nystrom, Ara Osterweil, Viva Paci, Elena Razlogova, Katie Russell, Masha Salazkina, Ned Schantz, Hélène Sicard, Yumna Siddiqi, Marc Steinberg, Will Straw, Alanna Thain, Haidee Wasson and William Wees. These colleagues have provided a steady font of support, while also consistently inspiring me to push further and think more deeply. I know how lucky I am to work among them. In Montreal, I would also like to send a special thanks to my research assistant Pete Schweppe, whose sharp eyes have been responsible for many finds discussed here.

Beyond Montreal, I am indebted to a number of scholars who have listened to, read and/or commented on various aspects of this project over the past several years. These include Mark Andersen, Stefan Andriopoulos, Nicholas Baer, Tim Bergfelder, Janelle Blankenship, Cornelius Borck, Erica Carter, Lucie Cesálková, Sema Colpan, Robin Curtis, Scott Curtis, Edward Dimendberg, Paul Dobryden, Noam Elcott, Karin Fest, Mary Francis, Laurent Guido, Tom Gunning, Malte Hagener, Markus Hallensleben, Karin Harasser, Vinzenz Hediger, Andreas Huyssen, Brian Jacobsen, Tony Kaes, Andreas Killen, Trond Lundemo, Siegfried Mattl, Rob McFarland, Arndt Niebisch, Lydia N'Siah, Sabrina Rahman, Joachim Schätz, Thomas Schlich, Werner Schwarz, Kai Sicks, Gabe Trop,

Johannes von Moltke, Jeffrey Winthrop Young, Joshua Yumibe, Yvonne Zimmermann, Michael Zrya.

Finally, I wish to acknowledge several scholars – in particular Jeanpaul Goergen and Leonardo Quaresima, but also Barry Fulks, Martin Loiperdinger, Irmbert Schenk, William Uricchio and Peter Zimmermann – whose archival work on Ruttmann and the avant-garde has laid the groundwork for subsequent research. Whatever intellectual debates this book might engage in, it is written with a deep appreciation of previous work in the field and a humble awareness that mine is hardly the last word.

Books also require material support, and this one has benefited from generous grants from the Social Science and Humanities Research Council of Canada (SSHRC) and the Fonds québécois de recherche sur la société et la culture (FQRSC). The research for this book also relied fundamentally on the infrastructure of the Moving Image Research Laboratory (MIRL) at McGill University, which was made possible by a generous grant from the Canadian Foundation for Innovation (CFI). Material support also means access to archives – an absolutely essential factor in this project, since so many of Ruttmann's films are still unavailable for public viewing. I am especially grateful to Jutta Albert, Ute Klawitter and Carola Okrug at the Filmarchiv-Bundesarchiv; Gerrit Thies and Julia Riedel at the Deutsche Kinemathek; and Monique Faulhaber at the Cinémathèque Française.

Earlier versions of chapters 1 and 2 were published in *Cinema Journal* and *New German Critique* respectively.

Contents

Introduction: Avant-Garde, Advertising and the Managing of Multiplicity

One would be hard pressed to think of a figure as ambivalent for Weimar film studies as Walter Ruttmann. On the one hand, Ruttmann figures in countless articles, book chapters and course syllabi as a major innovator of experimental film and a key representative of Weimar modernism. His abstract Opus films (Opus I-IV, 1921-1925), which held pride of place in the famous film screening of "absolute film" in Berlin in 1925, have been celebrated by critics from the 1920s to the present as pioneering works in avant-garde form and milestones in the history of animation.[1] Similarly, Ruttmann's urban portrait Berlin. Die Sinfonie der Grossstadt (Berlin. Symphony of a Great City, 1927) – the film that secured his international fame in the 1920s – has long counted as a defining work of early documentary,[2] a towering statement on Weimar modernity and the quintessential representation of urban modernism in the interwar period.[3] Ruttmann's experimental style has influenced subsequent filmmakers from Oskar Fischinger to Len Lye and beyond, and his city film has spawned numerous imitations and "remakes," both then and now.[4] Indeed, Ruttmann's importance as a pioneer in experimental moving image art is only growing in our current digital media climate as scholars search for origins and precursors to the proliferation of experimental, non-narrative forms.[5] But there is also another side to Ruttmann as the "one who stayed." Unlike many of his contemporaries such as Hans Richter and Fritz Lang, Ruttmann went on, after the seizure of power by the National Socialists, to make some eighteen films for the new regime – and nineteen "fascist" films if one counts his Italian film Acciaio (Steel, 1933) – between 1933 and 1941. Although once largely ignored and still unavailable for viewing outside of archives, this segment of Ruttmann's filmmaking career has garnered increasing interest since the 1980s, particularly in Germany, where scholars have devoted extensive attention to Ruttmann's post-1933 work for German steel companies, Nazi ministries, weapons manufacturers and other agencies.[6]

The ambivalence surrounding Ruttmann's career – and its difficult fit within traditional narratives of the avant-garde – might help to explain the relative dearth of attention to these commissioned films in English-language scholarship, which has focused almost entirely on the Opus films and the Berlin documentary. Indeed, given Ruttmann's importance for Weimar modernism alone,

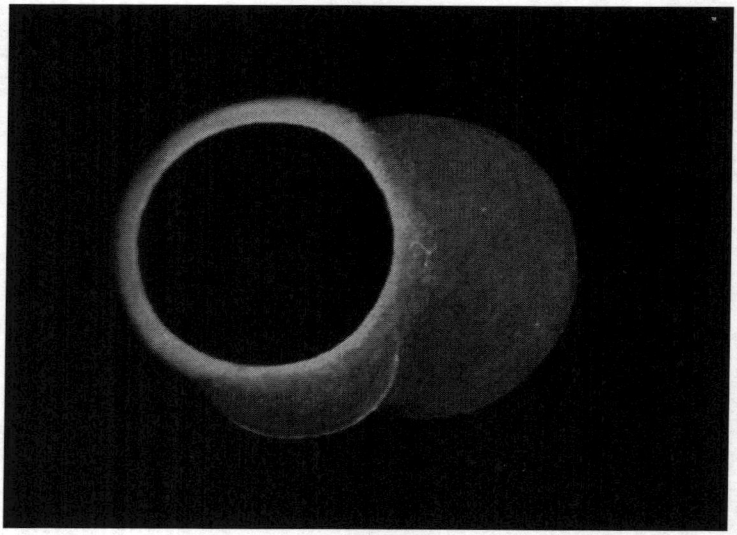

Still from Walter Ruttmann, LICHTSPIEL OPUS I *(1921)*

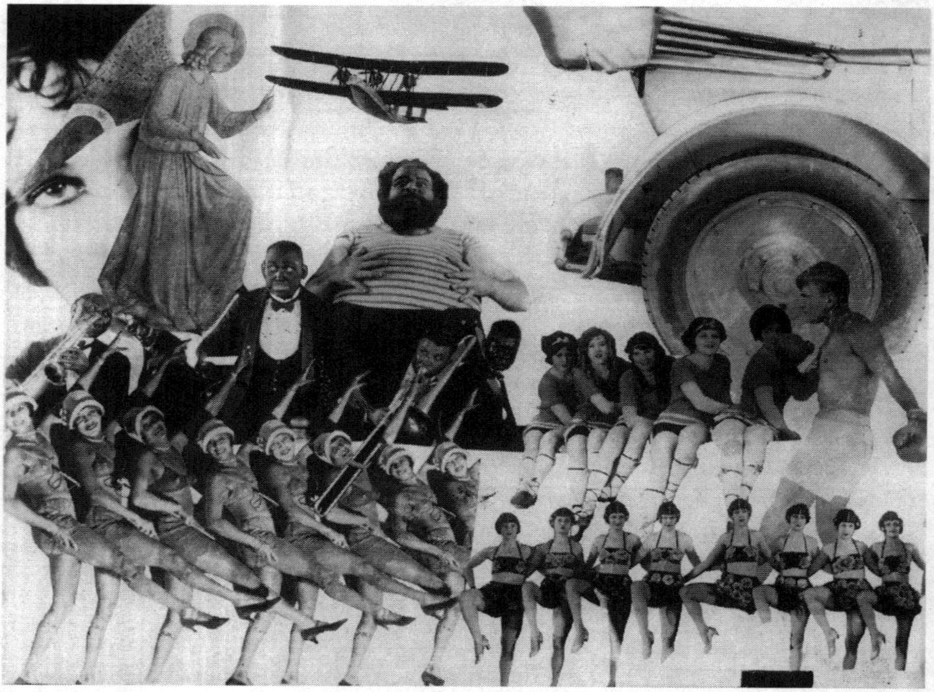

Advertisement for BERLIN. DIE SINFONIE DER GROSSSTADT *(1927)*

it is astounding that – unlike the cases of mainstream directors such as Fritz Lang, F. W. Murnau and G. W. Pabst, or experimental directors such as Oskar Fischinger, Lotte Reiniger and Hans Richter – he has *never* been the object of a book-length study in English.[7] To date, three books have been published on Ruttmann: Adrianus van Domburg's monograph *Walter Ruttmann in het beginsel* (1956), Jeanpaul Goergen's sourcebook *Walter Ruttmann. Eine Dokumentation* (1989) and a second sourcebook by Leonardo Quaresima entitled *Walter Ruttmann. Cinema, pittura, ars acustica* (1994).[8] While Van Domburg's study still presented Ruttmann principally as a paragon of artistic modernism, the more recent volumes by Goergen and Quaresima, both of which include scholarly essay collections, reflect the ambivalence described above in their examinations of Ruttmann both as a central figure of the interwar avant-garde and as a collaborator in National Socialist propaganda.[9]

As the first English-language book to examine Ruttmann's work both before and after 1933, the present study takes into account both of these phases – and "faces" – of Ruttmann, but I also want to propose a different approach to his filmmaking. For all of the rediscovery of Ruttmann's fascist films in recent years, scholars have continued to be informed by presuppositions stemming from the vision of Ruttmann as a high modernist. As a result, scholarship on Ruttmann's post-1933 work has been largely preoccupied with what might be called the "Mephisto" question. How could an avant-garde artist of Ruttmann stature – a paragon of "absolute film" who participated in left-wing groups such as the Volksverband für Filmkunst (People's Association for Film Art) and played a major role in the famous Congress of Independent Film of 1929 alongside Sergei Eisenstein, Béla Balázs and Alberto Cavalcanti[10] – so readily collaborate with a totalitarian regime?[11] Scholars have come down on various sides of this question. While some critics have seen Ruttmann's work under fascism as a compromise that allowed him to continue practicing a progressive modernism in an inhospitable climate, or even to subvert the ideological project of Nazism,[12] others – building upon the well-known critique of Ruttmann by Siegfried Kracauer – have interpreted his post-1933 work as the development of a fascist aesthetic, a reactionary modernism or (to invoke an oft-cited term from Barry Fulks) a "Nazi Sachlichkeit" already portended in the rigid formalism of his "new objective" films such as BERLIN.[13] What these positions share is the assumption that we should approach Ruttmann first and foremost as an *auteur*: a high modernist filmmaker, painter and musician whose work situated itself within an international avant-garde scene.[14] This assumption is certainly not wrong. Ruttmann did study the high arts of architecture and music before becoming a painter and ultimately a filmmaker; he did take part in the debates concerning the status of film as an "art";[15] he did consider his early abstract films forms of "visual music" (and accompanied screenings of OPUS I himself on the cello); and he did stand in dialogue – in some cases in rivalry – with international experimental filmmakers such as Eisenstein, Abel Gance and Dziga Vertov. But there was also another aspect to Ruttmann's career altogether, one present already in the Weimar years and visible in his copious body of work – only now coming to light – in advertising and other commissioned forms. Indeed, as Thomas Elsaesser and Malte Hagener point out, Ruttmann's strictly "independent" work was, in purely quantitative terms, a marginal phenomenon. The vast majority of his films consisted, rather, in commissions from private and state agencies: from product manufacturers, shipping companies, public service groups, professional associations, film companies, government offices, medical associations and others. Such commissions account for well over half of Ruttmann's Weimar output, including some of his earliest work and even the quota film BERLIN, SINFONIE.[16] And they account for all of his films after 1933.

Viewed through the lens of traditional auteurist film studies, one might be tempted to see this work in advertising as a compromise, a means of securing funding for his more "serious" experiments or a set of necessary constraints under which Ruttmann could – like later filmmakers such as Peter Kubelka – practice the genuine art of experimental aesthetics. But such an assumption is problematic on several accounts. To begin with, this would be a "compromise" that nearly all of the Weimar avant-garde participated in; from Hans Richter to Lotte Reiniger, from Guido Seeber to Oskar Fischinger, most German avant-garde filmmakers worked in advertising and related forms of commissioned filmmaking. Although these filmmakers followed various trajectories after the seizure of power by the Nazis – some leaving Germany for good, some leaving and coming back, and some staying on – *all* of them made "sponsored" films both before and after 1933.[17] Indeed, such work in sponsored film characterized a good portion of the filmic avant-garde both within and outside of Germany, encompassing filmmakers such as Joris Ivens, Len Lye, Dziga Vertov, Sergei Eisenstein, René Clair and many others.[18] Rather than downplaying this activity as somehow antithetical to the spirit and mission of the avant-garde and its artistic experiments, we might rather attempt to rethink – as Hagener has done – interwar avant-garde film culture as a sphere that could unite multiple and often contradictory identities, projects and aesthetic programs.[19] While some currents could emphasize the opposition of aesthetics to the instrumental logic of capitalist modernity, others – in particular the constructivist currents prevalent in Russia and Germany – understood the practical implementation of avant-garde aesthetics in engineering, magazine layout, advertising and other spheres as a palpable realization of the scenario of "art becoming life" that Jacques Rancière has seen as central to modern design discourse.[20] Taking this context into account, the present study on Ruttmann sets out not from the assumption that experimental aesthetics and practical applications were at cross-purposes, but rather from the question of how we might read them together. If, as Elsaesser and Hagener have argued, Ruttmann "saw in commissioned films not a limitation of his artistic freedom, but rather his genuine calling,"[21] how did this professional identity as a maker of advertising and other commissioned forms enable and even encourage certain forms of experimentation in abstraction, rhythm and montage?

This question is not entirely new. One of the impacts of "postmodernism" – articulated by scholars such as Andreas Huyssen in the 1980s – was to draw renewed attention to the historical imbrications between the historical avant-garde and the forms of mass consumer culture that arose in the wake of WWI.[22] But the question concerning the links between avant-garde filmmakers and advertising has gained a new resonance in film studies today with the recent emergence of archival and materialist histories that challenge the once-dominant auteurist paradigms by opening up the field to all of those areas of film production beyond narrative and classical documentary: to advertising and industrial films, to educational and public service films, to management and instructional films, and numerous other categories of moving images intended (to borrow the title of one recent important volume) to be "useful."[23] As the term suggests, while these films might still be received in a certain sense as art (particularly if, as is the case with the surrealist cult of outmoded commodities, their use-value has subsided), their status as aesthetic artifacts cannot be separated from their value as "practical" or "applied" films, commissioned for specific purposes and screened with specific ends in mind. Accordingly, much of the methodological discussion surrounding this new film history – following in particular upon several programmatic publications by Elsaesser – has emphasized the need to trade in traditional aesthetic and auteur-centered accounts for meticulous investigation into context: commissioning bodies, occasions for particular commissions, intended audience, purposes and so forth.[24]

Drawing on such work, this book takes Ruttmann seriously as a commissioned filmmaker.[25] In part, such a project entails a revision of the familiar – and in English-language scholarship nearly exclusive – focus on Ruttmann's four OPUS films and BERLIN. DIE SINFONIE DER GROSSSTADT. While not ignoring these canonical works in the following pages, this study also seeks to embed them within a broader analysis of Ruttmann's filmic production that has remained unknown to most English-speaking readers: his Weimar advertisements, his hygiene and medical films, and his industrial and propaganda films after 1933. In so doing, I take seriously the requisite (and not always answerable) contextual questions of financing, screening and intended audiences.[26] But my argument in this book also looks beyond those questions in several respects. First, I assume that "commissioned work," while created for a particular occasion, can also exceed the immediate purpose of its commission. This is not the familiar argument of subversion; whether working for a tire manufacturer (Excelsior) or the German Wehrmacht, Ruttmann, I argue, did take his commissions seriously. But as works of a celebrated avant-garde filmmaker, which often premiered in prominent cinemas such as the Ufa-Palast am Zoo, those commissioned films also existed within a broader context of modernity and engaged with many of the key questions of modernity studies regarding rationalization, perception, contingency, power and discipline.[27] Without a doubt, the immediate occasions of Ruttmann's commissioned films affected fundamentally the ways in which they could and did frame these broader questions of modernity. Accordingly, the point of a study such as this one is not to play one level off against the other, but rather to examine how the commissioning occasion of the film at hand and the broader context of German and European modernity are *intertwined*: i.e. how did Ruttmann's commissioned works enfold questions of modernity into their more immediate contexts and projects.

Secondly, as already suggested, this book seeks to reexamine the *aesthetics* of Ruttmann's commissioned work. To this end, it starts out from the hypothesis that Ruttmann's aesthetic experimentation occurred not despite the financial, practical and ideological conditions under which he made his films, but rather in tandem with those very conditions. In other words, I am arguing that Ruttmann's aesthetics were compatible with commissioned work. But this compatibility should be understood not simply in the sense that his aesthetics could be "co-opted" to commercial and propagandistic ends, as one says – often ignoring the avant-garde's actual history – that the aesthetics of experimental film have today been co-opted by digital pop culture. Rather, Ruttmann's signature aesthetic innovations in abstract animation and montage were – from the "beginning" – bound up with "practical" research. This suggests a different view of early experimental cinema than what is sometimes espoused. From a post-Frankfurt School intellectual perspective, being avant-garde might appear tantamount to opposing the instrumental rationality of the culture industry.[28] But while such a viewpoint might work for much experimental work of the post-WWII period,[29] it does not get us far with the interwar experimental art, particularly as it developed in "design" and constructivist milieus such as Russian Constructivism, Dutch De Stijl, the circle around Hans Richter's *G* and the Bauhaus. Like the experimental science, engineering and psychology of its day, experimental art in these circles was carried out *within a horizon of possible – even expected – "applications."* That is, the "practice," the "use" or the "application" always already inhabited the "experiment" *in potentia*.[30]

The analogy to science becomes particularly plausible if one examines carefully the multiple relations between avant-garde design and the science of advertising that emerged as a new professional sphere in the 1920s. As I explore further in the first chapter below, one of the areas in which Ruttmann himself was positively received – and one that has never been considered in film-historical scholarship on Ruttmann – was precisely in the trade literature of advertising. As advertising experts such as the Verein deutscher Reklamefachleute (Association of German Advertising Experts, VdR) began to discover film as a medium for advertising in the mid-1920s, Ruttmann's animated advertisements were often singled out for attention in professional journals such as *Die Reklame* and *Industrielle Psychotechnik*.[31] That reception forms part of a much broader cross-fertilization between experimental (avant-garde) art and advertising design during the period, when groups like the Bauhaus taught courses in the principles of advertising layout.[32] As Frederic Schwartz has argued, this interest in the science of advertising among avant-garde artists was also closely bound up with the avant-garde's redefinition of aesthetic production, one leading away from notions of disinterested or inspired creation and toward ideas of "expertise" and expert intervention in social life.[33] But we can also turn Schwartz's observation around and emphasize that not only was the avant-garde interested in advertising psychology; many advertising psychologists also had a keen interest in the kinds of experimental aesthetics we associate with the avant-garde. The early 20th century saw the rise of an entire new class of advertising designers – including Peter Behrens, Jupp Wiertz, Wilhelm Deffke and Lucien Bernhard – who reformed the aesthetics of posters and trademarks to conform to the kind of minimalist, simplified high-contrast designs we associate with constructivism. But such designs did not occur in a bubble; advertising psychologists, who regularly discussed these "applied" artists in their writings, were also articulating the principles of this streamlined aesthetics in articles for journals such as *Die Reklame*. These psychologists based their prescriptions for advertising aesthetics on countless laboratory experiments carried

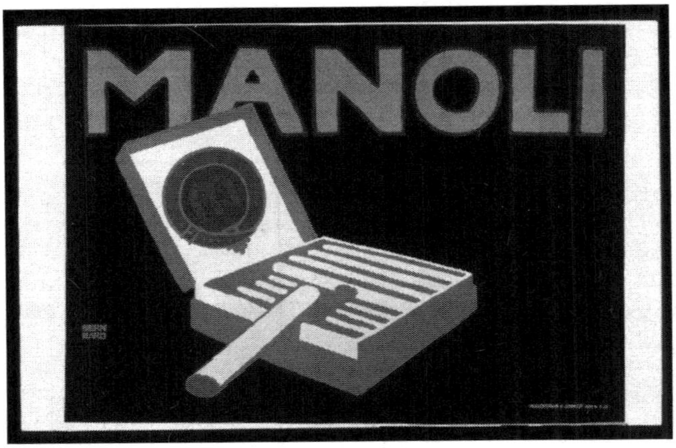

Lucien Bernhard, advertising poster for Manoli cigarettes *(1910)*

out for example in the new Institut für Wirtschaftspsychologie (Institute for Economical Psychology) founded in 1920 in Berlin. In so doing, they assumed (years before Benjamin or Kracauer) a new type of visual culture, one in which "fleeting glances" and distracted attention had become the rule within a public sphere marked by the "flood" of visual information.[34] Most importantly, they contributed every bit as much as their avant-garde counterparts to the redefinition of the "artist" for the commercial age, insisting that disinterested aesthetics had to give way to new forms of "Nutzkunst" (useful art), "Gebrauchskunst" (applied art) and "Gebrauchsgraphik" (applied graphic design).[35] Within this context, it seemed quite logical to expect a link between experimentation and its "applications": between experimental psychology and the new "applied" psychotechnics of the 1920s or between the experimentation design and its application in advertising posters.

It is, then, little wonder that advertising psychologists looked to a figure such as Ruttmann when they became interested in film, for his "applications" of experimental film in advertising resembled their own applications of experimental psychology to the design of poster advertisements. Conversely, it is hard to imagine that Ruttmann – who began his career not only as a painter but also as a designer of advertising posters – was unaware of the discussions about art linked to the new field of advertising, and the habitus of the "applied artist" those discussions helped to promote.[36] Ruttmann in fact wrote a great deal on the question of film as "art" in his early years, and his thinking on the subject was anything but a defense of traditional aesthetic categories. Like many of his contemporaries, Ruttmann did call for the creation of a "film art" appropriate to its medium and thus freed from its subservience to narrative and theater, arguing as early as 1917 that film should follow the turn of abstract painting rather than attempting to copy the stage.[37] But Ruttmann also consistently argued against elitist conceptions of "art" removed from the interests of life, writing for example – in his earliest published text on the topic – in 1925:

> Film, this monster brimming with vitality [Lebendigkeit], ecstatic among so many possibilities for life [Lebensmöglichkeiten], has no need to seek canonization from the tribunals of philological art. If film does not fit into the registry of "art," that is not its fault – and it is justified in demanding that we expand our concept of art in its direction.[38]

It was precisely this perceived *vitality* of film, its apparent proximity to "life," that preoccupied Ruttmann in the 1920s. It underlay both his conviction that film was the "art of our time" (Kunst unserer Zeit) and his insistence on redefining the very concept of "Kunst."[39] Perhaps no sphere better embodied that scenario of "art becoming life" than advertising design, and although Ruttmann wrote comparatively little about his own early advertisements, they clearly

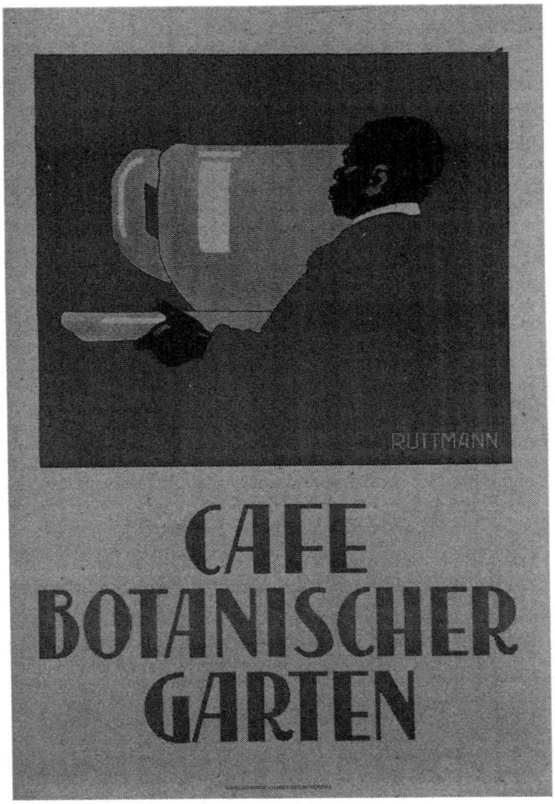

Walter Ruttmann, advertising poster for Café Botanischer Garten *(ca. 1910)*

constituted one – and not the least important – manifestation of film's *Lebensmöglichkeiten.*[40]

But the significance of advertising to understanding Ruttmann's work goes beyond questions of design and experimental aesthetics to touch on Ruttmann's very professional identity as a filmmaker and the concept of the medium that undergirded it. As the historian Corey Ross has argued, the industry of advertising "experts" that arose after the war also played a decisive role in changing ideas about political and social power in the 1920s. The key question here was one of *managing* the complexities of a new and seemingly unruly mass democratic arena. Having experienced the importance of propaganda for mass politics and mobilization during the Great War, Weimar social scientists and policymakers came to see the techniques of advertising and propaganda not as antidemocratic forces, but rather as crucial tools for reaching a mass audience and thus for organizing the centrifugal forces of the new mass democratic public sphere – a sphere marked by expanding claims to participation in public life, by an increasing awareness of the power of public opinion, and above all by the pervasive presence of technological media.[41] Advertising, along with the related field of propaganda,[42] promised to help assure the orderly functioning of this new political sphere by managing the flows of information and economies of attention. All of these questions, moreover, also informed the intense preoccupation with advertising by the emerging National Socialist movement, which drew centrally on the science of advertising psychology in articulating its own program of propaganda: its methods of "trademarking" and "product branding,"[43] its strategic use of filmic images,[44] and its understanding of mass media and their role in governing a mass populace.[45]

Advertising, that is, was not simply about managing images and information (visual culture), but also carried with it the implicit and sometimes explicit promise to help manage the new arena of mass politics. In this sense, advertising and related disciplines were part and parcel of the broader techniques of regulation that Michel Foucault has grouped under the term *governmentality*: forms of knowledge and power based on the management of populations, their economic activity, their health, their movements, etc.[46] The new sciences of governmentality were thus sciences of mass society, aware of the need for tools with which to comprehend and regulate the masses. Key among these was the science of statistics that arose in the 19th century.[47] Indeed, as Ian Hacking has shown, statistics – as a means of conceptualizing mass society through the identification of regularities and probabilities – is fundamentally bound up with a new awareness of masses: an "avalanche of numbers" that changed the ways in which policy-makers, social scientists and individuals understood society and the place of the individual within it.[48]

Such statistical methods were central to advertising psychology and its efforts to calculate "normal" or "probable" reactions to advertising displays and to reach the widest public possible.[49] But as Mary Ann Doane has argued, they also formed a critical epistemological framework in which the cinema itself emerged as a mass art form. With its sheer variety of images, captured on film in countless "actualities" from the Lumière Brothers on, the institution of the cinema embodied the experience of multiplicity in mass modernity in a particularly powerful way. As such, Doane argues, the cinema's photographic images could both contribute to the anxieties surrounding contingency – i.e. the proliferation of idiosyncratic details – and offer a means of escape from modernity's rationalizing tendencies.[50]

In this book, I argue that Ruttmann was, perhaps more than any other filmmaker of his generation, intuitively aware of such questions surrounding mass modernity and sought to fashion film – a medium defined by the concatenation of numerous images and shots – as an instrument for regulating multiplicity. As anyone who has watched BERLIN. DIE SINFONIE DER GROSSSTADT knows (and as John Grierson long ago pointed out), Ruttmann was centrally concerned with the masses, their regularities, their flows and their possible ordering.[51] As I argue in chapter 2, his "symphony" films drew on statistics in order to fashion the cinema as a means of such conceptual ordering of mass society. That project is thoroughly bound up with Ruttmann's professional identity as an "expert." Like advertising theorists, Ruttmann wanted his filmic advertisements to intervene in a public sphere marked by the proliferation of images and information, and indeed understood film as a means of training and regulating perception and attention within this arena. But increasingly in his later hygiene films and his propaganda films after 1933, Ruttmann also presents film as a means of managing *populations*, of intervening in biopolitical processes. It should thus hardly seem surprising that he would draw on contemporary forms of "expertise" for conceptualizing and managing mass society, its populations and its visual information. From advertising design to statistics to National Socialist models of Gleichschaltung (alignment or coordination), moreover, these were *the same forms* of "expertise" espoused by Ruttmann's many sponsors. Throughout Ruttmann's career, I argue, his signature filmic experiments drew on such forms of expertise in order to legitimate the medium as a means of managing the multiplicity of mass society: of training and guiding perception, conceptualizing the city, winning audiences over for products, influencing public health, and – after 1933 – commanding audience allegiance to the new regime.

Examining Ruttmann's exchanges with these domains of "expertise" produces a different picture of his professional identity as a filmmaker. But it also entails a different approach to the "intermediality" of his works. Although the notion of "absolute" film lends itself to Greenbergian accounts of modernism as an effort to reduce art to its "medium specificity," Ruttmann in fact conceived film from the beginning in terms of its intermedial relations to music, dance and painting,[52] and scholars have long been fascinated by his ability to cross the boundaries between artistic media: between painting and film in the OPUS films,[53] between musical and visual rhythm in the OPUS films and BERLIN,[54] and between image and sound montage in works such as WEEKEND (1930) or TÖNENDE WELLE (RESOUNDING WAVES, 1931).[55] This idea of Ruttmann as a multimedia artist is summed up in the title of Leonardo Quaresima's catalogue *Walter Ruttmann. Cinema, pittura, ars acustica*. Within this framework, film historians have often cited Ruttmann's early unpublished essay "Malerei mit Zeit" (ca. 1919) as evidence of his leading position within an international project among Futurists, Dadaists and other artists to overcome static painting through the dynamism of movement arts in the early 20th century.[56] But while such a framing certainly explains one aspect of Ruttmann's work, he also drew on many other media – particularly visual media – beyond the realm of high art. In his early work, these include the tradition of scientific curvature mentioned several times in the essay "Malerei mit Zeit," as well as the art of poster design that he adapted to his earliest advertising films. But they also include several modes of visual representation from the applied sciences such as cross-sectional representations, visual statistics (or Isotype), blueprints, maps and engineering designs. As an "artist" who sometimes accompanied his own films musically, Ruttmann was indeed interested in the interstices between painting, music and film, but as an "expert" who wanted film to contribute to the regulation of mass society, he was also interested in these other types of "useful" images, all of which stem from the tradition that Gottfried Boehm has labeled "images as instruments of knowledge."[57] As I explore in the chapters below, Ruttmann sought to adapt such practical visual forms to film in order to define a role for filmic images as a medium for managing mass society and its multiplicities. *This* form of intermediality sought to position film and its operations as an instrument not of artists but of experts, and examining it more carefully allows a different picture to emerge. Whereas Deleuzian film scholars describe modernist film in terms of the "action image," the "affect image" and the "perception image" (usually aligning the avant-garde with the third category), I argue that Ruttmann sought, in adapting the visual traditions of science to film, to create another kind of filmic image: a *management image,* which would allow film to participate in the logic of governmentality.[58]

It is here, I believe, that we can best understand the "politics" of Ruttmann's aesthetics. Rather than assuming that Ruttmann's post-1933 work amounted to a corruption of a purportedly "pure" aesthetics of experimentation from his early career, I would suggest that Ruttmann practiced experimental aesthetics, both before and after 1933, as an *applicable* art, one that could be used in product commercials, cultural publicity pictures, social and hygiene films, city advertisements, industrial films and wartime propaganda. Ruttmann himself summarized this view of film in 1928 in a text entitled "Die absolute Mode" ("The Absolute Fashion"):

> Film is – thank God! – not simply an artistic affair, but also and above all a human-social affair! It is the strongest advocate for the spirit that seeks to reunite vital and artistic interests, for that spirit that today deems jazz more 'important' than sonatas, posters more 'important' than paintings. Art, *living* art, is no longer what we learned it was in school: no longer a flight from the world into higher spheres, but rather an act of entering into the world and explaining its nature. *Art is no longer abstraction, but rather the taking of positions* [*Stellungnahme*]*!* Any art that does not contain a pronouncement belongs in the antiquities museum. Of course, it is a matter of indifference what this pronouncement applies to: feminine beauty; socialism; or technology, nature and their various imbrications. What is important is simply the fact of taking a position.[59]

Coming at the end of the 1920s, Ruttmann's statement was clearly meant on one level to explain his own turn away from abstract animation and toward photographic images with his BERLIN film, and the text has often been read as a public renunciation of his early avant-garde aspirations. But the text affords insight, I believe, into a professional identity that Ruttmann had been fashioning for some time, one in which the filmmaker participates in social processes by placing aesthetic expertise in the service of other causes, be it product advertising ("feminine beauty") or political propaganda (e.g. "socialism"). Scholars have sometimes wondered what exactly Ruttmann had in mind with the term "Stellungnahme" (taking positions), given the filmmaker's own formalist tendencies.[60] Part of my point in this book is to argue that the concept referred to something broader than political committment: at stake here was rather the very act of "applying" film aesthetics to useful tasks, of reuniting "art" and "life." This notion of the artist as an intervener in social life might help to explain, more than any specific political positions that Ruttmann may or may not have espoused, his own willingness to participate in both advertising and, later, fascist propaganda. Ruttmann's own stated "indifference" to the objects of those interventions is, of course, precisely what makes him such a problematic filmmaker for histories of the avant-garde. But that "indifference" was also perfectly in keeping with the professional ethos of advertising theorists in Weimar, who sought to legitimate advertising and propaganda as *formal techniques* applicable to multiple ends.[61]

To point out this relational continuity in Ruttmann's professional identity, however, is not to argue that nothing changes in his films between the Weimar Republic and National Socialism. On the contrary, the regime change in 1933 did have immediate consequences for the ways in which the management of mass society was conceptualized. As recent historians have emphasized, although "biopolitics" – understood as the projects, techniques and methods for managing populations – is a feature of modern mass societies from the 19th century to the present, both the means and the ends of biopolitics *did* change drastically in Germany in 1933, when open discussion and public dissent were silenced, public policy was orchestrated from the top down, individual rights and pleasures were subordinated to the interests of the collective, and race-based eugenics became an official part of a governmental policy designed to support concept of the populace as a "Volkskörper." Thus Edward Dickinson has argued:

> What was critical [for the destructive dynamic of Nazism] was not the expansion of the instruments and disciplines of biopolitics, which occurred everywhere in Europe. Instead it was the principles that guided how those instruments and disciplines were organized and used, and the external constrains on them. In National Socialism, biopolitics was shaped by a totalitarian conception of social management focused on the

power and ubiquity of the *völkish* state. In democratic societies, biopolitics has historically been constrained by a rights-based strategy of social management.[62]

Nazism and its genocidal policies were thus both part of a broader logic of modern biopolitical management and, as several recent historians have argued, something quite distinct from the welfare states that existed before and after the National Socialist period, even if all of these formations shared in the logic of governmentality and biopolitical management that characterized mass modernity as a whole.[63] Adapting these insights to film history, we could say that what changed in Ruttmann was not the interest in management of mass society and its visual culture *per se*, and not the desire to adapt forms of "expertise" to the cinema, but rather the *framework* in which such adaptations took place and the ends to which they were put.[64] As I argue below in chapters 3 and 4, Ruttmann's post-1933 films display a new concept of governmentality: one characterized by a model of the population not as an aggregate mass with its regularities and differences, its typologies and contingencies, but as a *Volkskörper* rooted in the land and the "race"; one in which ideas about governing and regulating the masses sought not to manage differences but to eliminate them and unify the populace through policies of *Gleichschaltung*; one in which advertising no longer has to balance government policy with the procurement of individual pleasures, but rather functions to make individuals aware of their "duty" to the state and the *Volk*. Ruttmann's post-1933 films "enacted" these transformations, as it were, in their representations of the masses as a racialized *Volkskörper* or as raw material to be molded to the ends of the state; in the way they rethought advertising as an "educational" exercise of power; and above all in the way they positioned the cinema itself as an instrument for molding spectators to the dictates of the new regime.

Thus even as I emphasize the continuities in Ruttmann's professional identity and his efforts to draw on modern forms of "expertise" in order to fashion film as an instrument for managing the multiplicity of mass society, I also want to insist on the real differences between his Weimar work and his later output. This means attending to the specificities of Ruttmann's "fascist" films. Conversely, it also means attending to the specificities of his *Weimar* films. While Ruttmann's filmmaking might have displayed a certain "instrumental" logic before 1933, subsuming those films under notions of proto-fascism or Nazi Sachlichkeit *avant la lettre* would fail to account for the very real engagement with multiplicity, difference and plurality visible in these films and which continues to make them so interesting to Weimar scholars.

In order to support this reading of Ruttmann, the book is divided into four chapters arranged according to representative periods and concepts. Although each of these chapters focuses on a select group of films, the goal here is not to provide exhaustive coverage. Readers looking for a biography of Ruttmann's life or an exhaustive description of the dozens of films he directed, co-directed, collaborated on or imagined during his twenty-three years as a filmmaker are better served by the informative source books by Goergen and Quaresima.[65] In particular, because I am interested here in the way that Ruttmann's work conceives of film as a medium for managing visual culture, this book has comparatively little to say about his important experiments with sound.[66] I have also left out any extended discussions of Ruttmann's many collaborations on the works of other filmmakers such as Lotte Reiniger's DIE ABENTEUER DES PRINZEN ACHMED (THE ADVENTURES OF PRINCE ACHMED, 1926), Fritz Lang's NIBELUNGEN (1924) or Leni Riefenstahl's TRIUMPH DES WILLENS (TRIUMPH OF THE WILL, 1935). And several important films, including the full-length fiction film ACCIAIO, receive little or no attention.[67] Finally, as already suggested, readers looking for a narrative of the avant-garde as an inherently counter-cultural or progressive phenomenon are bound to be disappointed. What this book *does* offer is a detailed analysis of four representative periods and themes that can help us to rethink Ruttmann's experimental aesthetics as forms and operations bound up with modern strategies for managing the multiplicities – visual, informational, populational – of mass society.

Chapter 1 focuses on the context of post-WWI advertising psychology already mentioned in order to reassess Ruttmann's early abstract animation. Examining Ruttmann's animated product advertisements in relation both to his OPUS films and to the new theories of advertising design, I propose a new reading of abstract filmmaking as a form profoundly compatible with the experimental science of advertising and its notions of instrumental visual representations. In particular, I show how the oscillation between abstraction and figuration in Ruttmann's animated advertisements – which repeatedly take up the signature forms of his OPUS films while transforming them into figurative representations – echoes the precepts of advertising psychology, which sought to apply the findings of experimental psychology to the real world of the advertising marketplace. Drawing on Ruttmann's early unpublished text "Malerei mit Zeit" ("Painting with Time"), this chapter also examines how Ruttmann's animation sought to effectuate a training of spectatorial attention for an era of acceleration and information overload by drawing on the visual tradition of movement curves. Ultimately, Ruttmann's advertising films present their products precisely as a means of navigating the "curves" of modernity's accelerated informational flows by entering into "resonance" with the waves of accelerated movement. A key term in the advertising discourse of the time, "resonance" offered a model for ordering and governing movement: one that would make advertising and its visual representations as efficient as a Fordist factory.

Chapter 2 then examines Ruttmann's turn toward photographic images in the second half of the 1920s, focusing in particular on his development of "cross-sectional" montage. Tracing the history of the "cross-section" (Querschnitt) from a mode of scientific illustration to a form of sociological analysis based on a statistical epistemology, I show how the figure was imported into Weimar visual culture as a model for conceptualizing mass society and managing a visual sphere characterized by the increasing proliferation of photographic representations. Drawing on illustrated journals such as *Der Querschnitt*, Ruttmann's "cross-sectional" montage in films such as BERLIN sought to manage the contingency associated with "indexical" representations by underscoring the similarities and regularities between people, animals, technologies and objects from different spheres. Such a form lent itself well to Ruttmann's project in the 1929 film MELODIE DER WELT (MELODY OF THE WORLD), an extended advertisement for world cruises offered by the Hamburg-Amerika shipping line (HAPAG) that touted the company's ability to bring about a new "understanding" between the peoples of the world in the wake of WWI. By transforming the company's narrative journey around the world into a "cross-sectional" catalogue of visual analogies between different peoples and their forms of culture, Ruttmann attempts to imagine a similar function for film: a medium that could manage the world's multiplicity by balancing difference with statistical regularity.

Building on this analysis of Ruttmann's "cross-sectional" films as statistical conceptualizations of mass society, chapter 3 then turns to the application of statistics to populational representation in Ruttmann's hygiene films from the early 1930s. Comparing the anti-syphilis film FEIND IM BLUT (ENEMY IN THE BLOOD, 1931) with Ruttmann's first Nazi propaganda film BLUT UND BODEN. GRUNDLAGEN ZUM NEUEN REICH (BLOOD AND SOIL. FUNDAMENTALS FOR THE NEW REICH, 1933), I show how these films sought to apply Ruttmann's "statistical epistemology" to problems of biopolitics. In particular, by adapting statistical forms such as graphs, charts and the recently developed conventions of Isotype to film, Ruttmann here refashioned the medium and its "statistical montage" as a tool for encouraging viewers to see themselves as part of a biopolitical population. However, this chapter also demonstrates the profound changes that Ruttmann's biopolitics undergo from Weimar to National Socialism – and from a semi-private commission by reformist anti-syphilis groups to a public commission by the newly formed Office of the German Reich Peasant Leader (Stabsamt des Reichsbauernführers). Where a film like FEIND IM BLUT still seeks to persuade individuals of their vested interest in statistical information about syphilis, BLUT UND BODEN de-individualizes spectators, treating them as representatives of a racialized *Volkskörper* whose health and degeneracy becomes the spectator's direct responsibility. Within this configuration, Ruttmann's cross-sectional montage still functions to insert individual images and stories into a greater statistical whole, but the valorization of the contingent, the detail or the idiosyncratic is no longer possible.

My final chapter then turns to Ruttmann's many "steel" films of the 1930s and 1940s in order to examine how Ruttmann re-imagines film after 1933 as a means of conceptualizing and managing the new "Volkskörper." Like other scholars who have considered these films, I am interested in the ways in which they display a vestige of Ruttmann's Weimar aesthetics – abstraction, animation and the attention to elementary forms – in the many images of molten steel and factory technology. However, rather than interpreting this correspondence as evidence that Ruttmann used advertising to "smuggle" experimental aesthetics into Nazi cinemas, or (on the contrary) as an invitation to read Ruttmann's Weimar films as proto-fascist, I argue that such abstraction comes to serve a new purpose after 1933: namely as the iconography of a particular power of "form-giving" or a "Formgefühl" (feeling for form) attributed to the German race in the art history and anthropology of the time. Steel production comes to embody this "form-giving" power, which Ruttmann's films – like the literature of the steel industries that commissioned them – trace from ancient Germanic swordsmiths to modern factories. But this forming of steel for society also becomes a figure for fascist leadership, which Goebbels famously conceptualized as the power to "give form" to the *Volk*. Ruttmann's many classroom scenes, alongside his predilection for animated plans, designs and blueprints in these films, suggest a view of the medium as an instrument for this disciplinary constitution of the audience as a "Volk."

Following this trajectory from Weimar to Nazism, it would be easy to condemn Ruttmann (as both Siegfried Kracauer and John Grierson did) for his cultivation of an abstract formalism – or in the terms of this study a formal "expertise" – that could be co-opted by any and all political ends. Or one might fault him (as Bazin could have done) for his contribution to an instrumental montage aesthetics that lent itself to the propagandistic manipulation of viewers.[68] It is not my intention to defend Ruttmann against such critiques here. Like other scholars, I am wary of notions of "inner immigration," especially when one considers the extent to which Ruttmann's post-1933 films actively espoused elements of Nazi ideology. This book unabashedly examines the imbrications of Ruttmann's experimental aesthetics with National Socialist models of governance, with the championing of warfare, and even with a racialized model of the body politic after 1933. But I hope the book can also point beyond such questions (which have, understandably, preoccupied histories of German film in the interwar period) to reopen a discussion about what exactly "experimental" aesthetics meant. Writing in 1933, Grierson argued that Ruttmannesque cross-sectional montage failed to attain the "higher reaches of art" because of its emphasis on pure mechanics without moral ends.[69] If my contention is correct, such moral ends were never the point for a filmmaker like Ruttmann, who sought rather to see how film could be fashioned as an instrument, what it could *do*. Ruttmann was no more preoccupied with hierarchizing its possible applications than were the experts of advertising and propaganda with the ends to which its own findings would be applied.[70] Film, in this understanding, was a tool for "experts," susceptible to multiple applications, and precisely therein resided its legitimation. This is not to say that we should avoid condemning Ruttmann's political opportunism, but that we should read that opportunism as part and parcel of one historical conception of the medium – and of the avant-garde's role in shaping that conception – that has yet to be fully understood.

1. Absolute Advertising: Abstraction and Figuration in Ruttmann's Animated Product Advertisements (1922-1927)

Introduction

Of all the domains of "sponsored film" recently rediscovered, product advertising has received perhaps the least amount of attention in English-language scholarship.[1] And yet, the sphere is rife with possibilities for the kinds of archival investigations suggested by Elsaesser: investigations into commissioning companies and contexts, into distribution and forms of screening, and not least of all into the theories and discourses of consumerism that informed both the production and circulation of these films. Moreover, product advertising is a particularly relevant field for anyone wishing to comprehend avant-garde film culture of the 1920s. Nearly all of the major proponents of avant-garde film in interwar Germany – including Ruttmann, Reiniger, Seeber, Richter and Fischinger – collaborated with advertising producers such as Julius Pinschewer.[2] Most, if not all, of this work employs the signature forms we have come to associate with experimental cinema, from abstract animation (Ruttmann, Fischinger) to silhouettes (Reiniger) to montage (Ruttmann, Seeber, Richter), which these artists placed in the service of advertisements for products as diverse as chocolates, tires, alcohol, flowers, cigarettes, skincare products, perfumes and illustrated magazines.[3] Nor would it be correct to describe this use of experimental aesthetics for advertising as "secondary" or derivative; as Ingrid Westbrock long ago argued, advertising film provided a consistent forum for experimentation in the 1920s and many of the major innovations in experimental film (in color, sound and montage) were actually first tried out in advertising films.[4]

Only recently has much of this work become available for researchers outside of archives, and only a handful of publications have devoted extended attention to its role within the avant-garde film culture of the interwar period.[5] No doubt, this dearth of research is in part the result of tacit assumptions, in avant-garde history, that such advertising commissions represented a "compromise" of artistic integrity or simply a means of financing the artists' more "serious" projects in visual music.[6] But if we approach these films outside of such assumptions, a different picture begins to emerge, one suggesting – as Jacques Rancière has argued in a different context – that modernist formalism and advertising design in fact shared some fundamental goals and principles. In a well-known essay comparing Mallarmé's graphic poetry and the trademark designs of Peter Behrens, Rancière has argued that modernism, in both its "high" and "low" forms, was traversed by an ethos of design, where the "surface" (the page, the poster or – we should add in this context – the screen) came to be seen as a space for proposing new modes of collective life: a space for forging "types" that could help to reorder perception and redistribute the shared space of a world where the traditional forms of religious and courtly ceremony no longer held sway.[7]

For anyone wishing to investigate the ramifications of Rancière's reading of modernism for film and moving images, Ruttmann offers an ideal case study. While histories of avant-garde film stress Ruttmann's beginnings as a painter in the Munich art scene before the war, it is worth recalling that he was also a graphic designer and poster artist and in fact made his living, at least in part, by designing advertising posters.[8] Ruttmann would go on, of course, to become one of the pioneering figures of abstract film, whose LICHTSPIEL OPUS I, first screened in May 1921, is by many accounts the first abstract film ever shown publicly. But Ruttmann was also among the first experimental filmmakers – along with Lotte Reiniger – to delve into product advertising with his film DER SIEGER. EIN FILM IN FARBEN (THE VICTOR. A FILM IN COLORS), an advertisement for Excelsior tires completed one year after LICHTSPIEL OPUS I in April 1922. And advertising would continue to form a major part of Ruttmann's oeuvre throughout the 1920s, including at least six animated product advertisements made for Julius Pinschewer between 1922 and 1927,[9] as well as other animated advertisements that have been lost.[10] Examining the surviving animated advertisements in both their contextual and formal dimensions, this chapter suggests a different understanding not only of the place of advertising film within modernist film culture, but also of the aesthetics of advertising film – and indeed of abstract animation itself, its uses and its possible meanings in the 1920s. Far from being understood uniformly as a resistance to the culture industry, abstract film could and did appear both to filmmakers and advertising theorists as a form rife with financial and industrial possibilities, a means for harnessing film's effect on spectators, and a nodal point around which a filmmaker like Ruttmann could lay claim to a certain type of professional expertise. As I will show, Ruttmann's animated advertisements draw on these understandings of abstract film, while ultimately blending abstraction and figuration to stage a loss and retrieval of meaning that was part and parcel of early advertising theory itself.

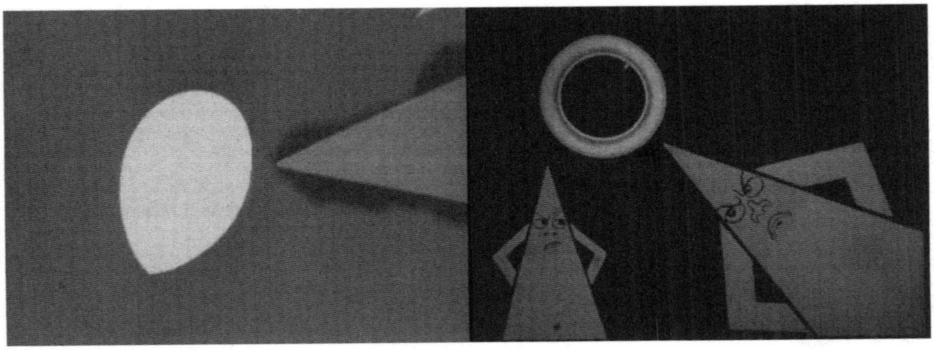

Stills from Ruttmann, Lichtspiel Opus I *(1921) and* Der Sieger. Ein Film in Farben *(1922)*

Absolute Film and the Psychophysical Image: Ruttmann's Opus Films

Seen against the backdrop of debates about Ruttmann's formalism, what makes his animated advertisements particularly interesting is the way in which they seem to hover between abstract "absolute" formalism and denotative referentiality, constantly moving back and forth between abstract-elementary forms and recognizable objects and thus highlighting the fluid border between the two. Throughout Ruttmann's advertisements from this period, one finds precise echoes of the forms operative in his Opus films, but those forms now morph into identifiable faces, bodies and objects. Thus in Der Sieger, the dance of round and angular forms from Lichtspiel Opus I becomes a struggle between anthropomorphized spikes and Excelsior tires; similarly, the round and paisley shapes from Lichtspiel Opus II (1922) become two arguing heads in the 1922 advertisement for Kantorowicz liqueur, Das Wunder. Ein Film in Farben (The Miracle. A Film in Colors); the spirals from Opus IV (1925) become the serpent in the Garden of Eden in the 1925 flower advertisement Das wiedergefundene Paradies (Paradise Regained); and the geometric shapes from Ruttmann's later Opus films become the stairs on which the ravaged German nation climbs to health in Der Aufstieg (The Ascent), a 1926 advertisement for the "Gesolei" exhibition on health, welfare and physical fitness.[11] Nor is Ruttmann alone here; examining the range of advertising work by experimental filmmakers, one can find similar correspondences in works ranging from Reiniger's 1922 Nivea advertisement Das Geheimnis der Marquisin (with its echoes of her early ornamental silhouette shorts) to Fischinger's cigarette

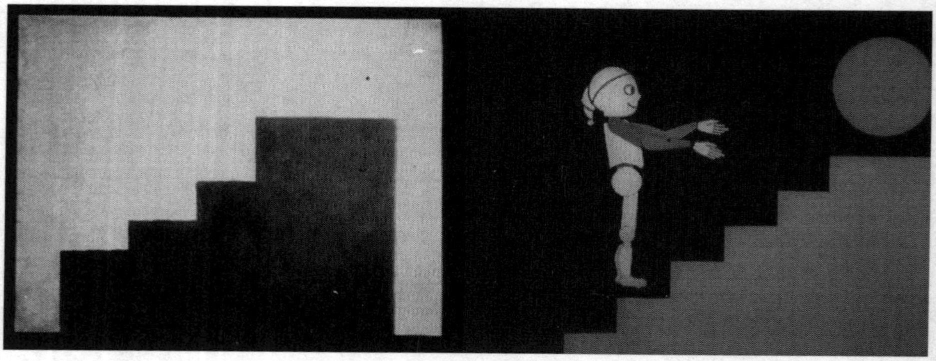

Stills from Ruttmann, Opus II *(1922) and* Der Aufstieg *(1926)*

advertisement Muratti greift ein (Muratti Steps In, 1934), which portends the aesthetics of his Komposition in Blau (1935).

In asking what made possible the translation of experimental forms from abstract film to advertising, it is worth reconsidering, here at the beginning, Ruttmann's "absolute" films themselves. In his 1926 study *Expressionismus und Film* (*Expressionism and Film*), the critic Rudolf Kurtz described the abstract work of Richter and Ruttmann, not surprisingly, as an effort to do away with the "psychological" dimensions of spectatorship – i.e. all of the processes of cognition, association and temporal ordering by which spectators normally identify things and people and piece together stories – in order to access elementary forms and laws of movement. But if abstract film emptied out the "psychology" of spectatorship, it nonetheless left room for, and even cultivated, a "psychophysical" dimension, in which the film elicits an elemental reaction from spectators. As Kurtz described it:

> Despite its rejection of the possibility for psychological comprehension, absolute art doubtlessly exerts effects on audiences in certain cases. Only this is not an act of contemplation that perceives forms in their pure relations to one another, but rather a mental process sufficiently familiar from psychophysics: the spectators feels his way into the mathematical forms [fühlt sich in die mathematischen Formen ein] and answers them with corresponding sensations. This process occurs at an unconscious and compulsory level; the elementary lines and form relations lead the spectator's sensation in their directions, making him move with their movements and guiding him through their various degrees of clarity – so that a mental counter-image arises that corresponds to the struggle, harmony or reconciliation of the forms on the screen.[12]

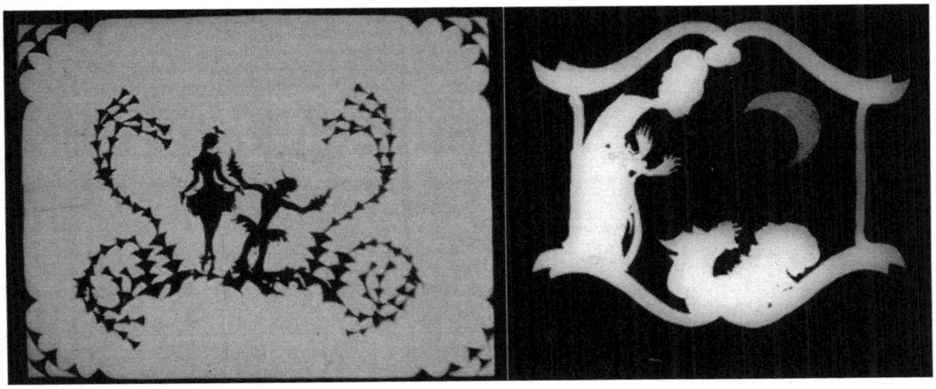

Stills from Lotte Reiniger, Das Ornament des verliebten Herzens *(1919) and* Das Geheimnis der Marquisin *(1922)*

Kurtz's reference to "psychophysics" here is hardly fortuitous; already in the late 19th century, the idea that the sight of movement could provoke a tendency toward counter-movements within the spectator was a standard axiom of psychophysical research, invoked by scientists such as Charles Féré and Théodule Ribot – under the term "psychomotor induction" – to explain all sorts of phenomena from telepathy to the predilection for popular spectacles of movement such as sports.[13] This emerging model of spectatorship also came to inform a widespread understanding of film as a medium of visual movement that could affect spectators psychosomatically inducing "counter-movements" at the micro-physiological level.[14] As late as 1927, a writer for the journal *Filmtechnik,* in an article entitled "Von der Psychomechanik des Zuschauers" ("On the Psychomechanics of the Spectator") could still rely on this psychophysical explanation to argue that movement shown on the screen could elicit tendencies toward elementary counter-movements in spectators: "When we see a movement, it calls forth in us a need to produce our own movement in turn. When executed correctly, it 'hits' its target and infects us. [...] These are qualities that make man an appropriate object for film's effects."[15] But while it could theoretically be applied to any form or genre of filmmaking, this notion that visual movement could call forth counter-movements in spectators proved particularly attractive for describing the desired effects of *abstract* film, which was widely understood as an effort to bracket out psychological "content" precisely in order to isolate and amplify such psychophysiological mechanisms. Not only for theorists such as Kurtz, but also practitioners such as Hans Richter saw absolute film among other things as a field for cultivating the psychophysical power of moving images. As Richter explained in a 1924 text "Die schlecht trainierte Seele" ("The Badly Trained Soul"): "This film here offers no 'stopping points,' at which one could look back through memory. The viewer is – exposed – forced to 'feel' – to go along with the rhythm."[16]

My point, in rehearsing such arguments, is not to maintain that Richter or Kurtz were empirically correct in their assessment of abstract film's ability to affect spectators. But such statements do tell us something about the ideas and motivations informing the very emergence of "absolute" film in the 1920s. That emergence was motivated not simply by artistic questions, but also by a desire to trade in psychological understanding for psychophysical effects. In this, absolute film can be read, at least in part, as the culmination of a broader media paradigm shift already begun in the 19th century, which has been the focus of much recent media archeology. Like the visual practices and discourses examined by Jonathan Crary, these films were created for an *embodied* spectator, one for whom the faculties of attention, sensation and affect mobilized in acts of visual consumption had become the new terrain of social power.[17] Like the modernist poetry examined by Friedrich Kittler, moreover, these films carried into aesthetic production a "flight of ideas" inaugurated by psychophysics. Kittler saw Hermann Ebbinghaus's use of meaningless syllables to measure quantitative memory capacity as the paradigmatic incarnation of a new regime of materialist media experience, one that would find its aesthetic continuation in the experimental "nonsense" poetry that emerged some 20 years later in works by Kurt Schwitters or Christian Morgenstern.[18] A similar relation between art and science can be observed in absolute painting and film, which operates with many of the same parameters on the visual level. The attention to elementary forms, for example, as well as the effects of primary colors and color combinations, were standard components of psychophysical experimentation – and scientists invented all sorts of apparatuses for testing them, such as the "form board" devised by Edouard Séguin in 1866 and subsequently used in children's education and in performance intelligence tests, or the "Farbenkreisel" (color wheel) designed to test the perception of color combinations. Both devices were still being used in the 1920s in the field of psychotechnics for intelligence and aptitude testing, as suggested by their inclusion in publications such as *Methoden der Wirtschaftspsychologie* (*Methods of Economic Psychology*) by the German psychotechnician Fritz Giese.[19] Indeed, one could point to numerous similarities between the modernist textual phenomena noted by Kittler and the visual experimentations of absolute filmmaking. Just as Mallarmé discovered the importance of the white page for defining the black of letters, so Hans Richter highlighted the relativity of black and white through the sudden reversal of figure and ground in his first rhythm film, a motif he would return to in his *Filmstudie* (*Film Study*) of 1926.

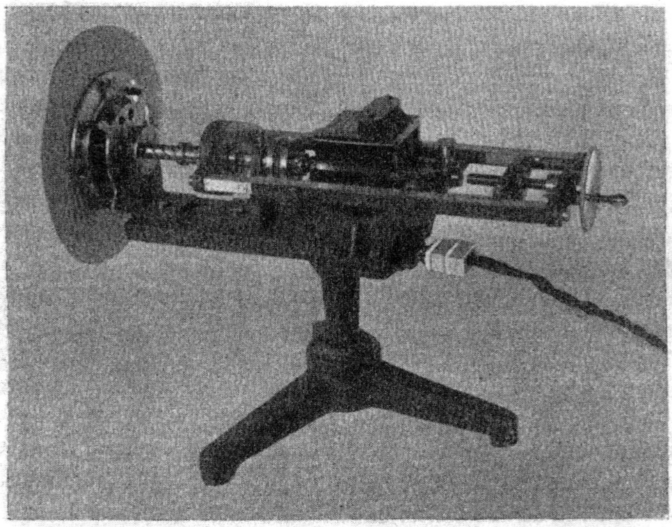

Color wheel, illustration from Fritz Giese, Methoden der Wirtschaftspsychologie *(1927)*

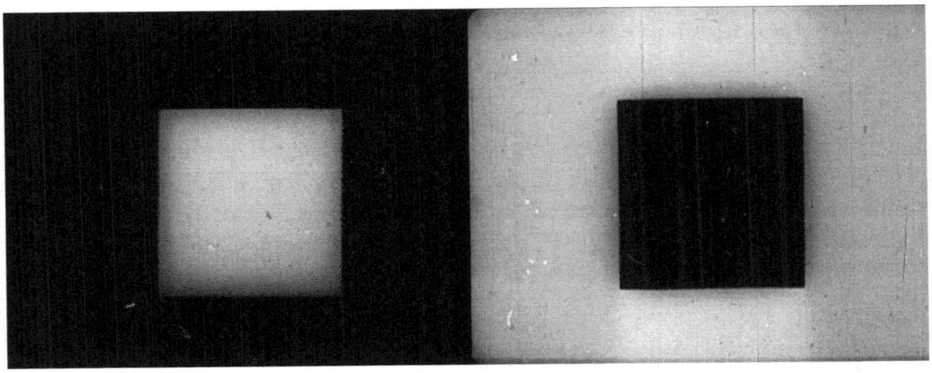

Stills from Hans Richter, Rhythmus 21, *reversal of figure and ground*

Advertising Psychology and the Uses of Abstraction

Seen in this light, the absolute film of the 1920s would appear less as a mode of resistance to mass culture than as one part of a broader elaboration of new techniques of spectatorship, where the viewer figures as an embodied object of psychophysical testing rather than as a hermeneutic interpreter. It was precisely this status as a forum for perceptual experimentation, moreover, that made abstract film, in the eyes of contemporary observers, an obvious realm to combine with advertising. For perhaps no other domain of applied science in the 1920s adopted the lessons and tools of psychophysics more enthusiastically than advertising psychology. That science emerged in the wake of World War I – almost simultaneously with the emergence of abstract film – from its status as a branch of psychotechnics to become a major field of independent scientific research during the Weimar Republic, one marked by the opening of institutes and laboratories (e.g. the Institut für Wirtschaftspsychologie [Institute for Economic Psychology] founded in 1920 in Berlin), the proliferation of specialty journals (such as *Die Reklame, Seidels Reklame* and *Industrielle Psychotechnik*), and a host of books and articles on advertising psychology.[20] Drawing explicitly on the pioneering research of figures such as Ebbinghaus and Hugo Münsterberg (particularly his *Psychologie und Wirtschaftsleben* [*Psychology and Economic Life*] from 1912), theorists within this new branch sought to forge a new science of advertising spectatorship by meticulously testing – via rapid-flash windows of tachistoscopes – the psychophysical effects of such material factors such as composition, contrast, color, typography, letter spacing, image size and ad placement.[21]

In conducting such tests, these advertising theorists were in part reacting to a new experience of visual culture in the Weimar Republic brought on by the increased presence of advertising itself. Among other changes introduced by the social democratic government was a thoroughgoing relaxation of prewar advertising laws, which opened up public institutions such as the German railway, the post office, public transportation systems and streets to use for advertising displays. As a result, print advertisements – once confined to street corner columns – began to turn up everywhere: in train stations and rail cars, in the roofs of tramways and the interiors of subway stations, at street crossings and along traffic routes, on postal delivery vehicles, construction fences, mailboxes, tram tickets, stamps and anywhere else a bit of surface space could be found. The period was also marked by a significant expansion of electric signage, along with the invention of numerous new advertising technologies, many of them strikingly cinematic, such as mobile advertising vehicles and special projectors for projecting colorful slide advertisements onto walls ceilings or sidewalks. To contemporary observers, it seemed as if *every surface* had now become fair game for advertising.[22] Where later observers would decry the "Bilderflut" or flood of images occasioned by the spread of illustrated magazines, advertising trade literature already spoke of a "Reklamehochflut" or "flood of advertising" in the early 1920s.[23] Within this context, advertising theorists also assumed – long before Benjamin and Kracauer – a new mode of distracted and divided visual attention. Thus in one of the earliest texts on advertising layout, the head of the

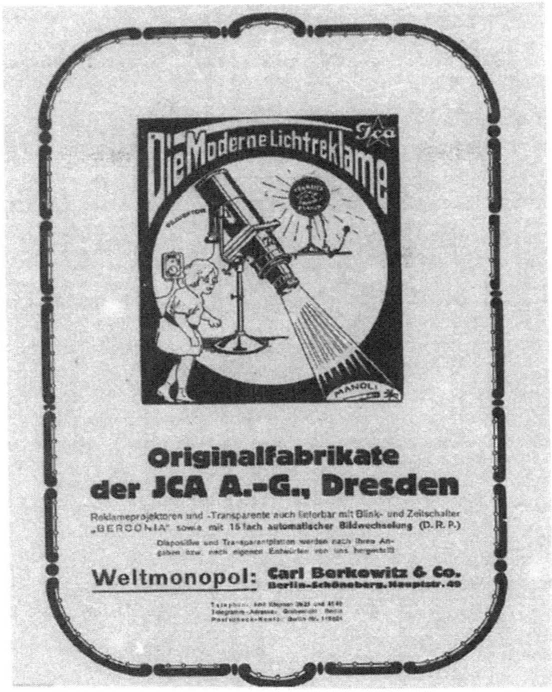

Advertisement for mobile publicity projector, from Die Reklame *(1922)*

new Institut für Wirtschaftspsychologie, Walther Moede, argued that all advertisements had to conform to the "principle of the fleeting glance" (Prinzip des flüchtenden Blickes), which stipulated that consumers would only perceive advertising content for a fraction of a second.[24]

In reaction to this new configuration, these theorists called above all for a reductive visual aesthetic, one not a little reminiscent of the "elementary" forms of abstract film itself. Specifically, they argued that advertisements should strive for clarity and rapid recognition through the reduction of images to simple geometric forms, the adoption of streamlined typographies, and the strategic use of high contrast.[25] Such principles were put to use in the trademark designs by Wilhelm Deffke and others,[26] but they also came to characterize the aesthetics of poster design, most famously in the so-called "Sachplakate" (objective posters) of Lucien Bernhard, which simplified shapes and colors to the extreme to draw attention to the object advertised.[27] A case in point can be seen in a celebrated advertisement by Bernhard for home movie projectors by the Heimlicht Company, in which the family members, projector and light were reduced to abstract white geometrical shapes over a black background. The advertisement

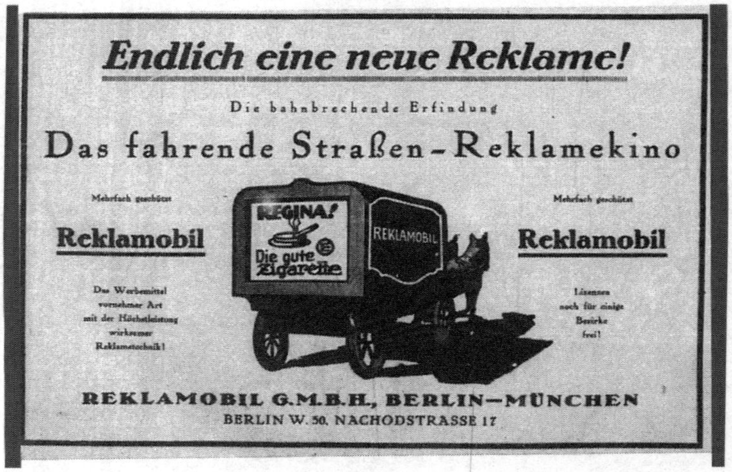

Advertisement for "Reklamemobil," from SEIDELS REKLAME *(1920)*

was singled out for special mention in 1920 by the editors of SEIDELS REKLAME, who lauded Bernhard's use of "spherical human figures" (Kugelmenschen) and the "effects of black and white" (Schwarz-Weiß-Wirkung).[28] Looking back in 1927, Fritz Giese would also take Bernhard's advertising as a model of effective advertising layout in his *Methoden der Wirtschaftspsychologie,* where he walked readers through the simplification of a complex image through the reduction of detail and the reversal of black and white.

Such black and white reversals recall, once again, the work of Richter. But advertising theorists also meticulously discussed and tested the effects of contrasting colors. Wilhelm Ostwald's color theories, according to which "harmonious" color compositions could be achieved through the exact determination of the brightness of adjacent colors, generated widespread interest advertising circles.[29] But more often advertising theorists latched onto ideas about complimentary and contrasting color tones derived from the theories of Michel Eugène Chevreul via late 19th-century experimental psychology and now understood as a means of maximizing the advertisement's effect on consumer attention.[30] Walther Moede, for example, cited the "law of contrast" (Gesetz des Kontrastes) as the key to effective advertising design and recommended not only the use of black and white but also "Farbenkontrast" (color contrast).[31] Similarly, the editor of SEIDELS REKLAME, Robert Hösel, described a series of experiments designed to determine which color combinations would produce the most effective contrast between text and background on posters.[32] In one of the first book-length presentations of experimental advertising psychology, Theodor König would then argue in 1922 that the greatest effect on consumer attention could

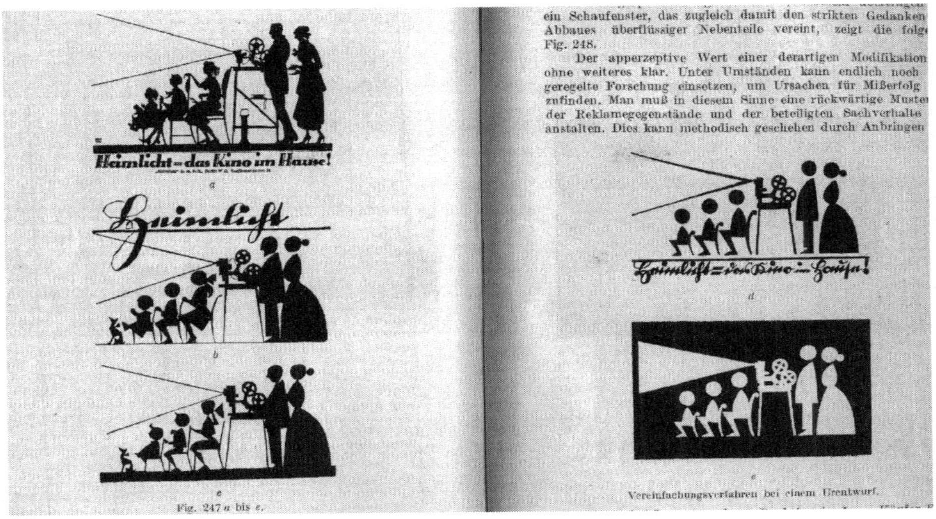

Lucien Bernhard, Heimlicht *advertisement (showing successive stages), from Fritz Giese,* Methoden der Wirtschaftspsychologie *(1927)*

be achieved by contrasting the complimentary primary colors of green and red or yellow and blue.[33]

It is perhaps no accident that the same color combinations show up quite frequently in Ruttmann's animated color advertising films, suggesting that he was at least minimally aware of the latest science on fashioning words and images in terms of their effects on the attention. Ruttmann's awareness of the principles of advertising design would, moreover, hardly be surprising when one considers the intense research into color taking place simultaneously at the Bauhaus, where the study of color – often based on the theories of Chevreul – played a key role in the preliminary course, and courses in advertising, typography and even experimental film formed part of the school's curriculum.[34] Bauhaus teachers frequently employed color wheels of the type described above (including a device developed by Ludwig Hirschfeld-Mack, who also screened abstract color projections at the "absolute film" matinee in 1925) to illustrate the effects of color combinations, and it is surely no accident that the well-known children's block set designed by Alma Siedhoff-Buscher to familiarize children with primary forms – itself reminiscent of "form board" tests – employed the same primary colors combinations of red, green, yellow and blue.[35] Ruttmann knew members of the Bauhaus including Paul Klee and Lyonel Feininger from his days as a student in Munich.[36] Moreover, it was a Bauhaus student, Lore Leudesdorff, who would serve as Ruttmann's principal assistant on several Opus films and advertising films in the mid-1920s.[37] According to Jeanpaul Goergen,

Ruttmann in fact met Leudesdorff in the offices of Edgar Beyfuß, the head of the Ufa Kulturfilmabteilung, when Ruttmann was first working on securing a contract for his films with Pinschewer.[38] Leudesdorff herself would later recall bringing to Ruttmann's advertising films specific knowledge gained from her Bauhaus courses, including "new techniques of colors and forms" (das Neue an Farben und Formen).[39]

As Frederic Schwartz has argued, the interest in psychophysics and advertising among Bauhaus artists, along with the predilection for the metaphor of the artist as "engineer," formed part of a widespread tendency, during the 1920s, to redefine the role of the artist as a potential "expert" in social and media questions rather than a hermetic creator withdrawn from social concerns.[40] This cult of the artist as "expert" was particularly pronounced among the constructivist circles of the Weimar avant-garde – one thinks here of the group around Hans Richter, Werner Graeff and the constructivist journal *G. Material zur elementaren Gestaltung* (*G. Material for Elementary Construction*) – and it also informed the frequent collaborations of avant-garde filmmakers with advertisers. Those collaborations in fact signaled the filmmaker's entry into a very specific kind of "expert" culture. As Corey Ross has shown, the emergence of a professional caste of "advertising experts" in the Weimar Republic (the most prominent association bore the title Verein deutscher Reklamefachleute [Association of German Advertising Experts, VdR]) was centrally bound up with a question and process of legitimation: having witnessed the new prominence ascribed to propaganda as a means of mobilizing public opinion during the First World War, Weimar scientists and policymakers came to see advertising and propaganda as crucial forces within the mediatized public spheres of modern mass democracies. Advertising theorists capitalized on this newfound prominence to legitimate their own role as "experts" in mass psychology and as a key professional class, alongside work scientists and psychotechnicians, within the management of the new industrial consumer society.[41]

It is against this background, moreover, that one can understand the transformations in the area of film advertising after 1918. Although filmic advertisements can be traced back to the earliest years of cinematography (the first known advertising film in Germany dating from 1897),[42] the period after WWI oversaw a veritable explosion in advertising film production, with over 80 companies operating in Germany alone by the end of the 1920s.[43] These companies and their major players stayed abreast of the latest developments in advertising theory and competed fiercely for their reputations as experts in the newly defined professional sphere of filmic advertising. As one writer described it in an article for *Die Reklame* from 1925, "Not every person – no matter how talented – is an expert in this field. Not every person can master the difficult instrument of propaganda, and this goes especially for filmic propaganda, since this form must be treated in a very specific way."[44]

Within this new field of professional film advertisers, the most prominent player was surely Julius Pinschewer. Having started making advertising films in the 1910s, Pinschewer went on to become a major producer of propaganda film during the war years, before founding one of the most successful advertising enterprises of the Weimar Republic in 1918 (and he would continue to produce advertising films after his flight to Switzerland in 1933).[45] Pinschewer held numerous contracts, many exclusive, with major cinemas, variety stages, schools, exhibitions and trade fairs throughout Germany, and even with the on-board cinemas of the cruise ships belonging to the Hamburg-Amerika shipping line (HAPAG). By 1926, Pinschewer could claim that his films were seen by 3,000,000 spectators weekly.[46] It was Pinschewer who inaugurated the trend of avant-garde advertising films in Weimar, beginning with his collaborations with Ruttmann and Reiniger in 1922. Given the increasing prominence of advertising in the mass-mediated public spheres of the new democracy, working with Pinschewer's company – as so many of the experimental filmmakers of the period did – meant a legitimation of the public role of film itself within the new republic, and a confirmation of the filmmaker's status as a professional with expertise analogous to that of scientific experts in advertising.

That Ruttmann himself was understood at least partly in this sense can be gathered, among other things, by the reception that his advertising films received in advertising circles. While we do not have record of the precise circulation of Ruttmann's advertising films for Pinschewer, based on what we know about advertising film distribution at the time (and on the considerable investment Ruttmann's color films demanded from the commissioning companies), we can assume that they were screened in large and mid-sized theaters throughout Germany.[47] They were likely also shown – as examples of innovative advertising design – in trade fairs and other special venues for industry experts. This is suggested among other things by the attention Ruttmann's films generated in the trade literature of the advertising industry. As film itself came to figure more prominently within discussions of advertising in the mid-1920s, advertising theorists took an increased interest in the use of abstract film on account of its perceived psychosomatic effects on spectators, and they held out particularly high hopes for the films of Ruttmann. Typical, in this respect, was an article published in *Die Reklame* – the official organ of the VdR – in which the author praised Ruttmann as the most prominent representative of a "new type of color film advertisement" (neuartigen Buntfilm-Werbung). With their "wave-like movement" (Wellenbewegung) and play of primary colors, the writer argued, Ruttmann's films "exert a lasting hold on spectators" (fesseln nachhaltig).[48] Precisely what was at stake in this argument can be seen in another article on advertising film for the journal *Industrielle Psychotechnik* (the journal of the Institut für Wirtschaftspsychologie mentioned above), in which the advertising theorist Käthe Kurtzig distinguished three prevalent forms of advertising film: the humorous cartoon caricature (the most widespread form at the time), the graceful silhouette in the style of Lotte Reiniger, and what she dubbed the "absolute" advertising film – a designation she almost certainly took from the much discussed matinee Der absolute Film (1925), where Ruttmann's Opus II, III and IV had their public debuts a year earlier.[49] It was Ruttmann's animated advertisements that formed the model for the final category, and Kurtzig duly illustrated her article with still from Der Aufstieg, Ruttmann's 1926 advertisement for the Düsseldorf Gesolei exhibition of body culture and social welfare. Such abstract film, she argued, drew its efficacy above all from the psychophysical power of rhythmical movement:

> Absolute film, this latest type of artistic film, offers no rounded stories. Rather, it attempts to give visible expression to ideational content through the movement of ornaments and figures; it works above all through the rhythmical power of movement, which brings the spectator into resonance with its movements [den Zuschauer zum Mitschwingen bringt] and allows him not simply to see and understand events on the screen, but also to experience them.[50]

If Kurtzig's conception of Ruttmann's absolute film and its usefulness for advertising sounds like the descriptions of Rudolf Kurtz cited above, this is hardly a coincidence. Like the author of *Film und Expressionismus*, she held out the hope that absolute film, by peeling off the layers of narrative and psychological associations, could enhance film's psychophysical force, its ability to make spectators "move with" (mitschwingen) the images on the screen.

It was precisely this notion of "mitschwingen" that attracted advertising theorists to absolute film in their desire to harness spectatorial attention. The same year as Kurtzig's article for *Industrielle Psychotechnik*, another advertising theorist Fritz Pauli caused a small sensation in the advertising world with the publication of his treatise *Rhythmus und Resonanz als ökonomisches Prinzip in der Reklame* (*Rhythm and Resonance as Economical Principle in Advertising*).[51] Drawing on contemporary research in work science and engineering, Pauli argued that rhythmical presentations of advertisements (in print, electric signage and film) could lend them a quasi-hypnotic power over spectators by adjusting the movements of the spectators' nervous systems to the rhythms of the advertisements itself: "Such a rhythm functions hypnotically to leave an inextinguishable impression with no unpleasant side effects; for every consumer is immediately calibrated to the resonance of these lights and syllables."[52] Like Kurtzig, Pauli located the efficacy of abstract rhythm in the experience of "mitschwingen," the power of the advertisement to make spectators "move with" the rhythmical presentation. When "the advertisement's oscillations" ("Werbeschwingungen") are correctly calibrated, he argued, the spectator himself becomes "a part of the oscillating system" ("Teil des Schwingsystems").[53] Little wonder, then, that Pauli would take interest in Ruttmann's abstract rhythmical films. Writing the same year for *Die Reklame,* he singled out Ruttmann's DER SIEGER and DAS WIEDERGEFUNDENE PARADIES for offering what he described as "the novel use of forms and colors for effects along with a clearly recognizable approach to rhythmical organization."[54]

Interestingly, Ruttmann himself would adopt similar language of "Schwingen" to describe the effects he sought to attain with his "optical music." Describing his BERLIN film in 1927, Ruttmann wrote: "And if I have succeeded in bringing the audience into oscillation [zum Schwingen zu bringen], to make them experience the city of Berlin, then I have attained my goal."[55] Scholars have often commented on Ruttmann's conceptualization of film as a means of provoking the experience of movement. Jeanpaul Goergen, for example, describes Ruttmann's project in BERLIN as follows:

> In fact, Ruttmann does not see himself [...] as a reporter. [...] He attempts rather to bring about a new artistic reality; he observes Berlin with an aesthetic gaze and attempts to transmit his artistic feelings to the spectator. He wants to intoxicate spectators, to set them into motion [zum Schwingen bringen], to trigger vibrations.[56]

As we have seen, however, the desire to provoke movement ("Schwingen") in resonance with the rhythmical image was not simply an "aesthetic" endeavor opposed to reality, but rather the object of intense advertising research, which understood "Schwingen" and "Mitschwingen" as an eminently useful economical phenomenon. This was a form and a language of advertising expertise: one that Fritz Pauli explicitly adopted from engineering treatises such as Heinrich von Schieferstein's "Die Ausnützung mechanischer Schwingungen im Maschinenbau" ("Harnessing Mechanical Oscillations in Mechanical Engineering," 1925), and one that Ruttmann likely adopted from advertising experts such as Pauli.[57] That Ruttmann understood animated advertising as a forum for generating such forms of "resonating" spectatorship is also suggested by several of his later animated advertisements. In the 1926 Gelosei advertisement DER AUFSTIEG, in which an allegorical "Michel" figure representing the German nation climbs back to health after the ravages of war and inflation, the character's restored vitality is marked by his ability to turn flips in resonance with the isorhythmical waves flowing at the bottom of the image. Similarly, in an advertisement for AEG radio equipment from the same year, SPIEL DER WELLEN (PLAY OF THE WAVES), a European listener, receiving the sound of an African drumbeat via his radio headphones, smiles as he rocks back and forth in pleasurable resonance with the waves of the radio. Although serving the immediate purpose of

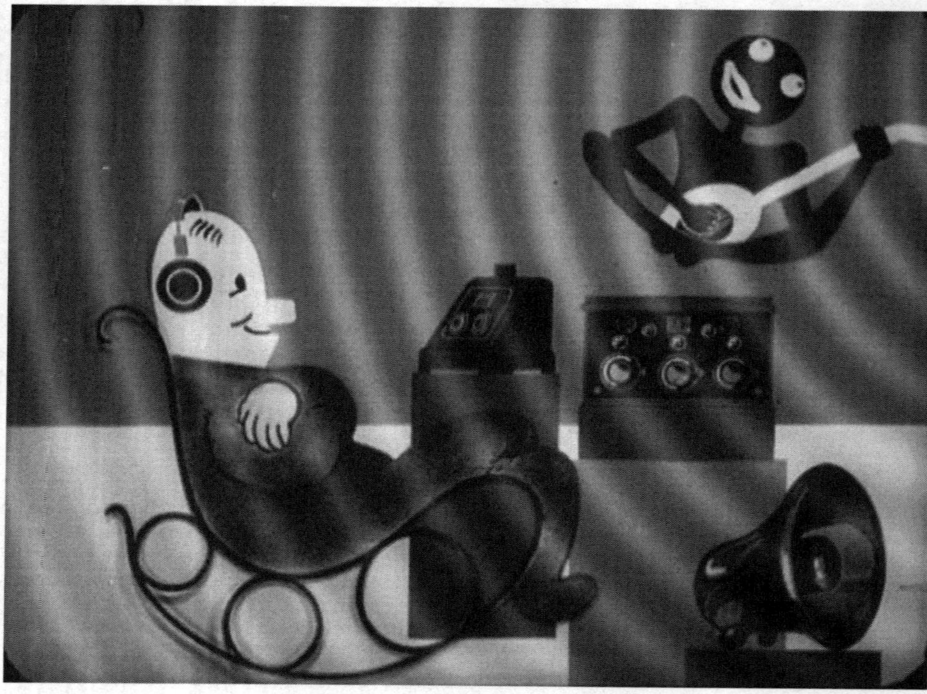

Still from Ruttmann, SPIEL DER WELLEN *(1925)*

advertising radio equipment, the image also offers an intermedial corollary for the filmic *dispositif* Ruttmann sought to create with advertising film: one that – like Fritz Pauli's calibrated advertisements – would cause spectators to move in resonance with the representations unfolding on the screen.[58] Thus Ruttmann's abstract "Wellenbewegung" represented something more than a mere artistic phenomenon; it was, rather, part and parcel of an expert research on advertising design.

From Abstraction to Figuration: Ruttmann's Animated Advertisements in Context

Interestingly, for all of their enthusiasm for abstract forms, colors and rhythms, none of the advertising theorists who discussed Ruttmann acknowledged the extent to which his advertising films had, in fact, deviated from the central precept of "absolute" cinema through the reintroduction of identifiable objects. This too, however, could find a justification in advertising theory. Indeed, the one point on which advertising psychology contradicted the "flight of ideas" inaugurated by psychophysical testing was precisely the question of meaning and recognition. Theodor König, for example, in the same book cited above, identified three principal goals for a successful advertisement: capturing the attention, producing pleasure and stimulating memory. And he argued – even as he extolled at length the benefits of Ebbinghaus's experiments in meaningless syllables for advertising research – that the use of *identifiable* objects was critical to all three phases. First, while novel impressions can stimulate our curiosity, the qualities of familiarity (Vertrautheit) and meaningfulness (Bedeutsamkeit) capture the attention more effectively because the objects thus recognized speak to spectators' interests.[59] Secondly, in terms of pleasure, König argued that, alongside other factors such as harmony of form or the use of humor, the very familiarity of objects served to stimulate spectatorial pleasure: "According to a well-known psychological law, the pleasure we receive from the very act of recognizing something is easily transferred to that object itself."[60] Finally, and in direct distinction to Ebbinghaus, König argued that while meaningless syllables might provide the ideal zero-degree material for testing perception and memory, in actual practice, representations allowing for meaningful associations were much more affective at *stimulating* memory. Customers, he argued, perceive and retain meaningful words much more effectively than "concatenations of meaningless syllables [Verbindungen sinnloser Silben]."[61] The same logic, moreover, applies to images: "Memory can and must be supported by images, drawing and diagrams that are, to the greatest extent possible, meaningful and easy to perceive and understand."[62] Similarly, for trademark design, König argued: "Trademarks should be meaningful, for the figures that are retained and distinguished from others are above all those that provoke an associative chain of thoughts and a process of interpretation."[63]

Within certain parameters, then, advertising theory actually sought to *temper* the evacuation of meaning that characterized both modern psychophysics and much experimental art. But I would hasten to add that this was not in order to return to any 18th-century model of spiritualizing or interiorizing hermeneutics. Rather, the call for "meaningful" associations was made in the very interest of increasing the advertisement's material efficacy with actual consumers: only a combination of signifiers and signifieds, only a mix of abstraction and identifiable content, could elicit the maximum productivity of the attention and of memory that advertisers sought and thus guarantee the advertisement's real-world success.

At this point, we can better understand how Ruttmann's advertising films – with their slippage between abstraction and figuration – took up ideas from advertising theory as it had developed by the 1920s. Indeed, according to Rudolf Kurtz, Ruttmann's absolute films themselves already contained something

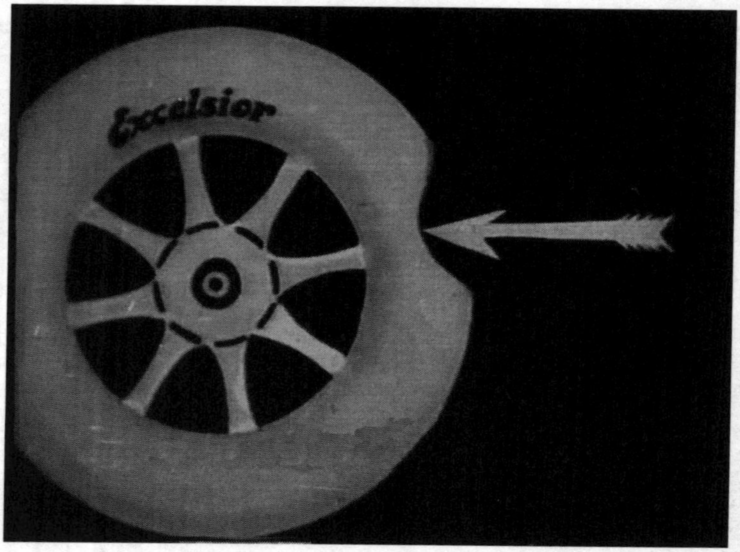

Still from Harry Jäger, IM LANDE DER APPACHEN *(1919)*

of this mixture of abstraction and recognition key to the successful advertisement. In the endless multitude of rounded, wave-like and pointed forms populating Ruttmann's films, as well as their lively interaction on the screen, Kurtz saw a far greater degree of what he called "organic associations" or "organic reminiscences" (organische Anklänge) – and thus far greater room for psychological operations – than in the reductive geometry of Viking Eggeling and Hans Richter: "The strong attraction of Ruttmann's films lies in their psychological impulses, which continually account for their efficacy. His compositions are animated by a drama in which the actors are mathematical forms that contain a wealth of organic associations."[64] This tendency toward psychological associations might account for the ease with which Ruttmann's elementary aesthetics were adaptable to figurative animation, as for example in the sequence he created to depict Kriemhild's dream in Fritz Lang's NIBELUNGEN (1924), where his familiar abstract shapes morph into silhouettes of a falcon and two eagles. But Kurtz also sees it as a factor that lent itself particularly well to advertising. "Just how great a wealth of expression is contained in these colorful forms in movement can be seen in the fact that Ruttmann had considerable success with an industry advertising film in this style."[65]

While one may or may not agree with Kurtz's assessment of Ruttmann's OPUS films and their effects on spectators, it does suggest what was at stake in Ruttmann's *advertising* films. For what those films repeatedly thematize is precisely the line between abstraction and "organic" associations – associations

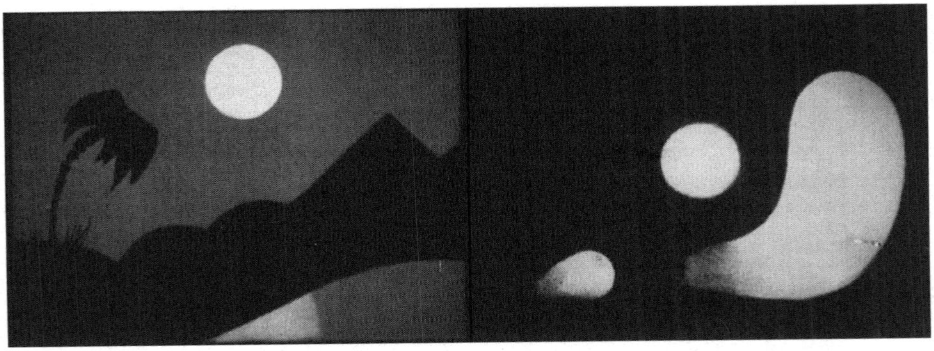

Stills from Ruttmann, DER SIEGER. EIN FILM IN FARBEN *(1922). Tropical lagoon replaced by abstract forms*

they continually make and undo before our eyes. A case in point can be seen in Ruttmann's first advertising film DER SIEGER, a tire advertisement commissioned by the Hannover Gummiwerke Excelsior. For his film, Ruttmann borrowed motifs from a previous advertisement for Excelsior tires by Harry Jäger entitled IM LANDE DER APPACHEN (IN THE LAND OF THE APACHES, 1920). Drawn in a black and white caricature style, Jäger's animated film showed a group of men in an automobile being attacked by bow-wielding Indians but escaping when the Indians' arrows prove no match for the resistant Excelsior tires. Where Jaeger's film relied on a well-tried adventure scenario, however, Ruttmann's film looks back to the design aesthetics of advertising posters to construct a drama of elementary forms. Following a title card reading "Der Sieger: ein Film in Farben," the film opens onto a clearly identifiable image of a tropical landscape, over which a sun then rises, reflected in the lagoon below. But hardly have we had time to absorb this harmonious image – with its static and balanced composition of palm tree, sun, water and mountain – when it is immediately transformed by a dark and menacing storm cloud into an abstract field of frenetic explosions followed by a dance of circular and paisley forms in primary colors of red, blue and yellow.

This transformation has everything to do with pleasure. For DER SIEGER will recount precisely the effort to reinstate the lost idyll of the establishing image on a higher, industrial plane, and the Excelsior tire will form the agent of that sublation. As the tropical lagoon disappears in the opening sequence, only the form of the circle remains, no longer denoting a sun, but simply constituting one element among others in an abstract graphic conflict of colored shapes. Soon, however, this circle – the dominant form of Ruttmann's film – will morph back into an object, namely the Excelsior tire, which rolls over abstract waves, geometrical rectangles, and finally a new industrial landscape, all presented in various

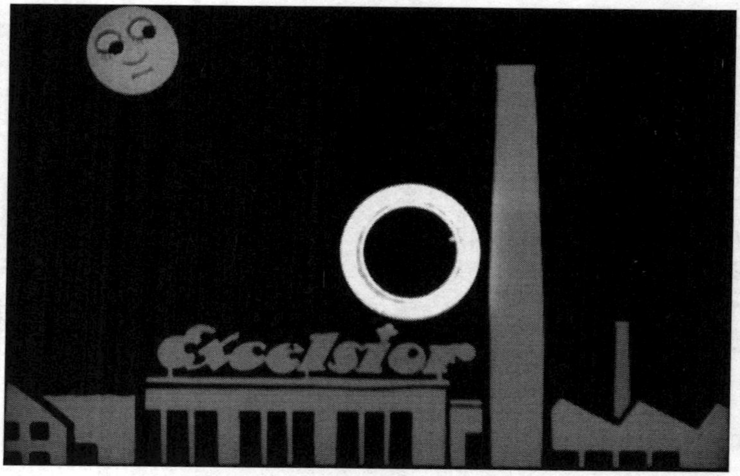

Still from Ruttmann, DER SIEGER *(1922)*

combinations of red, green, blue and yellow. Throughout these transformations, the tire – here recalling Jäger's scenario – is characterized by its bouncy elasticity and its corresponding ability to withstand the shocks of Ruttmann's angry spikes. But seen within Ruttmann's new abstract technological environment, this theme of elasticity takes on new connotations, recalling George Grosz's contention, in his 1917 poem "Man muß Kautschukmann sein" ("One Must be Like Rubber"), that modern consciousness had to become as elastic as rubber in order to adapt to the jolts of the technological environment, with its traffic accidents, explosions and dizzying heights.[66] Indeed, in an image reminiscent of Freud's postwar description of consciousness as a protective shield, the elastic tire now encircles the sun itself, which smiles in glee as if happy to be shielded from the kinds of storms that destroyed the former paradise. Finally, at the end of the film, the tire will literally become a new sun, filling the screen with its glowing yellow halo. As the culmination of a narrative of paradise lost and found, Ruttmann's sunny tire is thus associated with much more than simply a smooth ride; the pleasure this ad promises is one of psychic stability, the pleasure of adapting to the perceptual shocks of war and industrial modernity – shocks which, as Janet Ward has shown, included the exponential increase in advertising itself with its constant claims on consumer attention.[67]

Most importantly, however, this loss and restoration of stability is echoed, on the formal level, by a drama of the disappearance and restoration of identifiable objects: the passage from the representation of familiar things to one of abstract forms and back again. Such a back-and-forth movement, as I argued above, echoes a tension between abstract shapes and meaningful forms (or "organic associations") already present in advertising theory itself. But within the context of Ruttmann's narrative of paradise lost and found, this tension cannot but also recall Wilhelm Worringer's theory of the dualism between "abstraction" and "empathy" in visual art. In his study *Abstraktion und Einfühlung* (*Abstraction and Empathy*, 1908), Worringer associated naturalistic representations with a relation of trust and "familiarity" (Vertraulichkeit) between the observing subject and its environment, while he understood abstraction as a compensatory activity undertaken in reaction to a sense of anxiety before a chaotic or threatening external world.[68] Worringer attributed such an anxiety above all to "primitive" cultures, but he also saw it at work in the burgeoning avant-garde movements of the early 20th century (e.g. cubist painting), and compared it the signature modern pathologies discussed in the psychological literature of his day, citing the well-known condition of agoraphobia ("Platzangst") as an explanation for the elimination of three dimensional space in the abstract surface.[69] In unmaking and remaking the perceptual world of objects on the surface of the filmic canvas, Ruttmann's film rehearses, as it were, Worringer's conceptual opposition, passing from an aesthetic of empathy to one of abstraction and back again. And the tire, as the successor to Ruttmann's abstract circle, figures as the agent of this process.

Riding the Curve of Modernity's Information Flows

Of course, Ruttmann's abstraction differs from that described by Worringer in that it occurs not only at the level of spatial forms, but also at the level of *temporal* movement. In his much-discussed essay "Malerei mit Zeit" ("Painting with Time"), an unpublished text written shortly after WWI, Ruttmann described his own transition from painting to film as an effort to introduce movement into visual art. But he also emphasized his desire to isolate and visualize abstract trajectories of movement, a project he understood as a reaction to a potentially "hostile" environment, namely one characterized by a the acceleration of perception and a surplus of information:

> Telegraphs, high-speed trains, stenography, photography, high-speed press machines, etc. […] have brought about a speed in the transmission of intellectual results previously unknown. For the individual, this speed with which information is transmitted results in a state of continuous inundation by material that can no longer be processed by traditional methods.[70]

Nearly all of the media and technologies described here – most explicitly the train and the rotary press – would play key roles seven years later in Ruttmann's

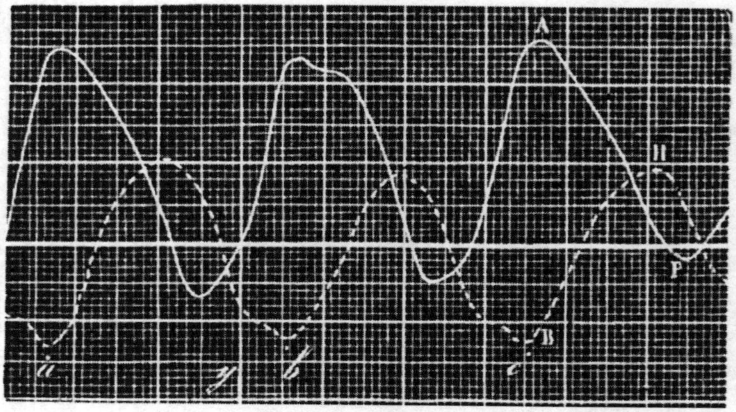

Marey, curve showing the movements of a pigeon's wing, from La méthode graphique dans les sciences *(1885)*

Berlin film as the catalysts of a process in which perception literally becomes blurred by acceleration.[71] But already in his 1920 essay, Ruttmann saw this technological transformation as the key factor underlying his own explorations in abstract animation. For it is above all in reaction to this sense of accelerated information flows, he argued, that art needed to abstract from the contingent details of individual images to focus on *lines of movement*:

> [A]s a result of the increased speed at which individual data is cranked out, the gaze is now diverted from individual contents to the overall trajectory of a curve formed from the various points, a phenomenon that unfolds in time. Thus the object of our observation is now temporal development and the physiognomy of a curve caught in continuous transformation, and no longer the static disposition of individual points.[72]

Ruttmann's language of "curves" here recalls a long tradition of abstract representations of movement stretching back into the 19th century: namely the scientific motion curves, by which 19th-century physiologists sought to represent abstract trajectories of movement and change. Such curves came in many forms: the rhythmical curves of breathing and heartbeat registered by pneumographs and sphygmographs; the trajectories of force and fatigue inscribed by dynamometers; the paths of bodies isolated by Marey's geometrical chronophotography or the chronocyclegraphic studies of Frank and Lilian Gilbreth. But as visual representations, all of these "curves" shared a labor of *simplification*: the effort to bracket the contingent details of individual bodies so as to visualize the elementary arc of a movement or a development.[73] However, this is not to argue

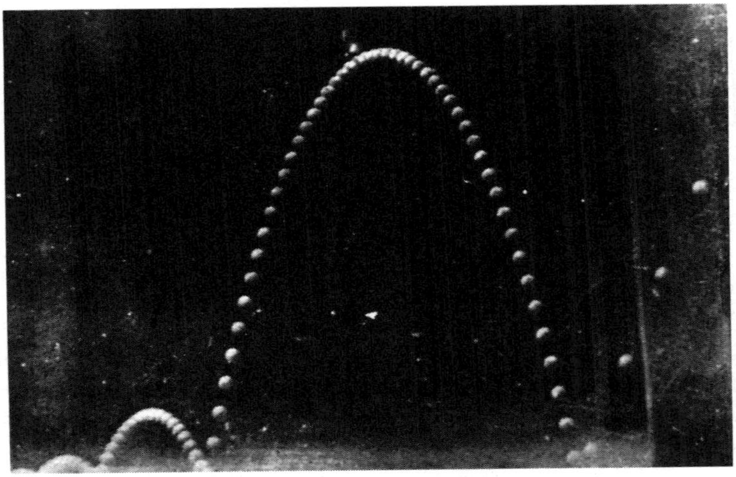

Etienne-Jules Marey, trajectory of a bouncing ball (1886)

that Ruttmann sought simply to transpose the epistemological project of 19th-century motion "curves" onto film; on the contrary, as his description of the curve's "continuous transformation" suggests, Ruttmann's motivation for temporal abstraction was not to isolate trajectories of movement for study in a static image, but to create a new vocabulary of abstract movement-patterns unfolding in time (Ruttmann goes on to provide a long list of such movements with names such as "wave-like" (wellenförmig), "dance-like" (tanzartig), "snake-like" (schlangenartig), "galloping" (galoppierend), "raging" (tobend), etc.) In other words, at stake, in Ruttmann's filmic abstractions, was no longer an epistemological project, but rather an *experiential* one. This was, to be sure, a Bergsonian project, with precursors in the widespread use of color organs of the 1910s or in Loïe Fuller's light and electricity dances.[74] But it was also motivated by a desire to adapt vision and spectatorship to the information overload that threatened to overwhelm subjective perception. While such a project clearly resonates with Worringer's view of abstraction as a reaction to a hostile environment, that environment is now defined explicitly by technology (mass media and rapid transportation) rather than nature, and the central quality of its "chaos" is a temporal one linked directly to the modern experience of acceleration. This was, we might recall, the same experience that informed the development of advertising psychology itself, with its constant search for new ways of capturing the fleeting attention of consumers caught between myriad impressions in movement.

Coming back to DER SIEGER, one could thus argue that the real pleasure promised by Ruttmann's tire – an emblem of acceleration if there ever was one – consists precisely in its promise to navigate this new industrial world by overseeing the restoration, as it were, of the lost paradise of the opening image on a higher industrial plane. In this narrative of paradise lost and found, moreover, DER SIEGER establishes a pattern that will be repeated in different variations in several of Ruttmann's subsequent advertising films, in which pleasure is constantly evoked through an eminently Freudian narrative of restoring a state of harmony existing before the tension or conflict introduced by the play of graphic forms.[75] This narrative finds its most explicit expression in Ruttmann's 1925 ad DAS WIEDERGEFUNDENE PARADIES, which recounts a modified version of the expulsion from the Garden to promise viewers that flowers will literally "awaken memories of paradisiacal pleasures." But the promise of pleasure is also present in film such as DAS WUNDER, where alcohol has the magical power to resolve conflict; in the 1926 film SPIEL DER WELLEN, where the AEG radio receives waves from an African landscape transporting the latter into the protected space of a European radio-listener's headphones; or DER AUFSTIEG, in which the Gesolei exhibition promises to restore the nation to its healthy state before the ravages of warfare and hyperinflation. Thus, these films repeatedly stage moments of anxiety linked to the destruction of pleasurable origins through graphic conflict only to promise their restoration on a higher plane by means of industrial products. At the formal level, this back-and-forth between pleasurable stasis and unpleasurable conflict finds its parallel in the very tension between the unfamiliar world of abstract forms and figurative images of familiar things. Like Freud's child, Ruttmann's advertisements thus constantly throw away the object only to reel it in again in a repetitive back-and-forth trajectory between empathetic description and defensive abstraction, where the commodity and the trademark figure as the agents of a new trust in the world of things and three-dimensional space.

Pleasure was, not surprisingly, a central preoccupation for proponents of the advertising film and their conceptualization of the audience. In a 1926 article for *Die Reklame,* for example, Fritz Pauli argued that the darkened movie theater had the unique advantage over billboards, newspapers or radio of completely monopolizing the spectator's captive attention:

> [T]he audience *has* to register the advertisement, whether it wants to or not. One can deliberately oversee the advertisements section of a newspaper; one can more or less avoid the sight of traffic and electric advertisements; one can take off one's headphones during radio advertisements or simply turn off the receiver; but it is not easy to close one's eyes in the movie theater.[76]

However, Pauli continued, such a compulsory claim on the attention could backfire if didactic or boring films failed to please spectators through humor or

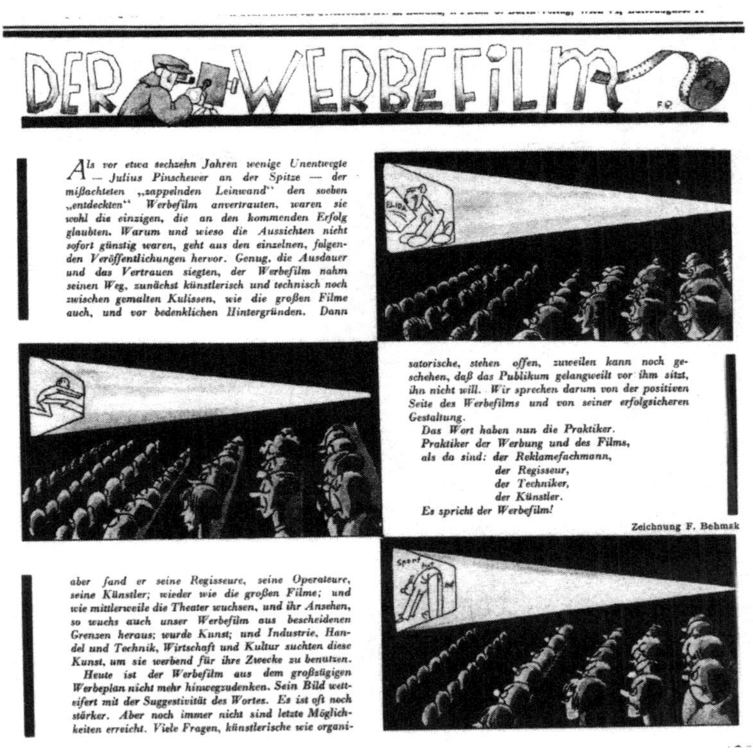

DER WERBEFILM

Als vor etwa sechzehn Jahren wenige Unentwegte — Julius Pinschewer an der Spitze — der mißachteten „zappelnden Leinwand" den soeben „entdeckten" Werbefilm anvertrauten, waren sie wohl die einzigen, die an den kommenden Erfolg glaubten. Warum und wieso die Aussichten nicht sofort günstig waren, geht aus den einzelnen, folgenden Veröffentlichungen hervor. Genug, die Ausdauer und das Vertrauen siegten, der Werbefilm nahm seinen Weg, zunächst künstlerisch und technisch noch zwischen gemalten Kulissen, wie die großen Filme auch, und vor bedenklichen Hintergründen. Dann aber fand er seine Regisseure, seine Operateure, seine Künstler; wieder wie die großen Filme; und wie mittlerweile die Theater wuchsen, und ihr Ansehen, so wuchs auch unser Werbefilm aus bescheidenen Grenzen heraus; wurde Kunst; und Industrie, Handel und Technik, Wirtschaft und Kultur suchten diese Kunst, um sie werbend für ihre Zwecke zu benutzen.

Heute ist der Werbefilm aus dem großzügigen Werbeplan nicht mehr hinwegzudenken. Sein Bild wetteifert mit der Suggestivität des Wortes. Es ist oft noch stärker. Aber noch immer nicht sind letzte Möglichkeiten erreicht. Viele Fragen, künstlerische wie organisatorische, stehen offen, zuweilen kann noch geschehen, daß das Publikum gelangweilt vor ihm sitzt, ihn nicht will. Wir sprechen darum von der positiven Seite des Werbefilms und von seiner erfolgsicheren Gestaltung.

Das Wort haben nun die Praktiker.
Praktiker der Werbung und des Films,
als da sind: der Reklamefachmann,
der Regisseur,
der Techniker,
der Künstler.
Es spricht der Werbefilm!

Zeichnung F. Behmak

Caricature of film audiences, from Die Reklame *(1927)*

interesting tricks: "Audiences do not wish to feel cheated, as it were, out of their time or their ticket price. […] They wish to be amused, thrilled or educated in an interesting way. When this is the case, they feel entertained and regard the product being advertised with favor."[77] Pauli's argument here was echoed more or less verbatim in numerous other books and articles from the time,[78] and it found an illustration the following year on the title page of a special issue of *Die Reklame* devoted to advertising film, on which a caricature drawing compared bored, angry and entertained audiences to suggest that pleasure played a central role in the success of filmic advertisements. Nor was Pinschewer himself unaware of such theories, as he would later resort to the same argument to explain the prevalence of animation in advertising film:

> A particular advantage of film advertising resides in the fact that spectators sitting in the darkened room cannot avoid paying attention to the film. Precisely for this reason, the advertising content should be presented in a pleasurable form. This is also the reason why people prefer to clothe advertising film in the form of animation [Trickfilm], for animation satisfies the need for relaxing entertainment.[79]

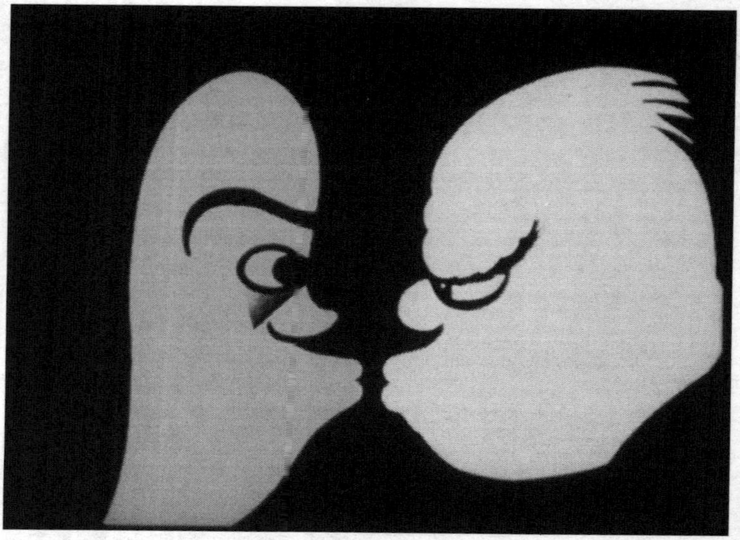

Sill from Ruttmann, DAS WUNDER *(1922)*

It was also in the interest of stimulating such pleasure that product advertisements resorted from the beginning to strategies of humor, a topic much discussed in the literature on advertising and one of the principal motivations for the widespread use of caricature animation in film advertisements of the 1920s. As one writer for SEIDELS REKLAME put it in 1927, "Audiences today want humor. The animated film offers the possibility of conjuring up the most grotesque Chaplinades, the most fantastical improbabilities on the screen."[80] In particular, advertisers called for the use of gentle humor typical of German print caricature traditions as opposed to the biting satire of Dada and expressionist cabaret. Typical, in this respect, was a 1927 article by the animator Lutz Michaelis, who argued that the advertising animator "should ensure that he does not develop aggressive humor (satire); rather, his figures should be based in a jovial humorous characterization. (To draw on a crass comparison, Wilhelm Busch's caricatures are funny and jovial, while George Grosz's every pen-stroke is caustic and aggressive)."[81]

Although Ruttmann's experimental advertisements sought to distinguished themselves from the caricatures of animators such as Michaelis and Harry Jäger, he was not averse to employing such moments of gentle humor – for example in the Kantorowicz film, where the bickering faces begin to kiss one another lovingly after consuming the liqueur from the bottle conjured up by a magician. But as I have argued, his films also sought to produce pleasure at the formal level through the play of abstraction and empathy, by which Ruttmann continuously staged perceptive reactions to the new technological conditions with which these advertisements were concerned. If Ruttmann's commodity objects promised pleasure, this was above all through their promise to navigate this new world of accelerated information, and more precisely to restore a sense of trust in the new landscape of people, objects and information in motion. Ruttmann's advertisements not only participated, with their targeted stimulation of attention through color and movement, in the shocks of this new media environment, but also promised to help spectators come to terms with that environment in and through acts of consumption.

Conclusion: Experimental Advertisements and the Governance of Perception

In conclusion, I might add that although I am focusing on Ruttmann in this book, the play of abstraction and empathy I have followed here was not entirely unique to his films, but found many imitators in the world of film advertising during the interwar years. From Ewald Schumacher's 1925 advertisement FLAMMENTANZ (DANCE OF FLAMES), where the flames produced by the gas fuel transform from abstract forms into personified dancers and back again, to the cigarette commercials by Hans Fischerkoesen (e.g. SCHALL UND RAUCH [SOUND AND SMOKE], 1933), Wolfgang Kaskeline (ZWEI FARBEN [TWO COLORS], 1933) and Oskar Fischinger (MURATTI GREIFT EIN, 1934), with their play of abstract movement and recognizable objects, the alternation of abstraction and figuration constituted an important strategy of filmic advertisement in the 1920s. Given the involvement of avant-garde and experimental artists in these films, one could easily read them as neglected examples of what Gilles Deleuze has called "liquid" or "gaseous" perception in modernist experimental cinema; according to Deleuze, a good deal of early experimental filmmaking attempted to overcome territorialized modes of instrumental perception to attain – or "regain" – a Bergsonian realm of pure fluctuation or universal variation underneath.[82] Above all Vertov, Deleuze argued, sought "to reach 'another' perception, which is the genetic element of all perception."[83] But in order to understand the full stakes of the preoccupation with abstract movement in experimental advertising films of the 1920s, it is also crucial to read them within the context of advertising culture – and more specifically to see their relation to theories of advertising pleasure. It was precisely in the back-and-forth movement between abstraction and familiar objects, between the loss of meaning and its recuperation in the commodity, that the pleasure and efficacy of these films resided.

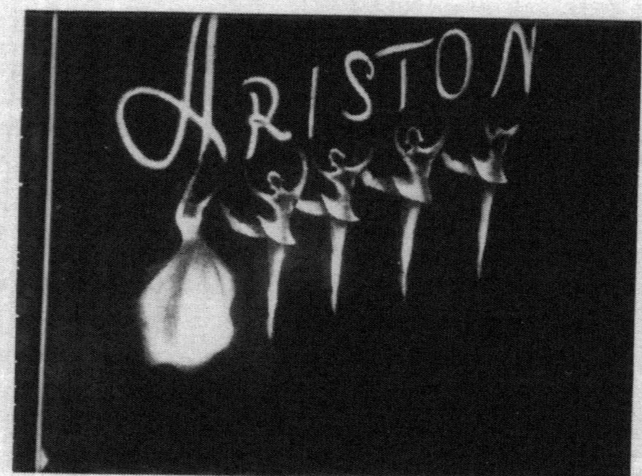

Still from Hans Fischerkoesen, SCHALL UND RAUCH *(1933)*

Far from challenging that efficacy or undermining the "usefulness" of the image, the avant-garde filmmakers who participated in product advertising in the 1920s affirmed it. If these filmmakers were attracted to advertising, this was not on account of a financial compromise or as part of a campaign of subversion, but because advertising provided a forum in which to demonstrate the filmmaker's expertise, and the relevance of that expertise for a technological-industrial society. Abstraction, movement and rhythm, that is, were not simply artistic elements, but also scientific and practical ones: the building blocks of "management images" that might regulate perception, attention and audience reactions. Reducing the image to its "psychophysical" potential, Ruttmann's "absolute" film promised to harness this governing power of the image. As we will see in the following chapters, Ruttmann's subsequent turn toward photographic images and montage might have constituted a break in appearance from his abstract animation, but he would continue to fashion cinema as a tool for managing mass culture throughout his career.

2. The Cross-Section: Images of the World and Contingency Management in Ruttmann's Montage Films of the Late 1920s (1927-1929)

Introduction

In the last chapter, I argued that abstract design was never simply an aesthetic phenomenon, but also the object of psychophysiological research, much of it carried out within the new science of advertising psychology. The participation in advertising on the part of Ruttmann and other filmmakers could hardly be written off as a compromise of aesthetic principles; it was, rather, a logical extension and application of their own experiments in abstract film design, which were carried out within a horizon of application. In a broader sense, we saw that Ruttmann understood reduction and abstraction as a potential answer to a problem of perception in modernity. Drawing on the convention of the scientific "curve," he saw the aesthetics of abstraction as a means of training perception to operate within the new technological and mass-mediated public spheres of the early 20th century, spheres defined above all by acceleration and the increasing accumulation of mental and visual "data."

One could easily carry this analysis of "perception training" over to the film that sealed Ruttmann's international fame in 1920s and since, his magnum opus BERLIN. DIE SINFONIE DER GROSSSTADT (BERLIN. THE SYMPHONY OF A GREAT CITY, 1927), in which Ruttmann used montage to depict the teeming life of the metropolis from morning until nightfall.[1] As has often been pointed out, Ruttmann's first full-length film, despite replacing animation with photographic images, retained a schematic "musical" quality in its imitation of the symphonic form, its division into five "acts" of varying intensities, and its calibration of visual montage with the musical score by Edmund Meisel. Upon the film's premiere, critic Herbert Jhering spoke of Ruttmann's "Bildmusik" (image music) in BERLIN,[2] and Béla Balázs would invoke the term "optische Musik" (optical music) to describe BERLIN in his book *Der Geist des Films* (*The Spirit of Film*, 1930).[3] Subsequent scholars have largely followed in the same path.[4] Such a musical quality, moreover, would appear to have informed Ruttmann's very planning of the film. As Goergen notes, rather than basing the film on a linear script, Ruttmann employed a kind of card catalogue for the individual scenes; each card included not only a description of the scene's content, but also, as one

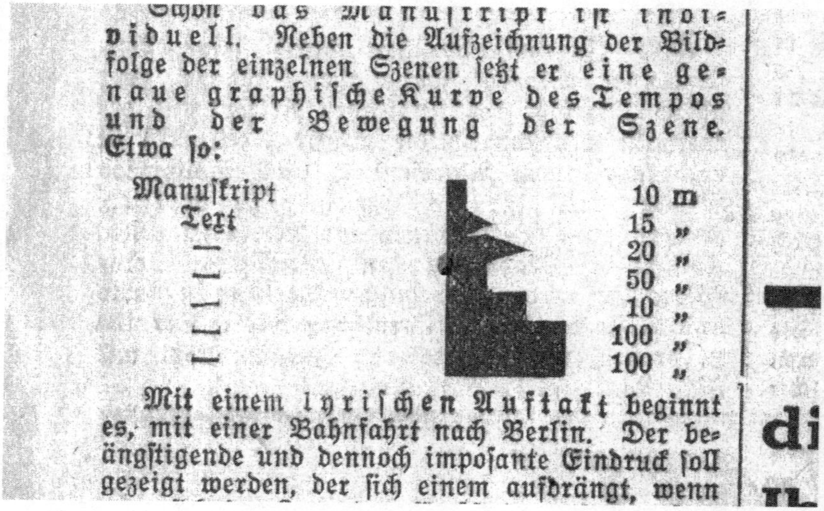

Schon das Manuskript ist indi-
viduell. Neben die Aufzeichnung der Bild-
folge der einzelnen Szenen setzt er eine ge-
naue graphische Kurve des Tempos
und der Bewegung der Szene.
Etwa so:

Manuskript 10 m
Text 15 „
— 20 „
— 50 „
— 10 „
— 100 „
— 100 „

Mit einem lyrischen Auftakt beginnt
es, mit einer Bahnfahrt nach Berlin. Der be-
ängstigende und dennoch imposante Eindruck soll
gezeigt werden, der sich einem aufdrängt, wenn

Excerpt from "manuscript" for BERLIN. DIE SINFONIE DER GROSSSTADT, *from Clarus, "Der Schöpfer des abstrakten Films Walter Ruttmann,"* FILM-KURIER *(1926)*

writer for the journal *Filmkurier* described it in an article from September 1926, "a precise graphic curve representing the scene's tempo and movement."[5]

Once again, however, this use of motion curves served not simply an aesthetic purpose, but also a practical one. For BERLIN deals with the same motifs of acceleration and information overload that Ruttmann cited as the motivations for his desire to adapt scientific curvature to film in his "Painting with Time" essay of 1919. Indeed, the very media and technologies cited in that essay – including high-speed trains, rotary presses and telegraphs (to which we can add typewriters and telephones) – all figure centrally in BERLIN as catalysts of acceleration and a resulting surcharge of visual and mental information. Within this context, it should hardly be surprising to see the film thematizing the transformation of perception from a perception of individual "contents" to one of lines and curves. An obvious example can be seen in the film's much discussed opening, in which animated circles and rectangles reminiscent of the OPUS films begin to rotate at an ever-increasing velocity before giving way – via a graphic match – to the train montage, where telephone wires, windows and the ties of the railroad tracks all appear to blend into abstract lines due to the accelerated motion of the train.

This motif of abstract lines will return even more explicitly in a later sequence in Act 4 just after the lunch break, where the film explores the theme of the press. There, Ruttmann shows us a kind of animated rotary press that appears to

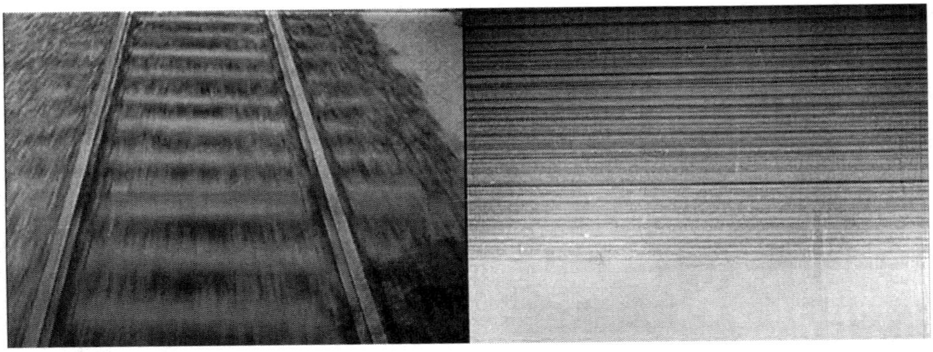

Stills from Ruttmann, Berlin. Die Sinfonie der Grossstadt *(1927). Railway ties and telephone lines from opening montage*

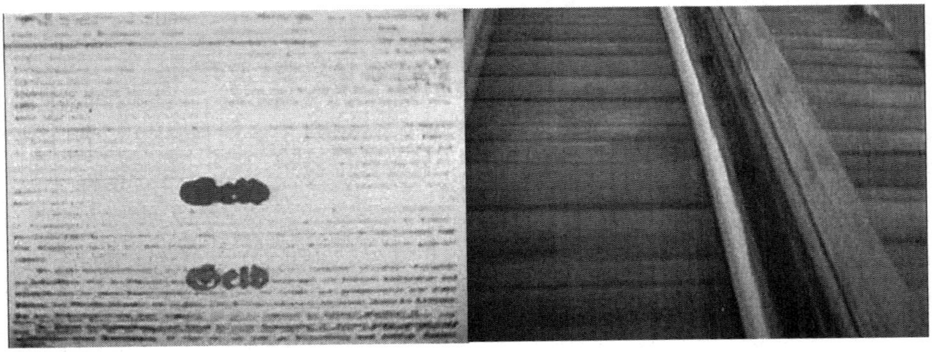

Stills from Ruttmann, Berlin. Die Sinfonie der Grossstadt. *Newspaper text and railway line*

spin out the headlines "Krise" (crisis), "Mord" (murder), "Börse" (stock market), "Heirat" (wedding) and "Geld" (money), with the last term repeated at an ever-increasing tempo as the rest of the newsprint blurs into a curve of continuous motion. When the film then cuts to the tracks of a rollercoaster, in which the rail ties imitate the blurring the text in the previous image, the argument is clear enough: "Seeing" in the accelerated milieu of the city must undergo a transformation similar to that of "reading" in the era of newspapers;[6] both must learn to "ride the curves" of modernity's information flows, taking in the essential information at lightning speed while not allowing themselves to become overwhelmed by the mass of letters, words, images, and information now circulating. This is, we might recall, precisely the transformation in perception that advertising theorists assumed in their efforts to create more efficacious posters for a public sphere marked by fleeting glances and information overload; like a newspaper headline, the advertising poster, reduced to its most elementary components, was meant to be perceived in the blink of an eye by a mobilized spectator with no time to linger over individual details. As a writer for SEIDELS REKLAME had stated already in 1921, "It has become a commonplace to demand of the advertising poster that it be identifiable and comprehensible in a single glance for people driving by in an automobile."[7] In this sense, one could see the famous transition from animation to montage in the opening of BERLIN not only as a statement of formal or artistic continuity (as most writing on the film does), but also as a statement of *continuity in perception training*: Ruttmann's first photographic film "applies," as it were, the training in "curve" perception from his OPUS films to the vision of the city.

But for all of its continuities with Ruttmann's early animation, the turn to photographic images and montage clearly also marked a turning point in Ruttmann's Weimar career. Against this background, the film has generally been read as a prime example of late 1920s "Neue Sachlichkeit" (New Objectivity), understood as a reconciliation of artistic production with industrial modernity after the more critical phase of Expressionism. In film-historical scholarship, BERLIN is remembered above all as a prime example of a documentary form particular to this period: part of a series of "city symphonies" including Alberto Cavalcanti's RIEN QUE LES HEURES (NOTHING BUT HOURS, 1926), Dziga Vertov's CHELOVEK S KINO-APPARATOM (MAN WITH A MOVIE CAMERA, 1929) and the collective film MENSCHEN AM SONNTAG (PEOPLE ON SUNDAY, 1929).

Although arguably the best known of these films next to that of Vertov, Ruttmann's BERLIN has also been the object of harsher critique. While the film seems to lack the poetic sensibility of Cavalcanti and the sense of spontaneity visible in PEOPLE ON SUNDAY, Ruttmann's detached formalism also appears to preclude any sustained attention to economic exploitation and class disparities in the city. The latter charge, made first and most famously by Siegfried Kracauer upon the film's release in 1927,[8] has become a mainstay of Ruttmann criticism ever since.[9] But nearly all of these discussions have been framed by an assumed opposition between documentary value and "formalism" – i.e. by the notion that the film's musical structure, combined with Ruttmann's predilection for formal visual parallels and contrasts in his montage, would subtract from the documentary value of the individual photographic shots. Thus Jeanpaul Goergen could write: "Ruttmann is only interested in using these facts of Berlin life as a musician would use notes. But precisely herein resides his artistic mistake, for one cannot compare a note with the objective impression registered by a single film frame."[10] Indeed, even Ruttmann's occasional defenders tend to accept this opposition between formalism and documentary value as a given. For example, in their *New History of Documentary* (2006), Jack Ellis and Betsy McLane explain:

> Yet BERLIN may have more value as a document than do those *documentary* films made with more explicit social biases and programs. Though composed according to artistic insights and intuitions and the requirements of form, what it offers essentially is a visual description. From this film we can learn a great deal about the appearance of life in Berlin in 1927.[11]

Here, the documentary content of Ruttmann's film is said to exist *despite* his use of formal operations, residing entirely in the presence of photographic images (lots of photographic images) that capture the reality of Berlin. If Ruttmann manipulated these images through his "formalist" montage, the authors argue, such formal operations were less manipulative than the "biases" of Vertov's political montage.

In the present chapter, however, I reconsider Ruttmann's turn to montage in the late 1920s to argue that something else was at stake. More than any of his contemporaries in the "city symphony" genre, Ruttmann has become associated with a particular type of montage: namely the "cross-section" or *Querschnitt,* by which filmmakers could show several actions occurring simultaneously in different locations. Although film historians still identify this term primarily with BERLIN and MENSCHEN AM SONNTAG, the concept of the *Querschnitt* in fact had a much wider usage and resonance in the print and visual culture of the Weimar Republic, as well as a much longer history as a mode of visual representation and as a means of social analysis. Taking this broader history into account, this chapter argues that Ruttmann's "cross-sectional" montage was not simply a "formalist" or "aesthetic" phenomenon, but also a tool for managing the "flood" of photographic representations in the late 1920s. Like abstraction, moreover, cross-sectional montage lent itself to advertising, and while BERLIN remains Ruttmann's best-known cross-section film, the cross-section form found perhaps its most characteristic expression in his subsequent film, MELODIE DER WELT (MELODY OF THE WORLD, 1929), an extended montage advertisement commissioned by the Hamburg-Amerika shipping line to advertise its world cruises. Following a detour through the history of the "cross-section" as a concept and a mode of visual culture, this chapter then closes with an extended analysis of MELODIE DER WELT as an advertisement for a particular kind of visual "ordering" of the world in the 1920s.

Montage and the Ordering of the Archive

Like Ruttmann's animated short films, which now reside on YouTube next to those of Richter and Fischinger as well as numerous amateur imitations, the "city symphony" form has also gained a newfound resonance today with the transition from analogue to digital media. In his study of new media, Lev Manovich credits the city symphony – in this case Vertov's MAN WITH A MOVIE CAMERA – with having anticipated the "database" logic of digital media: the tendency – visible in computer art but also in the cinema of Peter Greenaway – to emphasize paradigmatic over syntagmatic relations, presenting the world as a inventory of possible choices rather than a causal chain of narrative events.[12] One could make a similar analysis of Ruttmann's BERLIN film. As we saw, the film was based on an actual database – in the form of a card catalogue – rather than a linear script. Moreover, while the finished film does contain a rudimentary chronological axis in the form of the advancing workday (which brings about an alternating intensification and relaxation of the rhythms of work and leisure), this longitudinal perspective, presented as a series of five "shifts" rather than a continuous development, serves Ruttmann above all as a pretext for spreading out laterally on a paradigmatic axis; through cross-sectional montage, the film compares numerous analogous gestures, actions and phenomena: from the various openings of windows at the beginning of the film, to the simultaneous forms of marching, traffic flows, machine movement or leisure activities. A similar tension marks the collective film MENSCHEN AM SONNTAG; while this film revolves around the loose narrative of two couples undertaking a Sunday outing to Berlin's Lake Wannsee, it also repeatedly interrupts this narrative line to illustrate the simultaneous life – the 4,000,000 inhabitants of Berlin explicitly mentioned in the film's closing titles – teeming all about them. In this way, the film makes conscious, the various other "choices" that the filmmakers might have made for their story – most notably in a celebrated sequence illustrating a series of anonymous snapshots taken by a photographer on the beach.

The connection between such cross-section films and contemporary "database art" is also suggested by works such as Harun Farocki's installation GEGEN-MUSIK (COUNTER-MUSIC, 2004), in which Farocki uses footage from Ruttmann and Vertov as a counterpoint to his own exploration of the vast archive of images produced by the thousands of surveillance cameras strewn about contemporary cities such Lille.[13] The "archive" is, of course, a central theoretical figure in our digital media age, one that the genre of "found footage" film – or what

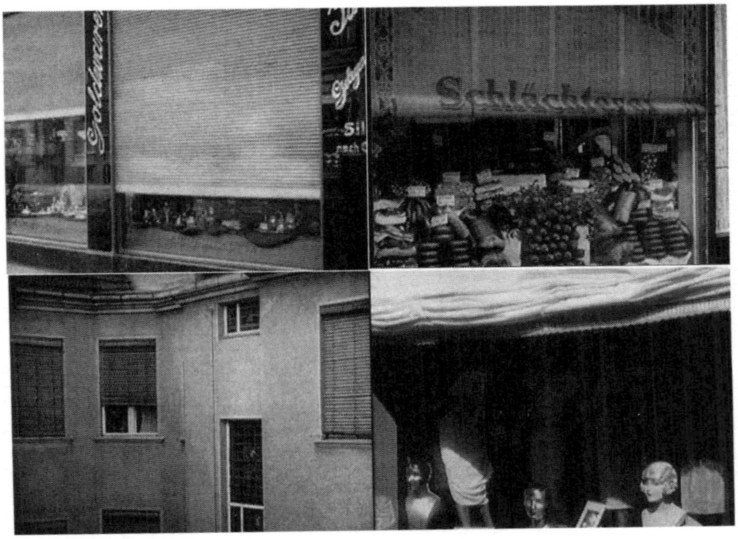

Stills from Ruttmann, BERLIN. DIE SINFONIE DER GROSSSTADT.
Analogous actions, opening blinds

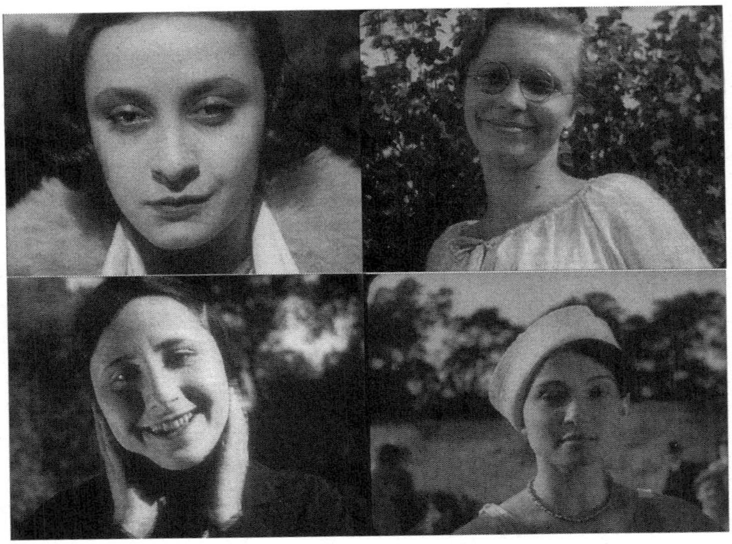

Stills from MENSCHEN AM SONNTAG *(1930). Photography sequence*

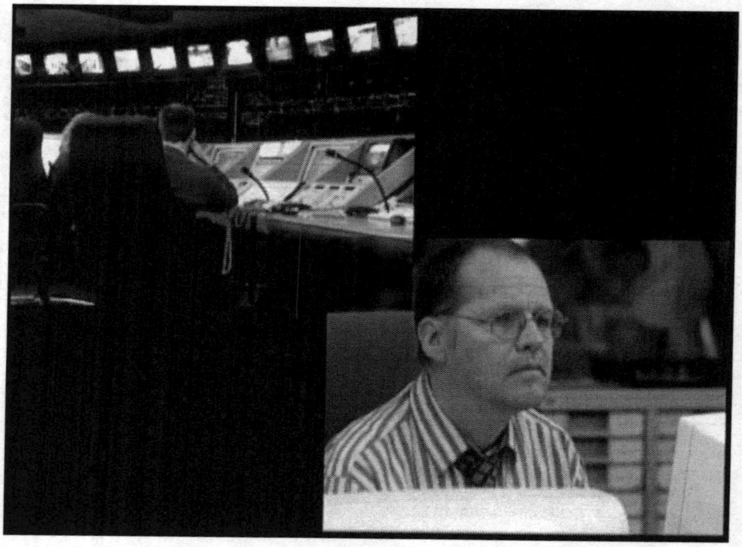

Still from Harun Farocki, still from GEGEN-MUSIK *(2004). Scene from Lille TGV control station*

Christa Blümlinger dubs "archival film art" (*Archivfilmkunst*) – practiced by Farocki, Matthias Müller, Gustav Deutsch and others attempts to work through.[14] Looking for precursors to such archival explorations, film historians such as Blümlinger have suggested the work of Ruttmann's contemporaries Walter Benjamin and Aby Warburg, whose signature modernist archival projects sought to transform linear development – the history of 19th-century capitalism in Benjamin's PASSAGENWERK (ARCADES PROJECT) and the migration of gestures and bodily expressions across different historical epochs and domains of visual culture in Warburg's MNEMOSYNE ATLAS – into the mode of simultaneous spatialized montage.[15] But part of what I wish to argue in this chapter is that the "cross-section film," and Ruttmann's work in particular, was also fundamentally concerned with a growing "archive" of visual representations and their possible ordering in the 1920s.

Indeed, this is true in a quite literal sense when one examines the history of the term "Querschnittfilm." Surprisingly, although one can find the term *Querschnitt* used already in the early 1920s to describe a certain form of montage, none of the works considered hallmarks of the *Querschnittfilm* today – neither Ruttmann's BERLIN nor MENSCHEN AM SONNTAG – received that generic designation when it appeared. Rather, the term *Querschnittfilm* (cross-section film) was first used for a particular kind of *Kulturfilm* launched by the Kulturabteilung (Cultural Section) of the Ufa Studio in 1928 and designed precisely to

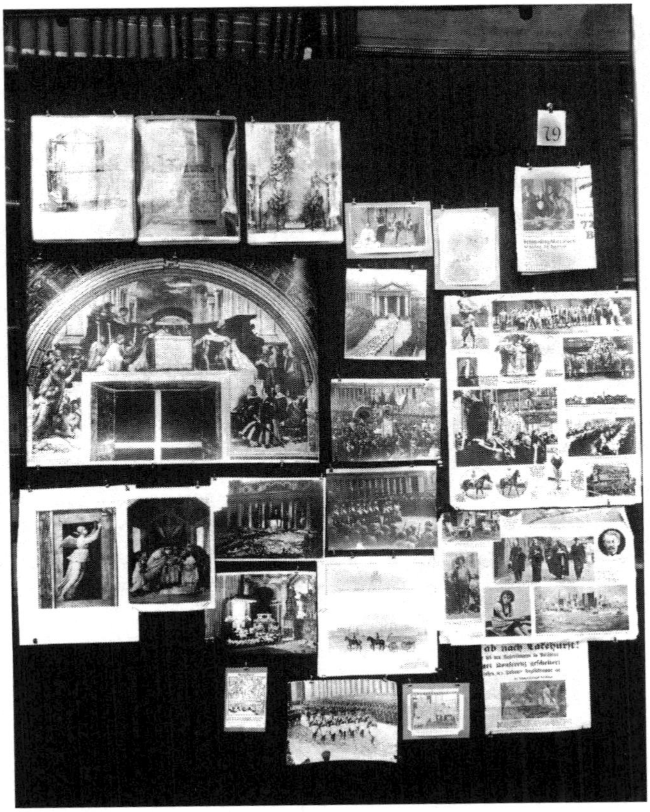

Aby Warburg, panel from Mnemosyne *atlas*

valorize the studio's growing film archive.[16] Under the title "Das Auge der Welt" ("The Eye of the World"), the Ufa proposed a series of six compilation films, on topics ranging from occultism in film to profiles of individual directors, all constructed via re-montage from footage stored in the expanding Ufa archive.[17] In the end, only one of the projected films – HENNY PORTEN. LEBEN UND LAUFBAHN EINER FILMKÜNSTLERIN (HENNY PORTEN. LIFE AND CAREER OF A FILMIC ARTIST, 1928), assembled by Oskar Kalbus from the Ufa Kulturabteilung – saw the light of day, but it was met with widespread acclaim by reviewers, almost all of whom spoke of the *Querschnittfilm* as a *new* genre designed to offer an overview of a given topic by means of representative examples.[18] The Porten film also inspired several other "cross-section" archival films such as RUND UM DIE LIEBE – EIN QUERSCHNITTFILM (ALL ABOUT LOVE – A CROSS-SECTION FILM, 1929), another Kalbus production designed to showcase various love scenes

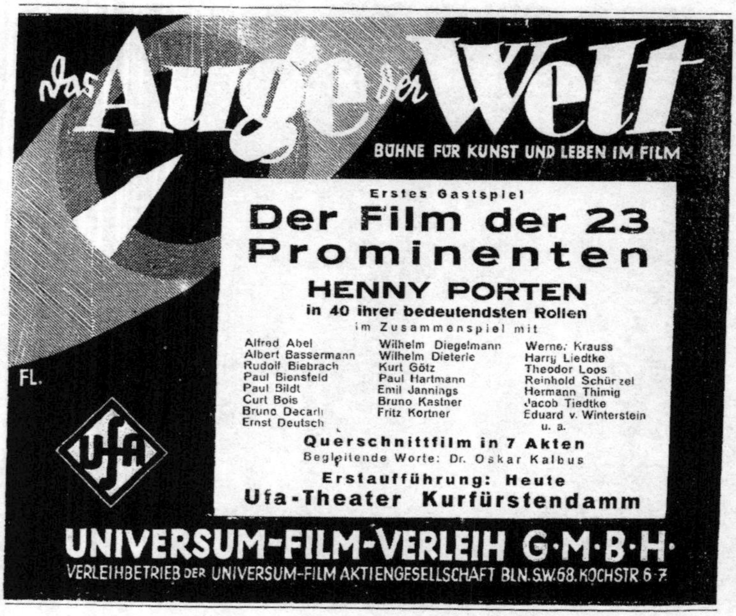

Advertisement for DAS AUGE DER WELT *(Ufa film series), from* Der Kinematograph *(1928)*

from German films; VON DER WUNDERTROMMEL BIS ZUM WERBETONFILM: EIN QUERSCHNITT DURCH 20 JAHRE PINSCHEWERFILM (FROM THE ZOETROPE TO THE SOUND ADVERTISING FILM: A CROSS-SECTION THROUGH 20 YEARS OF PINSCHEWER PRODUCTIONS), a compilation of selected historical advertisements by Julius Pinschewer for the 1929 Welt-Reklame-Kongreß in Berlin; Albrecht Viktor Blum's compilation film WASSER UND WOGEN, EIN QUERSCHNITTFILM (WATER AND WAVES, A CROSS-SECTION FILM, 1929);[19] and DIE WUNDER DER WELT (WONDERS OF THE WORLD, 1930), a compilation assembled from Ufa educational films by the head of the Kulturabteilung, Dr. Edgar Beyfuß.

As a phenomenon of re-montage, the *Querschnittfilm* was bound up with a new kind of thinking about the film archive in the late 1920s. Although calls for preservational film archives go back to the earliest years of filmic production,[20] it was during the 1920s that the awareness of a growing archive of film material gained broader institutional momentum, largely propelled by avant-garde circles, which would eventually lead to the founding of state-run film archives in the 1930s.[21] In Russia, this "archival impulse" resulted in the emergence of a new form of compilation film, pioneered by Esfir Shub, which sought to reedit archival footage (particularly that of newsreels) to instill it with revolutionary meaning. Analogous compilations were undertaken in Germany, particularly within the left-leaning "Volksverband für Filmkunst" (People's Association for Film Art), which – as Béla Balázs recalled – began buying up newsreels around 1928 and reediting them to instill a class-conscious message.[22] But the Ufa *Querschnittfilm*, although working within the same "archival" consciousness, clearly had a different objective: namely to educate audiences on the history of the film industry itself. Indeed, whatever critiques reviewers might have voiced concerning the Porten film, RUND UM DIE LIEBE and Pinschewer's historical review of advertising film, they unanimously praised the new genre of the *Querschnittfilm* for its ability to educate audiences, beyond its particular subject, about the history of film – of technology, style, acting and directorial techniques – in a pleasurable way.[23]

In choosing the term *Querschnitt* to describe these archival compilation films, the filmmakers were, in fact, adopting a well-known concept of Weimar print culture, where the *Querschnitt* designated a collection or anthology offering an overview of a given topic via representative examples. Countless book titles from the Weimar period – such as *Junge Baukunst in Deutschland: ein Querschnitt durch die Entwicklung neuer Baugestaltung in der Gegenwart* (*Recent Architecture in Germany: a Cross-Section through the Development of New Architectural Designs*, Heinrich de Fries, 1926) or *Fazit: ein Querschnitt durch die deutsche Publizistik* (*Upshot: a Cross-Section through Journalism in Germany*, Ernst Glaeser, 1929) – attest to the emergence of a new marketplace for forms of popularized knowledge within Germany's new democracy.[24] Designed for a mass audience in a society of mass media, such "Querschnitt" books clearly fulfilled a function – still central to our mass media landscape today – of information management: of filtering, via representative samples, fields too vast to be consumed in their entirety. It was precisely this function of the *Querschnitt* that the Ufa archival films sought to transpose from popular educational literature to film: as one reviewer for *Rund um die Liebe* described it, the new genre represented "an anthology of significant moments from German film literature [...] which have some theme in common."[25]

Only later was the generic term *Querschnittfilm* extended from these compilation films to include the experimental and documentary films such as Ruttmann's BERLIN. To be sure, the concept of *Querschnitt* had already been evoked to describe the kinds of paradigmatic editing that would come to play a dominant role in these films. Thus Béla Balázs, in his book *Der sichtbare Mensch* (*Visible Man*, 1924) describing what he called "simultaneism":

> The aim of simultaneism [Simultaneismus] is not to concentrate on one image from the wide world, but rather to show lots of *simultaneous* events, even if they have no causal relation to one another or to the main story. The goal here is to create a cosmic

> impression by showing a cross-section [Querschnitt] of life as a *whole*, a total image of the world [Totale der Welt].[26]

Balázs's description points forward in some respects to his own experiments in DIE ABENTEUER EINES ZEHNMARKSCHEINS (THE ADVENTURES OF A TEN-MARK BILL, 1926), which used the circular journey of a 10-mark bill to thematize the simultaneous forms of social life coexisting in the city,[27] and it would find its most sustained realization in Ruttmann's BERLIN and MENSCHEN AM SONNTAG. But it was only later, with *Der Geist des Films* (*The Spirit of Film*, 1930) that Balázs began to designate these city films specifically as "cross-section films" (*Querschnittfilme*). In doing so, Balázs inflects the generic designation away from associations with education and toward questions of dramaturgy when he classifies the *Querschnittfilm* as a particular variant of the "film without a hero."[28] After Balázs's intervention, the *Querschnittfilm* would come to be identified, internationally, with the dramaturgy of types and numbers characteristic of Ruttmann. Thus John Grierson, writing in 1932, could take Ruttmann as the prototype of a documentary approach showing a "cross-section of reality," one that attempted to capture the "mind and spirit of the time" in its insistence on the "mass nature of society" rather than the kind of individual drama presented in Robert Flaherty's NANOOK OF THE NORTH (1922).[29] This, of course, is still the dominant understanding of the *Querschnittfilm* today.[30]

From Science to Statistics: The Cross-Section and Mass Society

This tangled history of the term *Querschnittfilm* has led some observers to argue, in Antje Ehmann's words, that "a consistently describable 'genre' of the cross-section film does not exist."[31] But if we examine the concept of the *Querschnitt* from a wider historical angle, it become apparent that both the Ufa compilation films and experimental "Querschnittfilme" of Ruttmann and others could draw on a common set of associations surrounding the term *Querschnitt*, associations having to do with its history as a model of visual and conceptual ordering. Although the use of the term to designate an anthology format appears to be unique to the Weimar period, it had much older roots in various scientific traditions, including mathematics, surgical medicine, engineering, anatomy, architecture and geology. Most important, for my purposes here, is the tradition of the *Querschnitt* – and its older variant *Durchschnitt* – as a mode of scientific illustration that, simulating a cut through a body, allows the observer to perceive the internal contents and, crucially, analyze the relations between them.[32]

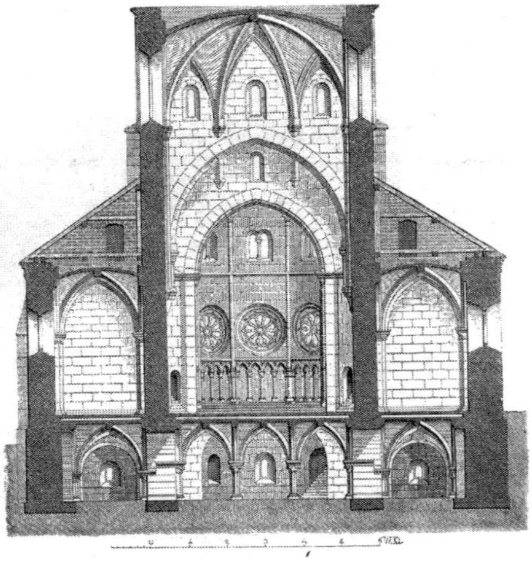

Architectural cross-section. "Kirche zu Trebisch. Querschnitt," illustration from Wilhelm Lübke, Geschichte der Architektur *(1884)*

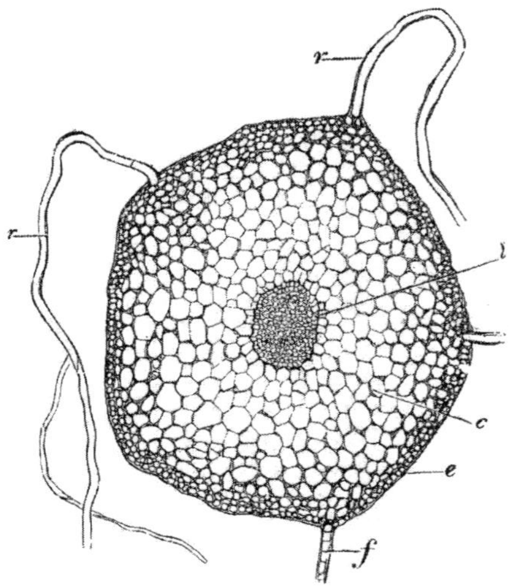

Cross Section of plant stem. Illustration from Strasburger, Lehrbuch der Botanik für Hochschulen *(1900)*

In architecture, the cross-section describes an imaginary cut through a building to reveal the relations between floors and rooms. In anatomy, zoology and botany, the term designates a dissecting cut that allowed the researcher to analyze the functional relations between organs, cells, nerves, tissue, etc.

With its conceit of opening up nature and revealing its hidden secrets, the scientific *Querschnitt* – which can ultimately be traced back to the anatomical drawings of the Renaissance – clearly belongs to a modern tradition of scientific illustration that Gottfried Boehm has dubbed "pictures as instruments of knowledge."[33] Given the epistemological aspirations attached to the filmic medium in its early years, moreover, it is hardly surprising that this association between the cross-section and the probing of nature's secrets would interest 1920s film theorists such as Balázs.[34] At the same time, there is an obvious difference between the scientific cross-section and the media of photography and film in as much as the latter were understood to have a phenomenological or indexical link to the real: like maps, blueprints and other schematic drawings, cross-sectional illustration was explicitly understood as a simplified model: an instrumental image that served to demonstrate, via the reduction of contingent and surface details and the inclusion of explanatory text, the functional relations between the elements it revealed.[35] Like many other forms of scientific illustration, the history of cross-sectional representation is marked by a gradual turn away from the conventions of aesthetic verisimilitude toward the abstract and the schematic in the interest of scientific legibility.[36] Moreover, to the explicit difference of filmic images, the cross-section implied the immobilization of nature, the freezing of movement for scrutiny by an analytic gaze.[37] Indeed, even when cross-sections were used to represent diachronic development, such visualizations took the form of a spatialization, where change appears on a line or a plane to be surveyed in a single glance; thus in geology, the *Querschnitt* designated a drawing of an imaginary cut through the surface of the earth, which used color codes to visualize the historical succession and development of geological strata. Like the scientific chronophotograph, such cross-sections immobilized development in order to place it at the disposition of an analytics gaze. Just how powerful this model of visual knowledge was can be seen in metaphorical usages of the term "cross-section" by modern writers such as Georg Simmel, who in his *Soziologie der Sinne* (*Sociology of the Senses*) from 1908 compared the human physiognomy, whose traits display the history of an individual's personality, with a "cross-section through geological layers."[38]

Around the same time Simmel wrote these words, the idea of the cross-section also entered into another branch of modern science that would have a decisive influence on Weimar and on the cross-section film: that of sociology, where it came to designate statistical as opposed to historical forms of social analysis. As one German sociologist stated in 1908: "History consists of longitudinal sections through life, while sociology consists of cross-sections."[39] With this importation into the new statistical science of sociology, the concept of the *Querschnitt* was extended beyond the sphere of scientific illustration to function as a metaphor for a new social epistemology related to the emergence of mass society. In

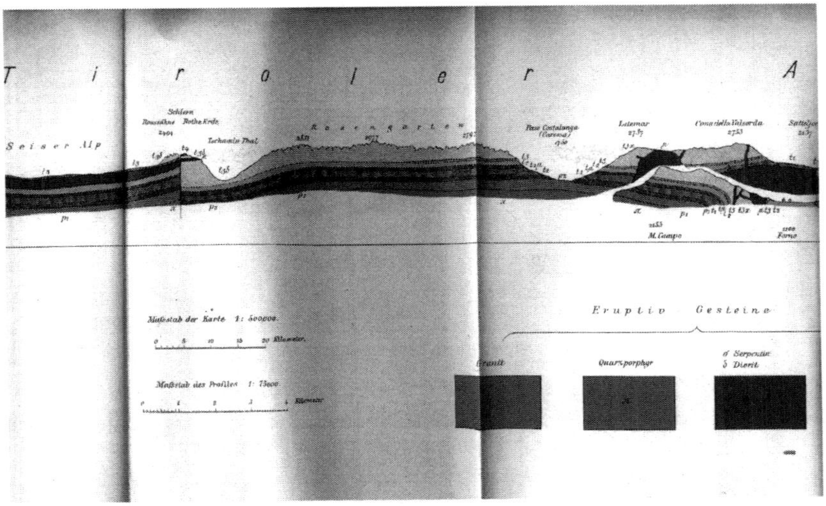

Geological cross-section. Illustration from August Rothpletz. Ein geologischer Querschnitt durch die Ost-Alpen *(1894)*

particular, the term came to designate the kinds of sampling research that characterized the social sciences in an era marked by the decline of deterministic thinking in favor of an epistemology based on the calculation of averages and statistical probabilities.[40]

The idea of "cross-sectional" analysis as the examination of social relations at a given moment clearly informed, on some level, the practice "cross-sectional" montage as it took shape in Ruttmann's filmmaking. But before turning back to Ruttmann, I want to consider how the transference of the "cross-section" from scientific illustration to social analysis helped to transform the trope as it entered into Weimar intellectual discourse. I do so by turning to Ruttmann's most famous critic, Siegfried Kracauer. In his well-known essay on Georg Simmel from 1919, Kracauer argued that Simmel's sociological method was characterized precisely by a preference for synchronic over historical modes of analysis, and he resorted to the metaphor of the *Querschnitt* to describe Simmel's characteristic efforts to tease out the correspondences between disparate social phenomena.[41] Surveying Simmel's numerous writings, Kracauer maintained that Simmel's anti-systematic approach constituted not a deficiency but an appropriate response to the increasing fragmentation of intellectual labor in late capitalism, one that sought to restore a sense for the "interwovenness" of all things.[42] Whether treating fashion, morality or the money economy, Simmel sought to dissociate his objects of study from the reified intellectual categories in which they were typically isolated by demonstrating their links to other (seemingly distant) phenomena. This was above all the case in Simmel's masterwork *Die Philosophie des Geldes* (*The Philosophy of Money*). There, Kracauer writes, "Simmel cuts one cross-section after another through the social and individual life of people in the age of a highly developed money economy. His observations [...] arise from the purely philosophical aim of bringing into consciousness the interwovenness of all the pieces of the world manifold."[43] For Kracauer, the cross-section thus functions to counter the increasing fragmentation of the world in order to suggest a totality no longer given in advance.

To this end, Simmel's principal sociological method involved not logical or causal explanations but rather the juxtaposition of distant phenomena by *analogy*. Simmel's thought, Kracauer argued, proceeds above all by "spreading a web of analogies across the world."[44] Through such analogical presentation, the sociologist "approximates" a totality that cannot be demonstrated deductively:

> One gets the distinct impression that Simmel always wants to arouse in us a sense of the unified connectedness of the manifold, that he wants to convey its totality (which is actually never available to him in its entirety), at least by approximation. And so he tends to prefer exploring the relations between objects that are entirely foreign to each other on the surface and that stem from radically different material realms.[45]

Such an effort to convey "totality by approximation" was, for Kracauer, precisely what made Simmel's sociology modern, adapting it to a world that no longer allowed for deterministic reasoning and in which any lawfulness underlying disparate phenomena must be established inductively, as it were, starting out from the mass of particular instances.

In adopting the "cross-section" as a metaphor for Simmel's effort to gesture toward a totality by means of analogies, Kracauer effects a transformation that I believe crucial for understanding its later transposition to photography and film in the 1920s. Whereas scientific "cross-sectional" illustrations purported to cut through a well-defined body to reveal its hidden components, Simmel's sociological cross-sections serve to constitute their body of knowledge in the first place. If Simmel's relational sociology could be described as a "cross-section" at all, this is because it implied (in Kracauer's estimation) that there is a larger body – a totality of interrelated social forms – to dissect. But since that whole is no longer given in advance, the cross-section as epistemological strategy now attains a level of uncertainty and even chance, its success in producing knowledge no more certain than the existence of the whole it seeks to verify. Thus Kracauer, who had himself studied architecture during the prewar years, claimed in a passage rife with the sense of loss and hope for redemption that characterized Weimar philosophy:

> It is only in the rarest cases that the architectural cross-section of a building reveals the structure of the entire house, the disposition of all the interior rooms. Some elements of the structure usually remain invisible. In order to discover them, one requires a longitudinal section or additional cross-sections. Yet one of these sections always does take precedence over the others, since it renders visible the layout of the structure's main volumes.[46]

In the absence of a pre-existing whole, Simmel's (and Kracauer's) cross-sections are thus more akin to a groping in the dark than to a self-assured scientific verification.

The Cross-Section and the Photographic Archive in Weimar Visual Culture

But while Simmel's groping cross-sections differed from the cross-sections of scientific illustration, they did point forward to the emerging theories of montage. "Simmel," Kracauer wrote, "is like a chemist who combines a substance unknown to him with all other substances, in order to get a picture of the essence and the properties of the body in question by means of its reactions to all of the remaining chemical substances."[47] Kracauer's understanding of social analysis as the study of the reactions between phenomena in combination – rather than the study of those phenomena in isolation – is not a little reminiscent of the signature montage theories of the Soviet school, which would strive precisely to define and control what happens in the interaction between two shots.[48] But as I argue in what follows, Kracauer's insistence on *analogy* as the operative figure in Simmel's thought provides a more specific framework for understanding a prevalent form of montage in *Querschnitt*-style photo and film presentations so popular in Weimar media. Benjamin Buchloh has argued that Weimar collage and photomontage aesthetics displayed two distinct tendencies: one, exemplified by early Dada art, based on "the order of the perceptual shock" and the other, exemplified by Benjamin and Warburg, based in "the order of the statistical collection or the archive."[49] It was the latter that came to dominate Weimar visual culture from the middle of the decade, and the analogy was one of its most prevalent rhetorical devices.

A case in point can be seen in the popular Weimar journal *Der Querschnitt*, which by all appearances seems to have been the catalyst for the kind of anthology-style print publications I discussed above. Although the journal began in 1921 as a forum for disseminating images of artworks from the gallery of Alfred Flechtheim, it quickly expanded into a general-interest publication featuring highlights from – in the words of editor Hermann von Wedderkop – "the most heterogeneous" domains of modern life, including fashion, travel, technology, music, architecture, politics, sex, hotels, cinema, drugs and many other topics.[50] Like Simmel's sociology, the journal asked readers to wade through diverse phenomena and draw connections between the spheres it treated, not only through its juxtapositions of heterogeneous articles, but also and much more explicitly through its signature photo montage layouts, which Wedderkop could describe by 1924 as the "specialty" of the journal.[51] *Der Querschnitt* constantly featured montage layouts, consisting of groups of photos juxtaposed on one or two adjacent pages with little or no textual explanation and often no apparent relation to the adjacent article. Through their compositional and thematic associations, such montages functioned precisely to suggest *analogies* between more or less distant phenomena: a jazz dancer and a Maillol statue, athletics from Africa and America, the gaping mouth of a tiger and an orchid, the wrinkled skin of an elephant and an aging hand, various forms of washing and grooming, cross-dressing from China and Europe, etc. If such analogies tended toward familiar conceptual categories in some cases, they could be quite provocative in others, as in a montage comparing a group of Muslims in prayer to a publicity photo for the popular Maciste films featuring a row of women in bathing suits.[52]

In establishing such visual resonances between heterogeneous phenomena, the photographic montages of *Der Querschnitt* bore a distinct resemblance to Simmel's experiments in intellectual chemistry, and both procedures can be understood as responses to a sense of lost totality that was pivotal to Weimar intellectual debates from Kracauer to Lukács and beyond. But beyond this intellectual context, such montage practices also responded to specific developments in visual media: namely the so-called "Bilderflut" ("flood of images") that increasingly characterized mass media experience in the 1920s. As we saw in chapter 1, advertising – posters, electric light advertisements and other forms – played a key role in this process. As the decade wore on, however, that role would be occupied more and more by photography, in particular illustrated journals. While photographic illustrations in journals date back to the 1880s (and the invention of the halftone process), journals only adopted photographic illustrations on a mass scale in the 1920s following the emergence of electronic photo transmission and the invention of lightweight cameras (1925), as well as more cost-efficient printing methods.[53] By the end of the decade, the critic Erich Burger, in his preface to a collection of film photos, could write:

> The days are over when the photo was merely an affair of museums, something to be enjoyed on holidays, an interlude for family festivals, or the filling for the gilded frames of couples in love. No more. The image, the photograph, has penetrated all spheres of our daily lives. At every minute, every second, images race before our eyes in a thousand forms, another one, another one, and yet another, on and on.[54]

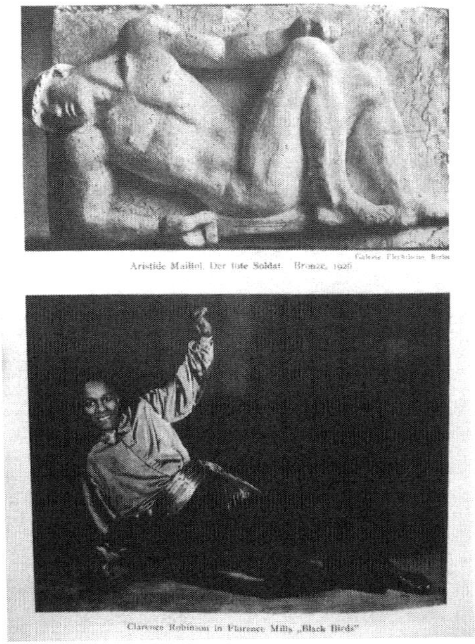

Photomontage from Der Querschnitt *6:11 (1926). Analogous montage of Maillol statue and Clarence Robinson*

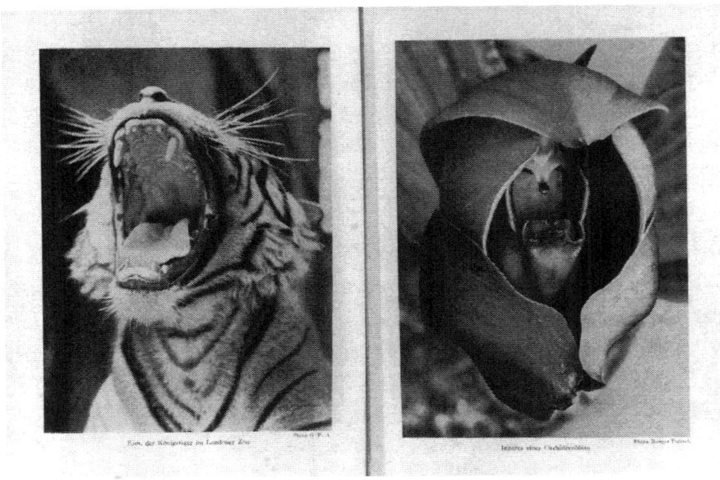

Photomontage from Der Querchnitt *6:3 (1926). Analogous montage of orchid and tiger*

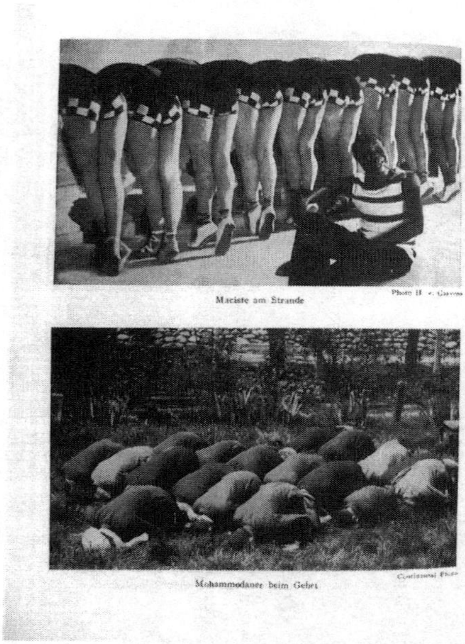

Photomontage from Der Querschnitt *6:7 (1926). Analogous montage of Muslim prayers and Maciste publicity photo*

Two years earlier, Kracauer himself, in his essay on photography from 1927, spoke of the "flood of photos" characterizing daily life and pointed in particular to their proliferation in illustrated journals. "The aim of such journals," Kracauer wrote, "is the complete reproduction of the world accessible to the photographic apparatus. They record the spatial impressions of people, conditions, and events from every possible perspective."[55] As is well known, Kracauer saw the ubiquitous presence of photography's "spatial impressions" as a threat to the more authentic temporal experience of memory. But as Mary Ann Doane has pointed out, he was also grappling with a particular problem of contingency, where the accumulation of photographs threatened to inundate observers with random details disconnected from any integrative law or structure of meaning (even as photography could also reveal the broader destruction of meaning in nature under capitalist production).[56]

It was this proliferation of contingent representations of the world in the 1920s that formed the backdrop for the emergence of *Querschnitt*-style montage. Again and again, the pages of *Der Querschnitt* emphasized their own contribution to the reproduction of the world through images of faraway places, peoples and forms of culture. But even as they flaunted the sheer endless variety phenomena accessible to the camera, the montage photo-layouts of *Der Querschnitt* promised to reduce the contingency of the details thus recorded by suggesting a greater regularity. This occurred, on the one hand, through the medium of photography itself; the kinds of visual analogies at the heart of journal's montages would be unthinkable without the ability to bring objects, images and people closer together in time and space and reduce them to a common scale, arranging them – as Warburg also did in his Mnemosyne panels – more or less symmetrically on the pages of the journal.[57] On the other hand, *Der Querscnitt* also heightened the impression of regularity with its insistence on compositional analogies. In suggesting a greater lawfulness, the journal's montage layouts recalled not only cross-sectional analysis in sociology, but also the scientific cross-section, with its schematic reduction of contingent detail. Or rather, one might say that they sought to strike a balance between the schematic and the contingent, flaunting their ability to reproduce anything while also gesturing toward yet-to-be-elucidated categories and correspondences.

Ruttmann and the Filmic Cross-Section: Berlin. Die Sinfonie der Großstadt

This tension between the schematic and the contingent would become even more pronounced in the time-based medium of film. Doane has argued that the very emergence of filmic technologies lent visual form to a much broader ambivalence about contingency in modern culture. Like the reproduction of the world in illustrated journals, early actualities implied that "anything and everything is filmable," what Doane describes as the "implicit thesis" of "indexicality" as such.[58] But in the case of moving images, this representation of contingency also related directly to film's status as a time-based medium; by virtue of their forward movement (in normal projection mode), filmic projections seemed to embody the modern experience of time as an irreversible process that, according to the second law of thermodynamics, led inevitably to the dissipation of order and meaning.[59] In Doane's estimation, this association between the projected moving image and the multiplication of contingent details constituted the cinema as a "site of awe and fear."[60] On the one hand, such heterogeneity seemed to offer an escape from modernity's incessant rationalizing tendencies, particularly the rationalization of time in industrial production. But it also fed into anxieties about the possible dissipation of meaning.[61]

Most importantly, Doane sees the ambivalence surrounding filmic images as part of a much broader reorganization of knowledge in the late 19th century, one in which new epistemological models of analysis turned toward inductive sampling and the establishment of probabilities in a world without pregiven order or totality.[62] Statistics, in particular, both acknowledged the presence of "singularity, particularity, contingency and chance" and sought – inductively through processes of sampling – to "constrain them within an overriding system" or social law.[63] It is surely no accident if these were the *same* social sciences to adopt the notion of the inductive "cross-section" in the late 19th century. As we saw in Kracauer's discussion of Simmel, that cross-section epistemology functioned precisely to suggest the presence of lawfulness and regularity even while taking account of the manifold and heterogeneous spheres of modern culture. Simmel's modernity, Kracauer argued, resided precisely in the way his sociology poised itself on the border between the particular and the general, the individual object and its relation to other objects.[64]

If, as Doane has argued, early film performed a similar balancing act with respect to time and movement, this tension informs the emergence of the *Querschnittfilm*-genre in a very specific way. Even as they flaunted their ability to capture everything on film, cross-sectional city films promised to manage the proliferation of moving images to which they contributed by gesturing toward a law-like regularity. This goes for a film like MENSCHEN AM SONNTAG, with its delicate interweaving of shots of contingency – the expanding wrapper of a drinking straw, a hat caught in a tree, etc. – and statistical stability (the 4,000,000 people who, as we learn from an intertitle at the end of the film, are all waiting for the next Sunday when they will repeat their leisure activities). But it also goes for Ruttmann's BERLIN, where the temporal structure of coordinated "shifts" seems to subsume the movements of individual shots into a system of coordinated repetition – not only the paradigmatic performance of similar actions by numerous people, but also the implied repetition of the actions shown in the film on subsequent workdays.

In this respect, it is hardly by chance that Ruttmann's film also makes heavy use of the forms of analogous montage familiar from the pages of *Der Querschnitt*. Throughout BERLIN, the editing draws numerous graphic and thematic parallels between the actions of different groups of people as they work, eat, sleep or relax, as well as those of people and machines or people and animals throughout the city. The result is a suggestion of a higher lawfulness; guided by the rhythms of the city, people, animals and machines seem to all perform similar actions *as if* following a predetermined order or obeying an objective law (a "social fact" in the language of statistics).

Ruttmann's analogous montage was, of course, a common feature of avant-garde and experimental filmmaking in the 1920s. As other critics have pointed out, it bears particular affinities with Sergei Eisenstein's theory of intellectual montage, in which the collision of two visual elements would evoke a third, undepictable concept.[65] Through montage, Eisenstein sought to create a cinema that would raise sensual images into the intellectual sphere, but also lend sensual form to intellectual ideas. In an article first published in German in the pages of *Der Querschnitt* entitled "Der Kinematograph der Begriffe" ("The Cinema of Concepts"), he thus described this conceptual mode of montage as "the synthesis of emotional, documentary and absolute film."[66] As we have seen, Ruttmann's BERLIN film similarly sought to combine the schematic quality of absolute film with the contingency of the photographic image. But Ruttmann's analogies differ from Eisensteinian conceptual montage in several significant ways. First, Ruttmann shows comparatively little interest in graphic "conflict," "collision" or dialectical oppositions. Rather, he overwhelmingly privileges visual analogies, where one movement resembles another.[67] Second, while intellectual montage in Eisenstein tends to occur in the form of non-diegetic inserts – most memorably in the guise of the slaughtered bulls inserted at the end of STATCHKA (STRIKE, 1926) to symbolize the oppression of the workers – it is difficult to speak of "inserts" in Ruttmann since everything we see forms a part of the diegetic world of BERLIN. A useful example here can be seen in the image of fighting dogs, which appear in the third act of BERLIN in parallel to arguing telephone operators and images of people fighting on the street. Where Eisenstein's bulls are introduced from without to inflect, in the manner of a non-diegetic soundtrack, our reading of the diegetic image, Ruttmann's dogs are part of the diegetic world – no less a part than the animals at the zoo who seem to nap on cue with their human counterparts after lunch.

Pushing this distinction further, one might borrow another conceptual tool from Kracauer's essay on Simmel, where Kracauer opposes the analogy characteristic of Simmel's groping montage to metaphor. Unlike the metaphorical thinker, Kracauer writes, "the analogy person never gives an explanation of the world, since he is not driven by a preconceived idea; he is content to identify the laws of the event and, by observing the many facets of the event itself, to pair together those things that have the same form."[68] By extension, whereas the metaphor assumes a hierarchy of elements compared, since one element is meant to "give sensuous expression to the essence of another," the elements juxtaposed by analogy "have equal status."[69] Rather than subordinating the sensuous symbol to the idea symbolized, the analogy retains the sensuous qualities of both terms, whose comparison only *suggests* the presence of a higher systematicity it cannot "explain." Adapting Kracauer's distinction to associational montage, one could argue that whereas Eisenstein's bulls function as a metaphor of class oppression, Ruttmann's animals function as analogies, gesturing – along with the humans they resemble – toward a greater whole that they do not explain.

Ruttmann's analogous montage thus displays a certain "statistical" quality in its suggestion of a higher order among the city's manifold appearances. Like a census operation, the multiple images in cross-section take stock of the city in

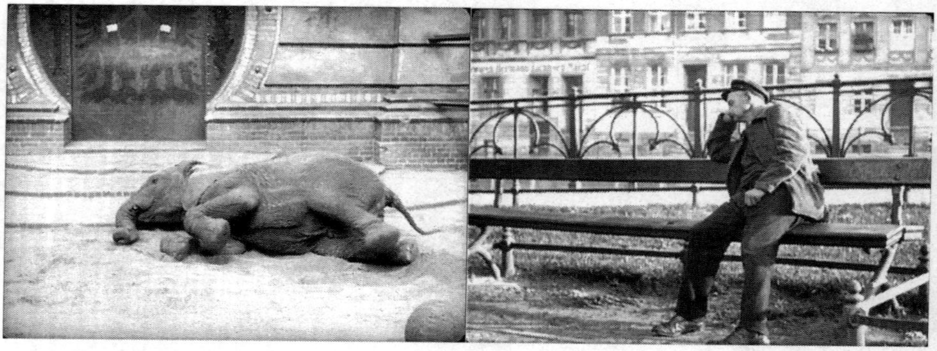

Stills from Ruttmann, BERLIN. DIE SINFONIE DER GROSSSTADT. *Analogous montage of people and animals napping during lunch hour*

both its multiplicities and its regularities. In certain cases, such as the section detailing the various rituals during the lunch hour, this visual epistemology does involve the juxtaposition of different classes. However, it does so not in order to emphasize or promote "conflict," but rather to conjure up an image of regularity: this is what people in the city – the "average man" conceived of as mean value of many people – do during their lunch break.[70] Indeed, it was precisely this "numerical" quality that impressed contemporary observers about Ruttmann's montage. Thus one reviewer could describe the montage of doors and windows closing at the end of the day as follows:

> In order to show that the businesses were closing, it would have sufficed to film one or two shop windows with their blinds being lowered, or a few doors from which employees emerge onto the street. […] But Ruttmann brings dozens of objects – over dozens of film feet – into play, showing them repeatedly closed, latched and snapped shut. […] Everything occurs in a standardized tempo and a nearly identical form.[71]

By means of such repetition, Ruttmann's montage emulates what statisticians had long termed the "law of large numbers," the idea that "social facts" can only be visualized by comparing numerous individual instances.[72] Thus where Ruttmann's animation sought to transpose the convention of the movement curve to animated film, his BERLIN, with its montage of individual photographic images, sought to convey a different kind of curve: namely the *statistical* curve of regularities resulting from the comparison of particular phenomena.

Even the "deviations" from the normal flow of city life in BERLIN can be read within this epistemology. Most obvious, among these, is the oft-discussed sequence of the woman jumping off the bridge. Suicide had, in fact, occupied a particularly important place in the history of statistics throughout the 19th century, where statisticians debated questions of free will and social laws by

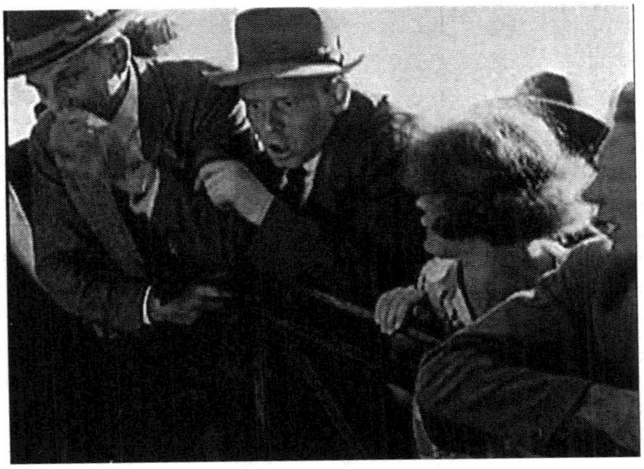

Still from Ruttmann, BERLIN. DIE SINFONIE DER GROSSSTADT.
Onlookers in suicide sequence

pointing to the constancy of suicide rates in given populations.[73] Durkheim's influential study on suicide from 1897 formed the culmination of these debates, arguing that suicide was not a "pathological" phenomenon that could be eliminated, but rather part of the "normal" statistical regularity of all societies. As Ian Hacking puts it, "Quetelet had made the mean of a population as 'real' as the position of an island or a star. At the time of Durkheim, the laws of deviation from the normal themselves became part of reality."[74] Whatever might be said about the free will or the pathology of the person committing suicide, it was nonetheless a "social fact," occurring with predictable statistical regularity.[75] In Ruttmann, the sequence of the woman on the bridge is arguably the only individualizing sequence in the film; unlike most of the other footage shot on location and often with hidden cameras, this sequence was staged with an actor and uses quasi-narrative techniques – such as shot-countershot, point of view shots and eyeline matches linking the woman's startled gaze to the water below (as well as false eyeline matches between her gaze and the tracks of a rollercoaster) – in order to convey her anxiety and the panicked responses of onlookers. However, this "individualizing" point of view lasts only a few seconds and is quickly reabsorbed after the woman's suicide when the film cuts to an image of a fashion parade in which the movements of the city appear to continue as if nothing had happened. The suggestion is that despite the tragedy of the suicide (viewed from the point of view of the woman and individual onlookers), the event itself is insignificant when measured against the "statistical stabilities"[76] of city life, and may well be a part of that stability (ultimately occurring no less "regularly" than thunderstorms or fights on the street).[77]

In its relativizing of individual drama, such a "statistical gaze" most certainly embodies the kind of "cool conduct" we associate with *Neue Sachlichkeit*,[78] and in a sense, this quasi-bureaucratic quality of Ruttmann's montage should hardly surprise us; commissioned as a "quota quickie" by the Fox Europa film studios, BERLIN might have been an experimental film, but it was never intended to be a radical statement on class exploitation or suffering. It is neither a revolutionary film in the manner of Vertov, nor a surrealist work in the manner of Alberto Cavalcanti, nor an anarchist work in the style of Jean Vigo. It is, rather, a representation of a mass metropolis commissioned by an American film company and realized by several "experts" in the film business: Ruttmann, the cameraman Karl Freund (who was serving as the head of Fox Europa) and the scriptwriter Carl Mayer (known for his work on the screenplay of DAS KABINETT DES DR. CALIGARI [THE CABINET OF DR. CALIGARI], but also for several films by F. W. Murnau).[79] Given Ruttmann's commission to make a film about the city itself rather than any particular inhabitants, it is little wonder that he would draw on the available epistemological framework of statistics in order to depict the city as a set of "social facts" (rhythms, shifts, traffic flows, rituals, gestures, etc.) beyond the agency of individual inhabitants.

To be clear, the argument here is not that Ruttmann's BERLIN offers any reliable statistical data about the city of Berlin in the 1920s – the kind of data one might find, for example, in the journal *Berlin in Zahlen* (*Berlin in Numbers*), launched in the same year as Ruttmann's film (1927) by the Statistisches Amt der Stadt Berlin (Statistical Office of the City of Berlin).[80] Ruttmann obviously chose to film some aspects and leave others out, and his visual "sampling" of urban phenomena did not follow any rigorous statistical methodology. But I am arguing that Ruttmann's montage "enacts," as it were, a certain statistical epistemology in its presentation of the city as an arena of multiplicity (of "numbers") and cues us to ask statistical questions (such as the question I posed about the suicide above). This attention to the "statistical" in BERLIN – its subordination of individual experiences and affects to the more "objective" level of social facts – contributes every bit as much as Ruttmann's interest in machines to make BERLIN. DIE SINFONIE DER GROSSSTADT a paragon of "Neue Sachlichkeit."

Understanding this project can also help to offer a more subtle response to Kracauer's famous critique, already mentioned, according to which Ruttmann adopted the formal procedures of Soviet montage while emptying those procedures of their political "content."[81] Kracauer was correct to point out the distinction between the political thrust of Russian montage and the "neutrality"[82] of Ruttmann's work. But this does not mean that Ruttmann's montage would have been understood as less experimental by observers of the time, or that it should be reduced to an empty formalism, unconnected to the "reality" of the city. It offered, as we have seen, a statistical approach to representing the city, which was never meant to be political in the manner of Eisenstein or Vertov. Ruttmann himself stated as much in a 1928 article on Soviet film where – in language remarkably similar to his text "Die 'absolute' Mode" that I cited in the introduction to this book – he explained that it was the *technique* of Russian film, rather than its politics, that interested him: "What is decisive is not the radical political leaning [Tendenz] of these films, but rather the radical and uncompromising way in which they take a position [das Radikale und Konsessionslose der Stellungnahme]."[83] Here again, Ruttmann openly declares his own model of filmmaking as a "positioning" (Stellungnahme) of film – an effort to reconnect art and life – distinct from the political commitment ("politische Tendenz") of Soviet film. To understand what this meant, we would do best to avoid reductive charges of aesthetic "formalism," but also the temptation to defend Ruttmann's images for their documentary value *despite* his "formalist" tendencies. Rather, we need to understand how Ruttmann's montage operations worked in tandem with the film's documentary project. One of the oft-repeated assertions about Ruttmann's "formalism" is that it consists in establishing "visual similarities and contrasts."[84] But as I have argued, the overwhelmingly dominant operation of Ruttmann's montage is that of *analogy*, not contrast. The latter operation was singled out by Vsevelod Pudovkin in his 1926 book *Film Technique* as the paradigmatic form of editing with which to underscore class antagonisms,[85] and the technique was often used in films about class conflict such as G. W. Pabst's Die freudlose Gasse (Joyless Street, 1925), where Pabst used cross-cutting to underscore the gulf separating the reveling upper classes from the hungry masses waiting in line for meat outdoors. But in Ruttmann, even when different classes are compared, they are shown engaged in analogous actions (as in one memorable sequence where a street beggar picks up a cigarette discarded by a middle-class man and continues to smoke it).[86] Rather than emphasizing conflict, such montage operations were meant to underscore the *regularities* of the city: its smooth functioning according to objective (statistical) laws beyond the agency of individual actors.

This emphasis on "functional" regularities was, as my reading above suggested, part of the legacy of the concept of the *Querschnitt* as it was adapted from scientific illustration and the social sciences into photography and film. That concept never really implied questions of social or political commitment,[87] but it did carry the memory and the promise of an ordering gaze: one that could reduce the contingency of particular instances and indexical images in the seemingly fixed coordinates of a functional structure. While the immobilized body of traditional science could no longer be taken as a given in the early 20th century, the *Querschnitt* did gesture toward a totality that would reduce the threat of contingency by locating elements within a paradigmatic system.

Melodie der Welt and the Ordering of the World

This aspect of the *Querschnitt* would be extended to a world scale in Ruttmann's next "film symphony," Melodie der Welt (Melody of the World, 1929). Commissioned by the shipping line HAPAG (formerly the Hamburg-Amerika Line) and the sound film syndicate Tobis Klangfilm, Melodie der Welt was intended as an advertisement – in the tradition of longer "Kulturwerbefilme" (cultural advertising film) – for HAPAG's tourist cruises.[88] To this end, the film takes up the interwar topos of "international understanding" (*Völkerverständigung*) in its opening titles:

> Placing its shipping network in the service of the spirit of community [Gemeinsamkeit] between peoples, the Hamburg-Amerika Line sent a film expedition around the world in order to increase understanding [Verständnis] for the diverse forms of human life and make visible the commonalities [das Verbindende] between people.[89]

This trope of international understanding was, of course, central to the self-fashioning of film as a popular medium in the wake of the Great War, when critics such as Balázs and directors such as Fritz Lang touted film as a "universal language" of gesture and facial expressions.[90] But the trope was also central to the tourist industry, which sought for good reason to promote a view of global space as an arena for safe travel free of armed conflict. HAPAG itself had been devastated by the war when over half its fleet of ships was confiscated by the United States and other allied nations (ultimately causing its president Albert Ballin to commit suicide in 1918), and the company had a vested interest in cultivating peaceful international relations as it sought to rebuild itself in the 1920s.

It was within this context that Melodie der Welt was commissioned. Specifically, the film was meant to celebrate HAPAG's resumption of world tours, and HAPAG duly marked the occasion with a Gala reception for diplomats, artists, industrialists and other VIP guests at the Hotel Esplanade following the film's premiere on 12 March 1929.[91] Although the company had been the world leader in world cruises before the war, it had been unable to provide world tours until the reacquisition of the ships *Resolute* and *Reliance* from United American Lines in 1926. In the spirit of international cooperation, and above all in order to retain American customers who might be put off by German nationalism, HAPAG kept the ships' American names rather than restoring the original German names (*Johann Heinrich Burchard* and *William Oswald*). Of the first tours in 1927, the most highly publicized of these was a 138-day world tour by the *Resolute* – the same ship featured in Ruttmann's film – which led from New York through twenty-eight countries in North Africa, the Middle East and

Asia.[92] Reports from the time emphasized both the continued cooperation with America (the presence of 332 American citizens on the ship, the celebration of Herbert Hoover's inauguration, etc.) and the peaceful conditions of the countries visited.[93] The tour was such a success that the company organized several expanded tours in the following years. It was the second world tour of the *Resolute* in 1928 – a 140-day journey through Africa, the Middle East, Asia and the Americas – that served as the basis for Ruttmann's film.[94]

As the film's opening title cited above suggests, this trip was, from the start, planned as a "film expedition," in which the HAPAG film crew led by Heinrich Mutzenbacher produced some 16,000 meters of film stock from various locations around the world. In accepting HAPAG's commission, Ruttmann was thus effectively making a "found footage" film, one that used a particular visual archive for a very specific purpose.[95] An obvious model for ordering this material would have been to narrate the journey chronologically in the fashion of previous Weimar travelogues such as Colin Ross's successful film MIT DEM KURBELKASTEN UM DIE ERDE (AROUND THE WORLD WITH THE MOVIE CAMERA) from 1924.[96] But Ruttmann chose instead to transform the chronological voyage into a cross-sectional "database" of world cultures, emphasizing the "commonalities" (das Verbindende) between the world's peoples.[97] Made up almost entirely of graphic, compositional and thematic analogies, the film's montage functions precisely to compare and assimilate various activities, rituals and cultural expressions: from labor, farming and warfare, to dance, athletics, cooking, music and arts. Indeed, Ruttmann's cross-sectional montage not only compares different ethnic groups, but also – in configurations reminiscent of nothing so much as the photomontages from *Der Querschnitt* – the actions of people and animals (flocking, fighting, sleeping, playing, eating, bathing, etc.) and bodies and machines (turning, pumping, pounding). Through such analogies, Ruttmann's montage creates the impression of global space as an arena of universal correspondences: between the "primitive" and the "modern," nature and culture, bodies and technology, leisure and work. In so doing, that montage suggests – inductively through the comparison of individual instances – a new "totality" on a global scale, one literally figured in the first image of the film, which shows a planet gradually illuminated by wandering spotlights. Preceded by an epigraph from Oscar Wilde reading "The true secret of the world resides in the visible, not the invisible,"[98] this opening image frames the film as an attempt both to shed light on the world – i.e. capture the world in the archive of filmic images – and reveal its secrets: secrets residing not in dark corners but rather in the correspondences and regularities amid the seemingly endless varieties of visible life captured in moving images. Rather than emphasize linear travel, then, Ruttmann's film flaunts its ability to visualize such paradigmatic similarities through cross-sectional montage.[99]

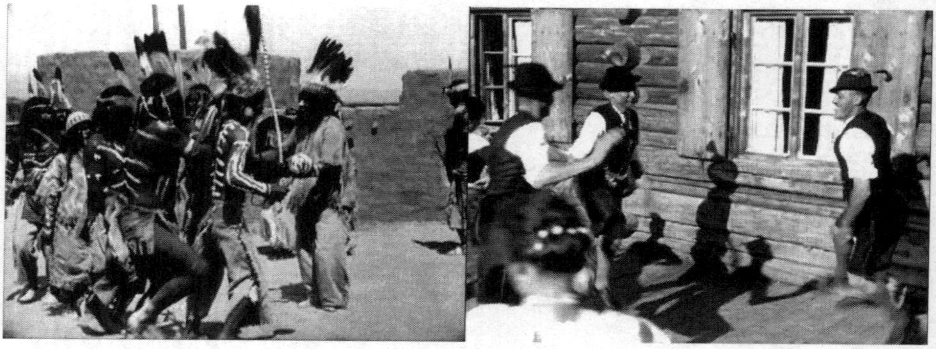

Stills from Ruttmann, MELODIE DER WELT *(1929). Analogous montage of Native American and Bavarian dances*

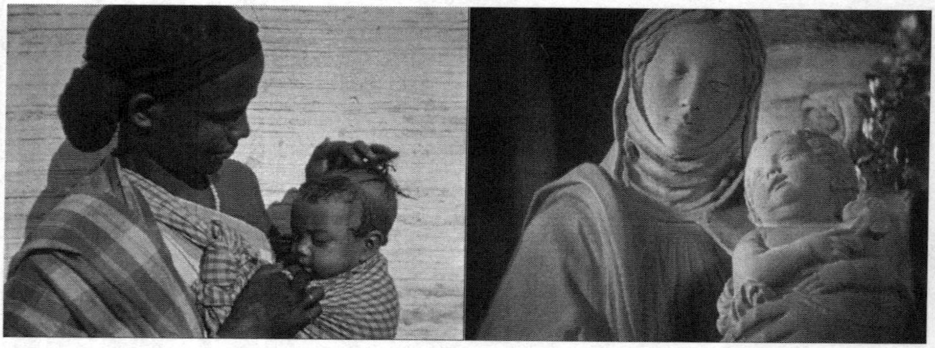

Stills from Ruttmann, MELODIE DER WELT. *Analogous montage of woman with baby and Madonna statue*

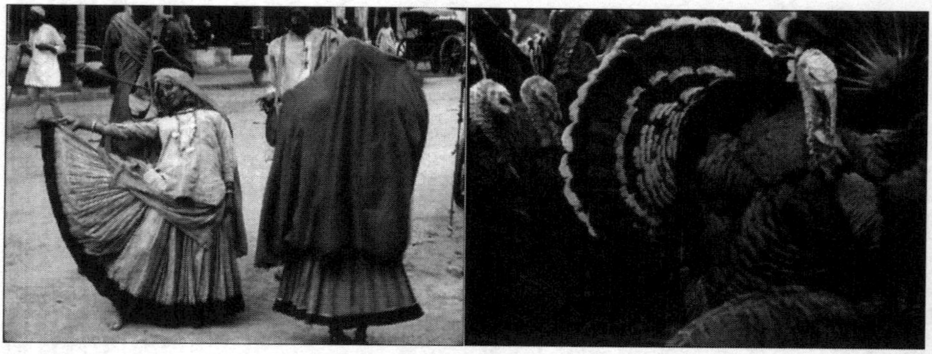

Stills from Ruttmann, MELODIE DER WELT. *Analogous montage of dress and turkey feathers*

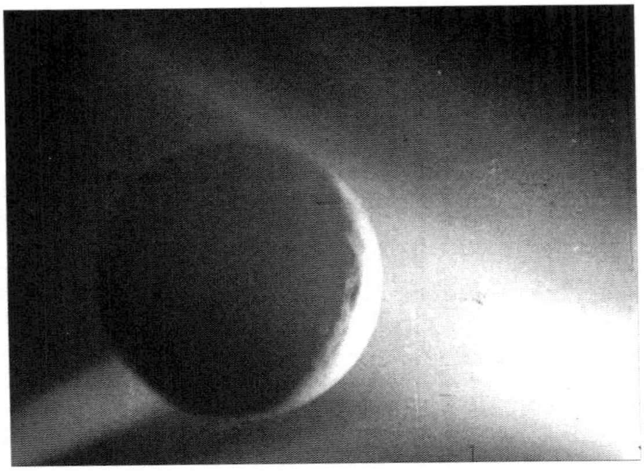

Still from Ruttmann, MELODIE DER WELT. *Planet illuminated by spotlights in opening sequence*

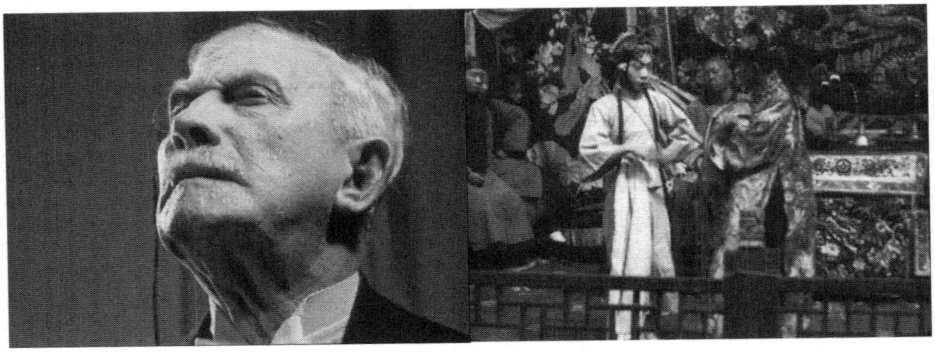

Stills from MELODIE DER WELT. *Mismatched montage of audience and spectacle*

This is not to argue that the film is devoid of all narrative development; most notably, the opening sequence, in which the character of a sailor is accompanied by his wife to the ship, serves as a narrative frame and even seems to suggest the travelogue format. The sequence also features typical narrative editing, most prominently in the form of shot-reverse shot configurations that establish the interaction between the couple. But this narrative editing quickly gives way to a system of analogous editing that dominate the rest of the film. To be sure, narrative editing does reappear in subsequent sections as shots of the sailor and his wife return sporadically like a leitmotif. Subsequent images of the sailor tend to reintroduce the shot-reverse shot configurations, where the sailor can be seen appearing to buy bananas from local children, enjoying the spectacle of Japanese geishas or tending the ship. Here, Ruttmann adopts Lev Kuleshov's famous lesson that narrative relations can be constructed from images taken worlds apart in order to make his sailor into a stand-in, as it were, for the film's audiences on their virtual travel through the world. However, Ruttmann also displays the artificiality of these narrative constructions by using two obviously different film stocks (in the banana sequence) or mismatched perspectives in the shots of the sailor and the spectacles he encounters. Indeed, this artificiality becomes even more evident in the only other sequence in the film to use shot-reverse shot editing. As we watch various stage spectacles parade over the screen, Ruttmann inserts images of spectators; but he noticeably mixes audiences and spectacles via false eyeline matches, so that a monocled European aristocrat can be seen "watching" the spectacle of Balinese theatre or Chinese opera. However, while these eyeline matches might appear as "false" from a narrative point of view, they support the film's other logic by extending the analogies between different forms of entertainment on the one hand and different types of audiences on the other. Here too, then, the film flaunts its ability to transform diachronic narrative into synchronic analogy, syntagmatic chain into paradigmatic comparison. Even more telling, in this sense, are the later appearances of the sailor's wife. After the opening sequence, the wife makes five more appearances in the film: in the sequences on warfare, mothers and children, women's morning rituals, varieties of hairstyles and cooking rituals. In none of these instances, however, does the reappearance of the wife reactivate the narrative editing of the film's opening; rather, she now appears as one female figure among others in a system of analogies: a "universal" woman bound to other women of the world by paradigmatic similarity rather than the narrative wife of the sailor awaiting his return.

While this analogical dimension dominates the film's visual montage, it also extends to Ruttmann's much-discussed use of sound. Upon its appearance, MELODIE DER WELT was billed and received as the first full-length sound film in Germany. Ruttmann, who would go on to create several sound-film experiments including the lost comedy sketch DES HAARES UND DER LIEBE WELLEN (WAVES OF HAIR AND LOVE, 1929), the imageless urban sound-montage *Weekend* (1930) and a composition of "mood" images set to Schubert in *In der Nacht* (*In the Night,* 1931), had already experimented with sound montage in his earlier film TÖNENDE WELLE (RESOUNDING WAVES, 1931), an advertisement for the Reichsrundfunkgesellschaft (German National Radio Company). Touting the newly formed national radio network, the film, now lost, used audio-visual montage to take listeners – via the voices of radio announcers from various stations in Germany – on a tour throughout the German Reich.[100] When Ruttmann then attempted to apply similar sound-montage experimentation to a longer film in MELODIE DER WELT, critics were nearly unanimously disappointed by the film's sparse use of synchronized sound and its heavy reliance on a musical score by Wolfgang Zeller.[101] But the film also employs – as did TÖNENDE WELLE

– what Ruttmann described as moments of "optical acoustical counterpoint" (optisch-akustischer Kontrapunkt), in which sound and image exist in an "intellectual connection" (in gedanklicher Verbindung) rather than simply reproducing extra-filmic perception.[102] Ruttmann's notion of audio-visual counterpoint clearly echoes the better-known sound film manifesto by Eisenstein, Pudovkin and Grigori Alexandrov, which had been published a year earlier in the *Vossische Zeitung* and the *Lichtbild-Bühne*,[103] and the notion would go on to play a particularly important role in Eisenstein's film theory, where it constituted yet another dimension of the dialectical conflict at work in film aesthetics at all levels. As Eisenstein explained in his "Dialectical Approach to Film Form": "Thus does conflict between optical and acoustical experience produce: *sound-film,* which is capable of being realized as *audio-visual counterpoint.*"[104] The similarity between Ruttmann's and Eisenstein's terminology in their prescriptions for sound film is surely due in no small part to the fact that both attended the Congress of Independent Film in La Sarraz in September 1929, where the question of sound film formed a central discussion topic.[105]

But here again, the differences between Ruttmann and Eisenstein are as revealing as their similarities; where Eisenstein saw counterpoint as a means of making palpable the dialectical conflict at the heart of film technology and film form, Ruttmann's counterpoint constructions – even if he described them in writing as a "struggle between image and sound" (Kampf zwischen Bild und Ton) – tend toward the analogical.[106] An example can be heard in a sequence on forms of racing, where the same sound of a cheering crowd is carried over through several analogous shots of different forms of racing, including boats, horses, dogs, hurdle jumpers, motorcycles, automobiles and skiers. One of Ruttmann's critics singled out this scene as an example of Ruttmann's tendency to "fudge [verfälschen] sounds" by "combining the sound of bicycle races with images of horse and automobile races" ("Sechstagerennen-Aufnahmen zum Kampf der Pferde und Autos zu nehmen").[107] However, this critique may have missed the point. For like the mismatched audiences in the opera sequence described above, this mismatching of sound and image in the racing sequence served another purpose: namely to highlight, via analogies between various audiences and various races, the broader concept of competitive racing. Another example of such analogical sound-image relations comes in the section on the languages of the world, where Ruttmann overlays an image of two men arguing with the sound of barking dogs. Here too, one might be tempted to read Ruttmann's dogs as metaphors in the tradition of Eisenstein's bulls (or the chickens that Fritz Lang inserts to symbolize women's gossip in FURY (1936)). But Ruttmann's audible dogs serve a more analogical function. Like the fighting dogs in BERLIN, or the images of fighting tigers and rams in the section of MELODIE DER WELT on wrestling and boxing ("Zweikampf"), the audible dogs in the section on languages stand in an analogous relationship to their human counterparts on the image track: each element (the image and the soundtrack) illustrating one – if only one – of the many forms of communication (human and animal) making up the languages of the world. While Ruttmann's "counterpoint" sounds of cheering crowds or barking dogs might have been "non-synchronous" with the image, they cannot be described as "non-diagetic": no less than the dogs and elephants in BERLIN, these sounds in MELODIE DER WELT were a part of the film's diagetic frame (which now encompasses the entire world). In their non-synchronicity, these audio-visual counterpoints did indeed create an "intellectual" relation between sound and image. But that relation was one of analogy more than conflict, a relation in which one element is *like* the other and both have equal status.

It was this overwhelming emphasis on analogies in MELODIE DER WELT that caused the film, like BERLIN before it, to be criticized for glossing over actual forms of social and economic conflict – in particular those of colonial relations – to present the world as a series of consumable spectacles for the Western gaze. Thus one reviewer for the leftist *Hamburger Volkszeitung* opined: "The dire situation of oppressed peoples, the exploitation of colored races – these melodies were entirely absent."[108] Another writer for *Die Welt am Abend* accused the film of promoting a "phony serenity" ("falsche Heiterkeit") and succumbing to the "danger of observing the world as a globetrotter."[109] Subsequent critics and scholars have made similar critiques,[110] and here too, Ruttmann's film stands in marked distinction to the work of Vertov, in particular the latter's 1926 film A SIXTH PART OF THE WORLD. Commissioned by the Russian state-owned trading company Gostorg, Vertov's film also used montage to create the effect of a simultaneous vision of different parts of the world (while focusing on the regions of the Soviet Union). But it did so with a very different political goal in mind: namely that of forging class consciousness – or in Vertov's words of providing "an opportunity for the workers throughout the world not only to see, but also, simultaneously, to hear one another."[111] Like MELODIE DER WELT, A SIXTH PART OF THE WORLD includes several images of colonial life from Africa and Asia. But unlike Ruttmann, Vertov's montage places colonized subjects in opposition to wealthy Europeans in order to underscore relations of colonial domination. In this way, the injustice of colonialism – exploitative labor relations, but also the use of "black people" for capitalist entertainment – functions as a master trope through which Vertov's film frames class relations throughout the world. To be sure, Vertov does draw numerous visual parallels – both between the various peoples of the Soviet Union and between those peoples and colonial subjects elsewhere. But this is always in order to oppose these elements to the dominant class and thus to present the world as a global theater of capitalist conflict (and the Soviet Union as the center from which this conflict will emanate to the rest of the world). Such a construction of global space obviously presents a stark difference to the one we find in MELODIE DER WELT, which – like the photomontages of *Der Querschnitt* – amalgamated the various images of the world into an archive of visual analogies, while downplaying any awareness of (economic, ethnic, colonial) conflict.

At the same time, the lack of colonial critique in Ruttmann's montage does not necessarily make MELODIE DER WELT a work of colonialist propaganda, at least not in the sense that this category existed in the interwar period. Ruttmann's film displays none of the nostalgia for Germany's lost colonial possessions that informed colonialist educational films of the 1920s such as Hans Schomburgk's VERLORENES LAND (LOST LAND, 1925) or Marin Rikli's HEIA SAFARI! (1928).[112] The film's global montages also differ from the imperialist visions of colonial diffusion evident in experimental films such as Marcel L'Herbier's L'INHUMAINE (THE INHUMAN WOMAN, 1924) or Humphrey Jenning's LISTEN TO BRITAIN (1942), where distant peoples appear as the recipients of a Eurocentric culture broadcast from an urban center to the colonial peripheries (via television or radio).[113] Rather, like the journal *Der Querschnitt*, MELODIE DER WELT constructs global space as a space of universal correspondences, in which we see little if any hierarchical distinction between the "European" and the "exotic," the "primitive" and the "modern," or makers and receivers of culture. Although dealing with images of peoples often classified at the time according to their place on an imaginary scale of historical development, both *Der Querschnitt* and MELODIE DER WELT resist any suggestion of hierarchies in terms of technology or cultural production, presenting the world, rather, as a great archive of simultaneous and comparable paradigmatic movements.

This emphasis on comparability is underscored by the other major theme of the film: that of rhythm. Like the parts of the great city in BERLIN, all the forms of cultural expression in MELODIE DER WELT appear synchronized by common rhythms, which run through the waves of the ocean, the pulse of the ship turbines, the beating of drums, the movements of animals, the dancing of human bodies and – in the culminating sequence of the film – the many rhythms of human and industrial labor. This presentation of rhythm resonates with a much broader discourse on rhythm and culture in the early 20th century. However, where Ruttmann's contemporaries in anthropology and ethnomusicology differentiated sharply between the rhythms of "primitive" and "modern" societies,[114] Ruttmann clearly offered a vision of a universal rhythm running from the most ancient to the most modern forms of culture: from grain stompers and weavers to pneumatic hammers and the engines of cruise ship. This, moreover, is precisely how the film was received. As one reviewer described it: "With startling precision, Walter Ruttmann reveals the rhythmical recurrence of the same habits in the existence of peoples: work, traffic, sports, war, theater – a series of

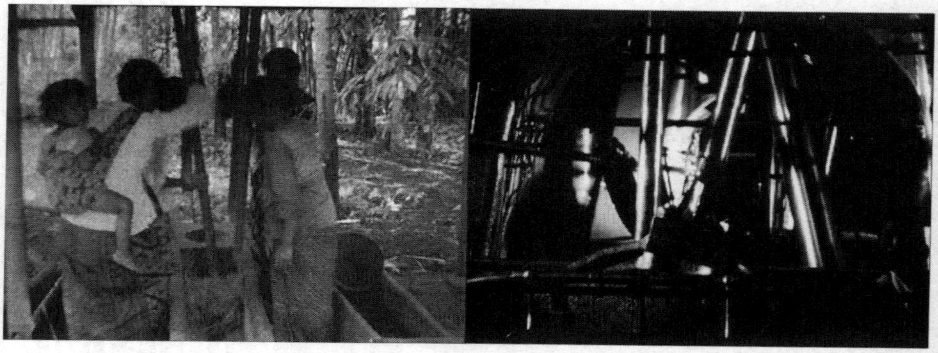

Stills from MELODIE DER WELT. *Analogous montage of grain stompers and ship engine*

optically continuous movements stretching over the entire earth from New York to Tokyo, from Berlin to Ceylon, and composed along symphonic principles."[115]

If this universalist vision of the earth and its peoples is not "colonialist," it can certainly be described as a "tourist" gaze. It was, in fact, similar to the tourist gaze that informed other promotional materials for the HAPAG world tours. As late as 1933, one can read in the introduction to a print documentation of one of the *Resolute*'s world cruises:

> If one is looking for an image to represent the worldly abundance [Weltfülle] encountered on the route of *Resolute* around the globe, one might think of a symphony in which the peoples of the world play their instruments. The American girl and the Siamese temple dancer, the New York factory worker at his conveyer belt and the rickshaw driver in Peking, the Italian in the streets of Naples and the Javanese man lounging beneath the palm trees, the Jew at the Wailing Wall in Jerusalem and the Benares Hindu wading into the Ganges wearing flowers – those are some of the figures from this orchestra of so many instruments, from which the melody of the world [Melodie der Welt] at all levels of human culture.[116]

Thus HAPAG, too, promised to offer an image of the world as harmonious symphony, in which political and economic discrepancies are deemphasized to the benefit of reassuring geographical correspondences. To this end, the HAPAG brochure (although structured along a linear path rather than cross-sectional montage) included many of the same motifs as Ruttmann's film. To be sure, the HAPAG brochure did include moments of staged authenticity and emphasize cultural differences within certain limits.[117] But those moments are subordinated to a model of tourism invested in presenting the world in terms of "commonalities" – a model on full display in Ruttmann's film.

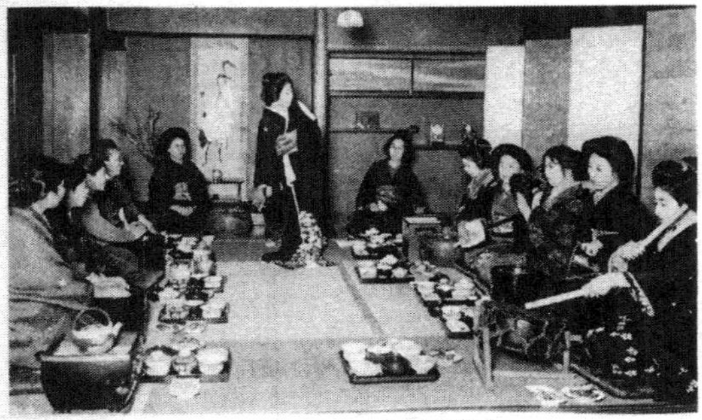

KIOTO · JAPANISCHE FRAUEN

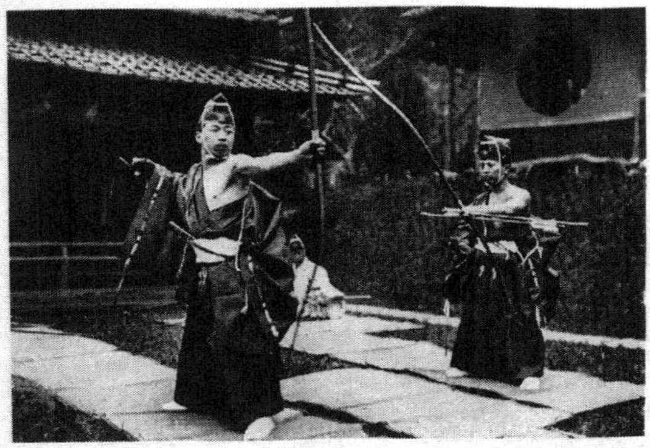

SAMURAIS · MITGLIEDER DER ALTEN JAPANISCHEN KRIEGERKASTE BEIM BOGENSCHIESSEN

Illustration from Hapag Weltreise 1933 mit dem Dreischrauben Luxus-Dämpfer 'Resolute' *(Hamburg-Amerika-Linie, 1933)*

More precisely, one might say that MELODIE DER WELT allows the photographic images to evoke difference and particularity in order, through montage, to show European viewers that other cultures are "just like us" and follow the same "universal" laws. As suggested above, this emphasis on universality and equivalence responded to the specific needs of a company like HAPAG which – rebuilding in the shadow of the Great War – had good reason to represent the world as a space largely free of cultural conflict.[118] As a "universal language," film was understood as a means for doing just this. The poet Kurt Pinthus, for example, certainly had the war experience in mind when he described film's "ethical possibilities" in 1922 as follows:

> Suddenly we find ourselves in foreign lands. We get to know the habits and dwellings of other peoples, how they work and how they live. People from every region of the earth pass before our gaze. As our knowledge of people is extended, so too, I believe, is our love of people. [...] We sense how all people from all parts of the world react with fear or joy to the same motifs; we become conscious of the fact that we all

> have fingers on each hand; and every woman experiences a sense of community at some level when she sees how the Indian mother raises her child and the Australian woman milks the cow. [119]

Such a "feeling of commonality" was, of course, precisely what HAPAG set out to evoke with its "filmic expedition," and in this sense Ruttmann's montage was perfectly appropriate to the task, showing for example – in a sequence that resonates with Pinthus's description – the parallels between a woman in Greece taking milk from the village goat herder, an American man buying milk from a boy with cows on the street and women in Germany buying coffee and cream from a street vendor. Such a touristic gaze functioned less to exoticize the other than to *familiarize* it, making it appear as part of a universal world community that could be experienced via a world cruise.

At the same time, MELODIE DER WELT is hardly exhausted, then or now, by its immediate function as an advertisement. As we have seen, questions of internationalism and *Völkerverständigung* (understanding among nations) were also central to the broader film culture of the late 1920s. Ruttmann's work on this film in fact kicked off an "international" phase in his own career that included participation in the famous Congress for Independent Film in La Sarraz, Switzerland, in 1929, several trips to France to work on Abel Gance's LA FIN DU MONDE (THE END OF THE WORLD, 1931), and a lengthy stay in Italy to make the feature film ACCIAIO (1933). Ruttmann's role in the La Sarraz congress – in which he met with Richter, Eisenstein, Cavalcanti and others to discuss the prospects of a society for independent film and collaborated on the lost film TEMPÊTE SUR LA SARRAZ (THE STORMING OF LA SARRAZ) – has often been cited as evidence that he was sympathetic to the *Völkerverständigung* project shared by much of the international film scene of the late 1920s.[120] The question of internationalism had also gained a newfound urgency with the emergence of sound film, a topic also discussed at the La Sarraz meeting and one that posed a direct challenge to the ability to distribute film internationally.[121] While later filmmakers would try to solve the problem by means of multiple versions in different languages and so-called "polyglot" films, Ruttmann was more interested in collecting the sounds of the world, including its languages but also its noises, which would stand – via his audiovisual "counterpoint" – in analogy to the images of the world.[122]

It was likely this nexus of sound film and internationalism that earned Ruttmann the invitation to work as chief assistant to Gance on LA FIN DU MONDE, the first major sound film in France. MELODIE DER WELT had in fact enjoyed great critical success in France, where critics almost unanimously praised Ruttmann's ability to interweave images and sounds of the world.[123] As one reviewer would later remember it: "Walter Ruttmann, composer of a double score for the eye and the ear in which sounds, sirens, machines and screams are combined with an extraordinary facility, has written the poem of analogy and correspondence, the romantic documentary of the unity of the human universe."[124] It was precisely this "unity" of the world that Gance also sought to demonstrate in La Fin du monde. Although the film's dialogue was entirely in French, its narrative was centrally about the question of international understanding; set against the backdrop of an impending planetary cataclysm through a wayward comet, the film focuses on the reformers Jean and Martial Novalic, who preach a new gospel of internationalism by sending out sound films made in every language of the earth in order to found an international government – modeled on the League of Nations – that would overcome nationalist warfare once and for all.[125] Although La Fin du monde was released only in a truncated version, we know from Gance's notes that the film was to include numerous sections of "world montage" reminiscent of Melodie der Welt – in particular a repeated section comparing forms of religious life to emphasize the unity of religious belief.[126] Thus if Gance sought out Ruttmann as the creator of the first full-length sound film, he clearly also saw in Ruttmann, as did his contemporaries in French cinema, an expert in world montage and someone well suited to projects of international understanding.[127]

As we have seen, however, such montage also sought to answer a greater problem of visual culture occasioned by the "flood" of photographic representations in the 1920s, a problem made all the more acute by images of the "world" – of other continents, other rituals and other cultural forms – that threatened to reveal the contingency and arbitrariness of cultural codes. While Ruttmann's audience may or may not have been able to afford a HAPAG cruise,[128] they very likely *were* familiar with the world of illustrated magazines. It was here that *Querschnitt* montage, with its all-important device of analogy, became useful for suggesting an order to the world's manifold appearances captured on photography and film, and thus containing – even as it acknowledged – the contingency of photographic representation.

It is this emphasis on order and regularity that has motivated the many critiques of Ruttmann's alleged formalism, and perhaps no film has received greater criticism in this respect than Melodie der Welt. Even at the time of its release, there was no shortage of voices to accuse Ruttmann of transforming film's visual experience – as one reviewer for the journal *Der Film* described it – into "schematism" ("Schematismus") and "exaggerated regularity" ("übertriebene Gesetzmäßigkeit").[129] Writing after WWII, the great film historian Georges Sadoul would later compare Ruttmann's use of analogies and chapter headings in Melodie der Welt to the "cataloguing mania of German university professors."[130] But it is important to understand such a "cataloguing" function of Ruttmann's montage in relation to the sheer variety of cultural forms and expressions – the "manifold forms of human life" evoked in the film's opening title – caught in photographic images. Ruttmann's film acknowledges and even presupposes such a "variety," the taming of which was the central *raison d'être* of his cross-sectional montage.

It was this balancing of variety and regularity, the particular and the lawful, that underlay the fascination with *Querschnitt* montage in the 1920s. In this sense it is perhaps no accident that, of all the films generally understood to represent the *Querschnittfilm* genre today, MELODIE DER WELT was the one most consistently associated with the term "Querschnitt" at the time of its release. While one review panned the film as "a cross-section stuck in empty doctrine" ("ein in leerer Doktrin steckengebliebener Querschnitt"),[131] others were more enthusiastic, seeing – in Rudolf Kurtz's words – "a cross-section through a fantastically colorful, multifaceted and dazzlingly heterogeneous world, which nonetheless creates the dramatic impression of a unified whole."[132] It was precisely this ability to weave disparate images into a seeming totality that Ruttmann's adherents praised in the film. "The significance of this cross-section," another reviewer wrote, "lies in its intellectual operation, the philosophical import of a technology which allows us to traverse the surface of a world with such speed that each retinal image combines with the former one. It allows us to superimpose the phenomena of the world in such a way that their contingent aspects cancel each other out, leaving only the essential."[133] This reviewer's description of Ruttmann's cross-sectional analogies as overlapping retinal images recalls modern theories of the persistence of images, by which the filmic spectator was thought to suture over the gaps of filmic reproduction to experience the projected image as one of continuous movement; but in the context of Ruttmann's statistical montage, the notion of superimposing images to arrive at essential traits also recalls projects such as Francis Galton's composite photographs, by which researchers hoped to transform the medium of photographic reproduction from an index of contingent details into an agent of statistical epistemology for the identification of types.[134] If *Querschnitt* montage promised to perform a similar epistemological feat, that promise was bound up with the project of transforming diachrony into synchrony: of overcoming the time of world travel to produce a near simultaneous display of paradigmatic similarities. Thus the French critic André Levinson could describe his experience watching MELODIE DER WELT as follows: "[Ruttmann's] images follow one another with such speed, they make such a brief appearance on the screen, that they seem to be superimposed, simultaneous, lined up for comparison, perceived at the same time." [135]

As I have argued, the desire to transform film from an art of linear narrative to one of paradigmatic comparison was also bound up, in the late 1920s, with questions of archive. Calling for the establishment of a *Reichsfilmarchiv* (state

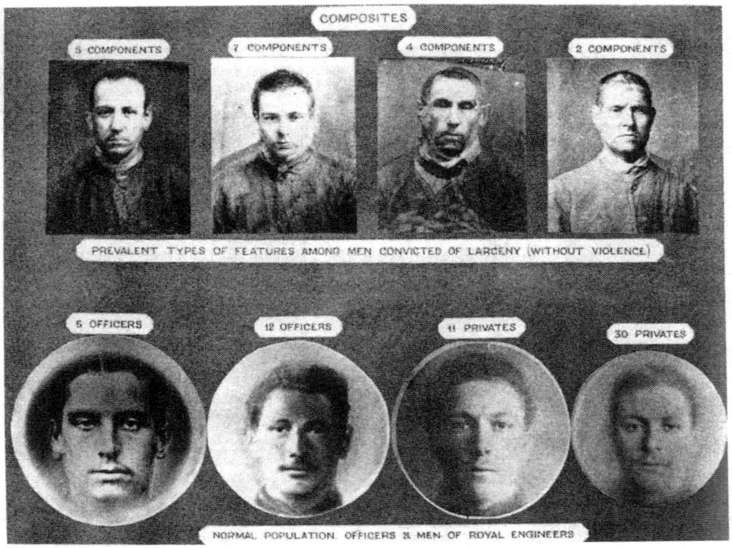

Francis Galton, example of composite photographs. Illustration from Inquiry into the Human Faculty and its Development *(1883)*

film archive) in a 1926 article for the journal *Lichtbild-Bühne*, the head of the Saxon Association for the Promotion of Film and Photography, Fritz Schimmer, explained that the "essential task of every archive [...] is to conserve and *order* objects that would otherwise be lost. [...] By comparing these objects with one another, the archive makes it possible to group them together or distinguish them from one another."[136] Clearly, the educational *Querschnittfilm*, as it was instituted by the Ufa in 1928, offered one such model for ordering archival images according to a cross-section of comparable moments or "samples" within the development of film.[137] But as we saw in the first part of this chapter, the very notion of the *Querschnitt* – as it became one of the key terms of Weimar visual culture – performed an operation of imaginary ordering amid the "flood" of photographic representations in the 1920s. Intervening within this cultural context, Ruttmann's cross-section montage promised to transform an archive of random details into a symphony of interlocking notes. Even while flaunting the camera's ability to record anything anywhere in the world, Ruttmann's analogous montage suggested an underlying system of order by performing, before the spectator's eyes, the kind of comparisons that Shimmer sees as the central to any archive.

Conclusion: Avant-Garde between Statistical Order and the Spark of Chance

This is not to argue that *all* uses of associative montage in Weimar experimental film displayed the same tendency toward quasi-bureaucratic "cataloguing" as Ruttmann's. One could of course point to many counter-examples, such as Hans Richter's ZWEIGROSCHENZAUBER (TWO-PENCE MAGIC, 1929). An advertisement for the *Kölnische Illustrierte Zeitung*, Richter's film represented the experience of reading illustrated magazines as one of joyful disorder. Using visual analogies linked via dissolves, Richter's film represents the illustrated paper as a series of graphic "picture rhymes" in a manner not a little reminiscent of *Der Querschnitt* and MELODIE DER WELT. However, far from reducing the contingency of the image, Richter's outlandish juxtapositions – the moon and a bald head, a criminal hold-up and a diver's outstretched arms, a monk ringing a church bell and a thief scaling a wall in the night, etc. – mock our desire to order the world or synthesize images. Like Borges's "Chinese encyclopedia," these analogies disrupt our established conceptual orders with the suggestion of an entirely different taxonomy, thus highlighting nothing so much as the "stark impossibility of thinking *that*."[138] Rather than knowledge, the operative mode of Richter's film is that of magic; in the tradition of the trick film stretching back to Méliès, Richter's film begins with the figure of a magician who, with a pass of the hands, conjures up both an optical device – the telescope through which we will first see the moon as the first image in the associative chain – and a paying audience. Such a conjuring trick, itself relying on editing, frames Richter's visual analogies as "tricks" rather than modes of scientific knowledge.

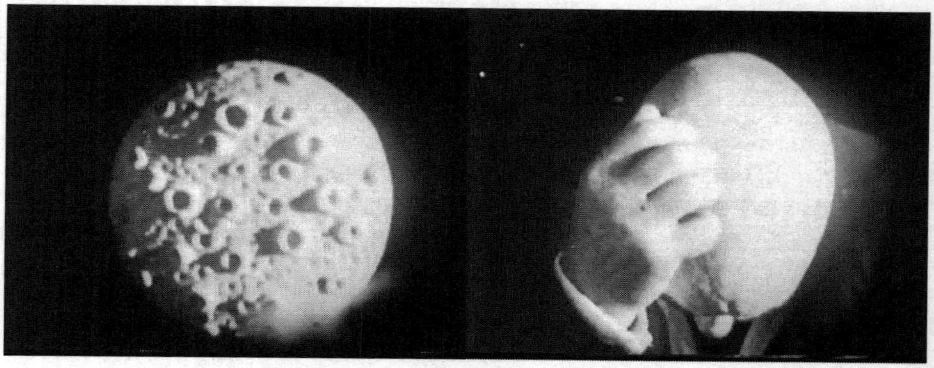

Stills from Hans Richter, ZWEIGROSCHENZAUBER *(1929). Analogous montage of moon and bald head*

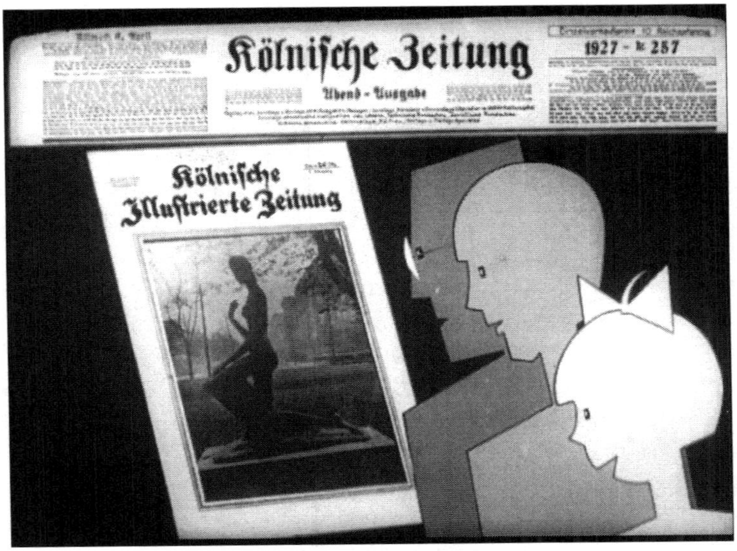

Still from Ruttmann, DORT WO DER RHEIN *(1927)*

Just how playful Richter's "picture rhymes" were can be gauged when one compares his film to a previous advertisement for the same journal made by Ruttmann himself. In his final animated advertisement DORT WO DER RHEIN (THERE WHERE THE RHINE, 1927), produced by Julius Pinschewer, Ruttmann presented the *Kölner Illustrierte* in the tradition of the industrial film, first showing the city of Cologne then a systematic rendition of the newspaper production process: reams of paper racing through the factory machines, folded newspapers stacked into piles, papers transported around the world, and a street vendor bringing the paper to customers on the street.[139] This presentation of newspaper production is then followed by catalogue-like list (not a little reminiscent of the chapter headings in MELODIE DER WELT) of the types of knowledge covered in the paper – trade and industry, politics, sports, technology, legal matters, and the arts – each accompanied by a trademark-like illustration. Finally, in a combination of animation and photographic images popular in advertising film in the 1920s, the film shows us a family looking at the *Kölnische Illustrierte Zeitung* as a parade of alternating photographic passes before their gaze. While this final parade of photographs suggests the heterogeneity of phenomena in the world, Ruttmann's schematic animations and encyclopedic categories promise to tame the contingency of images by subjecting them to a strict ordering schema, one offering – in conformity with the Weimar print anthologies mentioned at the beginning of this chapter – a "cross-section" of the world's knowledge.

Where Ruttmann's film thus figures the reading of the illustrated paper as a process of edification in the matter of popular *Querschnitt* books, Richter represents that reading experience as one of wonder, contingency and arbitrary associations. His analogous montages produce an effect not of systematicity, but rather the surrealist spark of chance: the chance congruence of a moon and a head, a monk and a thief, a sewing machine and the operating table. It is this ability to bring together incongruous phenomena that Richter's film attributes to montage in both print and film. Whereas Ruttmann represents the production of the illustrated journal through a vision of a Fordist factory, Richter shows us that production in the form of a hand with scissors, which forms an extension of the magician's hands from the opening scene. Emerging from a freeze-frame of the female burglar at the end of the film, this hand can be seen cutting the image of the burglar and laying it on a table. When the cutter's hands then pass over the image with the same gesture as the magician's hands at the beginning of the film, the image magically inserts itself (via another dissolve) into the layout of the newspaper, and we see the same visual analogies as juxtaposed photos in the newspaper in a layout reminiscent of *Der Querschnitt* and other journals.[140]

It is not always so easy to distinguish between "orderly" and "playful" (or the bureaucratic and magic) variants of analogous montage. Many manifestations of Weimar montage, including *Der Querschnitt* but also other works such as Hannah Höch's *Album* (ca. 1933), could accommodate both tendencies. Just as early cinema constituted a site of both "awe and fear," so cross-sectional montage itself must be understood in this dual relation to contingency, particularly the contingency of proliferating photographic representations in the 1920s. On the one hand, it could reactivate a longstanding ability of the cinema to promise an escape from modernity's incessant rationalizations. On the other, it was also bound up with a kind of archival desire and the search for order through statistical regularity. Both tendencies – the spark of chance and the demonstration of statistical regularities – participated in a greater balancing act between contingency and order in a world of proliferating images, one in which causal explanations no longer seemed adequate and totality was no longer a given.

3. Statistics and Biopolitics: Conceiving the National Body in Ruttmann's Hygiene Films (1930-1933)

Introduction

In the last chapter, I argued that Ruttmann's cross-sectional montage functioned above all as a means of ordering the images of the world that proliferated in the visual media of the 1920s according to a "statistical" epistemology, one that suggested higher laws even as it acknowledged the particular and the idiosyncratic. As we saw, such a project, while lending itself to the immediate goal of an advertisement for world cruises, also resonated with broader questions of Weimar modernism and with a broader understanding of film as a medium existing at the border between contingency and order. But statistics was not only a conceptual or epistemological tool of mass modernity; like experimental psychology, it was also a mode of knowledge created and practiced *within a horizon of applications*. More specifically, it was bound up with what Foucault has famously called "governmentality," the modern form of power that conceives of mass society as a "population" with its own laws and regularities (birth and death rates, rates of disease, economic activities, etc.).[1] If statistics offered the central means of conceptualizing such biopolitical phenomena, it always operated within a horizon of applications meant to influence them: of private and public campaigns for increasing birth rates, curbing alcoholism, reducing disease and "degeneration," enhancing public whealth and welfare, avoiding accidents, "directing the flow of population into certain regions or activities," etc.[2] As Ian Hacking puts it: "Statistics may think of itself as providing only information, but it is itself part of the technology of power in a modern state."[3] With the emergence of biopolitics, statistics became the key intermediary within a power relation no longer conceived of in terms of sovereign rights, but rather in terms of a population to be guided and influenced.

Given the horizon of applicability in which statistics operated, it should hardly come as a surprise that a filmmaker such as Ruttmann, whose filmic experiments drew upon such forms of expertise, would employ "statistical montage" to fashion film as a tool for biopolitical intervention. He did this, from the beginning of the 1930s on, through a number of sponsored "cultural films" (*Kulturfilme*), including FEIND IM BLUT (ENEMY IN THE BLOOD, 1931), BLUT UND BODEN. GRUNDLAGEN ZUM NEUEN REICH (BLOOD AND SOIL. FOUNDA-

TIONS FOR THE NEW REICH, 1933), ABERGLAUBE (SUPERSTITION, 1940) and EIN FILM GEGEN DIE VOLKSKRANKHEIT KREBS (A FILM AGAINST THE EPIDEMIC OF CANCER, 1941). While focusing on different themes (from syphilis to agrarian policy to medical superstition to cancer), all of these films can be described as "public hygiene" films since they all focus on the health of the population and, more importantly, seek to use film as a means of influencing it. Moreover, while the earliest of these films coincided with Ruttmann's "international" phase, they all conceive of the "population" in national terms. And like the state agencies that commissioned them, all of these films explicitly invoke statistics in the form of graphs, charts and Isotype illustrations to make their arguments about public health. As I argue in this chapter, these images of statistics function not only to conceptualize the problems these films were thematizing, but also to fashion *film itself* as a medium of biopolitical intervention.

It is perhaps no accident that Ruttmann chose the *Kulturfilm* as the format for such populational interventions. As has often been remarked, the German *Kulturfilm* was a unique national phenomenon; the result of a compromise between the educational-scientific aspirations of cinema reformers and the financial aspirations of popular film producers, the *Kulturfilm* emerged after WWI as a forum for the popularization of scientific, historical or social knowledge.[4] In generic terms, this dual genealogy translated into a hybrid form that tended to mix narrative drama and didactic presentations, while giving more or less weight to one aspect or the other.[5] Sexual "enlightenment films" such as ANDERS ALS DIE ANDEREN (DIFFERENT FROM THE OTHERS, Richard Oswald, 1919); travelogues such as Colin Ross's MIT DEM KURBELKASTEN UM DIE ERDE (AROUND THE WORLD WITH A MOVIE CAMERA, 1925); hygienic and athletic films such as WEGE ZU KRAFT UND SCHÖNHEIT (PATHS TO STRENGTH AND BEAUTY, Wilhelm Prager, 1925); and scientific films such as WUNDER DER SCHÖPFUNG (MIRACLES OF CREATION, Hans Walter Kornblum, 1925) combined traditions of the educational lecture, attractions cinema and narrative action in order to package the specialized knowledge (geographic, sexual, hygienic, scientific) of their commissioning agencies in popular forms for lay audiences.[6]

When Ruttmann took on his first commissions for cultural films at the end of the 1920s, he adopted a similar mix of narrative and non-narrative elements. But in Ruttmann, the non-narrative elements in films such as FEIND IM BLUT consist overwhelmingly of the kinds of cross-sectional montage he had developed in BERLIN and MELODIE DER WELT. In contrast to the earlier films, however, that montage no longer functions simply to establish regularities, but rather assumes – within the didactic framework of the *Kulturfilm* – a new pedagogical role: namely that of embedding individual stories within a broader social framework, and by extension asking viewers to see themselves as part of a national population and regulate their behavior accordingly.[7] In this, these films followed the logic of modern statistics generally, which – as Hacking reminds us, – helped to create "the determining classifications within which people must think of themselves and the actions that are open to them."[8] Ruttmann's hygiene films not only delimit such fields of classification, but also prescribe appropriate actions. Whereas BERLIN and MELODIE DER WELT sought to make sense of the world's manifold appearances, managing the multiplicity of impressions and visual images, these films directly interpellate spectators to become their own "managers": regulating their own lives in accordance with the films' populational findings.

Between the "symphony" films and the hygiene films, the function of statistics thus changes. For when Ruttmann's hygiene films invoke statistics – regarding rates of syphilis in FEIND IM BLUT, birth rates in BLUT UND BODEN or cancer rates in EIN FILM GEGEN DIE VOLKSKRANKHEIT KREBS – they do so in order to muster evidence for prescriptive arguments about individual comportment. These are eminently biopolitical prescriptions, concerned – as were the commissioning bodies – with regulating bodies, their sexuality and their collective health.[9] Within this context, statistics passes from a tool of conceptualization to one designed for the governing of populations, and in this sense, Ruttmann's hygiene films conformed perfectly the mandates of their commissioning organizations, which were bureaucratic agents of biopolitical governmentality in Foucault's sense.

Still, even within this biopolitical framework, one can observe a transformation between the Weimar and the Nazi variants of Ruttmann's hygiene films – a transformation I will explore in this chapter through a comparison of Ruttmann's 1931 film FEIND IM BLUT and his first National Socialist film BLUT UND BODEN. Whereas FEIND IM BLUT still addresses its viewers as individuals with a vested interest in managing their individual health (as well as that of their families), the National Socialist films subordinate individual interests entirely to those of the nation, rendering spectators responsible for the health or degeneracy of the *Volkskörper* (people's body). This transformation echoes a shift in the implementation of biopolitics itself in Germany, which – as historian Edward Dickinson has argued – *did* transform in 1933 from a predominantly reformist paradigm of social governance, based on the promotion of individual initiative and the management of social differences, to a totalitarian paradigm of population control based on top-down decrees and on the elimination of difference.[10] In terms of statistics, whereas the first variant musters statistics as evidence to persuade individuals how to act in their own interest, the second variant employs statistics to tell individuals what they must do in the interest of the *Volk*.[11]

Managing the Masses: Feind im Blut

From its planning stages on, Feind im Blut was indicative of the former model. Ruttmann's second long sound film (and the third he made with Tobis Klangfilm), Feind im Blut was commissioned jointly by the Deutsche Gesellschaft zur Bekämpfung der Geschlechtskrankheiten (German Society for the Suppression of Sexual Diseases, hereafter DGBG) and the Schweizerische Gesellschaft zur Bekämpfung der Geschlechtkrankheiten (Swiss Society for the Suppression of Sexual Diseases, hereafter SGBG). Like similar societies in other European countries and in the United States, the DGBG and the SGBG arose in the early 20th century to promote a new reform model of public hygiene based on notions of autonomous and enlightened self-cultivation, in which – as Anita Gertiser aptly puts it – authorities sought to animate "the individual citizen to take reasonable care of his or her own body."[12] Unlike the more radical and racist eugenic groups such as the Deutsche Gesellschaft für Rassenhygiene (German Society for Racial Hygiene), the DGBG was a pluralistic undertaking, with membership spanning from conservative to socialist and including not only doctors and politicians, but also moral reformers, feminists, leftwing thinkers and abolitionists.[13] What brought all of these factions together was a vision of democratic management for a pluralistic society based on autonomous self-care. After WWI, such reform groups began to see film as a key medium for dissemination of their ideals, producing an international body of films, largely forgotten today – such as The End of the Road (Edward Griffith, 1918) and On doit le dire (It Must Be Said, Marcus O'Galop, 1918) – all of which sought to persuade viewers to act rationally in their own interest by giving them the facts of sexual disease, its prevalence, its causes and its cures.[14]

It was within this context that the SGBG approached the Zurich production company Praesensfilm in January 1931 with the idea for Feind im Blut; the film premiered only three months later simultaneously in Berlin (on 17 April) and in Basel (on 18 April).[15] Praesensfilm, for its part, can hardly be described as a "reactionary" organization. Founded in 1924 by the Polish émigré Lazar Wechsler and the aviator Walter Mittelholzer, the company specialized in non-fiction and sponsored forms such as advertising, educational film and *Kulturfilm*. And by all appearances, Wechsler had a particular penchant for the "avant-garde." It was Wechsler who, shortly after the Congress of Independent Film in La Sarraz, hired Sergei Eisenstein (after Dziga Vertov had to back out) to make Frauennot und Frauenglück (The Happiness and Misery of Women, 1929), a film advocating the legalization of abortion. It was Wechsler who provided the backing for the communist film Kuhle Wampe, oder Wem gehört die Welt? (Kuhle Wampe, or Who Owns the World?, Bertolt Brecht and Slatan Dudow,

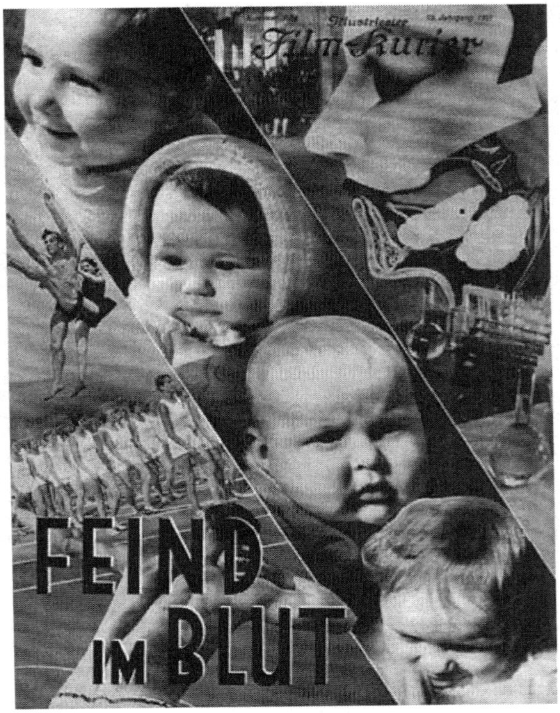

Poster for Ruttmann, FEIND IM BLUT *(1931), from* Illustrierter Film-Kurier *(1931)*

1932) after the original production company Prometheus went bankrupt. And it was Wechsler who approached Walter Ruttmann – who like Eisenstein had recently returned from the congress in La Sarraz – to make the commissioned film on the dangers of sexual disease.[16]

FEIND IM BLUT was thus the result of two distinct modern(ist) cultures: that of avant-garde film and that of medical-social reform. This double provenance was reflected in the film's performances. The Berlin premiere, for example, consisted of a special gala screening in the Atrium theater attended both by members of Berlin's film world and – as one report described it – by "leading authorities, executive boards, insurance groups and other representatives of the medical establishment."[17] That double provenance was also reflected in the film's overall structure, which combines elements of avant-garde and educational-scientific film.[18] Set in Berlin, the film follows several intersecting characters, while focusing in particular on two parallel stories: one of a medical student who hesitates to join his newfound girlfriend because of his fear that he has syphilis (before learning that he is in fact free of the disease) and another, more tragic, of a mechanic who provokes the suicide of his wife when he passes his syphilis to their

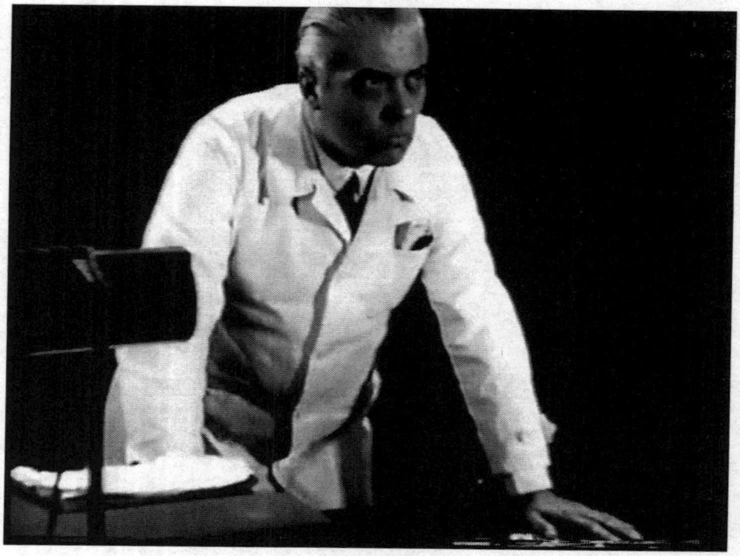

Still from Ruttmann, FEIND IM BLUT. *Doctor lecturing to students*

newborn child. But footage from these stories is alternated with lengthy didactic sequences set in the student's polyclinic, where doctors lecture to students and patients about the dangers of syphilis. On the one hand, the authoritative position accorded to the doctors – whose lectures are also aimed at the film's audience – clearly positions this as a film for public education, designed to fulfill the public mission of the DGBG and SGBG. Like those organizations, the film – with its sexual content and its many disturbing images of sexual disease – was aimed at an adult audience (and forbidden to minors).[19]

On the other hand, as an urban drama, the film is also imbued with topoi familiar from the avant-garde film culture of the late 1920s, particularly as the latter overlapped with social-realist filmmaking. Although it is difficult to verify whether Ruttmann collaborated with Vsevelod Pudovkin as some accounts suggest, the film does include echoes of contemporary Russian cinema. In particular, the opening and closing shots, which use associative montage to compare children's faces to fruit and flowers, could not but remind viewers of the famous opening montage of Alexander Dovzhenko's ZEMLYA (EARTH, 1930), with its famous comparisons of fruit, flowers and peasant faces. However, as the sequence continues, it becomes clear that Ruttmann's biopolitical montage has a different purpose from Dovzhenko's poetic exploration of peasant life cycles when the fruit, having grown rotten and worm-infested, is compared to the faces of disabled children.[20] FEIND IM BLUT also drew on German leftwing filmmaking. In particular, the film's melodramatic final sequence, in which the

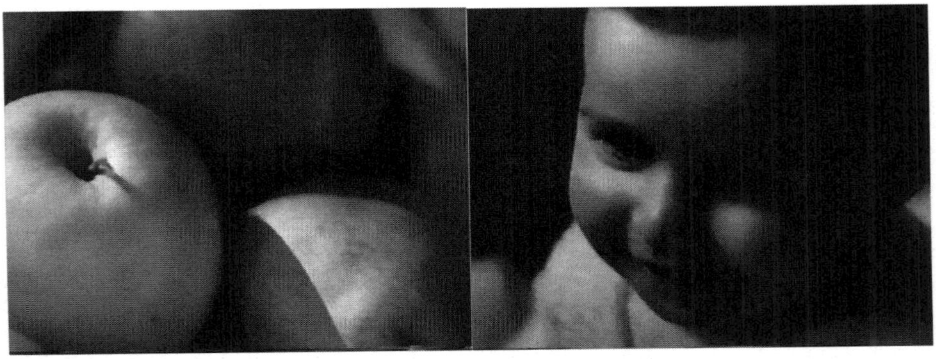

Stills from Ruttmann, FEIND IM BLUT. *Montage of fruit and children's faces*

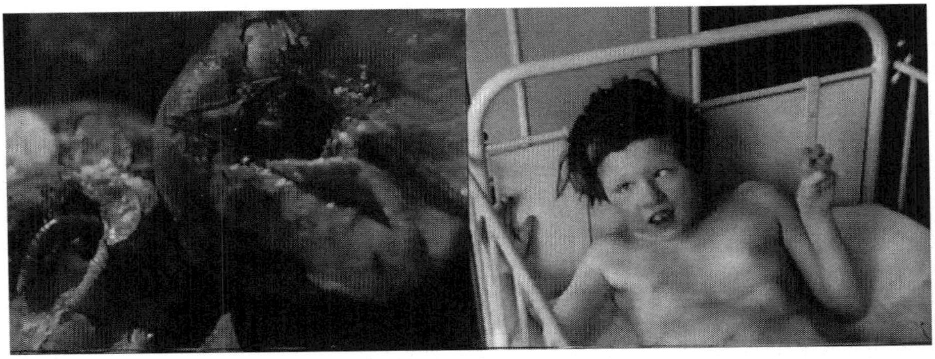

Stills from Ruttmann, FEIND IM BLUT. *Montage of rotten fruit and 'degenerate' children*

engineer's wife attempts to kill herself and her infected infant by turning on the gas in their apartment, recalls Phil Jutzi's popular melodrama MUTTER KRAUSENS FAHRT INS GLÜCK (MOTHER KRAUSEN'S JOURNEY TO HAPPINESS, 1929), in which the working-class mother kills herself and her tenant's infant by the same means at the end of the film.[21]

Perhaps most importantly for my purposes here, Ruttmann's representation of the city stands in an obvious dialogue with recent Berlin films, not least of all his own BERLIN. DIE SINFONIE DER GROSSSTADT. The film opens with a train ride into the city, and the morning sequences are all introduced by montages of urban tableaux reminiscent of the early sequences from BERLIN. However, in contrast to the former film (but closer in this respect to contemporary social-realism), FEIND IM BLUT portrays the city less as a space of perceptual dislocation than as a "milieu": the environment in which a disease like syphilis can spread. Thus the opening train ride, while containing individual shots of train parts reminiscent of BERLIN, nonetheless has its focus on a drama playing out inside the train car: namely a flirtatious meeting of a man and a woman in a closed cabin. One can make a similar observation concerning a lengthy nightclub sequence in FEIND IM BLUT. While the sequence recalls the entertainment portion in the last act of BERLIN, it also differs substantially; far from forming one form of rhythmical spectacle among others, the jazz club in FEIND IM BLUT, staged as a space of increasing drunkenness and licentiousness, functions to emphasize the causal relation between alcohol, sex and syphilis. What such comparisons suggest is that the problem being addressed in FEIND IM BLUT – the aspect of urban life in need of management – is not a problem of perception but one of behavior.

To date, what little research has been published on FEIND IM BLUT has tended to situate the film within the context of medical history.[22] In as much as I have classified the film as one of Ruttmann's "hygiene films," my own reading follows this precedent. However, within this broader context, I also want to emphasize a factor that situates this film more squarely within late Weimar film culture and Ruttmann's work in particular: its approach to statistics. The presence of a statistical optics is indicated already in the opening titles of the film before we see a single image, when the film introduces its main characters with the words: "Among many thousands of people, a mechanic, his wife, a student, his friend."[23] This statistical framework will continue into the film's prologue where we learn that there are 400,000 new cases of syphilis each year. But it also recalls MENSCHEN AM SONNTAG (PEOPLE ON SUNDAY) with its nearly anonymous characters chosen at random from among the 4,000,000 inhabitants of Berlin. Like MENSCHEN AM SONNTAG, FEIND IM BLUT is clearly at pains to keep the audience aware of these "thousands" of people, even as it follows the stories of its randomly chosen characters more closely. Indeed, it uses many of the same methods as its predecessor to keep that larger statistical reality in view. First, Ruttmann employs frequent long shots to frame his characters in compositions emphasizing the urban milieu surrounding them, especially in sequences taking place outdoors on the city streets as the student, the mechanic or the student's girlfriend move from houses to clinics to nightclubs.[24] This is true to the point where, like MENSCHEN AM SONNTAG, one can have trouble locating a character in the frame or following the action.[25] But in both films, this lack of visual focus is anything but accidental, for both films situate their "action" on two levels at once: the individual level of story and the statistical level of urban life. The loose focus also extends from the visual composition to the narrative level in several sequences in which Ruttmann spends as much or more time exploring the setting and the space as he does on the characters themselves. For example, in the above-mentioned nightclub sequence, which lasts over eight minutes, only a tiny fraction of the screen time is devoted to the meeting of the student and his girlfriend, while the majority of the sequence focuses on the musicians, the bartenders, dancers (including a cameo by the cabaret dancer Trudi Schoop), the accoutrements of drinking (where the rows of glasses recall the medical beakers from an earlier sequence) and the increasingly uncontrollable drunkenness of the patrons.

But Ruttmann conveys the broader statistical gaze onto Berlin above all through cross-sectional montage. Like MENSCHEN AM SONNTAG, FEIND IM BLUT repeatedly cuts to cross-sectional images of the city, its traffic and its anonymous inhabitants (morning street sweepers, prostitutes, etc.). While the actions shown in these images certainly appear to take place simultaneously with the action of the main characters, their geographical relation to the film's characters remains unspecified. Instead, they show us – like the "database" editing of BERLIN or MENSCHEN AM SONNTAG – spaces and characters that Ruttmann could just as easily have chosen for the main story. This cross-sectional logic also informs Ruttmann's representation of media, when a series of newspaper headlines and inserts suggests the widespread presence of syphilis, its consequences and its treatments throughout the city. But it comes to a head in a sequence toward the end of the film representing dozens of patients visiting doctors in the polyclinic. Cadenced by the sound of the recurring buzzer in the men's and women's waiting rooms, the sequence details various scenarios, symptoms and fates of those infected with syphilis, from mild and treatable cases to degeneracy and infertility.

Here again, a useful comparison can be made with MENSCHEN AM SONNTAG. In particular, the parade of patients in FEIND IM BLUT recalls the most celebrated sequence in the former film, in which we watch a parade of anonymous faces pass before a photographer's camera on the beach; like the photography sequence in MENSCHEN AM SONNTAG, the series of clinic patients in FEIND IM BLUT is clearly designed to insert the main characters into a larger pool of individuals, any of which might have served as the film's protagonist. (Both the student and the mechanic, after all, visit the same polyclinic as the other patients shown: the student coming in time to learn of his good health and the mechanic coming too late to save his wife, albeit in time to cure himself and his child). However, there is an important difference: whereas MENSCHEN AM SONNTAG conceived of the masses as a collection of urban types, FEIND IM BLUT conceives of its pool in biopolitical terms as a group of patients or potential patients: that is, as bodies susceptible to pathology. As a result, the statistical montage in FEIND IM BLUT takes on a didactic function entirely lacking in the city symphonies. For the comparisons of the mechanic and the student also serves to demonstrate the doctor's message that people should seek professional help as quickly as possible and avoid the services of charlatans. Unlike

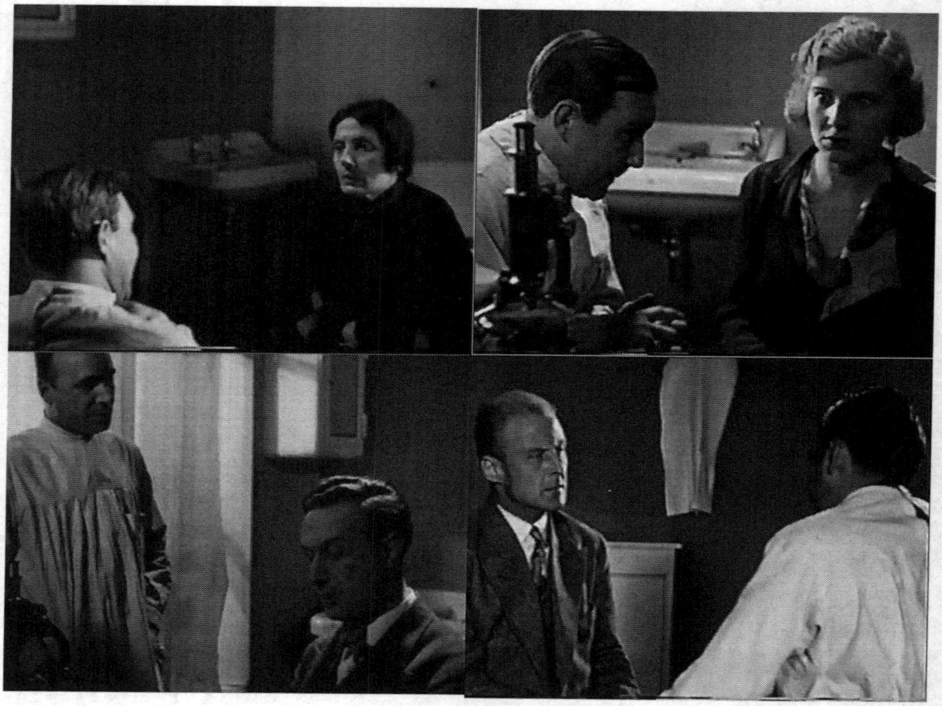

Stills from Ruttmann, Feind im Blut. *Parade of anonymous patients*

the student and unlike several of the patients, the mechanic suffers horrific consequences because he elects to consult an unaccredited "healer" (Heilkünstler) and have his baby delivered by a midwife rather than entrusting his and his family's health to the medical professionals.

It is these "professionals" who occupy the position of authority in the film, an authority established on the formal level as much as it is through the narrative; unlike the other characters, the doctors seem to hover between diegetic and non-diegetic status. Again and again, the scenes in which the doctors explain syphilis to the students and patients morph into *lectures for the film's audience* when the doctors disappear from view to become disembodied voice-overs speaking over images of graphs, charts, medical preparations and footage of syphilitic patients. In such sequences, Ruttmann's film transforms into the mode of an expository documentary, trading in narrative editing and cross-sectional montage for evidentiary editing, in which the images shown become evidence for the claims of off-screen voices.[26] In this, Feind im Blut sets up a hierarchical relation between sound and image that Ruttmann's earlier sound experiments explicitly avoided. This structure of authority within Feind im Blut was reinforced, moreover, by the structure of the film's screening, which – beginning in May 1931 – was preceded by a pre-recorded lecture by Dr. Hermann Roeschmann of the DGBG, who had already delivered the accompanying lecture in person at the film's Berlin premier in April.[27]

Although the pre-recorded lecture that accompanied FEIND IM BLUT has been lost, it is clear from the lectures presented in the film that medical authority here relied fundamentally on the evidence of statistics. From the first sentence of the first lecture – "As we have seen, the transmission of syphilis occurs in a majority of cases via sexual relations"[28] – the doctors employ the vocabulary of statistics ("a majority of cases") to explain the most frequent causes of syphilis, its typical patterns and phases of development, its rates of treatability, its relative frequency among different age groups, its costs to the state, etc. In several sequences, moreover, they explicitly point to statistical graphs as evidence of their claims, which Ruttmann – following well-established conventions of scientific and educational film – animates in order to render them filmic figures.[29]

If such graphs function as evidence for the doctors' lectures, they are also – within the wider structure of Ruttmann's film – meant to explain the dramatic stories recounted or evoked in the narrative, thus elevating individual cases to the status of larger statistical facts. During the cross-sectional montage at the clinic, for example, a doctor speaking to a father who has just lost his son shows the man a graph detailing the precise rates of syphilis per 100 inhabitants at various ages between fourteen and twenty, thus enfolding the father's tragedy into a broader problem of public hygiene. At another point, the film cuts from a newspaper headline about a twenty-year-old boy who committed suicide to a lecture in which the professor points to a graph showing that syphilis occurs most frequently in twenty-year-olds before gradually tapering off in the older population. Both the age (twenty) and the fate (suicide) of the person invoked here clearly resonate with the narrratives of the medical student and the mechanic at the center of FEIND IM BLUT, thus encouraging spectators to read the protagonists' stories, too, as part of a broader populational phenomenon outlined by the doctors.[30] More specifically, the protagonists' stories function, within this context, as models of how and how not to act. Thus between the symphony film and the *Kulturfilm*, statistics has transformed from a means of describing and conceptualizing urban life – making sense of its multiple impressions – to a tool for prescribing action: namely the action of taking care of one's health in a milieu rife with possibilities of contagion. In this sense, Ruttmann's animated graphs can also be understood as intermedial corollaries for his cross-sectional montage: like that montage, they bring order to the motley collection of bodies, movements and trajectories of populations. Or rather, one might say that they train us to read Ruttmann's montages of patients (or potential patients) as "statistical images," i.e. as presentations of possible cases and regularities.

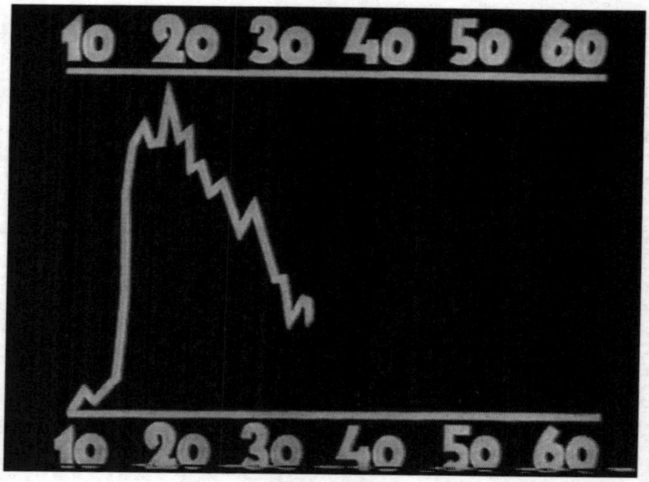

Still from Ruttmann, FEIND IM BLUT. *Animated statistical chart*

And yet, the graphs represent only one of the ways in which Ruttmann adapts the visual language of science to film. Other instances include schematic scientific drawings, which Ruttmann animates in order to illustrate the doctor's lecture concerning the normal progression of syphilis through the body. In their abstraction of contingent details and their emphasis on the "typical," such illustrations need to be distinguished from the 19th-century conventions of "mechanical objectivity" discussed by Lorraine Daston and Peter Galison, in which the recording of the particular and the idiosyncratic are valorized as indices of images free from artistic intervention and "untainted by subjectivity."[31] On one level, these illustrations might seem to harken back to the pre-19th-century tradition that Daston and Galison dub "truth to nature" with its valorization of "ideal" objects or "characteristic" exemplars.[32] But such illustrations are clearly no longer based – as were the images of 18th-century atlas illustrations – on the acquired wisdom and observational prowess of a sage artist. Rather, their scientific value as images of the "typical" came from elsewhere: namely from a statistical framework that sought to isolate the "normal" as the average of numerous particulars. This is precisely the value informing the animated scientific images in FEIND IM BLUT; like a statistical curve, those animations show us the normal progression of syphilis through the human body.

For Daston and Galison, the emergence of photography was not the cause of mechanical objectivity, but in as much as photography was understood as a mode of automatic reproduction (more or less eliminating the interventions of the artist's hand), it was often seen as a privileged medium for producing objective representations.[33] But in its relation to the contingent and to detail,

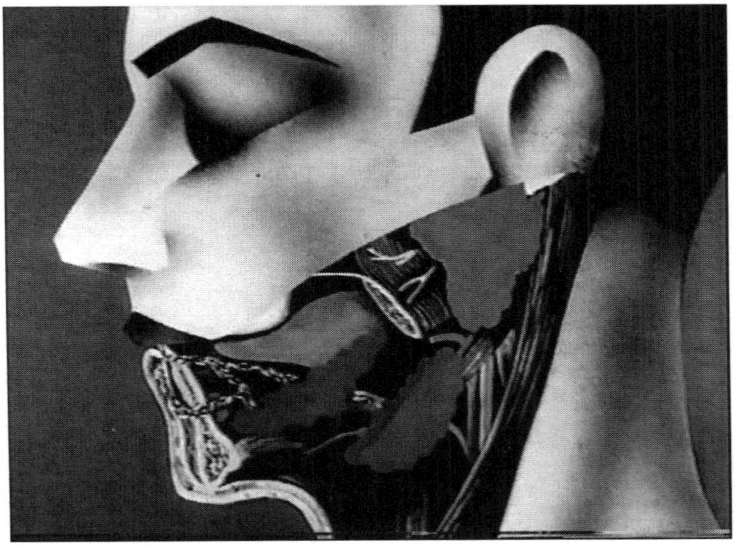

Still from Ruttmann, FEIND IM BLUT. *Animated medical illustration showing progression of syphilis in facial area*

photography also embodied one of the problems of mechanical objectivity, which produced objects "too particularized to be typical," thus threatening to rob science of a "universally valid working object."[34] Schematic scientific illustrations and animations of the type shown in FEIND IM BLUT clearly provided one answer to this problem; although not exactly a return to 18th-century modes of idealizing observation, such images did promise to overcome the contingencies and details of mechanical objectivity to produce a *typical* representation.[35] As Scott Curtis has argued, more over, such scientific illustrations generally functioned, in both print and film, *in relation* to photography and photographic images; while the "roughness" of the detailed photograph served to authenticate the "smooth" schematism of drawings and animations, the reduction of the these graphic illustrations also served to raise the photographic images up to the level of theoretical inquiry.[36] This is precisely what we see in Ruttmann. As I have argued, the animated "statistical" drawings in FEIND IM BLUT must be seen in relation to Ruttmann's cross-sectional montage. They teach us how to read that montage: i.e. to identify individual bodies as part of a statistical group or population susceptible to syphilis, to identify individual symptoms – no matter how overwhelming Ruttmann's often "disgusting" images might appear – as part of a more or less "normal" development of syphilis in the body, etc.[37]

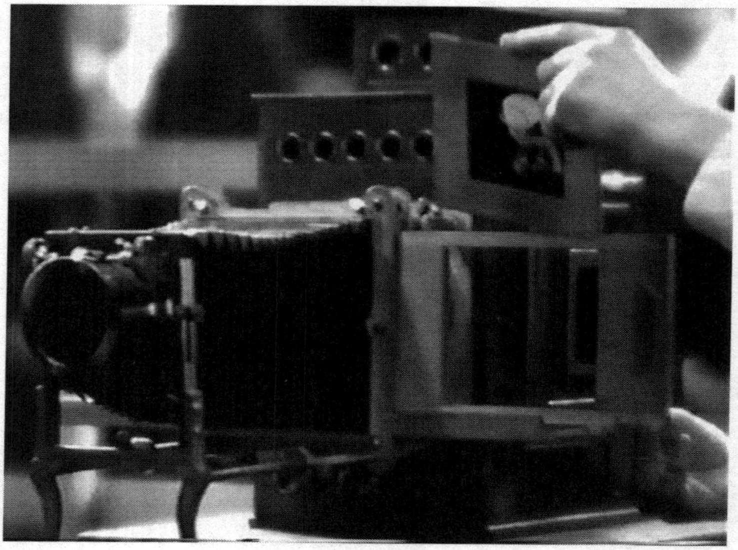

Still from Ruttmann, FEIND IM BLUT. *Lantern slide projector in medical classroom*

In animating such "typical" scientific illustrations, Ruttmann is clearly positioning film here as the successor to scientific drawing, an association that becomes unmistakable in several sequences highlighting the presence of a medical slide projector in the classroom. In one sequence, in which the student listens attentively as the doctor describes symptoms of gonorrhea (*Tripper*), Ruttmann dwells on the transformation of the classroom into a darkened theater. As one assistant pulls down the screen, another loads the medical slide – a schematic drawing of the male genitalia – into the lantern projector while a third assistant turns out the lights. A series of close-ups brings us into a detail shot of the projector lens before the film finally zeroes in on the scientific spectacle. From this point onward in the sequence, the medical spectacle and Ruttmann's own film are, as it were, melded into one, only now – in a transformation designed to highlight the superiority of filmic illustration to slide illustration – Ruttmann once again animates the image that he had just highlighted as a still slide in previous shots.[38]

Clearly the apparatus plays a key role here. Like other scientific films – but in distinction to Ruttmann's previous work – FEIND IM BLUT emphatically draws our attention to the projection equipment rather than hiding it.[39] This foregrounding of the apparatus should clue us in to the fact that FEIND IM BLUT is less about documenting city life than about advertising – as the film does explicitly in the prologue on the history of syphilis – for the medical establishment and its technologies. But it is also about depicting filmic projection itself as a part of the medical-technological *dispositif*.[40] This was, in fact, the very period in which film was beginning to find widespread usage in the medical establishment as a means of illustrating bodily processes and teaching medical procedures,[41] and Ruttmann's film was clearly also *about* the role that cinema could play in medical education. Within this context, the cinematic dispositif as depicted in FEIND IM BLUT fulfills a very specific function: namely to visualize statistical data. In this case, what that apparatus shows is the "typical" progression of a gonorrhea infection. As the professor's off-screen voice describes the various phases, their normal duration and their treatability, Ruttmann's animation shows us the progression of the pathological fungi as they make their way through the urinary tract to seminal vesicles and the testicles. Thus the cinema not only joins the medical lantern, but also surpasses its "predecessor" with its ability to visualize scientific knowledge – specifically statistical knowledge – in time.[42]

One other type of scientific image frequently thematized in FEIND IM BLUT is the wax "moulage," a cast of body parts for the demonstration of pathologies. Ruttmann repeatedly shows us moulages of faces with various syphilitic symptoms, beginning with the sore on the lip. These illustrations differ from the others in terms of their material presence (the doctor describes them as "sculptural" [plastisch] and we see the students passing around the moulages in their hands), and scholars have drawn attention to the proximity of the wax imprint to the filmic medium understood as an indexical trace of the real.[43] For my purposes here, however, I would emphasize above all the importance of the face for Ruttmann's statistical aesthetics. Nearly all of the moulages we see in FEIND IM BLUT are of faces, and many of them bear an obvious affinity to characters shown elsewhere in the film. Ruttmann himself underscores these relations repeatedly in the film's montage. In the first sequence of this sort, coming toward the beginning of the film, the students pass around a moulage of a woman's face displaying a syphilitic sore. As the professor announces that the symptom was "provoked by a kiss" ("hervorgerufen durch einen Kuss"), Ruttmann inserts a match cut leading from the moulage to the seductive lips of a woman with whom – as we soon learn – the student has just spent the night. As the sequence continues, the woman herself examines several photographic portraits of men's faces on her wall, including one of the student. As she then holds up the portrait of another man, the film cuts back to another medical moulage resembling the man in the photograph but showing more advanced syphilitic symptoms.

On one level, this associative montage of moulages and faces is clearly meant to underscore the dangers of seduction and make us question, as does the student himself, whether his night with the woman might have caused him to become infected. But the match cuts also reproduce and underscore the broader structural tension between the individual and the type informing Ruttmann's dramaturgy through and through. Scientific illustrations of the face were, of

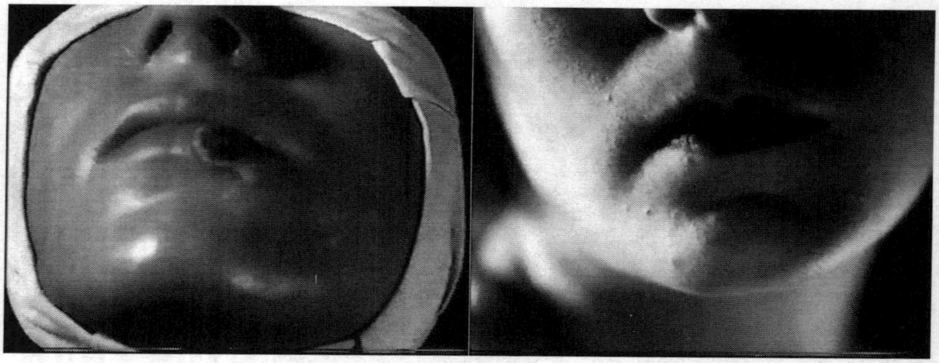

Stills from Ruttmann, FEIND IM BLUT. *Montage of medical moulage and woman's lips*

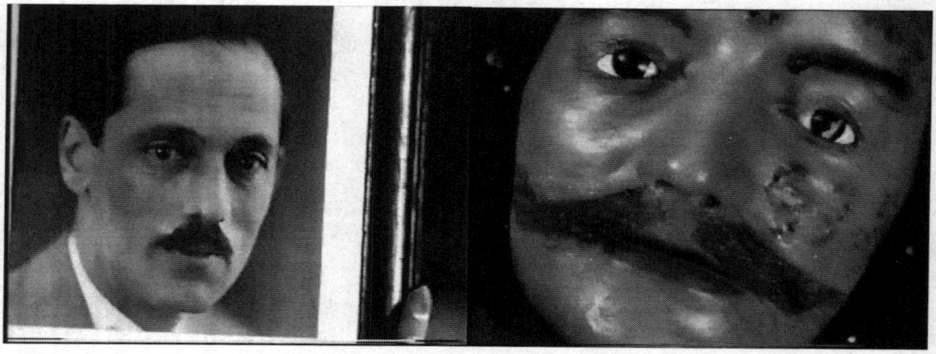

Stills from Ruttmann, FEIND IM BLUT. *Montage of photograph and medical moulage*

course, all about visualizing statistical types; Cesare Lombroso's photographic series of "typical" criminals and Francis Galton's famous composite photographs, which used superimposition to eliminate individual contingencies, both sought to highlight the "typical" features of certain human groups.[44] Medical faces, such as the moulage specimens shown in the film, could – and increasingly did – fulfill a similar function in their demonstration of "typical" pathological symptoms or stages; despite their verisimilitude (moustaches, hair, etc.), these were "specimens," designed to offer a "typical depiction of a common affliction" or (as in Ruttmann) typical stages of pathologies.[45]

By the late 1920s, however, this regime of the face existed alongside another one, particularly in film culture, where the face figured as the object of an emotive communion between spectator and screen.[46] For radical proponents of this latter view such as Jean Epstein and Béla Balázs, the face constituted the locus of

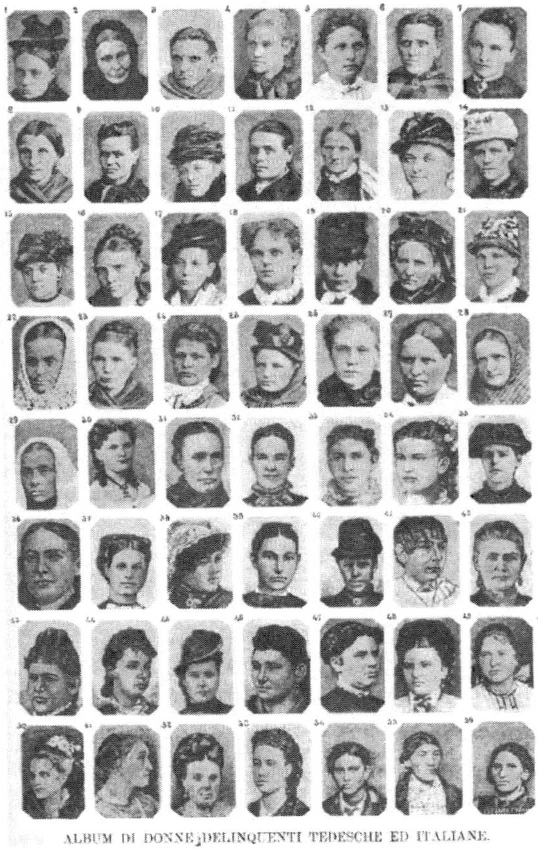

Cesare Lombroso, illustration from L'Uomo Delinquente *(1876).*
German and Italian female criminals

an inexpressible and emphatically non-rationalizable experience, and even directors such as Fritz Lang saw the face as the central means of eliciting emotional involvement from spectators.[47] On the one hand, Feind im Blut sought to solicit such emotional involvement, and to this end, Ruttmann hired several well-known character actors of the day including Gerhard Bienert (known from his roles in the above-mentioned Mutter Krausens fahrt ins Glück, Der blaue Engel [The Blue Angel], Der Hauptmann von Köpenick [The Captain from Köpenick] and Fritz Lang's M) and Ilse Stobrawa (Republik der Backfische [Republic of Girls], Revolte im Erziehungshaus [Revolt in Reform School]). But like other topoi, these faces hover, in the film, between melodramatic involvement and scientific scrutiny, just as they hover between

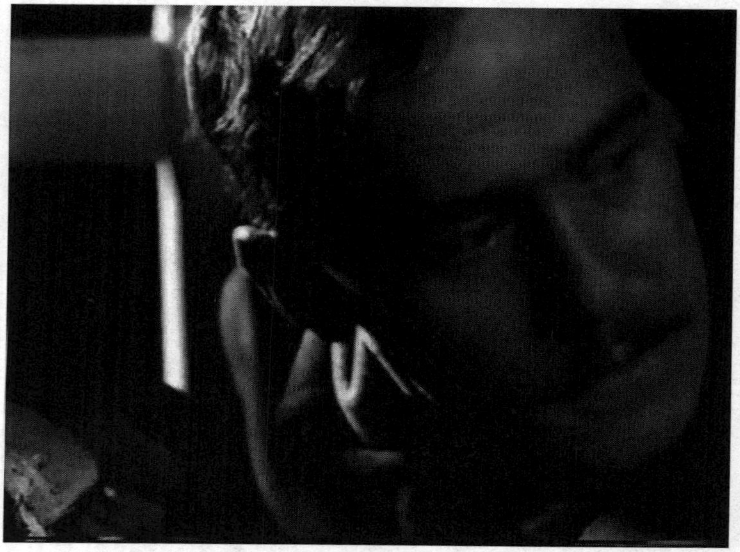

Still from Ruttmann, FEIND IM BLUT. *Gerhard Bienert*

photographic portrait and medical moulage. One could make a similar argument, of course, for a film like MENSCHEN AM SONNTAG, where the characters are represented both as individuals and as types (in the tradition of August Sander's portraits). But in FEIND IM BLUT, this double status of the face overlaps with the broader tension particular to the *Kulturfilm*, which – as we saw above – sought to interweave the dramatic and the scientific; while both films present a tension between the face as an expression of individuality and the face as a field of statistical information, only FEIND IM BLUT employs such statistics as part of a didactic argument about populations, sexual illness and degeneracy. Only the latter film asks us to adopt a scientific gaze that sees the face – every face – as a potential locus of pathology.

It is this scientific-medical paradigm – and the regime of the face that it entails – which ultimately wins out in Ruttmann, teaching spectators to see faces as specimens rather than individuals. Just as the opening montage of FEIND IM BLUT transforms Dovzhenko's poetry of the face into a medical gaze, so the film's entire dramaturgy teaches its audience to pass from affective-dramatic involvement – the kind of codes active, for example, in the melodrama of the suicidal wife – to scientific scrutiny. Where MENSCHEN AM SONNTAG reminds us that the faces we see are part of a mass of 4,000,000 urban inhabitants all following the same cycle of work and leisure, FEIND IM BLUT teaches us to see faces as part of a *population*, a biopolitical collectivity susceptible to the ravages of disease and contagion. Even as we identify with individual aspirations and tragedies, we learn, like the students before the moulages, to adopt a statistical medical gaze, seeing all faces as those of potential patients. This gaze differs, as I have argued, from Ruttmann's earlier statistical gaze in that it is no longer simply a matter of ordering the manifold or suggesting regularities, but rather of prescribing action: a regime of discipline and self-cultivation in a milieu full of sexual and pathological dangers.

At this statistical level – and above all in the film's overwhelming concern for syphilis's effects on reproduction – FEIND IM BLUT is a biopolitical and indeed a "eugenic" film,[48] and many of the arguments in this film would become staples of Ruttmann's eugenic films after 1933. For example, the film's warning about the machinations of charlatans would return centrally in both ABERGLAUBE (1940) and EIN FILM GEGEN DIE VOLKSKRANKHEIT KREBS (1941).[49] At the same time, it would be a mistake to reduce FEIND IM BLUT simply to a form of "proto-fascism" or "fascist" aesthetics – not only on account of the film's dialogue with experimental cinema and social-realist films of the period, but also because of the ways in which it does still acknowledge and even valorize contingency, particularity and difference. Despite the emphasis on medical statistics, the film still represents its population as a population of individuals, with their idiosyncracies, their individual situations and trajectories. While the scenario does homogenize this mass as a group of potential "patients" and suggest ways of reading their symptoms in relation to statistical norms, this is far from the kinds of monolithic (let alone racial) explanations that would come to predominate after 1933. Indeed, despite all of the film's emphasis on scientific statistics and biopolitics, the prevalent theme of contagion underscores the continued relevance of individuality. This was a film aimed at individuals, and the ideological weight of its arguments about the dangers of syphilis still presupposed the goal of individual desires and individual happiness, rather than – as we will see in later Ruttmann films – the need to sacrifice individuality to a *Volkskörper*. If Ruttmann's cross-sectional parade of patients suggests statistical regularities, these are nonetheless – and not unlike the series of portraits in MENSCHEN AM SONNTAG – still represented as a multiplicity of different patients.

The space of this multiplicity in FEIND IM BLUT is that of the city. As mentioned above, the city and its technologies are coded differently in this film than they were in BERLIN, appearing here as a milieu for sickness rather than simply the space of perceptual dislocation and re-ordering. But FEIND IM BLUT can hardly be described as a wholesale condemnation of the city. On the contrary, while the city is the backdrop of tragedy for the mechanic, it is also the backdrop of the happier story of the student and his girlfriend, who will presumably make their home in the city at the end of the film. While the city houses charlatans, prostitutes and other "dangers," it is also, as the home of the university and the polyclinic, a space of "progress." My point here is not to take such codes – backwardness vs. progress, contamination vs. hygiene, darkness vs. light – at face value, but simply to point out that, even within the film's own system of social and moral codes, the city in FEIND IM BLUT is a space of multiplicity: a noisy and messy space (quite literally on the sound track, which constantly emphasizes the noise of the city) characterized by a variety of people and criss-crossing trajectories.

Picturing the *Volkskörper*: BLUT UND BODEN

Things would change two years later with BLUT UND BODEN: GRUNDLAGEN ZUM NEUEN REICH (1933), where the city appears as a catalyst of racial degeneration. The first film Ruttmann worked on under the new regime, BLUT UND BODEN was commissioned – along with Ruttmann's next film ALTGERMANISCHE BAUERNKULTUR (ANCIENT GERMAN AGRARIAN CULTURE, 1934) – by the newly created Stabsamt des Reichsbauernführers (Office of the Reich Peasant Leader) under Walther Darré. Among the films analyzed in this book, BLUT UND BODEN is an exception since Ruttmann co-directed it with Rolf von Sonjevski-Jamrowski and Hans von Passavant – Ruttmann receiving the official credit for "Image and Sound Design" (Bild und Tongestaltung). Of the three figures, Ruttmann was by far the most experienced and best known. He was also the only figure who had not been a Nazi sympathizer (and Ruttmann never joined the Nazi party).[50] Whether or not this was the reason for surrounding Ruttmann with party loyalists is unclear, and it is difficult to determine with precision who was responsible for which aspect of the film. But Ruttmann's public status at the time, his expertise and experience,[51] along with the fact that the film directly recycles footage from his famous BERLIN film – would suggest that Ruttmann played a central role at a minimum in the film's technical production.[52] In fact, the only other prominent film personality involved in the film was the animator Svend Noldan, an important figure in the Ufa Animation Department who had gotten his start in Weimar experimental film (among other things as Hans Richter's assistant on RHYTHMUS 21).

The fact that both Ruttmann and Noldan – both of whom had been associated with left-wing circles – could be recruited by Darré's agency as early as 1933 is itself a testimony to the malleability of the interwar avant-garde.[53] As Hitler's chief advisor in matters of food production and agrarian politics, Darré was, along with Heinrich Himmler and Alfred Rosenberg, one of the chief proponents of "Blut und Boden" ("blood and soil") ideology and – after 1933 – the official responsible for the coordination (*Gleichschaltung*) of all people and associations involved in the production of agrarian goods under the heading of the Reichsnährstand (Reich Authority on Food Production).[54] In many ways, Darré's romanticism of *Boden* ("the land") was hardly unique to Germany; in the wake of the financial crisis, peasant and farming life became the object of an international revalorization with variants in the American farming movement and Soviet collectivization (the backdrop to Dovzhenko's EARTH).[55] But in contrast to these other "land" movements, the doctrine of "Blut und Boden" was – as Darré himself openly stated – based on an explicitly racial worldview, premised on the idea that the hereditary vitality ("blood") of "Nordic" or "Germanic" races was directly linked to the land.[56] In his 1935 treatise BLUT UND BODEN: EIN GRUNDGEDANKE DES NATIONALSOZIALIMUS (BLOOD AND SOIL. A BASIC CONCEPT OF NATIONAL SOCIALISM), for example, Darré maintained that, unlike "nomadic" races, paradigmatically represented by the "Jewish people," the "Germanic race" was sedentary and could only continue to produce healthy progeny if it maintained the continuity of its ties to the land.[57] The peasantry, he asserted repeatedly, formed the "Blood Source of the People" ("Blutsquelle des Volkes"). All of Darré's policies as Reichsbauernführer were meant to protect this "source" or racial vitality from the vicissitudes he associated with liberal economics.[58] Most central in this respect was the so-called "Hereditary Farm Law" ("Reichserbhofgesetz"), a protectionist law implemented in 1933, which sought to change the system of land rights and protect farms from foreclosure due to debts.

It was within the context of these agrarian reforms that Darré's office commissioned the film BLUT UND BODEN in 1933.[59] Premiering just two months after the passage of the Hereditary Farm Law on 23 November 1933 at Berlin's Marmorhaus to a crowd of invited guests (including Darré), and accompanied by a lecture by Karl Motz from the Stabsamt des Reichsbauernführers, BLUT UND BODEN was clearly commissioned to "sell" the new law to the populace.[60] By all appearances, the 30-minute film – which was released both in 35mm and 16mm formats and approved as a "Lehrfilm" (educational film) by the censors – was originally intended both for cinema screenings (in the preliminary program) and for nontheatrical screenings in clubs, associations and classrooms, particularly in rural settings.[61] The link between the film and the new law is also suggested by reports in the trade literature, which – in accordance with the new demands that film criticism conform to party doctrine – praised the film as "proof" (*Beweis*) of the law's necessity. Thus a reviewer for *Lichtbild-Bühne,* in an article appearing several weeks before the premiere of BLUT UND BODEN, explained:

> In a few weeks, the Office of the Reich Peasant Leader will premiere a thirty-minute film under the title BLUT UND BODEN, which can be described as the most timely political film ever made. At a time when the new laws of the Reich Authority on Food

> production are reinforcing Germany's rootedness in the soil [Bodenständigkeit], eliminating speculation and thus directing the attention of the entire world to Germany, this film, summarizing recent history through the example of one family, brings before our eyes the clear and unambiguous proof for the necessity of such a government policy.[62]

If the filmmakers and their allies in the press were so intent on underscoring the urgency of the new law, this is no doubt because that necessity did not go without question. While the law claimed to protect the nation's "blood source" by making German farms indivisible and inalienable hereditary properties (albeit excluding women from the hereditary chain and excluding families deemed to have "Jewish" or "colored" blood from the law altogether),[63] the conversion of farms to hereditary status was not mandatory and not necessarily desirable, since heredity was limited to the eldest son and the inheritor was now a "custodian" rather than a proprietor of the land (and was unable for this reason to gain access to loans).[64]

Despite this close link to the passage of the Hereditary Farm Law, however, BLUT UND BODEN was not exhausted by the immediate occasion of its commission. The film was also re-released in 16mm format in 1936, suggesting that it continued to find relevance as a cultural and educational film long after the passage of the law.[65] Like FEIND IM BLUT, moreover, the film itself follows the dual track typical of the German *Kulturfilm*. On the one hand, it recounts the melodramatic story of an uprooted family from the Eastern farmlands, forced to auction off its farm and move to an urban slum when it can no longer pay its creditors due to price reductions in German crops. On the other, this narrative line is constantly inserted into a broader argument about the plight of the German *Volk* (particularly the German farmer) under the Weimar government. Once again using evidentiary editing and direct voice-over commentary – this time with no pretention of the voice belonging to a character in the film – BLUT UND BODEN explicitly attributes the demise of German farming to the "liberalist" and "speculative" economic policies of Weimar, which opened up Germany's borders to a flood of cheaper "foreign goods" and forced German farmers to compete in a fierce capitalist marketplace.[66] Juxtaposing the volatile space of the market – paradigmatically represented in scenes of stock market and the auctioning block – with the stability and rootedness of the land, the film works with the same opposition that informed Darré's BLUT UND BODEN ideology generally and the hereditary farm law specifically: the opposition between the "continuity" ("Stetigkeit") of the race and the volatility of modern economic life represented by "mobile capital" ("bewegliches Kapital") or an unruly marketplace (regelloser Markt).[67] The very word "Bauer," Darré insisted, was the "the archetypal concept of all continuity" ("Urbegriff aller Stetigkeit").[68] This is

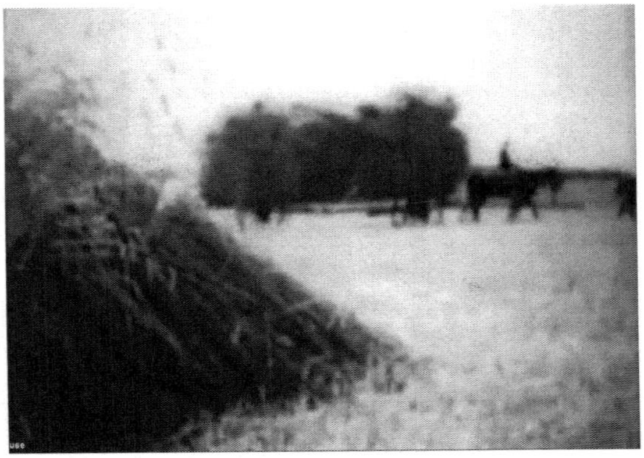

Still from Ruttmann, BLUT UND BODEN *(1933). Harvesting sequence*

precisely the image conveyed by BLUT UND BODEN, whose opening montage shows images of the farming community engaged in the age-old activities of harvesting and breadmaking. As the grandfather of the central family states when his grandson marvels at the family's 300-year history on the farm: "It should be five hundred years, indeed a thousand!"[69]

Like FEIND IM BLUT, BLUT UND BODEN relies heavily on cross-sectional montage – particularly in the sequences detailing the peasant family's uprooting to the city – to depict the family's plight as part of a national and collective tragedy. One of those cross-sectional sequences, coming just when the family arrives in the city, consists of footage lifted directly from Ruttmann's BERLIN film. Beginning with a truncated version of the famous train montage, the sequence quickly passes to the montage of newspapers with their sensational headlines of "Mord" ("Murder") and "Geld" ("Money"), followed by chaotic images of newsprint, traffic and bodies all moving in different directions in rapid montage and superimposition. The sequence is thus dominated by the same motifs of high-speed transportation and informational technologies that undergirded Ruttmann's earlier arguments about modernity and the acceleration of information flows. But rather than searching for a means of coming to terms with the multiplicity of city life, BLUT UND BODEN hammers home its detrimental character; in his remontage, Ruttmann sets the entire sequence to the kind of tempo and jarring juxtapositions that had characterized the train montage in BERLIN, and he even adds to the unruly quality of the impressions via the addition of superimpositions and canted angles. The sequence now presents the city simply as a cacophony of visual fragmentation and dissolution, a realm of uprooting – as we learn in a later sequence when the family's son tries to save a sun flower

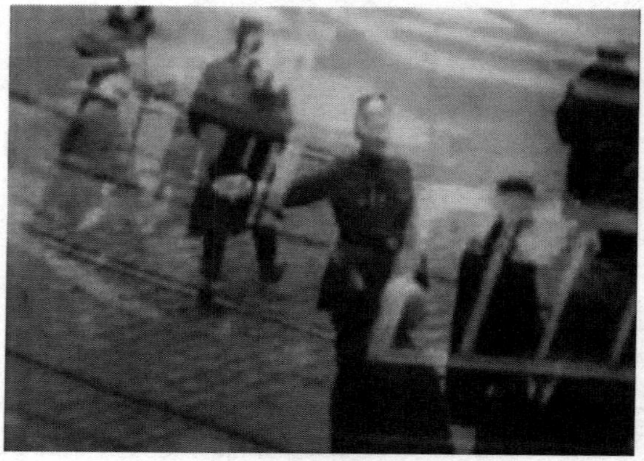

Still from Ruttmann, BLUT UND BODEN. *Recycled footage from* BERLIN. DIE SINFONIE DER GROSSSTADT

that couldn't take root in the concrete ground of the family's sunless *Hinterhof* (inner courtyard).

As in FEIND IM BLUT, this cross-sectional montage in BLUT UND BODEN also interacts with the visualization of collective trends via animated statistics. Now, however, the paradigmatic statistical image is no longer the graph, but rather an image more akin to the contemporary practice of visual statistics (*Bildstatistik*) or Isotype. Originally devised by Otto Neurath and Gerd Arntz as part of a socialist program of popular education in economic matters, such visual statistics were part and parcel of the search for a "universal" visual language in the 1920s. More specifically, however, they promised to make mass society legible and aid social planning by visualizing statistical phenomena via pictograms.[70] Not surprisingly, this pictorial statistics was quite often used to visualize biopolitical arguments. Thus in the Viennese pavilion of the Gesolei exhibition – the same exhibition for which Ruttmann had created his film advertisement DER AUFSTIEG (THE ASCENT) in 1926 – visitors could see pictograms illustrating the gradual improvement of birth and death rates in Vienna since the end of the war, the increase in the number of workers with accident insurance, or the number of individuals collecting a pension from the state.

In their combination of iconic figuration and abstract thought, Isotype pictograms recall, once again, various film experiments such as Ruttmann's analogies or Eisenstein's intellectual editing, and it is thus perhaps not surprising that they would interest experimental filmmakers such as Ruttmann and Noldan, just as they had long interested other members of the international avant-garde.[71] But in the place of Neurath's international scope – the term "Isotype" stood for "International System of Typographic Picture Education" – the pictograms in

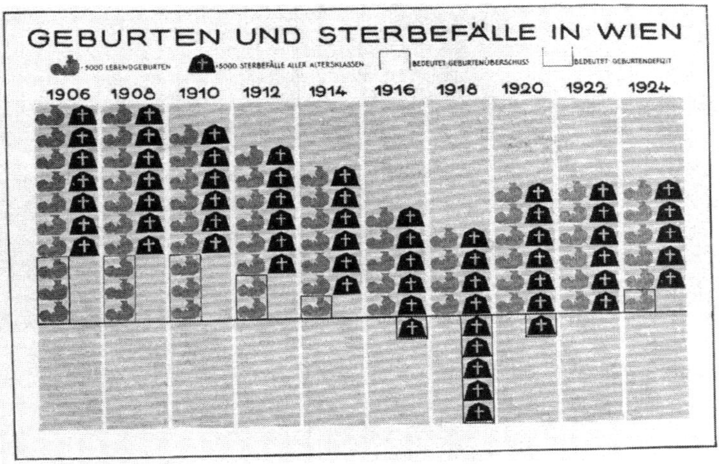

Isotype demonstration from Gesolei exhibition, from Gesolei. Amtlicher Katalog *(Düsseldorf 1926)*

Blut und Boden are placed in the service of a decidedly nationalist educational project. Thus an image of a family hesitating between two waiters illustrates the Weimar bourgeoisie choosing cheap foreign goods over homegrown products; farms being inundated by water or smashed by hammers illustrate the mounting debts and foreclosures; and animated caravans moving on the horizon illustrate the thousands of uprooted German farming families forced into a nomadic existence by the economic policies of Weimar.

Like the statistical charts in Feind im Blut, these statistical images in Blut und Boden show up precisely in the film's most didactic moments as "evidence" supporting the off-screen narrator's arguments. This function was hardly lost on the film's reviewers who unanimously praised the film's use of visual statistics. A writer for the *Süddeutsche Filmzeitung* described the film's "statistical data" ("statistische Angaben") as providing "proof" ("Beweismittel") of the detrimental effects of liberalist economics on the German *Volk*.[72] Or as another reviewer put it: "A simple plot […] provides the opportunity to introduce numbers that speak for themselves."[73]

Like the charts in Feind im Blut, moreover, the pictograms in Blut und Boden can be understood as corollaries to Ruttmann's cross-sectional montage, since both function to insert the family's tragic story within a larger collective development. In contrast to Feind im Blut, however, the pictograms in Blut und Boden underlie a racialized conception of the German populace as *Volkskörper* (people's body). This aspect comes to the fore in one the film's climactic sequences when the filmmakers introduce their main argument that migration

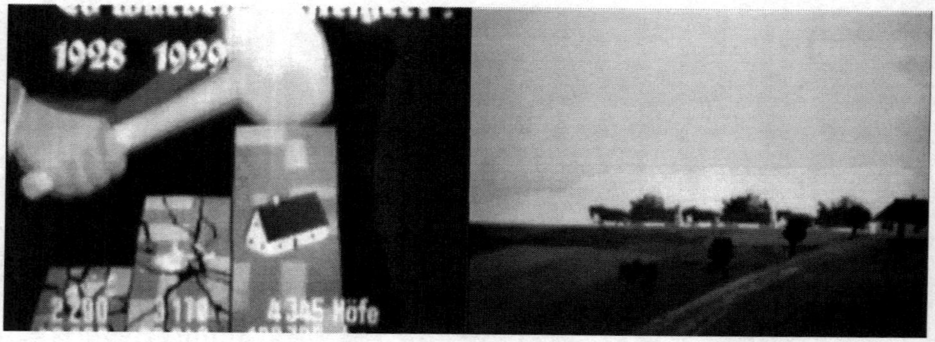

Stills from Ruttmann, BLUT UND BODEN. *Animated pictograms representing farms lost to debt and peasants moving into the city*

from farms into cities will lead to the demise of the race. In the first shot of the sequence, the bars on the windows of the dark *Hinterhof* morph into a series of crosses in superimposition, which then gives way to a full-screen title reading "Urbanization leads to the death of the people!" ("Verstädterung führt zum Volkstod!"). There follows an animated Isotype sequence showing cribs and infants over drawings of the "country" and the "city" filling the two halves of the screen. As the narrator outlines the decrease in birth rates among city-dwellers and the increase among the peasantry (which he calls the "life source of the German people" ["die Lebensquelle des deutschen Volkes"]), the cribs on the "city" side of the screen remain mostly empty, while the cribs in the "country" fill up beyond capacity. The animation then transitions into a schematic image of Berlin over which the off-screen voice projects a terrifying scenario of population decline; were the city shut off from "foreign immigration" ("Zuwandering"), we learn, the current population of 4 million would shrink to 3 million by 1960, 1.5 million by 1990, 500,000 by 2020 and only 90,000 by 2050 after four generations.

Such a use of visual statistics to visualize the health and degeneration of the "German people" is in keeping with the use of statistics by Darré and his associates. For just as Darré sought to distinguish the racialized notion of the German *Bauer* (farmer, peasant) in the Reichsnährstand from other merely nationalist images of the farmer or the peasant, so he explicitly distinguished his use of statistics from most applications of statistics on account of its specifically racial character. As he explained in his 1935 treatise:

> Today we produce statistics and balance sheets for every domain of our being as a people [unseres völkischen Daseins]. But we still have no statistics regarding the biological foundation of our people's life [unseres völkischen Lebens]. And we are even further from someday creating a biological budget for our people's body [Volkskörper] based on an accurate biological balance sheet.[74]

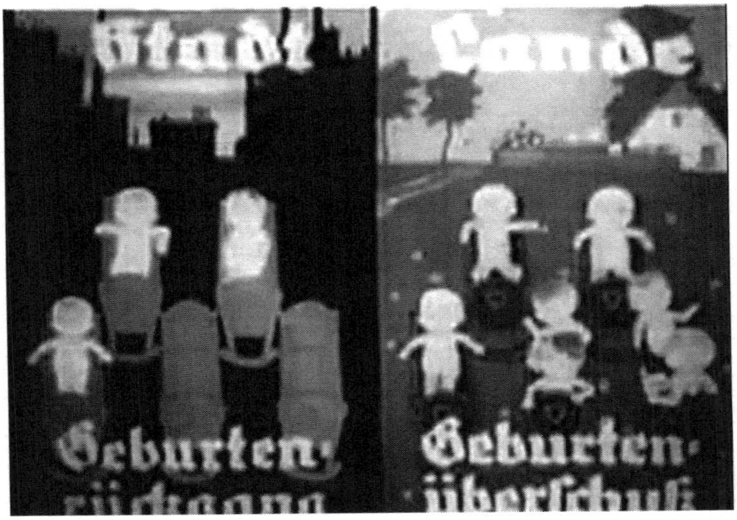

Still from Ruttmann, BLUT UND BODEN. *Pictograms representing birthrates in the city and the country*

Rather than measuring particular illnesses, Darré's racialized biopolitics sought to assess the vitality or "biological balance" ("biologische Bilanz") of the race itself, of the *Volkskörper* whose "blood" was directly dependent upon its rootedness in German "soil." He proposed to do this, above all, by measuring birth rates among different populations in urban and rural settings in order to show that a people's "level of hereditary force" ("Erbmasse") declined as families moved away from the land and into cities.[75] This is, of course, exactly what the animated pictograms of BLUT UND BODEN also set out to do, a message hardly lost on the film's reviewers. As one writer for the *Lichtbild-Bühne* dutifuly reported: "Seen in terms of populational politics [in der bevölkerungspolitischen Bilanz], this phenomena of inner-German migration from the country to the city exposes our entire *Volk* to mortal danger."[76] It is also what differentiates those pictograms from the graphs of syphilis rates a film like FEIND IM BLUT. Where the earlier film used statistics to persuade individuals and families to make certain choices (based on probabilities) in order to further their own happiness, the statistical images in BLUT UND BODEN interpellate viewers as members of a "Volkskörper," whose survival becomes their responsibility. That survival, the film argues as the above sequence continues, depends directly on a repopulation of the Eastern farmlands, "the territories that nature has given to us to settle" (unser naturgegebener Siedlungsraum). Just in case the link between population decline, racial purity and Eastern immigration was unclear, a title then closes the sequence with the words: "Only a bulwark of farms in the East can

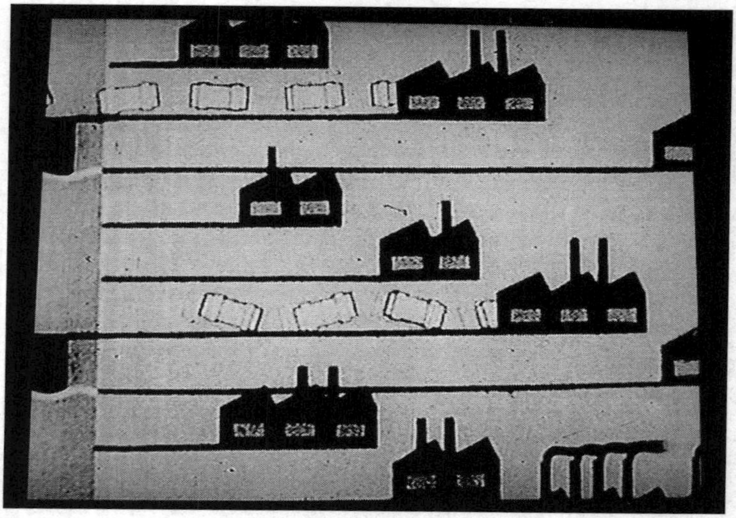

Still from Paul Rotha, A Few Ounces a Day *(1941)*

save and guarantee Germany's future against foreign infiltration into the *Volk* [völkische Überfremdung]."[77]

It is important to point out here that the use of animated Isotype images was not unique to Germany. Neurath had himself already experimented with filmic versions of Isotype in the 1920s and would go on to create several Isotype sequences for the wartime films of British documentarian Paul Rotha. In many ways, these films offer useful comparisons to Blut und Boden. In films such as A Few Ounces a Day (1941) and Blood Transfusion (1942), animated pictograms are used to emphasize the collective – indeed national – nature of the projects these films attempt to support (giving blood or saving materials to support the war effort). Like Blut und Boden, these films attempt to make viewers aware of their responsibility for a nation "under siege." But Ruttmann's film differs from its British counterparts – here again – for precisely the reasons laid out by Darré concerning agrarian policies. While both films use Isotype-style images to underscore nationalist projects, only Blut und Boden presupposes and promotes a racialized understanding of the nation as *Volkskörper*. The statistical images in Blut und Boden, in their projection of the slow death of the *Volkskörper*, are not simply nationalist. They function as evidence within an argument for racial survival.

In Darré's "blood and soil" ideology, that survival depended upon a belief in absolute "rootedness," the fixing of race and land and its protection from the vicissitudes of the capitalist marketplace. Such a conception leaves little room for models of governance based on the regulation or balancing of difference

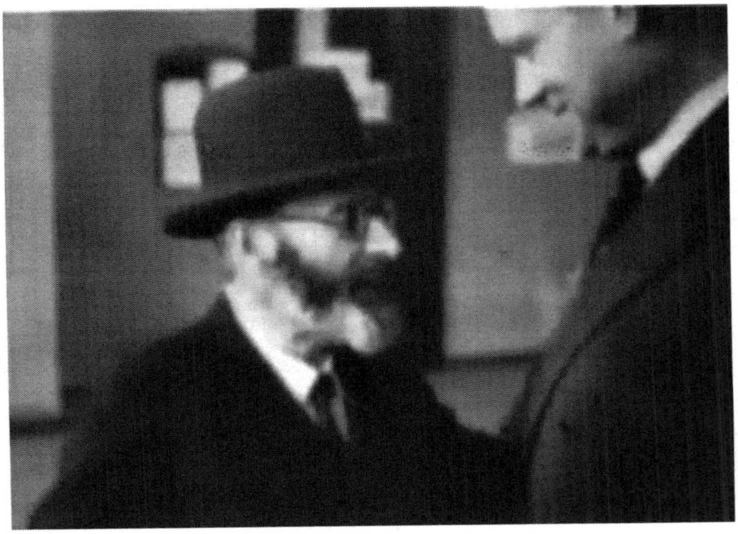

Still from Ruttmann, BLUT UND BODEN. *Jewish merchant*

and contingency, and for this reason, the city and the stock market can only be represented as spaces of instability, rootlessness and dissolution. In one of the first sequences of the stock market in BLUT UND BODEN, in which we see domestic products losing value while "foreign products" rise, we also see at least one face clearly coded as Jewish by the presence of a dense beard and round eyeglasses.[78] The paradigmatic representation of "difference" in BLUT UND BODEN, the "Jewish" face is also associated with the paradigmatic spaces of contingency (the city and the marketplace) and the paradigmatic form of economic and racial decline ("speculative" liberalism). Under the new regime, difference and contingency are no longer forces to be "managed," but to be eliminated through an authoritative cultivation of a healthy *Volkskörper* free of "foreign infiltration." This new strategy informs the use of statistics in BLUT UND BODEN through and through: far from functioning to balance order and contingency, and in contrast to the logic of "averages" still present in FEIND IM BLUT, the Isotype images of BLUT UND BODEN serve to demonstrate the existence of a German *Volkskörper* under assault. Indeed, this might explain the very appeal of the "Isotype" as visual form: with its identical, serialized bodies, the Isotype lent itself well to a representation of collectivity conceived of as identical and devoid of difference, one in which individuality and contingency are entirely absent from the field of vision. Both BLUT UND BODEN and Ruttmann's later film EIN FILM GEGEN DIE VOLKSKRANKHEIT KREBS – where an opening image of identical Isotype figures offers an image of the German populace in which every eighth person dies of cancer – employed such identical figures. No longer do such figures function to render "averages" legible; rather, their purpose lies elsewhere: in the visualization of a "people's body" under assault.

According to the historian Boaz Neumann, the *Volkskörper* under Nazism was not simply a "metaphor" or a figure for the state or the populace understood as an aggregate of bodies, but rather a lived reality, and one precisely meant to overcome the contingencies and entropic force experienced in the individual body:

> The Nazi corporeal ontology did not rest on the individual's body, since such a body was vulnerable to biological "whim." The individual body was one that invariably decayed. The Nazi corporeal ontology was based, instead, on a body that did not degenerate. This was the *Volkskörper*, whose existence was autonomous of this or that specific body.[79]

Whether or not Neumann's phenomenology corresponds to the actual historical experience of Nazism, his insistence on the "reality" of the *Volkskörper* does point toward a difference between the biopolitical paradigm of Nazism and the biopolitics of the Welfare state that preceded it; for National Socialist biopolitics *did* posit the existence of a racial *Volkskörper* transcending the individual body. Within this context, as Young-Sun Hong has shown, the very paradigm of "welfare" was also transformed from a model of welfare for individuals to a model that sacrificed individual well-being to the welfare of the *Volk*: one in which concepts of individual rights gave way to a political imaginary based on individual duty toward a racial community.[80] Within this biopolitical paradigm, groups such as Darré's understood themselves and their policies as so many efforts to "heal" the *Volkskörper* that had been weakened and debilitated by Weimar democracy with its individualism and tolerance for "foreign infiltration."[81] It is precisely this *Volkskörper* that the animated pictograms of Blut und Boden attempted to convey in its near destruction by Weimar economics and its regeneration in the countryside. Whereas 19th-century statistics might debate the existence of autonomous "social facts," regularities governing the behavior of individuals from a place beyond their control, the statistics in Blut und Boden – like the "biological balance sheet" called for by Darré – provided evidence for an autonomous "racial fact": a people's body whose life force had been sapped by Weimar economic policies, but which Nazism now promised to reconnect to its vital sources. Although Blut und Boden is ostensibly about economics and urbanization, it is, at bottom, about the hygienic life of this *Volkskörper*.

That body is on full display at the end of the film when the argument for the repopulation of the Eastern farmlands is followed by a montage of children's faces and marching youth. The sequence echoes the closing shots of Feind im Blut, which also ended with a parade of children's faces (there echoing the

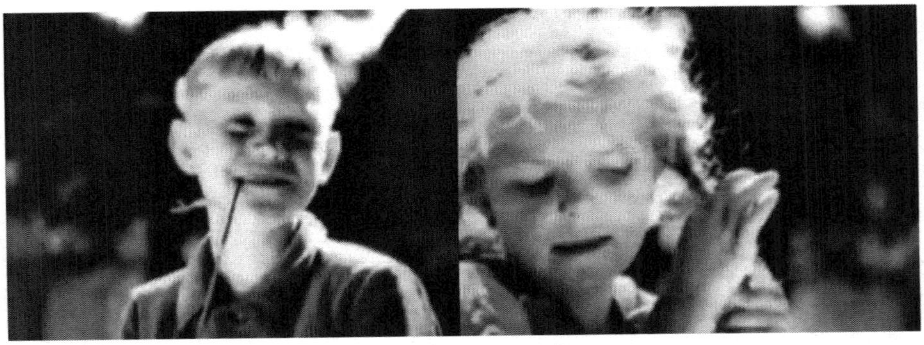

Still from Ruttmann, BLUT UND BODEN. *Children's faces in final sequence*

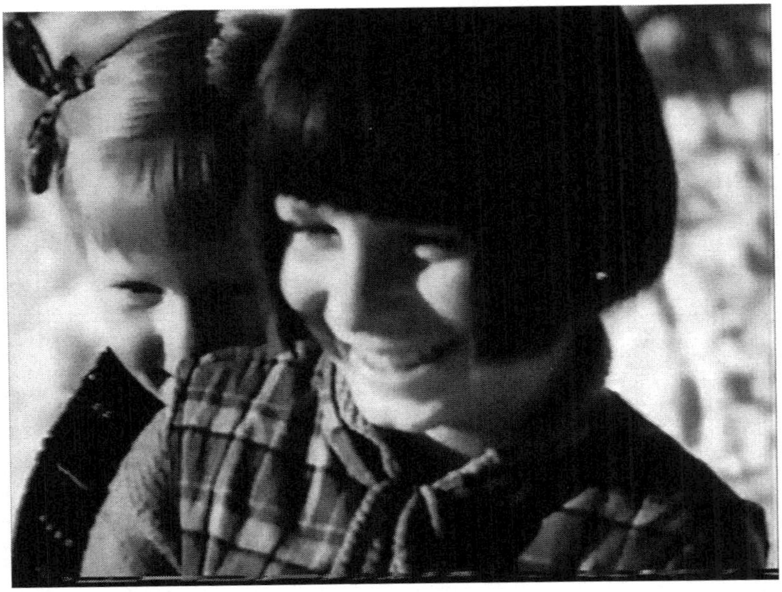

Still from Ruttmann, FEIND IM BLUT. *Children's faces in final sequence*

children's faces at the beginning of the film), and this parallel is hardly by chance. For both films sought to reinforce their respective biopolitical messages through images of a healthy future population. However, in contrast to FEIND IM BLUT, where we see various types of faces (including girls with Louise Brooks-style "bob" hairstyle [*Bubikopf*]), the faces in BLUT UND BODEN are clearly marked as "Germanic" with their uniformly blond hair. As the sequence continues, moreover, these faces will morph into marching columns of Nazi youth to the sound of Heinz Bolten-Becker's "Die Jugend marschiert" ("Youth on the March") with its couplet:

Always take note of this.
This is your homeland – keep it pure.
German soil, German blood
Should always be sacred.

[Merke Dir das eine immer gut.
Die Heimat ist Dein – erhalte sie rein.
Deutscher Boden, deutsches Blut
Soll stets dir heilig sein.]

It is precisely such "purification" of German blood that stood at the center of "Blut und Boden" ideology, and this notion of purity also informed the film BLUT UND BODEN with its visual statistics of the *Volkskörper*.

Conclusion: Experimental Film under Nazism – Continuities and Ruptures

As the first of Ruttmann's NS films, BLUT UND BODEN was also the most explicitly racial in its calls to protect the "Volkskörper" from "foreign infiltration." My point in this chapter, however, is not to argue that Ruttmann (who did not write the script and likely had little role in the film's ideological content) harbored any deep-seated racial beliefs, but rather to examine how he conceived of film – in analogy to the forms of expertise on which he drew – as an inherently "applicable" medium: one that he did apply no less to efforts to control the spread of sexual disease than to the advertisement of Nazism's agrarian policies. The fact that so many experimental filmmakers (from Richter to Reiniger to Noldan and beyond) were involved in sponsored film production suggests that this notion of "applicability" was compatible with a certain self-understanding of the avant-garde. Indeed, one could point to many other experimental filmmakers who remained in Germany after 1933 to place their expertise in the service of propaganda. These include not only Noldan, but also figures such as Guido Seeber, whose playful KIPHO film (1925) had been one of the sensations in both avant-garde and advertising circles in the 1920s.[82] Seeber's EWIGER WALD (ETERNAL FOREST, 1936) – an experimental *Kulturfilm* commissioned by the NS Kulturgemeinde under Alfred Rosenberg and which Seeber made together with the same Sonjevski-Jamrowski who co-directed BLUT UND BODEN – offers a lesson in applied experimental aesthetics; using dissolves and associative montage, the film represents the German forest as the metaphor for a national *Volkskörper* rooted in the German landscape, whose eternal life requires the sacrifice of the individual in a struggle against "foreign invasion."[83]

In claiming that a certain notion of "applicability" was part and parcel of experimental aesthetics, however, I am in no way suggesting that we cannot and should not judge the applications to which those aesthetics were placed. As we saw in the introduction, Ruttmann openly espoused a notion of "applied" aesthetics that was – like the forms of expertise on which he drew – "indifferent" to the object of those applications.[84] No doubt, it was this ethos of indifference that Kracauer picked up on when he faulted Ruttmann, and the vogue of "cross-section" montage films Ruttmann helped to spawn, for what he saw as the genre's "inherent neutrality."[85] Although Kracauer's critique should be situated in the post-WWII context in which it was formulated,[86] that critique undoubtedly still resonates today – all the more so when one examines closely the politics of films such as BLUT UND BODEN (or the wartime films I examine in chapter 4).

But even as we recognize Ruttmann's problematic "indifference," we would do well to avoid writing off his experimental montage as a mere aesthetic "formalism" that allowed itself to be co-opted by advertising and propaganda. As I have argued, Ruttmann's aesthetics were bound up with forms of knowledge and power from the beginning, and only by examining these imbrications can we gain a better understanding of where the continuities and ruptures lie. This chapter has attempted to do just that through an examination of two of Ruttmann's hygiene films made just before and just after the regime change, focusing in particular on these films' adaptations of visual statistics.

To be sure, both FEIND IM BLUT and BLUT UND BODEN have a different feel than Ruttmann's earlier Weimar montage films on account of their closer imbrications with biopolitics. Whereas BERLIN and MELODIE DER WELT used "statistical montage" to manage the multiplicity of photographic images, Ruttmann's hygiene films applied statistics to the management of populations. Introducing a level of didacticism through the format of the *Kulturfilm*, these films transform statistics from a descriptive to a prescriptive undertaking, in which spectators are asked to see their own bodies and their own lives within national trends and act accordingly to avoid certain results and bring about others.[87] This may explain why the principal intermedial corollary for the latter films is no longer photography with its valorization of contingency, but rather the graph and the Isotype. More than simply suggesting an underlying order, such visual forms generate knowledge about the population in view of regulating actions.

But even within this common biopolitical framework, there is a gulf separating the ends to which such biopolitical "management images" are put before and after 1933. Whereas a film like FEIND IM BLUT purports to provide information about populational tendencies in order to persuade audience members to act in their own interest, BLUT UND BODEN interpellates viewers as part of a racialized *Volkskörper.* In describing the modalities of power enacted in these films, one might say that FEIND IM BLUT, even in its most prescriptive moments, corresponds more closely to what Foucault dubbed the "care of the self"; in providing statistics about syphilis – its causes, frequency and cures – the film prescribes certain forms of self-regulation such as avoiding sexual temptation or excessive drinking, visiting medical "experts," and rejecting the advice of charlatans.[88] By contrast, the statistical images in BLUT UND BODEN, in their status as "evidence" for the existence of the *Volkskörper*, subordinate spectators' interests to that of a national body, making them responsible for its survival and its "purity." Both in Darré's ideology and in the film, the peasant-farmer (*Bauer*) is the model of this racial responsibility; as the narrator puts it at the beginning of the film, repeating a frequent definition of Darré: "The farmer is he who, aware of the hereditary rootedness of his race [Geschlecht] in the earth and the soil, tends to his land and considers this task as his duty to his race and his people."[89] Where FEIND IM BLUT seeks to "manage" differences, BLUT UND BODEN – in accordance with National Socialist biopolitics – can only represent difference as a threat to the race.[90] In the latter film, difference and contingency is identified with the city, the marketplace, "foreign" goods and "foreign" peoples (paradigmatically Eastern immigration) in distinction to the rootedness of the land seen as the milieu of a purified *Volkskörper.*

But despite the romanticization of the land within Darré's "Blut und Boden" ideology, there was nothing inherently anti-industrial about the notion of a *Volkskörper.* As we will see in the next chapter, Ruttmann's industrial films after 1933 could make a similar appeal to the people's body while championing industrial technology. In Ruttmann's many films on steel and weapons production, the medium of film is no longer represented simply as a means of verifying the existence of the *Volkskörper*, but rather appears as a tool for giving form to the *Volk*.

4. "Überall Stahl": Forming the New Nation in Ruttmann's Steel and Armament Films (1934-1940)

Introduction

If the decision to surround Ruttmann with party loyalists for the making of BLUT UND BODEN did stem from any suspicion of an eminent Weimar modernist, that suspicion was short-lived. Almost immediately after the completion of BLUT UND BODEN, Darré's Stabsamt des Reichsbauernführers rehired Ruttmann, this time as principal director, for a short cultural film entitled ALTGERMANISCHE BAUERNKULTUR (ANCIENT GERMANIC AGRARIAN CULTURE). Premiering on 14 April 1934 in a closed screening attended by Darré, Himmler and several other prominent figures from the Stabsamt des Reichsbauernführers and the Reichsnährstand,[1] the film went on to play in the preliminary program (*Vorprogramm*) at the Ufa-Palast am Zoo before touring German theaters the same year.[2] Employing several Weimar actors – most notably Fritz Rasp who had played in dozens of big-budget films, including a stint in Fritz Lang's METROPOLIS as the "Thin Man" – it told the story of a devoted member of the Hitler Youth (Claus) who defends the honor of the ancient Germanic people when a liberal professor ("Dr. Sandmann") depicts them as savages and nomadic peoples without a sedentary culture. Among other things, the film was notable for its interactive format. In a variation on the "prize contest" format often used in advertising films, in which audiences were prompted to solve a riddle or engage in some other similar activity, Ruttmann had the student address the spectators directly at the end of the film, calling on them to contribute to the propaganda campaign by sending in letters to the Reichsbauernführer:

> Tell us briefly how you would respond to Dr. Sandmann. Write out your answer and send it to the advertising department in the Central Office of the Reich Peasant Leader in Berlin. Your participation in this contest will help us to eliminate once and for all the historical lie that our Germanic ancestors were barbarians and nomads! Help us to reawaken the pride of the German *Volk* in its millennia-old culture of farming.[3]

In contrast to traditional prize films – for example the Viennese film WO SIND DIE MILLIONEN? (WHERE ARE THE MILLIONS?, 1925), which was combined with a contest to win a bicycle – ALTGERMANISCHE BAUERNKULTUR did not invite its audience to win anything.[4] Rather, like its predecessor BLUT UND BODEN, the film imposes a duty to the nation: a contribution to the collective defense of national heritage.

The National Socialists had little problem employing an experimental filmmaker like Ruttmann for such endeavors; as one of the foremost experts on advertising and the *Kulturfilm,* someone who could bridge the worlds of narrative film, experimental montage and animation, he was especially well qualified for such commissions. Accordingly, the same year he made ALTGERMANISCHE BAUERNKULTUR, Ruttmann was also tapped to provide a montage prologue to Leni Riefenstahl's TRIUMPH DES WILLENS (TRIUMPH OF THE WILL), glorifying the rise of the Nazi party. Although the prologue was ultimately discarded, Ruttmann's role was celebrated in the press at the time.[5] The following year, Ruttmann was then hired by Germany's leading film company Ufa – which had come increasingly under state control – to work as a filmmaker in its advertising section (*Werbeabteilung*).[6] Ruttmann would retain this professional identity until his death in 1941, making some 16 films at Ufa commissioned by private and state agencies, all of them short works (between 10 and 30 minutes) that would generally have had their first run in theaters in the preliminary program before going on to screenings in various non-theatrical settings.

Not one of Ruttmann's Ufa films promoted the kind of anti-urban ideology of BLUT UND BODEN. Rather, nearly all of them touted the triumphs of modern technology, medicine, hygiene and industrial production under Nazism. Indeed, many of Ruttmann's films from the mid-1930s were promotional films for cities such as Düsseldorf, Stuttgart and Hamburg.[7] In contrast to a film like BERLIN, however, these city films display a didactic and overtly nationalist quality. For example, the 1935 film STUTTGART. DIE GROSSSTADT ZWISCHEN WALD UND REBEN – DIE STADT DES AUSLANDDEUTSCHTUMS (STUTTGART. THE CITY BETWEEN FOREST AND VINES – THE CITY OF GERMANY ABROAD) presents the metropolis Stuttgart not as an arena of differences to be managed, but rather as the center of a unified Germanic identity. Commissioned by the city of Stuttgart, the film was clearly intended, as its title indicates, to celebrate Stuttgart as the "Stadt des Auslanddeutschtums" ("The City of Germans Abroad"),[8] an honorary name that the Nazis had recently bestowed upon Stuttgart as the home of the Deutsches Ausland-Institut (The German Foreign Institute, DAI). Founded in 1917, the DAI had been transformed after 1933, under the name "Deutsches Ausland-Institut der Heimat," into an organ for the propagation of National Socialism among Germans abroad, who were now encouraged to see themselves as part of a racial community.[9] Accordingly, the vision of the world presented in STUTTGART is – in contrast to that of the vast and decentered "database" constructed by MÉLODIE DER WELT – decidedly centralized, hierarchical and even racial: a vision of Stuttgart as the center of a worldwide German ethnic community (*Volksgemeinschaft*) held together by blood. Thus in the opening sequence, a school teacher touts the work of the Auslands-Institut der Heimat as follows:

> All the achievements of our brothers abroad – intellectual, organizational, economical – are collected here, where they are catalogued and made useful for the entire German people. We cultivate an endless number of relations in order to bind people of the same blood [Menschen gleichen Blutes] together across mountains, steps, rivers and oceans.[10]

Like a magnet, Stuttgart thus holds German identity together, extending the German nation out into the world and retaining Germans abroad within a community of "shared blood." Not surprisingly, the film ends with an image of the medium best suited to this end: radio. More precisely, Ruttmann shows us a series of maps over which animated radio waves appear to transport the voice of Stuttgart – audible in different languages on the soundtrack – from Germany out into Asia, Australia, Africa and South America.

It is precisely the idea of a national "Volksgemeinschaft" that underlies the film's subsequent presentation of the city. As the German-born character Hans returns after twenty-two years in America, his brother shows him the revitalized Stuttgart that unites tradition and modernity: traditional churches and marketplaces alongside modern mass architecture, traditional parades and modern athletics, traditional fountains and modern hygiene, traditional handwork and industrial factories. Such juxtapositions, reminiscent of Riefenstahl's presentation of Nuremberg in TRIUMPH DES WILLENS, also fulfill a similar function of grounding modernity in tradition and insisting on a continuity of "Germanness" in the face of recent crises. When Hans asks his brother how they achieved so much in the twenty-two years since his departure, the brother answers: "With motivation, proficiency and a sense for quality work. This has been our way down to the present day in manual labor as in industry, and this is why we have continued to improve steadily despite all the crises."[11] Stuttgart thus appears not as a space of manageable contingency, but rather – in the quintessential form of the Ausland-Institut der Heimat – as a bulwark against contingency and dissipation: the glue holding Germanness together against the twin threats of geographical dispersion and temporal dissolution. It was precisely within this framework of continuity that a film like STUTTGART could celebrate modern technology and modern architecture.

In addition to "city" films, Ruttmann's work for the Nazis ran the gamut of non-narrative forms from cultural, industrial and medical films to newsreels and advertisements for the military. Although commissioned by various private and state agencies, all of these films presented Germany as a *Volksgemeinschaft*, a "sworn community" demanding the sacrifice of individuals to the new state.[12] Thus in SCHIFF IN NOT (SHIP IN DISTRESS, 1936), an advertisement for the

Deutsche Gesellschaft zur Rettung Schiffsbrüchiger (German Society for the Rescue of Shipwrecked Sailors) later released under the title HELDEN DER KÜSTE (HEROES OF THE COAST, 1937), the narrator reminds the audience: "German seafaring is a concern of the entire people [Sache des ganzen Volkes]. Rescuing ships in distress is an honorable duty to the fatherland!"[13]

While such statements obviously served to demonstrate the conformity of the film's sponsors to the spirit of the times, they also had another pedagogical function for the film's audience. For SCHIFF IN NOT and HELDEN DER KÜSTE were also officially classified as "Lehrfilme" ("educational films") and deemed "appropriate to use in the classroom" by the board of film censors.[14] In this, these films were hardly alone: over half of Ruttmann's post-1933 films were explicitly classified as "Lehrfilme,"[15] and many others received the predicate "volksbildend" ("contributing to the education of the people"). The category of educational film was critical to National Socialist film culture. Shortly after the regime change, the newly created Reichsministerium für Erziehung, Wissenschaft und Volksbildung (Reich Ministry for Pedagogy, Science and National Education), charged with the central "alignment" ("Gleichschaltung") of school curricula, issued a decree in 1934 stipulating that schools should systematically integrate films into their curricula as part of a general education in National Socialist principles.[16] And the Nazis would make sure that all schools were equipped with 16mm projectors for showing films.[17] Schools were, thus, a key locus in the more general conception of the "educational state" ("Erziehungsstaat") that had come to replace the welfare state of the 1920s.[18] Surviving censor records would indicate that this broader "educational" circuit was an important part of the life of Ruttmann's post-1933 films, almost all of which were rereleased in portable 16mm versions, many of them accompanied by lectures. An even more telling indication provided by the censor cards is the fact that nearly all of the films classified as "Lehrfilme" were re-issued in multiple versions with spoken narration and with intertitles,[19] thus conforming to the criteria for educational films set by the Reichsstelle für den Unterrichtsfilm, which suggested the use of silent film in the classroom in order to allow for lectures by teachers.[20]

The imbrication of Ruttmann's films with Nazi education goes hand in hand with an ideological transformation in product advertising under National Socialism. Among Ruttmann's post-1933 films, one can find many advertisements commissioned by private companies such as Mannesmann steel works,[21] Beyer[22] and Henkel detergents and cosmetic products.[23] All of these films are at pains to code their products as modern: as models of Fordist efficiency (HENKEL. EIN DEUTSCHES WERK IN SEINER ARBEIT [HENKEL. A GERMAN FACTORY AT WORK], 1938), as agents of modern hygiene and Enlightenment for colonial subjects (e.g. the Beyer film IM ZEICHEN DES VERTRAUENS [UNDER THE SIGN OF

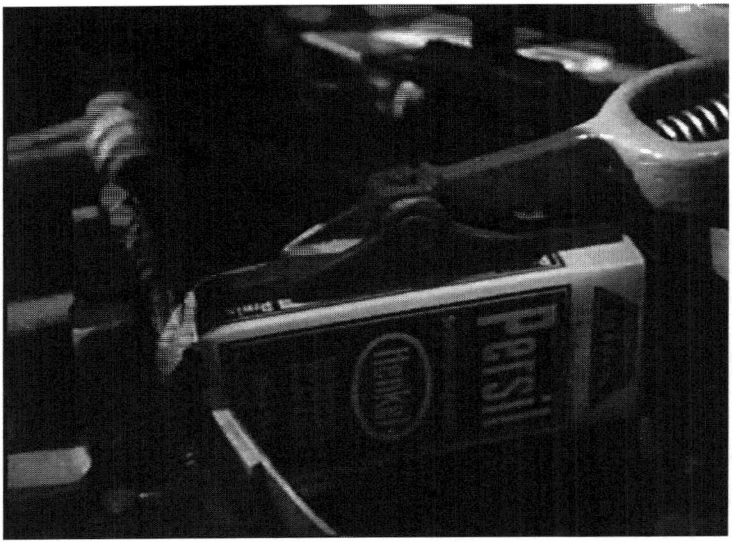

Still from Ruttmann, HENKEL. EIN DEUTSCHES WERK BEI DER ARBEIT *(1938). Factory production*

TRUST], 1937), or as essential elements in the production of mass infrastructure and housing (MANNESMANN, 1937). But in contrast to the product advertisements of Weimar, these product advertisements display an overt didacticism, striving to enfold their immediate advertising messages into a decidedly nationalist narrative of strength and vitality under the new regime. In the Henkel film, for example, two of the factory workers celebrate Germany's newfound independence from the "Zufälligkeiten der Weltwirtschaft" ("contingencies of global economics"), in particular the new policies of actively collecting raw materials through such activities as whale hunting.[24] More significantly, the film also reflects on the very status of advertising in a subsequent sequence in which a tour guide leading a group of housewives through the Henkel factory states:

> You see, ladies, advertising [Werbung] is different from mere "commercials" [Reklame]. Henkel advertising, in full recognition of the great educational value that advertising possesses, strives above all to serve consumers and allow them to enjoy all of the advantages of our products. It thus combines commercial interests with service to the general good.[25]

Such paeans to the "educational value" of advertising were designed to underscore a principle we already saw at work in the interactive "contest" at the end of ALTGERMANISCHES BAUERNKULTUR: advertising was now supposed to serve a national interest, where profits had to be subordinated to the interest of the state and the nation. In fact, this new tenor of advertising was the official policy of the Werberat der deutschen Wirtschaft (Advertising Council of the German Economy), the organization created by Goebbels in 1933 to oversee the "alignment" of advertising, which demanded not only that private advertising toe Nazism's ideological line, but also that it subordinate individual pleasure and company profits to the task of "educating" consumers in their duties as "Volksgenossen" of the new state.[26]

No industry was more important for this program of national fortification than steel. A key industry for the National Socialist efforts to "rebuild" Germany after the financial crisis, steel was the single most prominent motif in Ruttmann's post-1933 filmmaking, standing at the center of at least five films stretching from his 1933 Italian film ACCIAIO (STEEL) to his advertisements for the German weapons industry DEUTSCHE WAFFENSCHMIEDEN (GERMAN WEAPONS MANUFACTURERS, 1940) and DEUTSCHE PANZER (GERMAN TANKS, 1940). Not surprisingly, much of the secondary literature on Ruttmann's post-1933 films has focused on these "steel films." While some critics have read Ruttmann's preoccupation with images of steel production as a means of continuing to cultivate his artistic interest in formal experimentation despite the ideological constraints of the new regime,[27] others have interpreted Ruttmann's fetishization of steel technology as a more or less direct expression of Goebbels's "stählerne Romantik" ("steely romanticism") and Nazism's "reactionary modernism" in its use of modernist aesthetics to further National Socialist ideology.[28] Having emphasized the imbrications between experimental aesthetics with "practical" commissions throughout this book, my own reading tends toward the latter argument, emphasizing the compatibility between the aesthetics of Ruttmann's steel films and their ideological mission. However, as I explain further below, we should also push this argument further to ask how Ruttmann's steel films position the very medium of film as an agent of National Socialist governance conceived as national "education."

The titles of Ruttmann's wartime films already point to one of the principal reasons for the cult of steel under National Socialism: its association with weapons manufacture. This was an especially important topic for National Socialists, who saw the occupation of the industrial Ruhr region by French troops, the demilitarization of Germany and the continued interdiction of German soldiers in the Rhineland under the Versailles Treaty as the darkest episode in German national history. Thus while the "steeled body" formed a staple component of the Nazi imaginary generally (a topos regularly evoked by Hitler in his speeches to Nazi youth and famously articulated in the writings of Ernst Jünger), this was more than simply a psychoanalytic fantasy.[29] It was also and always connected with the status of the Ruhr, German steel production and especially weapons manufacture (which was revived en masse after 1933, followed by the return of soldiers to the Ruhr in 1936).

When juxtaposed the "Blut und Boden" policies that informed Ruttmann's 1933 film, this cultivation of the steel industry under Nazism points to a contradiction in Nazi thought and ideology, since the very industrial territories that a film like BLUT UND BODEN condemned as the cause of Germany's decline (the film singled out Ruhr cities like Wuppertal and Düsseldorf before calling on spectators to repopulate the Eastern farmlands) figured in Ruttmann's steel films as the centers of national prosperity. It is precisely this contradiction – i.e. Nazism's simultaneous embrace of agrarian romanticism and urban-industrial technology – that concepts such as Jeffrey Herf's "reactionary modernism" have sought to account for, and in this sense, it is hardly surprising that such terms have played a key role in scholarship on Ruttmann's National Socialist films. Like the Stuttgart film, Ruttmann's steel films are indeed at pains to reconcile the two currents. But it is also important to emphasize that Ruttmann's steel films draw on different ideological and visual conventions than a film like BLUT UND BODEN; whereas the former film's agrarian romanticism looked back to a tradition of peasant representation familiar from "Heimat" art, the celebration of steel had a clear filmic genealogy in the industrial film, a form dating back to the earliest years of the cinema and used to promote the production work of factories.

Indeed, much of Ruttmann's language in these films can be traced back to early industrial films such as the films for the Westinghouse Electric & Manufacturing Company (1904) or DAS STAHLWERK DER POLDIHÜTTE WÄHREND DES WELTKRIEGS (THE POLDIHÜTTE STEEL WORKS DURING THE WORLD WAR, 1916). This includes the frequent use of tracking and panning shots in Ruttmann's steel films,[30] which are entirely absent from films like BERLIN and MELODIE DER WELT. But it also includes the predilection for the dramatic use of light and dark on the factory floor, where the arrangements of beams, plates and molten metal form semi-abstract compositions that dwarf the figures of the workers.[31]

But if Ruttmann looked back to this tradition of semi-abstraction in the industrial film, he did so for a reason. For that tradition become particularly useful after 1933, when "abstraction" was officially discouraged – most famously in the *Entartete Kunst* (*Degenerate Art*) exhibition of 1937 – on account of its association with modernism.[32] As other scholars have pointed out, the tendency toward abstraction is still visible in many places in Ruttmann's National Socialist films: in the frequent use of mass ornaments (workers and Hitler Youth); in the image of an animated meteorite at the beginning of the steel advertisement METALL DES HIMMELS,[33] in the soap suds that fill the screen in the opening shot of the Henkel advertisement (later echoed by arrangements of dancing groups dressed in white), in the many images of isolated machine parts,[34] or – to name

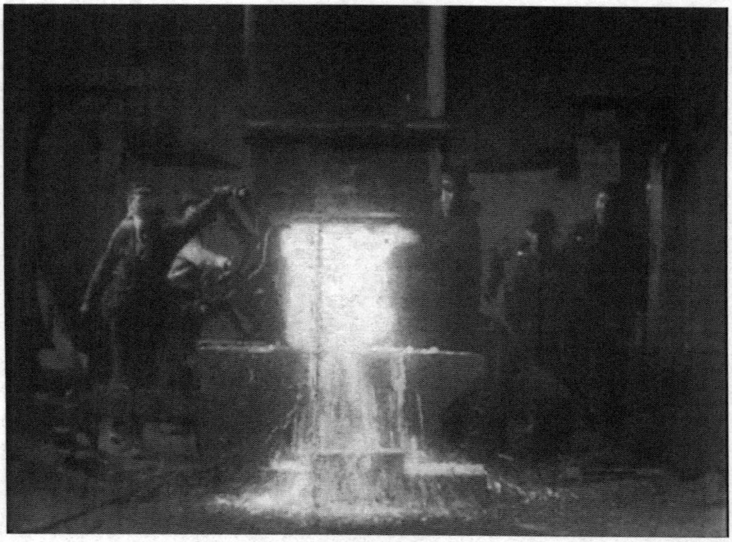

Still from WESTINGHOUSE WORKS
(American Mutoscope and Biograph Co., 1904)

the example most germane to the present chapter – in the many images of glowing steel plates and beams in Ruttmann's steel films from ACCIAIO on.[35] No doubt, such moments can be read as echoes of Ruttmann's abstract films from the 1920s (analogous in this sense to Ruttmann's widespread recycling of experimental montage forms after 1933), suggesting that the experimental aesthetics of Weimar were not simply suppressed by the Nazis. But those aesthetics did have to be reconciled with Nazi ideology.

Among other things, this meant reconciling any tendency toward abstraction with official aesthetic dictates, which – following Wilhelm Worringer – associated abstraction with primitivism and the "degeneracy" of modernist art. The case of Oskar Fischinger, whose abstract experiments were judged "contrary to the spirit of the times," has been discussed (although Fischinger himself produced several popular advertisements after 1933 before emigrating to the United States).[36] Ruttmann thematized the problematic status of abstraction under Nazism directly in ALTGERMANISCHE BAUERNKULTUR, where the Weimaresque "Professor Sandmann" condemns ancient Germanic art precisely on account of its "abstract" quality: "Before Charlemagne brought Roman Christianity to our ancestors," the professor argues, "they possessed absolutely no culture. All they had was an extremely primitive art of ornamentation with a tendency toward abstraction, which is of course common to all savage peoples."[37] In his defense of ancient Germanic culture, the protagonist Claus, significantly, does not

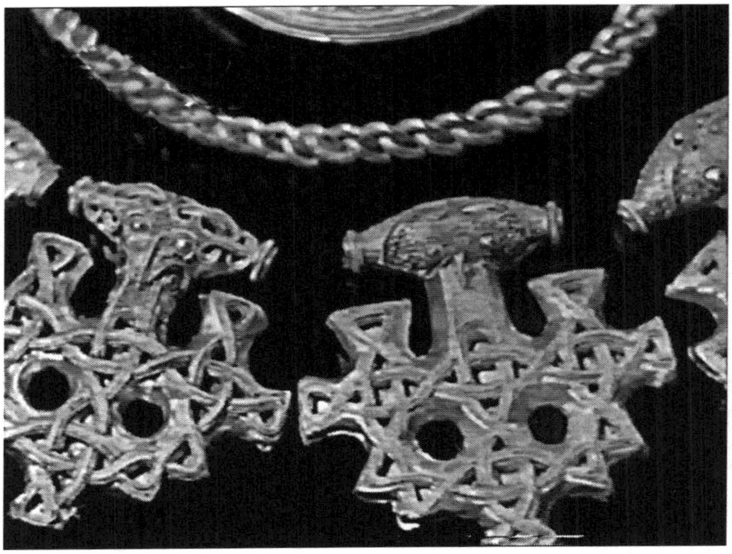

Still from Ruttmann, ALTGERMANISCHE BAUERNKULTUR *(1934). Ancient Germanic ornaments*

question the professor's association between abstraction and "savagery." But he does attempt to redefine the ornamental art of the ancient Germans, insisting that the surviving relics display a "Formgefühl" ("feeling for form") that belies any effort to reduce ancient Germanic art to abstract ornamentation. This notion of "form" and "forming" is central to the ideological project of ALTGERMANISCHE BAUERNKULTUR. As the film continues, Claus repeatedly evokes terms such as "Formgefühl," "Gefühl für Formenschönheit" ("feeling for the beauty of form"), "Schönheit der Form" ("beauty of form") and "Kraft künstlerischer Gestaltung" ("power of artistic forming") to describe the surviving pots, urns, tools, swords, jewelry and other relics, which Ruttmann displays on rotating and gliding platters like items in a shop window.[38]

The concept of "Formgefühl" was, in fact, a prevalent one in art-historical circles of the time. Although it had its origins in formalist analysis and empathy research, it had taken on nationalist and even racial connotations by the early 1930s. The art historian Heinrich Wölfflin, in his 1931 book *Die Kunst der Renaissance. Italien und das deutsche Formgefühl* (*Renaissance Art. Italy and the German Feeling for Form*), argued that Nordic art, despite the seeming diversity of historical styles and phases, displayed what he called "the continuous presence of an identical feeling for form characteristic of a people" ("die durchgehende Gleichheit eines volksmäßigen Formgefühls"), which he thought was rooted in the "soil" ("Boden"), the "race" ("Rasse") and "racial type" ("Rassentypus").[39] Following Wölfflin, the term would come to be invoked in art historical and philological studies under Nazism, particularly in scholarship on ancient Germanic culture. In his book *Deutsche Vorzeit* (1933), for example, the *völkisch* archeologist Hans Hahne argued that one could read the racial constitution of a culture from the "Formgefühl" visible in surviving artifacts:

> The trained eye has no trouble discovering quasi-mysterious relations between forms of the human body [Leibesformen], essential inner traits of races and tribes, and the corresponding artistic forms of vases and pots [Gefäßkunstformen]. Northern man is "jagged [zackig]," and so is his feeling for form [Formgefühl] and his manner of ornamentation. Other races have a feeling for form that is indistinct, placid, overly refined or stilted.[40]

Other publications would follow, such as Andreas Heusler's *Germanentum. vom Lebens- und Formgefühl der alten Germanen* (*Germanness. On the Feeling for Life and Form of the Ancient Germans*), which went through five editions between 1934 and 1941.

This insistence on a feeling for form and acts of "forming" as the characteristic of Germanic productivity points to one strategy for negotiating the problem of abstraction after 1933; for when Ruttmann's films feature abstraction at all, this generally occurs within a narrative of "forming," where the abstract appears above all in the guise of raw material for national production. As I explore further below, this motif figures prominently in nearly all of Ruttmann's steel films, from METALL DES HIMMELS to the wartime films for the Wehrmacht. And this association of steel production with the act of forming also suggests a modification of our understanding of the famous "steel body." For the main point of steel in Ruttmann's films resides not simply in its purported "hardness," but also and perhaps above all in its docile malleability: i.e. its ability to be molded and fashioned to the needs of a particular national project.

In this, steel production and the steel factory come to form not only a privileged topos in Ruttmann's later work in advertising and propaganda, but also an ideal embodiment of the modality of power that Ruttmann's work under Nazism sought to exercise: a filmmaking that treats audiences less as individual consumers than as raw material to be "formed" by mass media for participation in the new regime. Such "molding" was, of course, the very definition that Goebbels assigned to fascist politics, which he famously compared to the work of the sculptor giving form to the marble: "The true politician is an artist in the genuine sense of the word. Just as the sculptor measures, works and chisels raw marble, so the statesman forms a *Volk* from the raw material of the masses."[41] This totalitarian model of governance, understood as shaping the raw material of the masses, may or may not, as Philippe Lacoue-Labarthes has argued, represent the culmination of a German intellectual tradition of politics as aesthetic fiat stretching back to the 18th century and ultimately to ancient Greece.[42] But it was most certainly a different concept of governance from that based on statistics and probabilities that characterized the welfare state of the Weimar Republic. Ruttmann's industrial films, I argue below, take up this new model of governance; far from the balancing of multiplicity and regularity present in the Weimar films, the steel films stage the "forming" of the masses into a unified "Volk." To be sure, this concept of the collective is still informed by a biopolitics of the *Volkskörper* reminiscent of BLUT UND BODEN, but that biopolitics is increasingly superimposed with disciplinary operations, in which factories and schools become aligned as spaces for a general training of the population in the lead-up to war.[43] Within this configuration, these films suggest an understanding of film as a central tool for *forming* the masses into a unified *Volk.*

The Continuity of Germanic Production: METALL DES HIMMELS

Such "forming" stands at the center of Ruttmann's first German steel film, METALL DES HIMMELS (1935). Commissioned by the Beratungsstelle für Stahlverwendung (Advisory Council for Steel Usage), a public relations department of the German steel industry founded in 1927 with its headquarters in Düsseldorf, the film – which Ruttmann wrote and directed – premiered at the Ufa-Palast am Zoo on 24 February 1935 before going on to become one of Ruttmann's biggest international successes after 1933 (winning prizes in both Brussels and Venice).[44] With its heavy use of rhythmical montage, as well as its predilection for semi-abstract images of molten steel and glowing beams that seem to reduce the screen to a play of light and shadow, METALL DES HIMMELS recalls, on one level, Ruttmann's experimental work from Weimar – a connection even noted by German critics at the time.[45] But those experimental aesthetics are now placed in the service of a carefully constructed narrative of Germanness and the power of forming established from the beginning of the film in a prologue on the history of steel. Following credits presented in gothic script, the film opens onto an animated image of outer space showing stars, the spinning earth, the moon and several meteors. As one of these meteors then strikes the earth, an off-screen voice informs spectators that the ancient Egyptians and Sumerians gleaned their iron from craters, "thankful" ("dankbar") for the gift from the gods. Significantly, however, it is precisely *not* this "metal from the heavens" that will form the object of Ruttmann's film; for immediately following the image of the Sumerian crater, the film cuts from ancient Mesopotamia to ancient

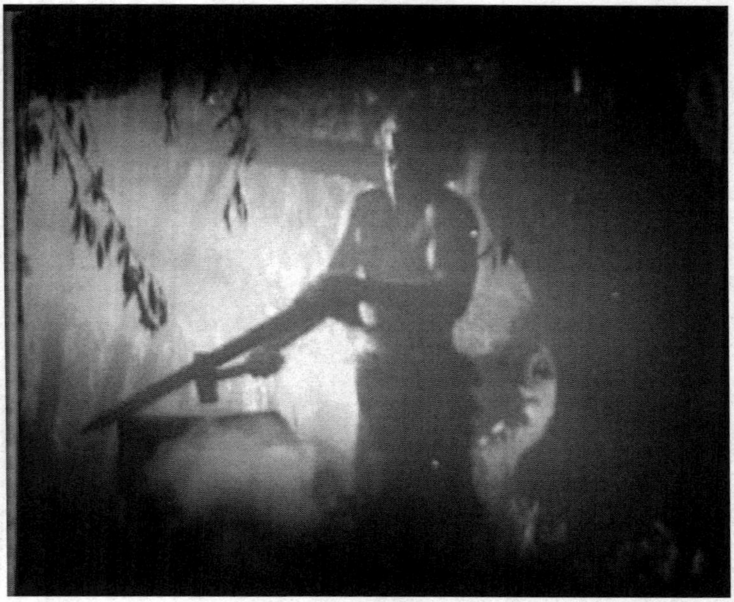

Still from Ruttmann, METALL DES HIMMELS. *Siegfried figure forging sword*

Germany where we see a blacksmith working at his forge as the narrator continues: "The Germans received no such gifts from the gods. But more than two thousand years ago, in southern Westphalia, a German subdued ironstone; placing it in the furnace, he forced [zwang] it to open up and deliver its glowing and malleable treasure: steel."[46] If this malleable substance offered a filmmaker such as Ruttmann opportunities for abstract compositions, it also supported a particular narrative of Germanic productivity and "will to form." Unlike the grateful Sumerians and Egyptians, the German actively sought out the earth's metallic resources and forced this abstract material to take on the forms desired.

Precisely what this "forming" entailed is suggested in the next image when a match cut takes us from the blacksmith's hammer blows to the image of warrior hammering out the final blows on his new sword. With his windblown blond hair, the figure is an unmistakable echo of the widespread "Siegfried" iconography that had appeared in German painting and film in the early 20th century, including a wartime propaganda film by Julius Pinschewer and, more memorably, Fritz Lang's NIBELUNGEN epic from 1924 (on which Ruttmann himself had collaborated).[47] Most importantly, the figure establishes the motif of weapons production that will dominate the rest of the prologue. Following the image of the Siegfried figure, Ruttmann then transports the spectator, via a rhythmical montage, from Siegfried's forge through shots of a medieval blacksmith to

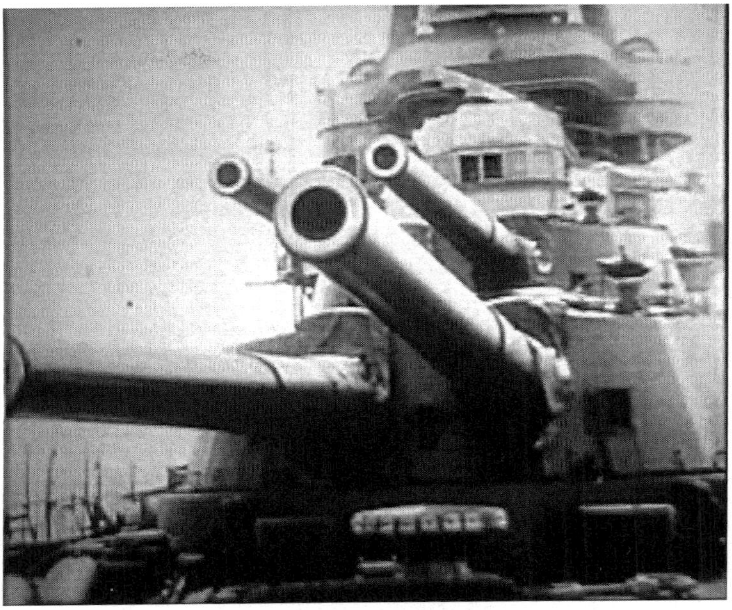

Still from Ruttmann, METALL DES HIMMELS. *Modern-day warfare*

scenes from industrial factories and finally scenes of the Great War: exploding shells, tank formations, battleships, and airplane fleets.

As the telos of this opening sequence, weapons manufacture figures not simply one form of steel production among others, but rather as the *raison d'être* of the Germanic steel industry. Moreover, as the prologue continues, the film presents steel production itself as the object of an international battle. Immediately following the war sequences, the film moves to the Weimar period with an animated image of the earth overlain with the title "Versailles." Unlike the images of the earth in MELODIE DER WELT, this globe is represented not as a space of understanding among different peoples, but rather as a theater of warfare. While the narrator describes how the European allies "destroyed" German steel production, leaving the country "defenseless" ("wehrlos"), an image reminiscent of the animated pictograms from BLUT UND BODEN shows a German factory crumbling in the background as allied factories spring up in the foreground, blocking our view. However, as we soon learn, the "men of the German steel industry" continued to believe in Germany's strength and, after the interlude of Weimar, returned the nation to its former position as the "leader in European steel production."[48]

In narrating German history as the history of steel production, Ruttmann was, in fact, following a precedent already established by the Beratungsstelle

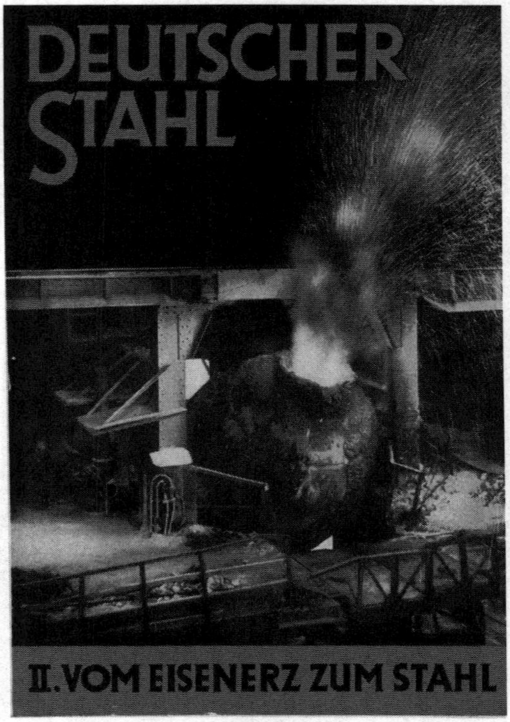

Cover of Deutscher Stahl, *special issue of* Stahl überall *(1934)*

itself. Among other forms of public relations, the group published monthly bulletin entitled *Stahl überall,* which ran from 1928 to 1936 and included essays by various industry experts. One issue from 1934 featured a lengthy essay by the historian Herbert Dickmann entitled "German Steel: Images from the History of German Iron and Steel Production" ("Deutscher Stahl. Bilder aus der Geschichte der deutschen Eisen- und Stahlerzeugung"), in which the author recounted the history of German steel production from 1000 A.D. to the early 20th century in order to emphasize "the tight bond linking steel to the people and the soil."[49] Another special edition of the journal from 1935 entitled *Stahlfibel* even recounts the legend of the "metal from the sky" before tracing the history of German steel production.[50] Richly illustrated, these publications included several images that clearly inspired the iconography of METALL DES HIMMELS (reconstructions of historical furnaces, workers guiding molten metal, exploding Bessemer converters, etc.).

Both the publications of the Beratungsstelle für Stahlverwendung and Ruttmann's film also sought to make readers aware of the ubiquity of steel in society

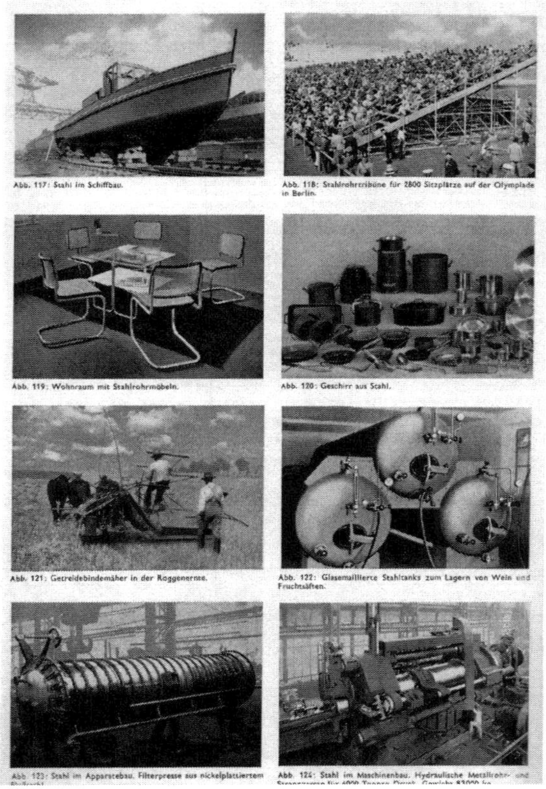

Illustration from Stahlfibel *(1935). Uses of steel in society*

and daily life. Thus the issues of *Stahl überall* included special issues on mining,[51] offices,[52] kitchens,[53] farming,[54] hygiene and medicine,[55] automobiles,[56] athletics,[57] and many other areas. Similarly, METALL DES HIMMELS is at pains to stress the pervasive use of steel in all sectors of German society. After the prologue, the film details the many uses of steel products in four sections: one featuring scenes of mining, factory work and architecture (including prominent shots of Berlin's first steel-framed high-rise building, the Shell-Haus from 1929); a second – reminiscent of the displays from ALTGERMANISCHE BAUERNKULTUR – showing and endless array of steel products (tools, appliances, kitchen utensils, lamps, luxury goods, etc.) on spinning platters or arranged in symmetrical formations for a tracking camera; a third section – recalling the final section of MELODIE DER WELT – consisting of a rhythmical montage that leads the audience from handwork (ironing, filing, sewing, etc.) to automated factories; and a final sequence (reminiscent of BLUT UND BODEN) featuring scenes of metal

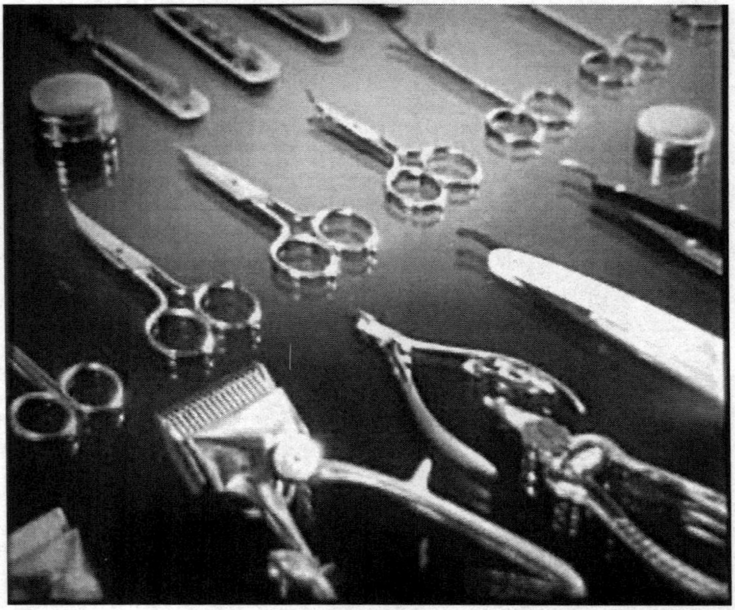

Still from Ruttmann, METALL DES HIMMELS. *Uses of steel in society*

in country life (ploughs, harvesting machines, grain sorters, etc.) before returning to a short montage of high-speed transportation (trains, airplanes, automobiles, ships) at the end. Taken together, these sections present steel as the glue holding all of German society together, a kind of monistic substance running throughout the various images and activities shown on the screen and binding them into a unified *Volk*. Summarizing this point, the film ends with the shot of a blacksmith pounding on an anvil as the off-screen narrator scans out the words "The German People! German Work! German Steel!" ("Deutsches Volk! Deutsche Arbeit! Deutscher Stahl!"). Shot from below and ominously surrounded by smoke, the blacksmith recalls the Siegfried figure from the prologue: the worker as warrior among a "people" totally mobilized for steel production.

The connection between Siegfried and the blacksmith in the closing shot also underscores the central rhetorical argument of this film: like ALTGERMANISCHE BAUERNKULTUR and STUTTGART, DIE GROSSSTADT ZWISCHEN WALD UND REBEN, and like many publications of the time, METALL DES HIMMELS is at pains to establish a continuity between the ancient and the modern.[58] More precisely, Ruttmann's film represents the Third Reich as a restoration of German production after the catastrophic "interruption" of the Versailles Treaty and the Weimar Republic. This rhetoric of continuity is visible in the film's many juxtapositions of tradition and modernity: the combination of farming equipment and

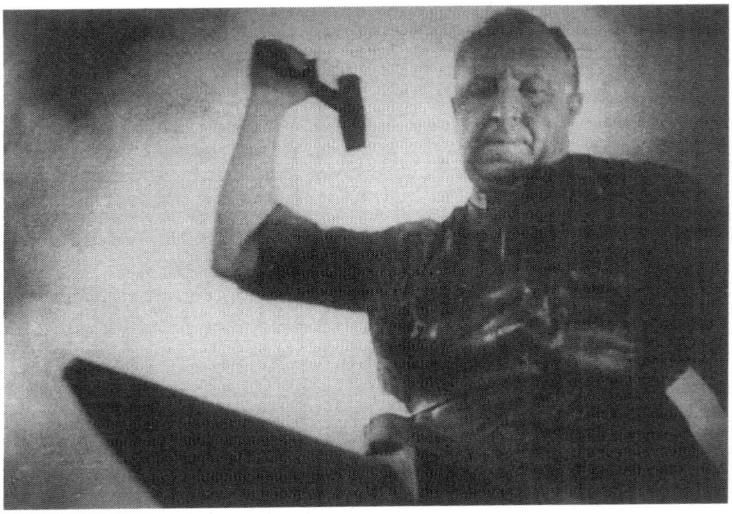

Still from Ruttmann, Metall des Himmels. *Blacksmith in final shot*

high-speed transport, of hand tools and industrial machinery, of swords and artillery shells, and of blacksmith and factory workers.[59] But it also informs Ruttmann's use of montage. On a technical and stylistic level, the montage sequences of Metall des Himmels resemble Ruttmann's Weimar work, particularly in their frequent use of rhythm and match cuts.[60] But such devices have been refitted, as it were, to support the narrative of historical continuity. Whereas the match cuts Berlin and Melodie der Welt underscored relations of analogy between different peoples, species, actions or cultural forms existing simultaneously, thus gesturing toward a higher order in an arena of difference, the match cuts of Metall des Himmels overwhelmingly tend toward relations of temporal *contiguity*, cuing spectators to read one form as a kind of "outgrowth" of the previous one. This rhetoric is first established in the montage of the prologue, where the ancient blacksmith's hammer blows are taken up by those of the medieval Siegfried, the smoke of Siegfried's forge is taken up by the smoke of an early modern metalworking shop, the giant water-powered hammer of that workshop is then taken up by the pneumatic hammers of early industrial factories, and the pounding the factory is taken up by the rapid fire of steel shells in WWI. In such sequences, Ruttmann's montage "passes the torch" – like the Athletes in the prologue to Riefenstahl's Olympia – from one time period to the next, suggesting that each form of steel production shown is a continuation of the activity in the past. This trend is also visible in later sections. In the sequence on forms of work, for example, the spinning wheel of a sewing machine is taken up, through a match cut, by the spinning action of an airplane propeller, which is then taken up by numerous spinning gears of the factory in abstract formations not a little reminiscent of Fernand Léger's *Ballet mécanique* or the opening to Fritz Lang's METROPOLIS. Combined with the frequent use of dissolves and smooth tracking (for example in the sequence displaying steel products), such match cuts suggest a restoration of continuity after the supposed "interruption" of German history under Weimar and the Versailles Treaty. Like the various forms of "Germanic" art held together by a common "Formgefühl," all of these shots appear as linked elements in a continuum of Germanic steel production rooted in a tradition of Germanic "forming" stretching back to pre-Christian times.

This continuity is further underscored in the film via Ruttmann's use of rhythm. Rhythm was, of course, ubiquitous in Ruttmann's films, and montage films such as BERLIN and MELODIE DER WELT had frequently thematized the rhythms of work and industry. As I have argued elsewhere, notions of rhythm in German experimental film of the interwar period were heavily influenced by ideas about work and rhythm derived from the economist Karl Bücher, whose book *Arbeit und Rhythmus* (*Work and Rhythm*), published in six editions between 1894 and 1924, proposed an influential understanding of rhythm as a means of maximizing energy, efficiency and productivity in acts of collective labor.[61] Hans Richter, for example, cited Bücher's ideas verbatim in his book *Filmgegner von heute, Filmfreunde von morgen* (*Opponents of Film Today, Friends of Film Tomorrow,* 1929): "Rhythm possesses a proven force. The cadence of marching enlivens the step. Oarsmen facilitate their rowing by means of rhythmical song. Threshers, blacksmiths and street pavers perform their hammering to a common rhythm."[62] In thematizing such rhythmical labor – as Richter did in his *Filmstudie* (1926) and Ruttmann did in the section on labor at the end of MELODIE DER WELT – experimental filmmakers sought to claim this enlivening power of rhythm for film, which they believed could involve the spectator bodily in the action on the screen. Such a notion of rhythm was also central, as we saw in chapter 1, to advertising theories of the 1920s, which sought to make spectators "resonate" ("mitschwingen") with the abstract rhythms on the screen.[63]

Ruttmann's rhythmical montage in METALL DES HIMMELS takes up this well-established tradition in its presentation of the rhythms of labor stretching from the first blacksmith's hammer to the rhythms of factory machines. But it once again places this motif in the service of a nationalist narrative of restored continuity. This reframing of rhythm becomes evident precisely when one takes into account the differences between Ruttmann and Bücher. While Bücher had sought to claim rhythm as a means of regulating energy and promoting efficiency, his book also contained a nostalgic critique of industrial labor as a dehumanizing form, and he located the moment of such dehumanization in the introduction of circular motion in the factory. In the transition from unidirectional

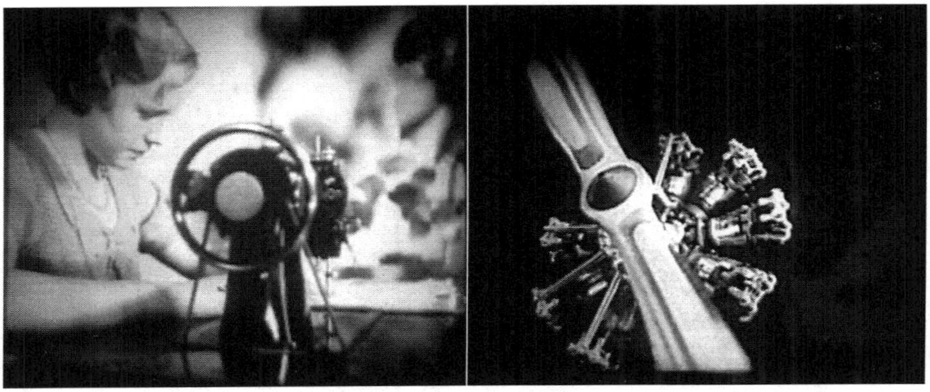

Stills from Ruttmann, METALL DES HIMMELS. *Montage of sewing machine and airplane propeller*

motion ("horizontal" or "vertical" motion) to "circular" motion, combined with the elimination of the hand's "idle backstroke," Bücher argued, the "traditional music of work" had disappeared.[64] For Bücher, this transition marked the moment at which modern man had become a servant to the machine, chained to a mechanism that no longer imitated the movements of the human body.[65] The iconography evoked by Bücher is prominently displayed in Ruttmann's film, particularly in the section on forms of labor, where the montage passes from shots of rhythmical hand work involving back-and-forth motions (ironing, woodcutting, sanding and filing) to shots of automated work of factory machines characterized precisely by continuous rotation (propellers, gears, pulleys). Replaying Bücher's history of technology, the sequence is characterized by the progressive automation of labor and the marginalization of the human body, beginning with the image of the sewing machine (in which the worker is reduced to steadying the cloth as the machine performs the labor). However, Ruttmann's sequence – and indeed the film as a whole – displays none of Bücher's critique of industrial technology. On the contrary, as we have seen, it represents modern mechanized steel production as the continuation and culmination of traditional labor on a higher plane. Unlike the famous montage of the sewing machine and the umbrella so prized by surrealist thinkers for its interruption of rational thought, Ruttmann's montage of a sewing machine and an airplane propeller is meant to celebrate the continuous increase in the power, productivity and efficiency of German work rhythms. Indeed, the film is at pains to establish a sense of continuity between rhythms of all sorts: from the undulating rhythm of the wheat swaying in the wind in the section on rural life to the accelerated rhythms of pistons and high-speed trains wheels. All are coded, in Ruttmann's montage, as the continuous rhythms of "German labor"

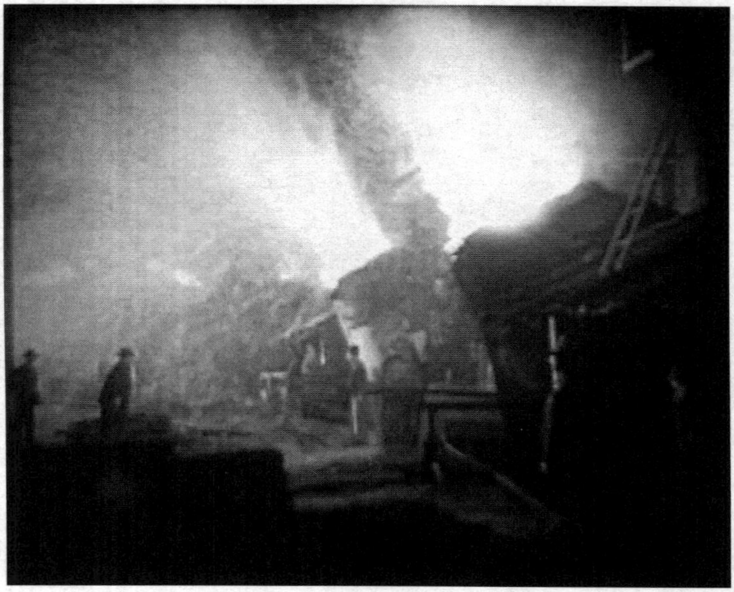

Still from Ruttmann, METALL DES HIMMELS *(1935). Bessemer converters*

("Deutsche Arbeit") that saved the steel industry and reestablished Germany's place among nations.[66]

To be sure, the process of automation does indeed appear to marginalize the worker in METALL DES HIMMELS, as factory workers are reduced to tending machines and guiding the steel in its trajectory from molten mass to formed product. In many sequences, such a marginalization is rendered strikingly in the compositions, where the human figures appear dwarfed by the giant formations of machinery, molten metal and glowing beams. But this marginalization is hardly presented as a problem in Ruttmann. On the contrary, workers appear here in Jüngerian fashion as de-individualized "types" – as disciplined as the steel they work on – sacrificing their individuality to the "Volk" as it reasserts its place in the struggle among nations after the interruptions of Weimar.[67]

This is, moreover, the same way in which the film sought to position spectators. If one were searching for a reflection on filmic spectatorship in Ruttmann's National Socialist films, one of the most obvious motifs would certainly be found in the disciplinary space of the classroom. Like FEIND IM BLUT, these films – including all three films examined in this chapter – frequently feature shots of classrooms, in which teachers explain to children the same arguments being made to the spectator in the film. In METALL DES HIMMELS, one such sequence occurs at the beginning of the section on steel products when we see a teacher

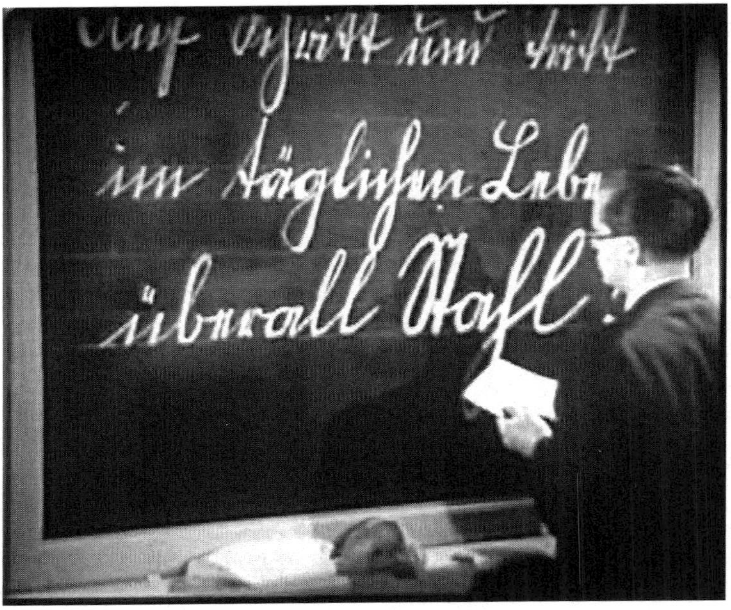

Still from Ruttmann, Metall des Himmels. *Classroom sequence*

administering a dictation exercise to a group of female pupils, who dutifully copy the shape of his Sütterlin handwriting as he traces the motto of the Beratungsstelle für Stahlverwendung – "Überall Stahl!" ("Everywhere Steel!") – on the blackboard. This, of course, is precisely the lesson of Ruttmann's film, and like the children copying from the blackboard, Ruttmann's spectator is supposed to learn to see steel as the essential glue underlying all the forms of daily life, but also as the result of a Germanic "forming" activity stretching from the most ancient blacksmiths to the work of industrial factories.

As we saw above, many of Ruttmann's post-1933 films – including Metall des Himmels –were, in fact, deemed appropriate for screening in schools and re-released as educational films. Thus in many cases, the audience of Metall des Himmels did likely consist of school children. But like most of Ruttmann's post-1933 films, this one also received the distinction of "volksbildend" from the censors.[68] Although it is unclear whether the film was shown in factories or in other non-theatrical settings, it was clearly considered to be "educational" in the broader sense in which the Nazis understood propaganda generally. With its ideological representation of German steel production as being rooted in a specifically Germanic "Formgefühl," the film was also an agent in a broader national education: one that would "mold" the masses into a self-conscious

"Volk," teaching them to see themselves as links in a long chain of steel producers. In this, METALL DES HIMMELS offers an example of the double sense of "educational" film that has informed discussions of the topic since the beginning of the 20th century.[69] Within this context, the images of the classroom in the film can be read as an indication of the broader disciplinary "dispositif" that Ruttmann's steel films imagine for the cinema. Like the school children shown in the film, the spectators of Ruttmann's film were conceived as raw material to be worked on. Whether showing as a theatrical release, in schools or in other non-theatrical settings, the film was meant to form audiences, like the malleable steel it represented, within the struggle of nations that had replace the paradigm of Weimar pacificism.[70]

The Surface of Nazi Design: MANNESMANN

If METALL DES HIMMELS suggested a vision of molten steel as a figure for the malleable spectator, Ruttmann's next steel film, MANNESMANN (1937), would unfold more fully the vision of film as a medium for shaping a public. Although commissioned by an individual company rather than a state agency, MANNESMANN shared the educational aspirations of its predecessor. After a gala premiere at the Ufa-Pavillon in Berlin in September 1937 (where it was screened for industrialists and other VIPs along with a 40-piece orchestra conducted by Wolfgang Zeller), the film went on to win prizes in film festivals in Venice and Paris, before being re-issued in 1938 as a *Kulturfilm* in both 35mm and 16mm versions under the title MANNESMANN. EIN UFA-KULTURFILM NACH DEM INTERNATIONAL PREISGEKRÖNTEN FILM (MANNESMANN. AN UFA KULTURFILM ADAPTED FROM THE INTERNATIONAL AWARD-WINNING FILM).[71] Like METALL DES HIMMELS, this rerelease of MANNESMANN received a rating of "volksbildend" and was deemed appropriate for use in schools as an educational film.[72] Like its predecessor, moreover, MANNESMANN features a prominent classroom sequence in a factory schoolroom labeled "MW" (Mannesmann-Werke), where a teacher lectures to a group of schoolboys on the resistance of Mannesmann steel parts; using images on the blackboard – which Ruttmann then animates – the teacher shows the pupils how steel pipes and girding in roads have to withstand changes in temperatures, exposure to the elements, the pressure of traffic and so forth.

This "resistance" was indeed the claim to fame of the Mannesmann brand. Founded in Remscheid in 1890 by the brothers Max and Reinhardt Mannesmann, the enterprise was famous for its signature method of producing steel tubes with no seams or welding. After moving to Düsseldorf in 1893, Mannesmann gradually grew during the prosperous decades around 1900 to become a principal supplier for companies such as Siemens and develop a worldwide empire of exports. It also became a vertically integrated company, acquiring its own steel works in 1929, a move that placed Mannesmann among the top steel producers in Germany alongside companies such as Krupp and Siemens. Within this marketplace, Mannesmann placed special emphasis on their pipes' resistance to heat, rust and pressure, thanks in part to new coating techniques the company had developed.[73] This – as the professor's lecture in the film was meant to illustrate – made their pipes particularly well suited to infrastructural applications for water, gas and oil.

In presenting MANNESMANN steel pipes, Ruttmann emphasized these same points, but he also recycled many of the topoi from METALL DES HIMMELS. The company's steel production is, first of all, presented as being grounded in an unbroken tradition of "Germanness." Beginning with an image of the Mannesmann factory, Ruttmann then uses a match cut to transition from a tracking shot of the steel factory columns to a tracking shot of the German forest as the narrator recounts the company's origins embedded within Germanic traditions: "Remscheid. In this town rooted in the soil of the Berisch regions, where blacksmiths have forced iron to become steel since ancient times, a feat was accomplished: that of forging a pipe without seams from a block of steel."[74] With this "grounding" of Mannesmann's signature technology in tradition and the landscape, MANNESMANN – like METAL DES HIMMELS – takes up a project that Ruttmann himself formulated as follows in a 1935 interview in the context of his Stuttgart film: "I would be happy if this idea [...] gave me the opportunity to create the epos of a German landscape, which would lead organically from the Stone Age through all of the nation's historical struggles to the joy of Germany's reawakening."[75] But the metaphor of the forest also implied something more. That metaphor was, in fact, a widespread topos in Nazi propaganda and advertising, which – looking back to publications such as Rudolf Düesberg's *Der Wald als Erzieher* (*The Forest as Educator*) – cast the forest as a model for a national community understood in *völkisch* terms as being based on rootedness, racial kinship and duty to the state.[76] This conception of the forest found filmic expression one year before MANNESMANN in the above-mentioned EWIGER WALD (ETERNAL FOREST, 1936), where Guido Seeber used tracking shots and dissolves to present the German forest as the "eternal" landscape and ground of the national *Volksgemeinschaft,* rooting modernity in tradition and technology in nature. The opening sequence of MANNESMANN, with its slow tracking shot and dissolve from steel posts to the forests of Remscheid, could not but recall Seeber's film. Like its predecessor, Ruttmann's film also sought to establish a sense of continuity between tradition and modernity – between ancient forests and

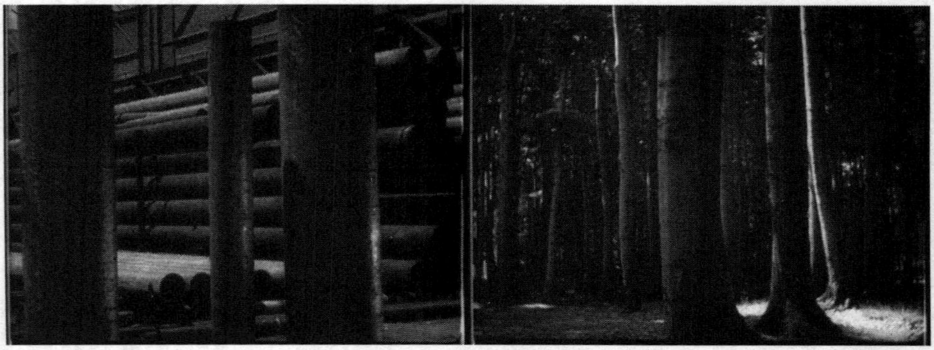

Stills from Ruttmann, MANNESMANN *(1937)*

modern steel pipes – that would vouch for Germany's "rootedness." If this was a "reactionary" modernism, it was, more precisely, a racinated modernism: one that sought to ground technological modernity in the soil and the blood.

Like METALL DES HIMMELS, moreover, MANNESMANN presents the company's steel pipes as a ubiquitous presence in German infrastructure and society. In successive sections, the film depicts the pipes as the essential element in road building and sewage, in gas and water canalization, in electric towers and cables, in oil extraction and refineries, and in numerous vehicles for land and sea travel. Like the former film, moreover, MANNESMANN frequently emphasizes the ubiquity of Mannesmann piping via contiguous montage. In the sequence on gas and water pies, for example, we see successive scenes from a bathroom where a woman can be seen bathing; a kitchen where a mother prepares a meal as the children drink from the faucet; a garden where a woman waters flowers as a child plays in the fountain; and a swimming pool with divers and frolicking bathers. While these images might suggest an analogical value in their status as so many examples of middle-class benefits of Mannesmann steel piping, they also and more importantly emphasize contiguity: following the clean water as it circulates from one location to another throughout society, the sequence illustrates the omnipresence of steel pipes in daily life, their linking of all spheres of work and leisure. Just as the film constructs a sense of continuity from "ancient times" to present steel production, it also insists on an unbroken continuity from one sector of society to another.

But Ruttmann's film is above all at pains to stress the "resistant" quality of Mannesmann piping. This is the point of the professor's lecture to the school children, and it is also the central message of Ruttmann's demonstrations to the film's audience. As we have seen, this presentation of steel pipes is, on one level, consistent with Mannesmann's own presentation of its product. But it also speaks to a larger theme of steel and modernity in Ruttmann. For just as the

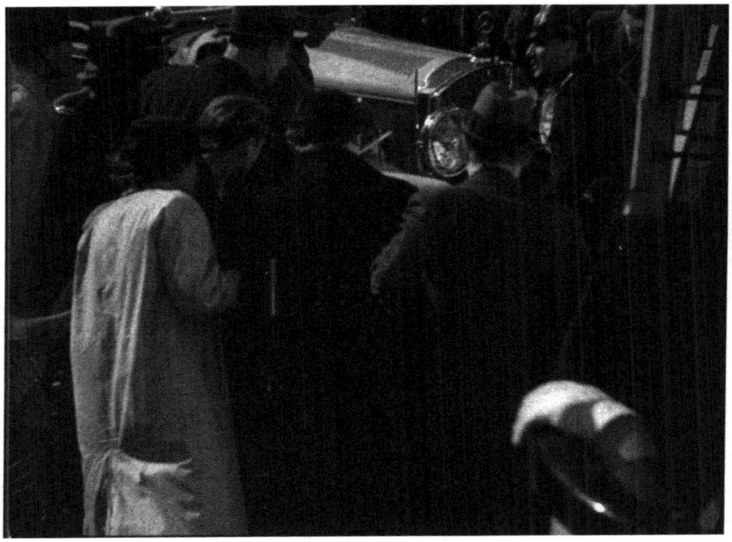

Still from Mannesmann

film anchors steel production in an ancient tradition, it also represents the resistance of steel as a means of surviving the shocks and contingencies of modern life. This becomes evident in a central sequence in Mannesmann depicting a traffic accident. Reminiscent of the Weimar street film, the sequence, shot in accelerated montage, focuses our attention on the onlookers. Rapid-fire images of heads turning to look at the accident, feet running in different directions, a wobbly bicycle, and concerned faces accompanied by distressed voices speaking of someone being "run over" ("umgefahren") all suggest that the accident has unleashed a general panic on the city street. Figuring frequently in films such as Die Strasse and literature such as Alfred Döblin's *Berlin Alexanderplatz*, the traffic accident was a staple modernist topos and perhaps the central embodiment of anxieties about contingency in the age of street traffic: a paradigmatic moment of resistance to modernity's ordering tendencies, the accident marked the limit of society's ability to master chance. One of the best-known examples occurs in the opening pages of Robert Musil's *Der Mann ohne Eigenschaften* (*The Man without Qualities*), when the sight of a man who has been run over evokes a series of reactions on the part of the onlookers. Significantly, one of these onlookers attempts to contain the shock of the accident by citing "American statistics" according to which 190,000 people are killed annually by automobiles, thus transforming the aberration of the accident – as Durkheim had done for suicide – into a "social fact." In Mannesmann, however, Ruttmann now takes a different approach. Immediately following the montage of the car crash, the film cuts to a scientific demonstration. Looking up from the scene of the accident, the crowd watches as a white-clad engineer drops a 146 kg weight from several stories up, which lands with a loud thud on a MANNESMANN cylinder. Another engineer then approaches the screen to reassure the audience: "You see, it wasn't so dangerous – just a slight dent – otherwise no harm!"[77] On the diegetic level, the connection between this scene and the preceding accident comes from the fact that we have just watched Mannesmann factories producing both cylinders and metal plates for the bodies of motor vehicles – thus suggesting that the automobiles in the accident resisted the crash no less than the cylinder in the demonstration. On a broader level, however, the demonstration is also meant to answer – both for the fictional onlookers and the film's audience – the fear of contingency evoked by the accident. Both the onlookers and the audience learn that steel resists the shocks of technological modernity because of its capacity to bend without breaking.

In addition to Musil and Döblin, the traffic accident in MANNESMANN, with its focus on the astounded onlookers, also recalls the famous suicide sequence from Ruttmann's own BERLIN film, discussed in chapter 2, in which the gawking onlookers amass on the bridge just after a woman throws herself into the river. There too, Ruttmann counters the threat of contingency with a return to order as the film cuts to an image of a fashion parade in which the movements of the city appear to continue as if nothing had happened – effectively suggesting that the city's "regularities" will persist despite such deviations from the desired flow of traffic. But there is a difference: whereas the BERLIN film (like *Der Mann ohne Eigenschaften*) sought to alleviate contingency through an appeal to statistical regularity, MANNESMANN promises to eliminate contingency through expert planning and production. Rather than simply suggesting the existence of a "social fact," the expert engineer in MANNESMANN assures the audience that the "authorities" – steel producers, engineers and ultimately the regime on display in the closing shot of the Nazi flag – have taken matters into their own hands. Rebuilding society on the basis of steel, the film suggests, will create a world in which the "accident" is rendered harmless.

It is this rhetoric of planning that governs Ruttmann's presentation of Mannesmann steel. For despite its "rootedness" in ancient traditions, the steel pipe appears in Ruttmann's film above all as the key to a *new* infrastructure of highways, gas lines, clean water, electricity, oil extraction and high-speed travel. The central quality necessary to such a thorough redesigning of the German landscape is steel's malleability. "Steel," as the first of several animated intertitles tell us, "submits to form" ("Stahl fügt sich der Form"). In this, the motif of steel production and steel usage also points toward the expected qualities of mass bodies – of workers and children – in Nazism's disciplinary regime: like the school children in the film taking down dictation, steel was meant to *con-form*

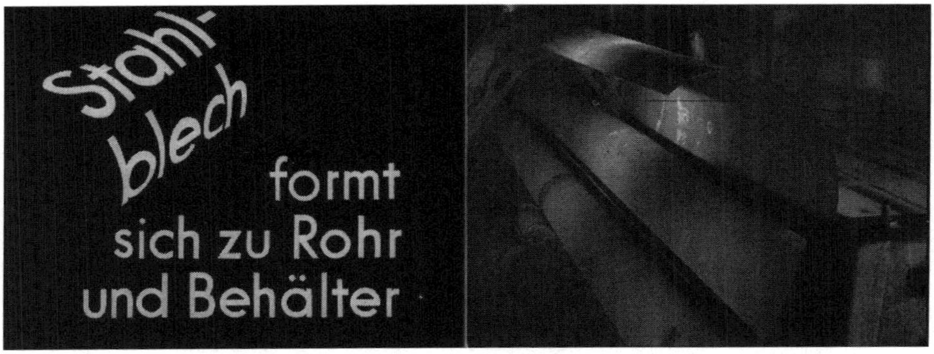

Still from MANNESMANN

to the dictates of the new and thoroughly planned society. Thus the central quality of the "steel body" in Ruttmann resides as much in its malleability as in its purported hardness: in its status as raw material that can be "forced" into the shape desired by the builders of the new society.

Ruttmann's film everywhere emphasizes such planning, and more importantly suggests an understanding of *film* as a medium for its execution. This is nowhere more the case than in the frequent use of animation. MANNESMANN contains more animation than any of Ruttmann's other post-1933 films, and nearly all of the animated sequences employ unmistakable elements of design. In several instances, Ruttmann introduces animated titles that figure the process of steel production in elementary forms. For example, in a title reading "Stahlblech formt sich zu Rohr und Behälter" ("Steel plates are formed into pipes and containers"), the word "Stahlblech" literally glides across the screen and spins around in a movement that prefigures the sheet of steel being bent into the form of a pipe in the next image. Similar animated titles will occur in the oil section (where the title imitates the movement of the oil being sucked out of the ground) and the electricity section (where the tile imitates the twitchy movements of electricity being channeled into electric wires). All of these animated titles recall Ruttmann's Weimar animation, not only in their general capacity to morph, but also in their hybrid status as image-texts, a technique he frequently employed for the titles of advertising films such as DER SIEGER (where the closing title "Excelsior" is "written" across the screen by a series of animated tires). Like the titles of these earlier films, and taking up a general topos of modernist design, the titles in MANNESMANN seem to hover between the status of letters, images and elementary forms.[78] However, in *prescribing* the movements of production shown in the live-action shots, the animated titles of MANNESMANN seem to have taken on a new function of "planning," appearing as a kind of elementary "blueprint" for the production processes of the new society.

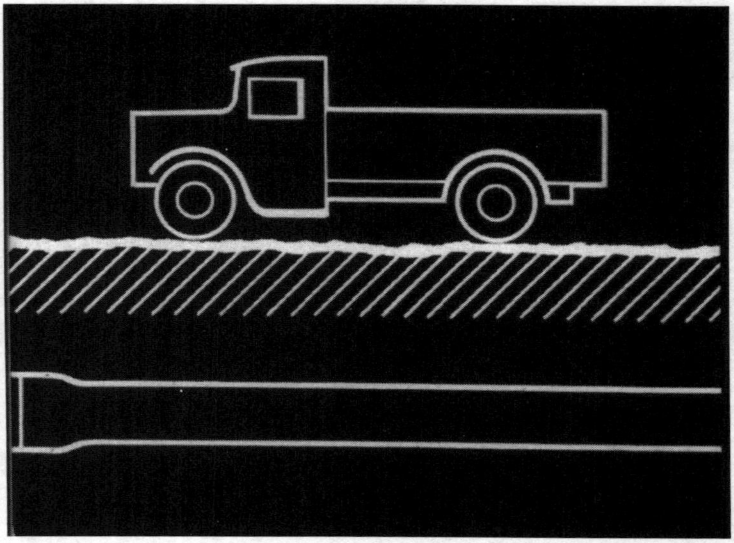

Still from MANNESMANN

This notion of the blueprint is further suggested by the other frequent use of animation in MANNESMANN, that of the "cross-section" – not the metaphorical cross-sectional of Ruttmann's Weimar montage, but rather more traditional scientific cross-sectional drawings. The first of these occurs in the classroom scene, when the professor draws a cross-section of a highway on the chalkboard to demonstrate the placement of Mannesmann piping underground and its resistance to the shocks of traffic. In Ruttmann's animation, we then see the animated pipe literally bend without breaking under the weight of the earth and the truck rolling along the highway. A second animated cross-section comes in the section on gas and water lines, when Ruttmann shows us the architectural schema of a housing unit in which pipes literally appear to grow and spread throughout the walls of the building. Finally, Ruttmann shows us a cross-sectional representation of a ship that fills with pipes before the covering once again appears to block our view into the interior and the ship is revealed as a commercial vehicle carrying Mannesmann products into the world. Like the animated titles, all of these animated cross-sections represent industrial processes – here the construction of roads, houses and ships – in elementary form.

Such animated representations – pulling the screen back in the direction of two-dimensionality – need to be seen, here too, in relation to the photographic footage of domestic scenes, street life, natural settings and factory floors. In their graphic and elementary quality, they once again reduce the contingency of the photographic image to suggest an underlying order. Only now, that

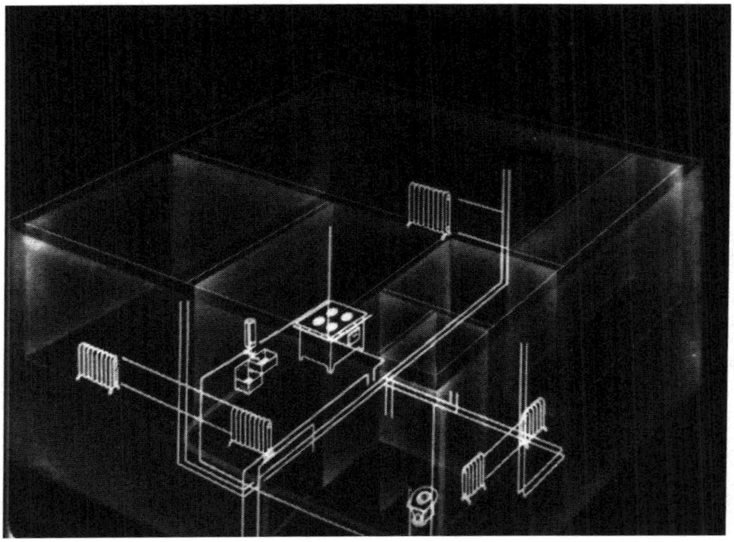

Still from MANNESMANN

order consists not of "regularities" or "social facts" established inductively, but rather appears as the result of conscious planning and production. Even more importantly, however, these animated sequences suggest a vision of *the film screen as the space for such planning*: a surface of design more akin to blueprints and cross-sectional diagrams than to the contingent photograph, and one which nonetheless differentiates itself from the traditional blueprint by virtue of its capacity for animation.

As we have seen, this use of the film screen as a design surface harkens back to Ruttmann's early work and links him to a broader current of modernism analyzed by Jacques Rancière. In his comparison of Mallarmé and Behrens, Rancière's main point, we recall, was that modernism was traversed by an ethos of design, in which aesthetics – poetry, painting or advertising design – could appear as a space for proposing new models for collective life in an era marked by the demise of older forms: a canvas for the drafting of new "types" for living. In likening the film screen to a blueprint, Ruttmann is undoubtedly still a "modernist," despite his efforts to root steel production in a timeless Germanic feeling for form, and one can certainly draw parallels between his Weimar animation and a film like MANNESMANN.

And yet, the latter film differs from the Weimar animation not only in its generic capacity as an industrial film, but also in its stark rhetoric of "planning" and its strict differentiation between "experts" (the teachers and the white-clad engineers) and audiences (the passive schoolchildren and the onlookers during the engineer's experiment). Ruttmann himself, one might conjecture, wanted to be understood as an analogous "expert" in film design, whose propaganda films could help to "form" audiences for life in the new regime. Beyond advertising the ability of Mannesmann steel to contribute to the design of a new infrastructure, MANNESMANN was advertising the ability of film – particularly the "sponsored" film – to discipline audiences: to shape reception, form viewing habits and generate planned responses.[79] Made as an advertisement but circulating as a cultural and educational film, MANNESMANN sought to claim the film screen – like the chalkboard and the blueprint – as a tool for "forming" the masses. In this way, the film proposes a very different model of governance than BERLIN or MELODIE DER WELT. Rather than simply "ordering" or identifying statistical regularities, Ruttmann's later films imagined film as a medium for the political "sculpting" that Goebbels understood as Nazism's modality of leadership: transforming the "raw material" of the masses into a unified "Volk."

Mobilizing the Steel Body in Wartime: DEUTSCHE PANZER

The pathos of "planning" in MANNESMANN would continue into Ruttmann's wartime steel films, while also being repurposed to depict a nation totally mobilized for war. Whereas a film like METALL DES HIMMELS could present weapons manufacture as the implicit telos of steel production within an international contest of nations, Ruttmann's wartime Ufa films DEUTSCHE WAFFENSCHMIEDEN and DEUTSCHE PANZER, both of which were screened at the Venice film festival in September 1940 before circulating as cultural and educational films, focused entirely on weapons production.[80] Commissioned by the Wehrmacht, these films – along with another lost film from the same year entitled DER WARTHEGAU (THE WARTHE DISTRICT) that appears to have celebrated the annexation of Poland[81] – formed part of a wave of military propaganda that ensued after the invasion of Poland in 1939, much of which focused in particular on the celebration of German tanks.[82]

Within this context, metal and arms production in particular became key topoi in the imaginary of a *Volksgemeinschaft* during wartime. The same year that Ruttmann made his wartime propaganda films, the Nazi party organized a campaign of national "metal donations" (Metallspende) for Hitler's birthday, in which they asked citizens to send in metal objects to be melted down for weapons production. The event formed the subject of another Ufa propaganda film from fall 1940, DIE GROSSE RESERVE (THE GREAT RESERVE) by Johannes Häussler and Walter Scheunemann. The film is now lost, but one reviewer described its contents as follows:

> Having grown to several tons, the collected metals are then taken to the foundries, where the pulsing power of the machines and the pounding of the giant hammers mold them into new forms. Suddenly, Uncle Otto's bowling trophy and that old copper bowl [...] are transformed into completely new things useful for the German people, such as grenade rings, cables, steel rope, steel straps, bullet rounds, gun barrels, torpedoes and canons! This job of transforming such apparently unimportant metals into useful objects is already in full swing. The soldiers on the front can count on the homeland [Heimat], for the homeland has the "great reserve." All of Germany has now become a giant weapons manufacturer, firmly clad with steel armor – and its will to victory is as hard as its steel![83]

This mobilization of the homeland for the war effort is also the central message of Ruttmann's films DEUTSCHE WAFFENSCHMIEDEN and DEUTSCHE PANZER. In this, all of these films could be understood as industrial counterparts to the contemporaneous melodramatic "homefront films" (*Heimatfrontfilme*) such as Eduard von Barsody's WUNSCHKONZERT (REQUEST CONCERT, 1940) or Rolf Hansen's DIE GROSSE LIEBE (THE GREAT LOVE, 1942),[84] which sought to enlist the efforts of the homeland in a common national battle. To this end, both DEUTSCHE WAFFENSCHMIEDEN and DEUTSCHE PANZER employ the conceit of the factory-worker-as-soldier, a totally disciplined citizen-warrior alongside the soldiers on the front. As the narrator for DEUTSCHE WAFFENSCHMIEDE puts it:

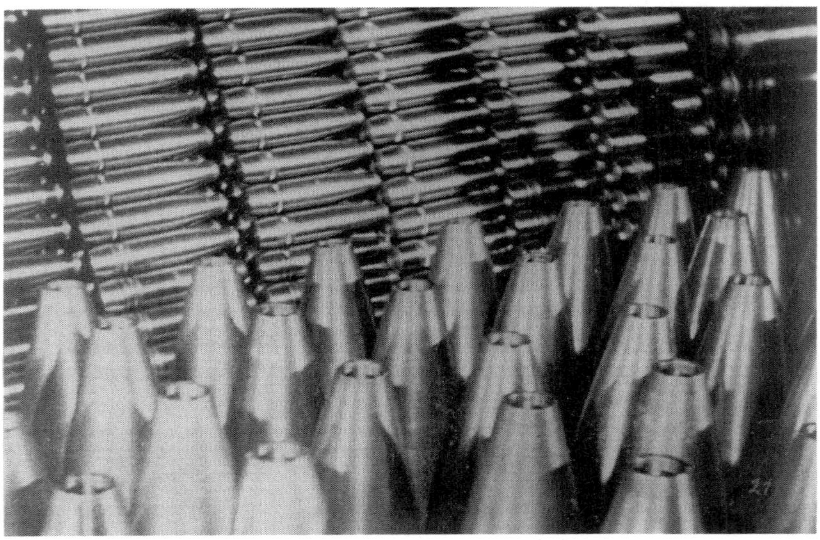

Still from Ruttmann, DEUTSCHE WAFFENSCHMIEDEN *(1940)*

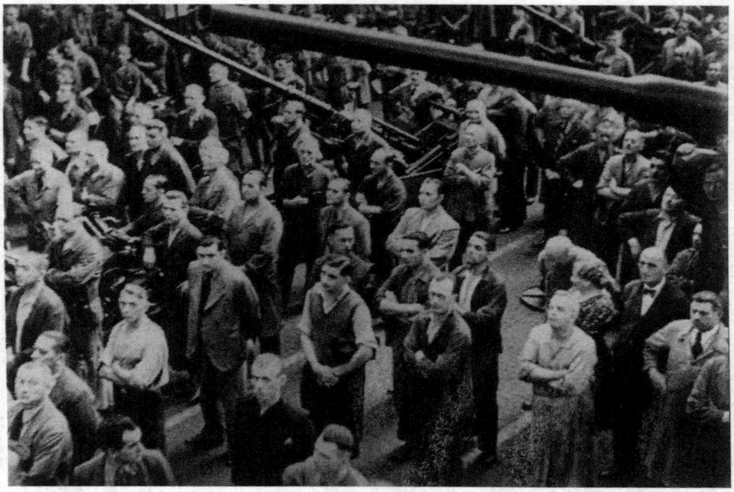

Still from Ruttmann, DEUTSCHE WAFFENSCHMIEDEN.
Factory workers as "sworn community"

> We are now a sworn community! Those are the Führer's words! Thus there are two soldiers today: the soldier manning artillery and the soldier manning the machine. They work man for man – in mines – furnaces – shipyards and factories – loyal to the command of the Führer![85]

A similar argument is made in DEUTSCHE PANZER at the end of the film, when a voice projected from the factory loudspeaker declares: "The men on the construction tables, who created this tank in tireless deployment [Einsatz], deserve the full recognition of the front and the homeland."[86] Within this framework, Ruttmann's films strive not only to meld the workers with the factory machinery as in the previous steel films (for example in a shot of a worker using the factory flames to light a cigarette in MANNESMANN), but to heroicize workers through repeated inserts of faces listening enraptured to the factory foreman or staring intensively at the production process.[87] Reminiscent of Leni Riefenstahl's mass choreography in TRIUMPH DES WILLENS, which repeatedly alternates between shots of mass formations and individual faces attentively looking toward the party leaders, Ruttmann's editing both individualizes workers and initiates them into the "sworn community" invoked by the narrator of DEUTSCHE WAFFENSCHMIEDEN. In contrast to the faces in FEIND IM BLUT, the worker-soldiers of Ruttmann's wartime films are not simply representatives of a biopolitical "population" with its statistical frequencies, but rather – like the enthralled children or the obedient workers of the Deutsche Arbeitsfront in Riefenstahl – members of a devoted *Volksgemeinschaft*.

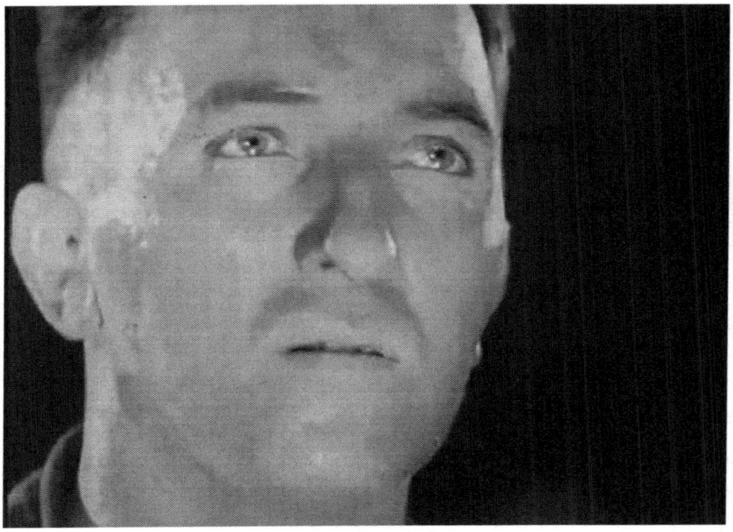

Still from Ruttmann, DEUTSCHE PANZER *(1940). Worker's face*

Above all, Ruttmann's wartime films sought to present an image of this "community" as a totally mobilized and coordinated national war machine. It is this notion of *coordination* – the *Gleichschaltung* of activities on the battlefield and the home front – that informs the presentation of national community in DEUTSCHE WAFFENSCHMIEDEN and DEUTSCH PANZER, finding its embodiment in the assembly process on the factory floor. In the following discussion, I focus in particular on the second film in order to demonstrate how this premium placed on coordination also impacted, once again, Ruttmann's self-presentation of the filmmaker as "expert," his use of montage and his presentation of film as a means of spectatorial training.

Of Ruttmann's wartime films, DEUTSCHE PANZER is the one most centrally focused on steel. From the opening credits with their monumental metallic hews to the many images of phallic drills, pumps and lathes moving rhythmically as they carve out the steel parts for the German tanks from blocks of metal on the assembly floor, steel forms the film's all-pervasive motif. Even more explicitly than the previous films, moreover, DEUTSCHE PANZER aligns this "forming" of steel parts with the activity of forging of a new national body through rigid discipline. This association becomes unmistakable in one prominent match cut, where Ruttmann juxtaposes the shot of a newly formed steel part being doused into water and spitting its last flames as it assumes its hardened form with a shot of young German athletes diving into a pool. As the sequence continues with shots of identically dressed Hitler Youth engaged in various group

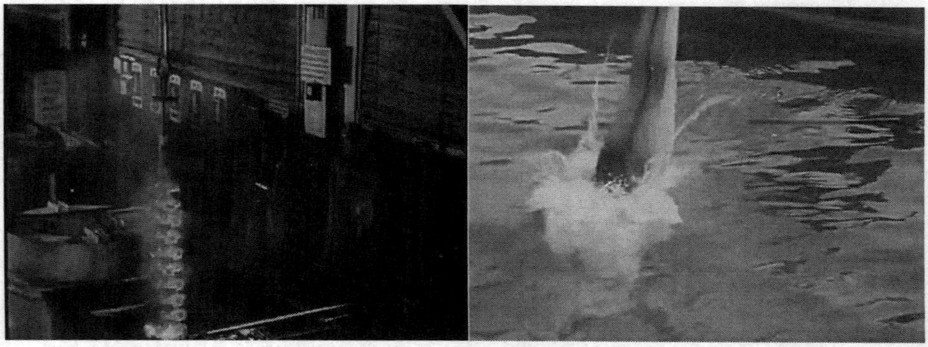

Stills from Ruttmann, Deutsche Panzer. *Montage of tank part and German athlete*

athletic activities, the argument is clear enough: athletic training is tantamount to a "steeling" of the docile body for battle, and young men are like tank parts that must be "formed" and assembled for national defense.

But Deutsche Panzer also, and perhaps more interestingly, thematizes training in another sense. Immediately after the athletic sequence, the film once again takes the audience into a classroom via another match cut between the Hitler youth lined up in military formation and a group of school children standing in formation in front of their desks. Only in this case, the classroom is part of a trade school designed to train students in the art of weapons engineering. As the children sit at their desks, the teacher shows them geometrical forms on the chalkboard and the camera then tracks and pans to take us from the classroom to an educational shopfloor below, where pupils receive hands-on training in the construction of model tanks from individual parts. Clearly, what we are seeing here is the training of tank designers rather than warriors on the front, the formation of worker-soldiers who will contribute to the war effort from the "construction table."

As an education in the construction of tanks from elementary parts, this training aims not to condition the body for battle, but to inculcate a capacity for what one can surely best call *montage,* understood as the assemblage and coordination of various parts within a larger system. Indeed, Ruttmann's film is all about a celebration of the engineer qua *monteur* as a quintessential player in the war effort, as one can see right from the beginning of the film. Following an opening image of a battlefield, where a line of tanks rolls toward the camera from the horizon, the film then takes us into the factory floor, where we see the lines of tank parts (metal hulls, canons, cogwheels, shells, etc.) in a series of lateral tracking shots. Such smooth tracking once again takes up the language of industrial film, but it also echoes the signature tracking shots used by Riefenstahl to film the geometrically aligned masses in Triumph des Willens. As in

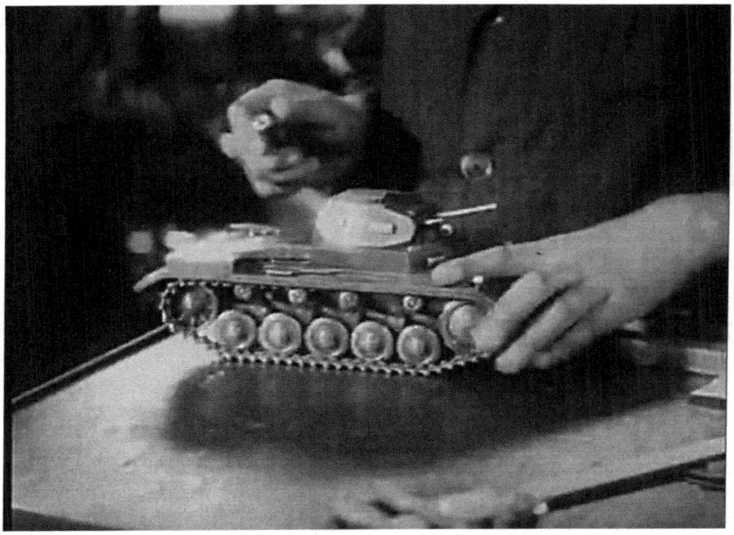

Still from Ruttmann, Deutsche Panzer. *Hands-on training in tank construction*

Riefenstahl, Ruttmann uses the tracking shot to emphasize the sheer mass of identical symmetrical formations arranged – like the tanks themselves – in military fashion. More significantly, these tracking shots of tank parts are immediately echoed, in Ruttmann's film, by a reverse tracking shot showing a line of identical engineer's drafting tables replete with design blueprints for the tanks – once again suggesting a vision of the engineer as "soldier" in the national battle. Into this configuration then comes the white-clad hand of the engineer himself, which can be seen tracing lines on the blueprint and unfolding the finalized plans for a completed tank.

Like the animated cross-sections of Mannesmann, the tank blueprints of the expert engineer in Deutsche Panzer fulfill a reflexive function. For it is the engineer's draft which, through the subsequent editing, appears literally to animate the weapons factory. After unrolling the finished design for the tank, the engineer's hand then folds it aside again to reveal – by means of a carefully constructed wipe – the first of many factory machines pumping in a coordinated rhythm as they realize the design laid out in the blueprints. Here too, one can draw a connection between the engineer and the artist. More specifically, the engineer's drafting table recalls the filmmaker's animation table, for example the table that Ruttmann himself had patented some 20 years earlier at the beginning of his career.[88] The artist as engineer was, of course, a recurrent topos among members of the constructivist avant-garde in the 1920s, who often depicted their aesthetics of *Gestaltung* (design or construction) and elementary

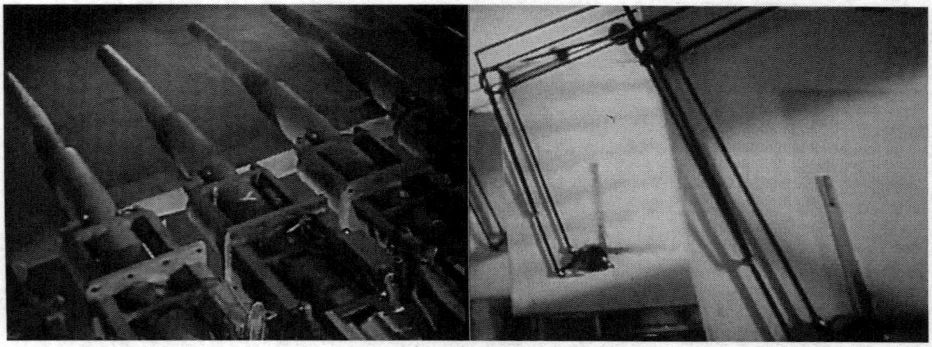

Stills from Ruttmann, DEUTSCHE PANZER. *Montage of tracking shots showing weapons and drafting tables*

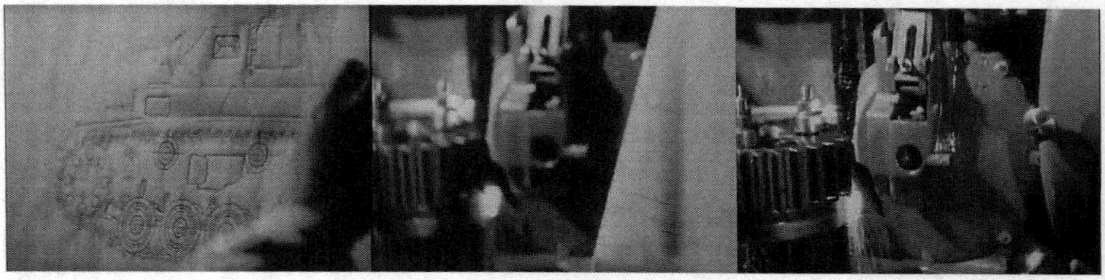

Stills from Ruttmann, DEUTSCHE PANZER. *Montage sequence: tank blueprints rolled back by engineer's hand to reveal factory parts in action*

forms as experiments undertaken within a horizon of practical application. The artist Werner Graeff, for example, in articles and illustrations for journals such as *De Stijl, G. Material zur elementaren Gestaltung,* or the Hungarian journal *Ma,* fashioned the image of the constructivist artist as an engineer who would intervene in the modern world through the design of automobiles and motorcycles. In its image of the drafting tables lined up in military ranks, DEUTSCHE PANZER mobilizes this well-established imagery of the artist-as-engineer for the nation at war. Armed with his drafting table, the artist-monteur would thus appear as the agent overseeing the coordination of tank production – a coordination carefully rendered in the tight montages of factory parts carving out the metal pieces of the tanks and workers assembling the final product.

However, the film is concerned not only with coordinating the activities of tank production, but also – as already suggested – with a broader coordination of the nation at war: i.e. the activities of factory (tank building), front (tanks on the battlefield) and homeland (the training of warriors and engineers). This function of national "coordination" is assumed above all by the radio in

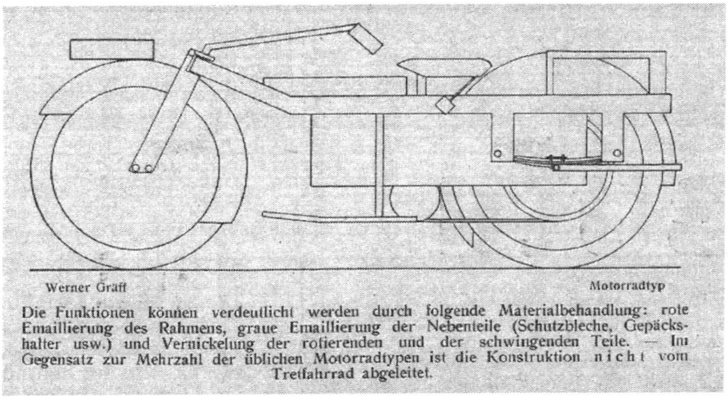

Werner Gräff, "Motorradtyp," from Ma *(1923)*

DEUTSCHE PANZER, which appears at the end of the film to announce a victory of the German tank division and recognize the role played by the "men on the construction tables" ("Männer am Konstruktionstisch") in Germany's war effort. Radio was, of course, one of the central media in Nazi fantasies of *Gleichschaltung* and the construction of a unified *Volksgemeinschaft*. As the Nazi radio propagandist Eugen Hadamovsky explained in his 1934 book *Der Rundfunk im Dienste der Volksführung* (*Radio in the Service of* Volk *Leadership*), radio could "create and make visible a *Volksgemeinschaft* linked by destiny, when millions of listeners in all of Germany's districts assemble before the loudspeakers as if they were marching together."[89] Molding the "millions of listeners" into a self-conscious "Volk," radio could thus fulfill the Nazi model of governance by transforming the solitary listener into a virtual soldier among other soldiers in disciplinary formation before the speaker. This is precisely what was visualized in a famous animated advertisement for the *Volksempfänger* (Nazism's home radio receiver), DIE SCHLACHT UM MIGGERSHAUSEN (THE BATTLE FOR MIGGERSHAUSEN, 1937), in which an army of radio apparatuses, summoned to action by a central antenna station, marches into the rural town of Miggershausen and issue the order: "Everyone participate in radio!" ("Nimmt Teil am Rundfunk alle!"). Radio becomes particularly important for mobilizing the home front for the war effort, as can be seen "home front films" such as *Wunschkonzert,* where the medium allows soldiers on the front and families at home to participate equally in war effort.[90]

Linking the heroic efforts of factory workers to those of the soldiers on the front, the radio loudspeaker in DEUTSCHE PANZER thus seems to connect the various parts of the nation within a collective military formation. As such, it offers another intermedial counterpart to the engineer's blueprints and, significantly, to Ruttmann's own filmic montage. Thus while DEUTSCHE PANZER thematizes the training in tank building, it also attempts to effectuate its own training of audiences in a certain mode of "coordinated" perception, one that would read the film's collection of images – from the factory, the battlefield, the athletic field and the school – as a unified and interconnected totality: an all-encompassing war machine, whose interlocking parts fit together with the snugness of a well-functioning tank. In this way, Ruttmann's spectators are enjoined to see themselves as members of a wartime disciplinary formation and their actions as part of this coordinated war machine.

Such a fantasy of the cinema recalls the famous theses on cinema and warfare by Paul Virilio. Among the many connections between war and cinema that Virilio outlined, not the least involves the parallels between the development of complex filmic techniques such as montage – in its capacity to weave together various times and locales – and the logistics of perception involved in modern warfare, where centers for information processing become necessary in order to coordinate the sheer mass of visual information that no single human eye or brain could process on its own.[91] To be sure, Virilio's provocative thesis on the parallels between technologies of war and the techniques of entertainment cinema are at times as reductive as the bleak historical metanarratives his readings tend to suggest. But the connections Virilio draws can, I believe, help us to understand the project of a wartime propaganda film like DEUTSCHE PANZER, which uses montage precisely to construct the vision of a national war machine based on the logistical coordination of disparate parts and different locals. Through devices of parallel and contrasting camera movement, wipes, eyelinematches and above all associative montage, the film encourages viewers to see shots taken in different locations as part of a coordinated system. More than a mere means of highlighting analogies between statistically comparable phenomena, the montage in DEUTSCHE PANZER is coded as an act of total mobilization, one relating weapons production to the production of engineers, Hitler Youth and worker-soldiers. Just as the film illustrates a certain training in the logistics of wartime engineering, so it attempts to effectuate a training in audience perception: to inculcate a mode of vision that constructs the nation as a war-machine, in which all of the parts must fulfill their dutiful task within a coordinated whole.

In contrast to Ruttmann's Weimar films, this montage of *Gleichschaltung* no longer allows for any acknowledgment of contingency, variety or individuation. Whereas montage films such as BERLIN, MELODIE DER WELT and even FEIND IM BLUT could still counterbalance their search for statistical regularities in mass society with a valorization of the heterogeneous detail, Ruttmann's armament films construct a vision of a social body totally planned, mobilized and coordinated from above by models, blueprints and the all-pervasive radio, one in which every part is meant to find its place and superfluous elements are quickly eliminated. The very motif of metalworking in DEUTSCHE PANZER seems to underscore this point. For in their endless repetition, nearly all of the machines in the tank factory share one central function: that of reducing machine parts to their elementary forms by scraping away excess material. This emphasis on the removal and disposal of excess should be understood as a symptom of the film's own desire to present wartime society and the war machine as an absolutely efficient management of energy and information, one in which friction, accidents, chance and individual details no longer have any place. If the motif recalls the image of Siegfried hammering out his sword in METALL DES HIMMELS, it also offers a distant echo of Ruttmann's early understanding of abstraction as a perceptual strategy for filtering out excess information. The difference is that the process of shaving away non-essential material and information is, after 1933, no longer seen simply as a means of individual adaptation to a world of mobile information flows, but rather stands in the service of a total mobilization, where parts are "formed" to find their place in a tightly coordinated system of interlocking gears and shots.

Conclusion: Molding the Masses

If Ruttmann's steel films have fascinated film historians, this is precisely because they seem to offer such echoes of his Weimar films while serving a very different ideological purpose. Like Ruttmann's OPUS films and his animated advertisements, the steel films show a predilection for elementary forms; like their animated predecessors, moreover, they display a particular fascination with morphing, where liquid material (paint or molten steel) appears to take shape as recognizable objects on the screen; and like Ruttmann's pre-1933 montage films, these films revel in clever "matches" of forms, movements, and actions. Such continuities between Weimar and National Socialism could be subsumed under terms like "Nazi Sachlichkeit," but Ruttmann's "experimental" aesthetics came to support a very different set of rhetorical and ideological arguments under Nazism: one bound up with contemporary notions of a Germanic "Formgefühl," a pathos of national planning after 1933, and the inculcation of an ethics of self-sacrifice for a society that was being "totally mobilized" for war.

This transformation was bound up with a new model of biopolitical discipline after 1933, one focused on the notion of "molding" and "sculpting" a people rather than basing public policy on the observation of statistical regularities. If Ruttmann showed such a predilection for steel, this was not only because of its formal qualities, but also – at least in part – because steel production embodied this new model of governing as molding. One might be tempted to describe steel production as a "metaphor" for Nazism's ideas about molding the national body, but the factory floor was itself a part – indeed a key part – of that process, a space in which both metal and bodies figured as raw material to be "molded" into an a coordinated national war machine.

Another key space within this process was the classroom, and with their repeated inclusion of classroom scenes – as well as the frequent comparisons of film to blueprints, plans and cross-sections – these films were at pains to represent Ruttmann's own medium as a *dispositif* for the execution of this "molding" process: a tool appropriate to an "educational state" in which individual welfare and individual pleasure were to be subordinated to a process of "education to community."[92] Like the Weimar films, Ruttmann's National Socialist films sought to conceive the medium as the locus of a certain "expertise," in which aesthetics could be made useful for sponsoring agencies. But this expertise no longer consisted in adapting perception to the flow of information or ordering the manifold appearances and data of mass culture. Rather, film now appears as a tool for national education. Even as they touted the benefits of steel production, these films also sought to advertise production in another sense: the production of the *Volk* by means of film itself.

Afterword: Of Good and Bad Objects

Like previous studies on Ruttmann, this one has had to contend with the "Mephisto" question I evoked in the introduction: namely, how to explain Ruttmann's turn from Weimar modernism to propaganda films under National Socialism. Was Ruttmann's commissioned work after 1933 simply a cover for pursuing aesthetic modernism? Was there a "fascist aesthetic" always already present in his Weimar films? While one can never fully ignore this question, I have tried to reframe its terms by suggesting that we approach Ruttmann less as a disinterested artist than as an "expert," who drew on other areas of expertise – motion studies, advertising design, statistics, traditions of scientific illustration, etc. – to fashion film as a "useful medium." In the process, this book has also followed the work of Malte Hagener and others to suggest that we need to expand and complicate our understanding of the interwar avant-garde, its history, its politics and its aesthetics. Part of that expanded view involves recognizing that for a large segment of the avant-garde, experimentation implied (and often entailed) practical applications in advertising and other spheres – applications that subtended the very definition of the avant-garde as a project for the reintegration of "art and life." Against this backdrop, one would do well to avoid seeing advertising or other commissioned work as a compromise of a purportedly "purist" or "absolute" – or inherently progressive – aesthetics of experimentation. As we have seen, the possibility for "applications" inhered in Ruttmann's experimental aesthetics *from the beginning*, just as they inhered in the experimental sciences on which he drew. For Ruttmann the nature of those applications played a secondary role to the effort to fashion the cinema as a means of expert intervention. They were, as he put it in his 1928 text "Die absolute Mode" ("The Absolute Fashion"), "a matter of indifference."[1]

Considering Ruttmann in this way, I believe, allows us to reformulate the questions of continuity and rupture posed above. On the one hand, Ruttmann was – as the title of this book suggests – concerned throughout his career with fashioning the cinema as a tool to manage multiplicity, and more specifically for the conceptualization and ordering of mass society. This might seem hardly surprising: as Grierson long ago recognized, Ruttmann's films were profoundly concerned with the mass nature of modern society and how to come to terms with it. But I hope that my analysis has elucidated more fully just what this concern meant for the way in which Ruttmann conceived of the medium: the forms of expertise his cinema drew upon, its intermedial positioning vis-à-vis other forms of visual culture, the tasks it envisioned for film as a means of governing and ordering perception, images and bodies, as well as the ways in which his cinema interpellated spectators as part of a mass. This is, I would suggest, the level at which we ought to look first for the "politics" of Ruttmann's filmmaking: by seeing how that filmmaking was bound up with ideas about governance, biopolitics and the regulation of perception and bodies in mass modernity.

On the other hand, I have also insisted on the differences – ideological and aesthetic – between Ruttmann's Weimar films and his films for National Socialism. While Ruttmann always drew on forms of "expertise" for the ordering of mass society, the way in which the masses and their governance could be conceived changed profoundly between Weimar and National Socialism. Whereas Weimar thought and culture valorized multiplicity and contingency, Nazism sought to eliminate contingency and reduce multiplicity through a restricted concept of a populace grounded in the "blood" and the "soil"; where Weimar policy used statistics to generate knowledge about probabilities and tendencies within the population, Nazism sought to verify the existence of a racial *Volkskörper*; whereas Weimar modernity sought to direct the movements of production and consumption through Fordist notions of efficiency and "resonance," Nazism sought to control them absolutely through a model of total mobilization, total discipline and total coordination (*Gleichschaltung*); finally, whereas Weimar's welfare-state democracy implied a government for individuals, Nazism demanded the sacrifice of the individual to the *Volksgemeinschaft*. If many of Ruttmann's post-1933 films can be understood as "fascist," this is not because they applied experimental film to social and political tasks (something he had been doing all along), but rather because they fashioned film as an instrument for governance according to fascist precepts, creating "management images" for *this* conception of the masses.

This reading of "fascist aesthetics" is obviously somewhat different from readings deriving from the Frankfurt School. Writing around the same time Ruttmann made METALL DES HIMMELS, Walter Benjamin famously hoped that filmic technology, and montage in particular, would inculcate a progressive form of reception, one that would oppose fascism's efforts to "aestheticize" politics with the (progressive) politicization of aesthetic experience via a Dadaistic rupture of continuity. Ruttmann's critics – building upon Kracauer's critiques – have often suggested that his montage, with its privileging of abstract or formal properties over ethical content, performed just the opposite function, aestheticizing and anesthetizing city life in BERLIN or the realities of war and destruction in films such as DEUTSCHE PANZER.[2] Of course, from the point of view of a film history invested in the notion of an autonomous high modernism, one could just as easily turn the equation around and reproach Ruttmann (along with his counterparts on the left) for "politicizing" a modernist aesthetics that should have remained autonomous.[3] It is this investment in high modernism, one suspects, that drives readings of Ruttmann's turn toward photographic realism as a move that "prepared the way for National Socialist art."[4] The argument in this book would suggest that neither "realism" nor "formalism" is inherently "reactionary," let alone "fascist," no more than statistics, bureaucracy or biopolitics are in and of themselves fascist phenomena. If we take seriously the intertwining of aesthetics and politics, understanding that experimental aesthetics were always bound up with possible "applications," then terms such as "aestheticization" and "politicization" make little sense; like the design aesthetics outlined by Rancière, Ruttmann's aesthetics were "political" from the beginning, bound up as they were with ideas about the regulation of perception and bodies in mass society.

Indeed, far from constituting an autonomous realm of aesthetic experience removed from power and politics, the "abstract" is the very locus of "useful" image making in Ruttmann; nearly all of the forms of scientific imaging that his films drew on – from motion curves to visual statistics to blueprints and cross-sections – were characterized precisely by their conceit of "abstracting" from the detail of normal perception and the "indexical" photograph, and this is precisely what made them models of expert management and regulation.[5] As we have seen, such moments of abstraction in Ruttmann's films – the statistical dimension in BERLIN and MELODIE DER WELT, the use of visual statistics and types in the medical films and the use of plans and blueprints in Ruttmann's steel films – repeatedly function as a means of ordering the motley collection of photographic images his montage brings together. In this way, his films "enact" modalities of governmentality in mass society from Weimar to National Socialism.

When Ruttmann's aesthetics are understood in this way, the appropriate question is no longer whether Ruttmann aestheticized politics or politicized aesthetics, but rather what kind of politics of the image is taking place: what kind of governance is being proposed, what kind of body politic imagined, what forms of "expertise" mobilized and so on. In a sense, such an approach might seem like a return to Susan Sontag's definition of the "fascist aesthetic" from nearly four decades ago, when she equated the term above all with certain motifs including the cult of death, the emphasis on purity and physical perfection, the championing of containment and control, the fascination with ecstatic participation, the submission to authority, etc.[6] Many of these ideological topoi can be found in Ruttmann's post-1933 films. But we can also go beyond such a motif study to argue that films such as BLUT UND BODEN, METALL DES HIMMELS and DEUTSCHE PANZER contain fascist elements to the extent that they attempt to *present Ruttmann's own medium* as a means of National Socialist governance, transforming the animation table into the drafting table for the new society.

Indeed, it is worth pausing here at the close of this book to compare the two tables from the beginning and the end of Ruttmann's career more closely in

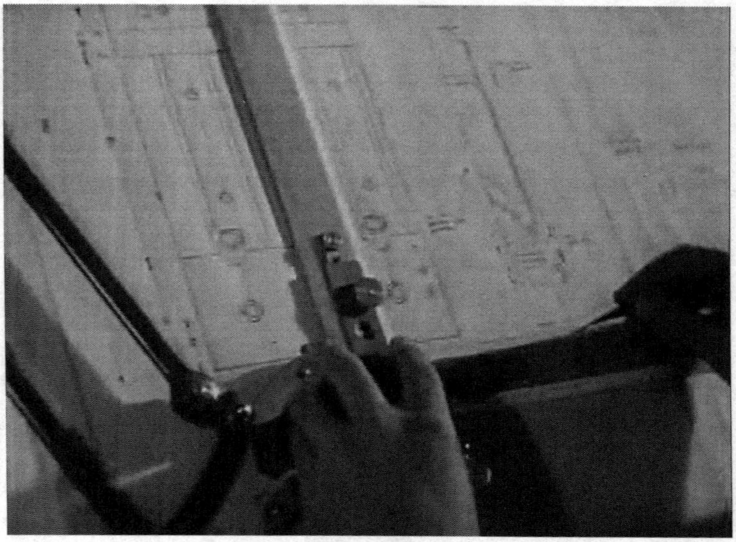

Still from Ruttmann, DEUTSCHE PANZER. *Drafting table*

order to consider how his conception of the filmic apparatus changed. In my reading of DEUTSCHE PANZER above, I suggested that the engineer's table in that film might be seen as a reflexive representation of the filmmaker at work, a kind of distant echo of the animation table Ruttmann patented in 1919. But there is a crucial difference in the two apparatuses. Everything about Ruttmann's animation table resisted finality. The table was to be equipped with three transparent plates, two of which were adjustable (one from right to left, the other up and down) so as to allow for the creation of movement parallel to the screen, movement in and out of depth, and the movement of objects in and out of focus (a technique Ruttmann used in films such as DAS WIEDERGEFUNDENE PARADIES and DER AUFSTIEG). In addition, Ruttmann called for adjustable lights and, most importantly, the use of slow-drying paint (*feuchtbleibende Farbe*) that would allow for the maximum transformation of the forms and objects represented at minimum cost. The goal of all of these movable and transformable components was clear:

> Through changes in the represented objects, combined with corresponding changes in the lighting of the glass plates, as well as changes attainable by means of adjustments in the placement of the plates, one can produce the most diversified [mannigfaltigsten], idiosyncratic [eigenartigsten] and vibrant cinematographic images in accordance with eminently individual artistic influences.[7]

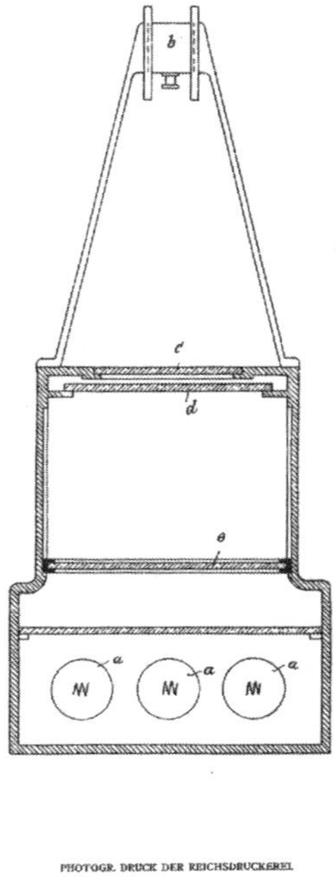

Ruttmann, schematic drawing of animation table (1919)

Compared to this apparatus of variety and transformation, the drafting table in DEUTSCHE PANZER presents a single goal – the tank, or rather a series of identical tanks – around which all national production is coordinated and synchronized. This comparison also speaks to a distinction in the aesthetics of Ruttmann's work before and after 1933. Although, as we saw, Ruttmann's steel films take up a certain interest in abstraction and morphing familiar from his Weimar advertisements, this interest is subordinated to narratives of "forming" in which molten material is only celebrated in as much as it can be subdued and "forced" to assume the form of industrial products or weapons understood as the expressions of national productivity and a Germanic capacity for forming. Within this context, the path between abstraction and figuration now becomes a one-way street; unlike Ruttmann's Weimar advertisements, which shuttled back and forth between abstract material (wet paint) and provisionally recognizable forms, his National Socialist films display processes leading from raw material (molten metal) to finished product (sword, tank, fighter or *Volk*), whose "beauty of form" these films were meant to display. In other words, the playful element of Ruttmann's Weimar advertisements, their pleasure in the making and unmaking of forms, has ceded to a rigidly controlled ideology of "forming" the nation according to the centralized schema of *Gleichschaltung*.

One could make similar comparisons in terms of audiences. As I suggested in chapter 1, a paradigmatic example of the spectator Ruttmann imagined for his rhythmical animation can be seen in the image of the AEG radio listener in SPIEL DER WELLEN (PLAY OF THE WAVES), smiling as he rocks back and forth in resonance with the radio waves. A similar movement can be seen in DER AUFSTIEG (THE ASCENSION), in which the Gesolei logo literally appears to order the frenetic and conflictual movements associated with warfare and inflation into isorhythmical waves, with which the central figure resonates as he turns flips on a hand bar. As representatives of "rhythmical" media experience, these figures can hardly be described as subversive or resistant to the culture industry (indeed they stand as icons of the supposed power of rhythm stimulate capitalist consumption). But they differ from the paradigmatic classroom audiences of Ruttmann's films after 1933. To begin with, they are individual figures, whereas Ruttmann later work imagines the audience as a collection of identical spectators lined up in disciplinary formation. Secondly, the earlier films insist – as did the advertising theory of the day – on the spectator's pleasure (all of the figures in the animated advertisements smile), whereas the National Socialist films will emphasize the spectator's duty to an authoritative state.

This transformation in Ruttmann's conception of the *dispositif* of sponsored film before and after 1933 underscores another point I want to emphasize in closing. While I have argued that Ruttmann's experimental aesthetics always occurred within a horizon of applications, this book is in no way intended as an effort to condemn experimental film culture, or Ruttmann's own experimental films, as a whole. Film theory was long invested in a project of depreciating filmic experience and deflating the "good object," an undertaking embodied perhaps most famously by Christian Metz's self-described struggle to overcome his own love for Hollywood cinema in order to "disengage the cinema-object from the imaginary and win it for the symbolic." Now that celluloid is no longer the dominant medium of moving images, cinephelia has returned in force, along with phenomenological and philosophical approaches that highlight film's power to transform everyday vision and consciousness. No doubt, this context helps to explain, at least in part, the renewed fascination today with Ruttmann's Bergsonian experiments in visual music. As someone who regularly teaches experimental film, I am familiar with – and still believe in – the ability of such experiments to expand everyday vision, and this book is not intended to delegitimate that experience. Indeed, far from seeing a "fascist" aesthetic at work in Ruttmann's Weimar films, my own experience of those films is still a mix of fascination (the OPUS films), exhilaration (BERLIN) and even delight (the advertisements).

On the other hand, as a film and cultural historian, I have attempted to say something more and something new about the networks of discourse and practice in which those films emerged, as well as the ramification of such an analysis for our understanding of experimental film culture between the wars. While this project has led me to argue for a continuity in Ruttmann's professional self-understanding as a commissioned filmmaker from Weimar and National Socialism, the recognition of this continuity, far from encouraging a wholesale condemnation of Ruttmann's Weimar films, can allow us to gain a more informed appreciation of their specificity. To my mind, a film such as BERLIN. DIE SINFONIE DER GROSSSTADT, with its intricate weaving of contingency and order, still stands as an icon of Weimar mass modernity in its complexity. It is precisely this complexity – along with the uncertainty and contingencies of democratic governance and economics – that Nazism sought to eliminate, and the reduction of complexity can be felt in Ruttmann's later films when they replace statistical probabilities with (racial) certainties, contain cross-sectional montage with didactic "demonstrations" and subordinate the particular to an all-powerful authority.[8] If there is a tragedy in Ruttmann's trajectory, it is not that his films were "fascist" all along. Nor is it that he "politicized" modernist art through sponsored filmmaking. Rather, I would argue that it is a more pedestrian one, residing in Ruttmann's own "indifference" to the objects of his applied filmmaking. On one level, this thought rejoins Kracauer's argument that Ruttmann's formalism betrayed an incapacity for ethical or political considerations. However, that problematic "formalism" is best understood not as an aesthetic phenomenon removed from "life," but rather as one that engaged with forms of power and knowledge specific to modern mass society. Rather than continuing to speak of Ruttmann as a "formalist," it might be more apt today to describe him as an "expert," one whose interest in modern forms of expertise led both to an astounding number of innovations and, ultimately, to his downfall.

Notes

Introduction: Avant-Garde, Advertising and the Managing of Multiplicity

1. From their initial screenings onward, the *Opus* films were celebrated as examples of avant-garde formalism. See Bernhard Diebold, "Eine neue Kunst. Die Augenmusik des Films" (1921), in *Film als Film*, ed. Birgit Hein and Wulf Herzogenrath (Cologne: Kölnischer Kunstverein, 1977), 16-17; Diebold, "Der gemalte Film" (1922), in *Walter Ruttmann. Eine Dokumentation*, ed. Jeanpaul Goergen (Berlin: Deutsche Kinemathek, 1989), 101; Adolf Behne, "Der Film als Kunstwerk" (1922), in *Film als Film*, 20-21; Rudolf Kurtz, *Expressionismus und Film* (1926), hg. Christian Kleining and Ulrich Johannes Bell (Berlin: Chronos, 1997), 100-103; Rudolf Schneider, "Formspiel durch Kino" (1926), in *Film als Film*, 28-29. Subsequent film historians canonized Ruttmann's abstract films, along with those of Viking Eggeling and Hans Richter, as pioneering works in the history of experimental or "underground film." See for example Friedrich Zglienicki, *Der Weg des Films. Die Geschichte der Kinematographie und ihrer Vorläufer* (Berlin: Rembrandt, 1956), 597. Birgit Hein, *Film im Underground* (Berlin: Ullstein, 1971), 27; Jean Mitry, *Le cinéma expérimental* (Paris: Seghers, 1974), 85; Hans Schleugl and Ernst Schmidt Jr., *Eine Subgeschichte des Films. Lexikon des Avantgarde-, Experimental- und Undergroundfilms*, vol. 2 (Frankfurt am Main: Surhkamp, 1974), 796-804; Standish Lawder, *The Cubist Cinema* (New York: New York University Press, 1975), 57-64; Hans Steike, "Walter Ruttmann," in *Film als Film*, 61-63; Malcolm LeGrice, *Abstract Film and Beyond* (Cambridge: MIT Press, 1977), 15-31; Michael O'Pray, *Avant-Garde Film. Forms, Themes and Passions* (New York: Columbia University Press, 2003), 17; A. L. Rees, "Frames and Windows: Visual Space in Abstract Cinema," in *Avant-Garde Film*, ed. Alexander Graf and Dietrich Scheunemann (Amsterdam: Rodolpi, 2007), 55-77; Laurent Guido, *L'Age du rythme. Cinéma, musicalité et culture du corps dans les theories françaises des années 1910-1930* (Lausanne: Payot, 2007), 152-153; Bruce Elder, *Harmony and Dissent* (Waterloo: Wilfrid Laurier Universtiy Press, 2008), 116-124; Joel Westerdale, "The Musical Pomise of Abstract Film," in *The Many Faces of Weimar Cinema. Rediscovering Germany's Filmic Legacy*, ed. Christian Rogowski (Rochester: Camden House, 2010), 153-167. Several film historians have argued that Ruttmann's *Lichtspiel Opus I* was, in fact, the first abstract film ever shown publically. See for example Zglienicki, *Der Weg des Films*, 597; Wulf Herzogenrath, "Wer war der Erste?," in *Film als Film*, 9-10; Jeanpaul Goergen, "Walter Ruttmann – Ein Porträt," in *Walter Ruttmann. Eine Dokumentation*, 22; Walter Schobert, "'Painting in Time' and 'Visual Music': On German Avant-Garde Films of the 1920s," in *Expressionist Film—New Perspectives*, ed. Dietrich Scheunemann (Rochester: Camden House, 2003), 238. For discussions of Ruttmann's *Opus* films within the history of animation, see Esther Leslie, *Hollywood Flatlands. Animation, Critical Theory and the Avant-Garde* (London: Verso, 2002), 46-75; Donald Crafton, *Before*

Mickey. The Animated Film 1898-1928 (Chicago: University of Chicago Press 1993), 232-234; Anika Schönemann, *Der deutsche Animationsfilm von den Anfängen bis zur Gegenwart, 1909-2001* (Sankt Augustin: Gardez! 2003), 114-121.

2. Even Ruttmann's earliest critics Siegfried Kracauer and John Grierson recognized the importance of Ruttmann in this respect. See Siegfried Kracauer, "Wir schaffens" (1927) in *Werke 6.1. Kleine Schriften zum Film 1921-1927* (Frankfurt am Main: Suhrkamp, 2004), 411-413; John Grierson, "First Principles of Documentary" (1932), in *Grierson on Documentary* (Berkeley: University of California Press, 1966), 145-156. For subsequent readings of BERLIN within the history of documentary form, see for example Matthew Bernstein, "Visual Style and Spatial Articulations in *Berlin, Symphony of a City* (1927)," *Journal of Film and Video* 36:4 (1984): 5-12; Jack Ellis and Betsy McLane, *A New History of Documentary Film* (New York: Continuum, 2006), 49-53; Patricia Aufderheide, *Documentary Film. A Very Short Introduction* (Oxford: Oxford University Press, 2007), 14-16. Other critics have read BERLIN as an extension of Ruttmann's early experimental work. See for example Jiri Kolaja and Arnold Foster, "*Berlin, the Symphony of a City* as a Theme of Visual Rhythm," *The Journal of Aesthetics and Art Criticism* 23:3 (1965): 353-358; David Macrae, "Ruttmann, Rhythm, and 'Reality': A Response to Siegfried Kracauer's Interpretation of BERLIN. THE SYMPHONY OF A GREAT CITY," in *Expressionist Film. New Perspectives*, 251-271.
3. Readings of BERLIN as a document of urban and/or Weimar modernity include Michael Minden, "The City in Early Cinema: *Metropolis, Berlin* and *October*," in *Unreal City. Urban Experience in Modern European Literature and Art*, ed. Edward Timms and David Kelley (Manchester: Manchester University Press, 1985), 193-213; Sabine Hake, "Urban Spectacle in Walter Ruttmann's *Berlin, Symphony of the Big City*," in *Dancing on the Volcano. Essays on the Culture of the Weimar Republic*, ed. Thomas W. Kniesche and Stephen Brockmann (Columbia: Camden House, 1994), 127-142; Anke Gleber, "Female Flanerie and the Symphony of the City," in *Women in the Metropolis. Gender and Modernity in Weimar Culture*, ed. Katharina von Ankum (Berkeley: University of California Press, 1997), 67-88; Anton Kaes, "Leaving Home: Film, Migration, and the Urban Experience," *New German Critique* 74 (1998): 179-92; Janet Ward, *Weimar Surfaces. Urban Visual Culture in 1920s Germany* (Berkeley: California University Press, 2001), 161-163; Carsten Strathausen, "Uncanny Spaces: The City in Ruttmann and Vertov," in *Screening the City*, ed. Mark Shiel and Tony Fitzmaurice (London and New York: Verso, 2003), 15-40; Derek Hillard, "Walter Ruttmann's Janus-Faced View of Modernity: The Ambivalence of Description in *Berlin. Die Sinfonie der Grossstadt*," *Monatshefte für deutschsprachige Literatur und Kultur* 96:1 (2004): 78-92; Eric Weitz, *Weimar Germany. Promise and Tragedy* (Princeton: Princeton University Press, 2007), 230-231; Nora Alter, "Berlin, Symphony of a Great City," in *Weimar Cinema. An Essential Guide to Classic Films of the Era*, ed. Noah Eisenberg (New York: Columbia University Press, 2009), 193-217; Sabine Hake, *Topographies of Class. Modern Architecture and Mass Society in Weimar Berlin* (Ann Arbor: University of Michigan Press, 2008), 242-274.
4. Recent "remakes" include Thomas Schad's BERLIN. SINFONIE EINER GROSSSTADT (2001) and Harun Farocki's GEGEN-MUSIK (2004).
5. On Ruttmann as a precursor to video art, see Holly Rogers, "The Unification of the Senses: Intermediality in Video Art-Music," *Journal of the Royal Musical Association* 136:2 (2011): 399-428. For a reading of Ruttmann as a pioneer of multimedia art, see

Gregory Zinman, "Analog Circuit Palettes, Cathode Ray Canvases: Digital's Analog, Experimental Past," *Film History* 24:2 (2012): 135-157.

6. The major catalyst for research into Ruttmann's post-1933 work was Barry A. Fulks, "Walter Ruttmann, the Avant-Garde Film, and Nazi Modernism," *Film and History* 14:2 (1984): 26-35. Subsequent publications on Ruttmann's films under National Socialism include Martin Loiperdinger, "Neue Sachlichkeit und Nationalsozialismus. Zur Ambivalenz von Walter Ruttmanns Filmen für das Dritte Reich," in *Perspektiven des Dokumentarfilms,* ed. Manfred Hattendorf, *Diskurs film* no. 7 (1995): 43-56; Peter Zimmermann, "Neusachlicher Technikkult und 'stählerne Romantik'. Walter Ruttmanns Symphonien der Industriearbeit," in *Geschichte des dokumentarischen Films in Deutschland. Band 3: 'Drittes Reich' 1933-1945,* ed. Peter Zimmerann and Kay Hoffmann (Stuttgart: Reclam, 2005), 231-241; William Uricchio, "Ruttmann nach 1933," in *Walter Ruttmann. Eine Dokumentation,* 59-65; Imbert Schenk, "Walter Ruttmanns Kultur- und Industriefilme," in *Mediale Mobilmachung I. Das Dritte Reich und der Film,* ed. Harro Segeberg (Munich: Wilhelm Fink, 2005), 103-128.
7. The only extended study on Ruttmann in English is Barry Fulks's dissertation *Film Culture and Kulturfilm. Walter Ruttmann, the Avant-Garde Film, and the Kulturfilm in Weimar Germany and the Third Reich* (PhD diss., University of Wisconsin, Madison, 1982), on which the above cited article was based. Another important study worth mentioning here is William Uricchio's dissertation *Ruttmann's "Berlin" and the City Film to 1930* (PhD diss., New York University, 1981).
8. Adrianus van Domburg. *Walter Ruttmann in het beginsel* (Purmerend: Nederlands Filminstituut, 1956); Jeanpaul Goergen (ed.), *Walter Ruttmann. Eine Dokumentation;* Leondaro Quaresima (ed.), *Walter Ruttmann. Cinema, pittura, ars acustica* (Trento: Manfrini, 1994).
9. Goergen's volume includes a lengthy biographical essay by Goergen himself focusing on Ruttmann's place within the international avant-garde, as well as essays by Fulks and Uricchio on Ruttmann's work after 1933. Quaresima's volume includes several essays on Ruttmann's work from the 1920s focusing on topics ranging from abstract animation to sound montage, as well as several essays on the *Kulturfilm* and on Ruttmann's modernist aesthetics under Nazism.
10. See Jeanpaul Goergen, "Walter Ruttmann – Ein Porträt," in *Walter Ruttmann. Eine Dokumentation,* 37.
11. See for example Uricchio, "Ruttmann nach 1933," 59.
12. Jeanpaul Goergen has suggested understanding Ruttmann's confinement to advertising film after 1933 as a self-imposed "isolation" that allowed the artist to continue persuing formalist aesthetics under certain constraints. See Goergen, "Walter Ruttmann – Ein Porträt," 41. Around the same time, Martin Loiperdinger argued that Ruttmann's experimental aesthetics in fact stood at cross purposes with Nazi ideology, even functioning to "ironize" the ideological projects of films such as METALL DES HIMMELS (1934) or DEUTSCHE PANZER (1940). See Loiperdinger, "Neue Sachlichkeit und Nationalsozialismus," 53. Similar arguments have been made for other avant-garde filmmakers. In her study on German advertising films of the 1920s and 30s, for example, Ingrid Westbrock argued that advertising offered a space where a filmmakers such as Fischinger could continue to experiment in abstract forms without being classified as "degenerate art." See Westbrock, *Der Werbefilm. Ein Beitrag zur Entwicklungsgeschichte des Genres vom Stummfilm zum frühen Tonfilm* (Hildesheim:

Georg Olms, 1983), 95-96. William Moritz made similar arguments about Fischinger and the animator Hans Fischerkoesen. See Moritz, *Optical Poetry. The Life and Work of Oskar Fischinger* (Bloomington: Indiana University Press, 2004), 51-54; ibid., "Resistance and Subversion in Animated Films of the Nazi Era: The Case of Hans Fischerkoesen," in *A Reader in Animation Studies*, ed. Jayne Pilling (Sydney: John Libbey, 1997), 228-240.

13. See Fulks, "Walter Ruttmann, the Avant-Garde Film, and Nazi Modernism"; Uricchio, "Ruttmann nach 1933," 60; Leonardo Quaresima, "Walter Ruttmann e la mobilità del moderno," in *Walter Ruttmann. Cinema, pittura, ars acustica*, 15-50; Schenk, "Walter Ruttmanns Kultur- und Industriefilme." For the term "Nazi Sachlichkeit," see Fulks, "Walter Ruttmann, the Avant-Garde Film and Nazi Modernism," 26; Schenk, 122. Both Schenk and Quaresima invoke Jefferey Herf's concept of "reactionary modernism" to argue that avant-garde aesthetics were compatable with a certain strand of Nazi thought and ideology, and Quaresima specifically criticizes Loiperdinger's efforts to pinpoint a subversive moment in Ruttmann's post-1933 films. See Quaresima, "Walter Ruttmann et la mobilità del moderno," 29. Quaresima also criticizes Fulks's notion of "Nazi Sachlichkeit" for its implications that Ruttmann's Weimar films were protofascist (25-26), but he himself insists on the continuity of a reactionary modernism – manifested in a struggle between organic and machinic forms – running throughout Ruttmann's Weimar work and his work after 1933 (34-48). For a critique of Goergen's take on Ruttmann's Nazi films as a form of "inner emigration," see Zimmermann, "Neusachlicher Technikkult und 'stählerne Romantik,'" 236.
14. For example, Goergen's essay "Walter Ruttmann: Ein Porträt" situates Ruttmann within a "großem kunsthistorischen Zusammenhang" (28), emphasizing Ruttmann's connections to figures such as Marcel Duchamp (20), Leopold Survage (20), Philippe Soupault (23), James Joyce (28), László Moholy-Nagy (31) and others. Ruttmann appears in turns as a Futurist, a Dadaist, a Surrealist, and a representative of high modernism.
15. See Ruttmann's texts "Kunst und Kino" (undated manuscript), in *Walter Ruttmann. Eine documentation*, 73; "Malerei mit Zeit" (undated manuscript), in *Walter Ruttmann. Eine Dokumentation*, 73-74; "Kino als Kunst" (1925), in *Walter Ruttmann. Eine Dokumentation*, 78; "Mein neuer Film" (1926), in *Walter Ruttmann. Eine Dokumentation*, 78.
16. Ruttmann's BERLIN film was commissioned by Fox Europa as a so-called "Kontingenzfilm" (contingency film) designed to help the company increase the number of American films shown in Germany. On contingency films in the Weimar Republic, see Sabine Hake, *German National Cinema* (London: Routledge, 2007), 32.
17. For an overview of the advertising work of Weimar avant-garde filmmakers, see Westbrock, *Der Werbefilm*; Sabine Hake, "Das Kino, die Werbung und die Avantgarde," in *Die Spur durch den Spiegel. Der Film in der Kultur der Moderne*, ed. Malte Hagener, Johann Schmidt and Michael Wedel (Berlin: Bertz, 2004), 193-206. For a more recent discussion of Seeber's advertising film in the context of Weimar advertising theory, see Michael Cowan, "Advertising, Rhythm and the Avant-Garde in Weimar: Guido Seeber and Julius Pinschewer's *Kipho* Film," *October* 131 (2010): 23-50; a similar discussion of Reiniger can be found in Cowan, "The Ambivalence of Ornament: Silhouette Advertisements in Print and Film in Early-Twentieth-Century

Germany," *Art History* 36:4 (2013): 784-809; on Richter, see Yvonne Zimmermann, "A Missing Chapter: The Swiss Films and Richter's Documentary Practice," in *Hans Richter: Encounters,* Exhibition catalogue, ed. Timothy O. Benson (Los Angeles: Los Angeles County Museum of Art, 2013), 108-119.

18. See Thomas Elsaesser and Malte Hagener, "6. September. Walter Ruttmann: 1929," in *1929. Beiträge zur Archäologie der Medien,* ed. Stefan Andriopoulos and Bernhard Dotzler (Frankfurt am Main: Suhrkamp, 2002), 326-327.
19. Malte Hagener, *Moving Forward, Looking Back. The European Avant-Garde and the Invention of Film Culture 1919-1939* (Amsterdam: Amsterdam University Press, 2007), 77-121. As Hagener argues, the relation between the avant-garde and industry was never defined by a simple opposition, but rather by a mutual dependency and a dialectics of attraction and repulsion that also defined the relation of "art" and "life" among the avant-garde (52).
20. See Jacques Rancière, "The Aesthetic Revolution and its Outcomes," ed. and trans. Steven Corcoran, in *Dissensus. On Politics and Aesthetics* (London: Continuum, 2010), 115. See also Hagener, *Moving Forward, Looking Back,* 62-68.
21. "[D]araus erklärt sich die Tatsache, dass [Ruttmann] in Auftragsfilmen keine Einschränkung seiner künstlerischen Freiheit erkennen konnte, sondern darin seine eigentliche Bestimmung sah." Elsasser/Hagener, "6. September. Walter Ruttmann," 342.
22. Andreas Huyssen, *After the Great Divide. Modernism, Mass Culture, Postmodernism* (Bloomington: Indiana University Press, 1986), viii. Huyssen argued for a distinction between "avant-garde" (which engaged with popular culture) and "high modernism" (which sought to distinguish itself from popular culture).
23. See *Useful Cinema,* ed. Charles Acland and Haidee Wasson (Durham: Duke University Press, 2006). Other important volumes include *Films That Work. Industrial Film and the Productivity of Media,* ed. Vinzenz Hediger and Patrick Vonderau (Amsterdam: Amsterdam University Press, 2009); *Learning with the Lights off. Educational Film in the United States,* ed. Devin Orgeron, Marsha Orgeron and Dan Streible (Oxford: Oxford University Press, 2012). In German, the most important publication in this area is 2005 series *Geschichte des dokumentarischen Films in Deutschland* (volumes cited individually throughout this book).
24. Elsaesser proposed that historians of sponsored film focus on what he dubs the three A's: *Auftraggeber* (the commissioning body), *Anlass* (the occasion and purpose for which it was made) and *Anwendung* (the film's intended use). See Thomas Elsaesser, "Die Stadt von morgen. Filme zum Bauen und Wohnen," in *Geschichte des dokumentarischen Films in Deutschland, Band 2. Weimarer Republik 1918-1933,* ed. Klaus Kreimeier, Antje Ehmann and Jeanpaul Goergen (Stuttgart: Reclam, 2005), 381-409. For further discussion of this concept, see Elsaesser, "Archives and Archeologies: The Place of Non-Fiction Film in Contemporary Media," in *Films That Work,* 23; Vinzenz Hediger and Patrick Vonderau, "Introduction," in *Films That Work,* 8-16. In the same volume, Hediger and Vonderau develop Elsaesser's paradigm to examine more broadly how industrial film, as a form, contributes to the governance of industrial organizations. Under the rubric of the three R's, they ask how films contribute to governance through recording (creation of memory and archives), rhetoric (the persuasion of workers to identify as part of the corporate community)

and rationality (improving institutional performance). See Vinzenz Hediger and Patrick Vonderau, "Record, Rhetoric and Rationalization," in *Films That Work*, 35-51.

25. Elsaesser/Hagener, "6. September. Walter Ruttmann," 344.
26. On the frequent difficulty of answering such questions, see Elsaesser, "Archives and Archeologies," 24.
27. Examples that will be treated in the chapters below include the frequent representations of "shocks" and "accidents" in advertising films such as DER SIEGER (THE VICTOR, 1921) or MANNESMANN (1937); the concern with contingency that runs throughout Ruttmann's photographic films from the Weimar era; the question of information overload (the so-called "Bilderflut") in MELODIE DER WELT; the reflection on the face in FEIND IM BLUT; or in the much-debated question about the relation between technology and nature in Ruttmann's films after 1933.
28. Indeed, even in books on "useful cinema," there is still a tendency to define experimental and avantgarde work by its resistance to usefulness. See for example Michael Zryd, "Experimental Film as Useless Cinema," in *Useful Cinema*, 315-336.
29. Obvious exceptions can be seen in pop art, but also for example, among the Japanese avant-garde of the 1960s. See Yuriko Furuhata, "Animating Copies: Japanese Graphic Design, the Xerox Machine, and Walter Benjamin," in *Animating Film Theory*, ed. Karen Beckman (Durham: Duke University Press, forthcoming 2014).
30. On this point, my argument overlaps with Hagener's suggestion that we cease to see the "realist" turn of the late 1920s and 1930s as the historical "defeat" of the avant-garde, but rather consider the two phases in terms of research and application. As Hagener writes: "A more useful division to describe some aspects of the changes between the 1920s and 1930s would thus be to replace the binary opposition of abstraction vs. realism with the transformation from the laboratory (research pure and simple, not necessarily determined by its use-value) to engineering (applied science)." Hagener, *Moving Forward, Looking Back*, 67. Ruttmann himself appears to have valorized the model of experimental film as a laboratory throughout his career, going so far as to call for a state-funded laboratory for systematic research on film techniques in 1930. See Walter Ruttmann, "Technik und Film," in *Walter Ruttmann. Eine Dokumentation*, 87-88. But I also want to insist that such research *always* occurred, even in the early phases, within a horizon of possible "applications."
31. See Fritz Pauli, "Das Problem des Werbefilms," *Die Reklame* 19 (1926): 617; Richard F. C. Béringuier, "An der Peripherie des Reklamefilms." *Die Reklame* 20 (1927): 429; Käthe Kurtzig, "Die Arten des Werbefilms," *Industrielle Psychotechnik* 3 (1926): 314.
32. On advertising at the Bauhaus, see Frederic J. Schwartz, "The Eye of the Expert: Walter Benjamin and the Avant Garde," *Art History* 24:3 (2001): 414-415; on experimental film at the Bauhaus, see Leslie, *Hollywood Flatlands*, 38.
33. Schwartz, "The Eye of the Expert."
34. See for example Walther Moede, "Psychologie der Reklame," *Die Reklame* 13 (1920): 244-245. Theodor König, *Reklame-Psychologie, ihr gegenwärtiger Stand – ihre praktische Bedeutung*, 2nd ed. (Munich and Berlin: R. Oldenbourg, 1924), 46-47. For more on this context, see chapter 1 below.
35. For the term "Nutzkunst," see for example Robert Hösel, "Reklame und Kunst," *Seidels Reklame* 5 (1920): 299. See also Hösel, "Expressionistische Reklameentwürfe," *Seidels Reklame* 6 (1921): 37-40; König, *Reklame-Psychologie*, 172-173. *Gebrauchsgraphik*

was the German title of an international journal devoted to advertising design founded in 1924.

36. On Ruttmann's origins in poster art, see Goergen, "Walter Ruttmann – Ein Porträt," 18.
37. Ruttmann, "Kunst und Kino," 73. On the dating of this text, see Goergen's notes, p. 73. See also Clarus, "Gespräch mit Ruttmann" (1926), in *Walter Ruttmann. Eine Dokumentation,* 79; Ruttmann, "Berlin? – Berlin!" (1927), in *Walter Ruttmann. Eine Dokumentation,* 79; ibid., "Der neue Film" (1927), in *Walter Ruttmann. Eine Dokumentation,* 80.
38. "Der Film, dieses vor Lebendigkeit strotzende und vor allzu vielseitigen Lebensmöglichkeiten oft noch taumelnde Monstrum, hat es nicht nötig, mit der Heiligsprechung durch ein philologisches Kunstgericht zu kokettieren. Wenn der Film nicht in die Registratur 'Kunst' hineinpaßt, so liegt die Schuld nicht bei ihm – und er kann verlangen daß der Kunstbegriff nach ihm erweitert wird." Ruttmann, "Kino als Kunst," 78. All translations are mine unless otherwise noted.
39. Ruttmann, "Mein neuer Film" (1926), 78. Elsewhere in the same text, Ruttmann wrote: "Nach Jahrhunderten, in denen künstlerische Interessen immer mehr zu Vereinsgelegenheiten verkümmerten, ist plötzlich durch den Film wieder ein Instrument auf die Welt gekommen, das zu Allen spricht und überall Resonanz findet. Gerade aus diesem Grunde wird natürlich bezweifelt, daß der Film Kunst sei. Denn man hat sich daran gewhöhnt zu glauben, daß 'Kunst' ein Ding ist, das nur für Wenige, besonders dazu Geschulte existiere. Aber er ist Kunst." Ibid.
40. Increasingly, Ruttmann would conceive the problem of "film art" in terms of a need to reconcile art with commerce. Thus in a text from 1929, he wrote: "Es ist klar daß dieses prinzipiell feindliche Verhalten zwischen der Kunst und dem Geschäft unrentabel ist. Denn beide sind aufeinander angewiesen. Die Kunst bereitet das Geschäft von morgen vor, das Geschäft nährt sich von der Kunst von gestern. Einen Kompromiß von gestern und morgen auf ein Heute wäre das richtige." Ruttmann, "Der isolierte Künstler," in *Walter Ruttmann. Eine Dokumentation,* 85. Around the same time, Ruttmann wrote another text on advertising film, in which he fondly recalled his own work in advertising from the early 1920s before adding: "Es wäre sicher ein großes Verdienst, durch Interessierung der großen Industrie- und Kapitalgruppen für diese Werbemöglichkeit dem Film neue Mittel und neue Impulse zuzuführen." Walter Ruttmann, "Moderne Werbung im Film" (1929), in *Walter Ruttmann. Eine Dokumentation,* 86.
41. Corey Ross, "Mass Politics and the Techniques of Leadership: The Promise and Perils of Propaganda in Weimar Germany," *German History* 24:2 (2006): 184-193.
42. The terms "Reklame" and "Propaganda" could and were used interchangeably in the 1920s, although they were already beginning to differentiate according to the object of the advertisement: products (Reklame) vs. ideas or institutions (Propaganda). See for example, König, *Reklame-Psychologie,* 29. The National Socialists would later forbid the term "Reklame" altogether and differentiate strictly between "Werbung" (commercial advertising) and "Propaganda." Ralf Forster, *Ufa und Nordmark. Zwei Firmengeschichten und der deutsche Werbefilm 1919-1945. Schriftenreihe der Cinémathèque Municipale de Luxembourg* 17 (Trier: WVT, 2005), 21-24.
43. See Sabine Behrenbeck, "'Der Führer'. Die Einführung eines politischen Markenartikels," in *Propaganda in Deutschland,* ed. Gerald Diesener, Rainer Gries (Darmstadt:

Wissenschaftliche Buchgesellschaft, 1996), 51-78; Holm Freibe, "Branding Germany: Hans Domizlaff's *Markentechnik* and Its Ideological Impact," in *Selling Modernity. Advertising in 20th-Century Germany,* ed. Pamela Swett, Jonathan Wiesen and Jonathan Zatlin (Durham: Duke University Press, 2007), 92-93, 98; Michael Imort, "'Planting a Forest Tall and Straight Like the German *Volk*': Visualizing the *Volksgemeinschaft* through Advertising in German Forestry Journals, 1933-1945," in *Selling Modernity,* 102-126.

44. Peter Zimmermann, "Filmpropaganda und Warenästhetik," in *Geschichte des dokumentarischen Films in Deutschland. Band 3,* 505-510.
45. Corey Ross, "La professionalisation de la publicité et de la propagande dans l'Allemagne de Weimar," *Vingtième Siècle* 101 (2009): 25-26; Ross, "Visions of Prosperity: The Americanization of Advertising in Interwar Germany," in *Selling Modernity,* 66-72.
46. See Michel Foucault, *Security, Territory, Population. Lectures at the Collège de France 1977-1978,* ed. Michel Senellart, trans. Graham Burchell (New York: Picador, 2004), 87-114; Foucault, "Governmentality," in *The Foucault Effect. Studies in Governmentality,* ed. Graham Burchell, Colin Gordon and Peter Miller (Chicago: University of Chicago Press, 1991), 87-104.
47. Ibid., 99,
48. See Ian Hacking, *The Taming of Chance* (Cambridge University Press, 1990), 5.
49. See for example König, *Reklame-Psychologie,* 3.
50. Mary Ann Doane, *The Emergence of Cinematic Time* (Cambridge: Harvard University Press, 2002), 13-25.
51. See Grierson, "First Principles of Documentary," 149.
52. In his earliest known manuscript, Ruttmann called for an "artistic film" that would conform to the "Möglichkeiten und Forderungen seines Materials." Ruttmann, "Kunst und Kino," 73. But Ruttmann's point was less to cut all ties with other media than to separate the cinema from the philological arts of literature and theater (here echoing numerous other writings of the time). A bit further on, he insists on film's affinities with painting and dance: "Denn die Kinematographie gehört unter das Kapitel der *bildenden Künste,* und ihre Gesetze sind am nächsten denen der Malerei und des Tanzes verwandt. Ihre Ausdrucksmittel sind: Formen, Flächen, Helligkeiten und Dunkelheiten mit all dem ihnen innewohnenden Stimmungsgehalt, vor allem aber die Bewegung dieser optischen Phänomene, die zeitliche Entwicklung einer Form aus der andern." Ibid.
53. See for example, Schobert, "'Painting in Time' and 'Visual Music'"; Bruce Elder, *Harmony and Dissent,* 116-125.
54. See for example Diebold, "Eine neue Kunst. Die Augenmusik des Films"; Kolaja and Foster, "'Berlin, the Symphony of a City' as a Theme of Visual Rhythm"; Alter, "Berlin, Symphony of a Great City," 199; Carlo Piccardi, "Rapporti tra suono e vision nel cinema di Ruttmann," in *Walter Ruttmann. Cinema, pittura, ars acustica,* 93-136. Ruttmann's earliest critics sometimes even faulted him for overemphasizing musical analogies. Thus Willy Haas, after seeing BERLIN, proclaimed: "Wir wünschen keine Übertragung der symphonisch-musikalischen Möglichkeiten, keinen Wagnerianismus des Films der Zukunft. Was immer kommen soll: er muß streng und organisch aus den technischen Gegebenheiten der Filmphotographie selbst wachsen." Cited in Goergen, "Walter Ruttmann – Ein Porträt," 28.

55. See for example Jeanpaul Goergen, "Il montaggio sonoro come 'ars acustica,'" in *Walter Ruttmann. Cinema, pittura, ars acustica,* 177-192; Sergio Freire, "Early Musical Impressions from Both Sides of the Loudspeaker," *Leonardo* 13 (2003): 67-71; Dieter Daniels, "Sound and Vision in Avantgarde & Mainstream" (2004). *Media Art Net,* http://www.medienkunstnetz.de/themes/image-sound_relations/sound_vision/1/, accessed 04.01.2013.
56. Goergen, for example, compares Ruttmann to Leopold Survage and even cites a lost Ruttmann painting in the tradition of Duchamps's *Nude Descending a Staircase.* See Goergen, "Walter Ruttmann – Ein Porträt," 20-21.
57. Gottfried Boehm, "Bilder als Instrumente der Erkenntnis," in *Wie Bilder Sinn erzeugen. Die Macht des Zeigens* (Berlin: Berlin University Press, 2008), 94-114.
58. On action, affect and perception images, see Gilles Deleuze, *Cinema 1: The Movement Image,* trans. Hugh Tomlinson and Barbara Habberjam (London: Continuum, 2005), 58-105 (on the avant-garde and the perception image, see especially pp. 82-86).
59. "Der Film ist – Gott sei's gedankt! – nicht nur eine künstlerische, sondern vor allem eine *menschlich-soziale* Angelegenheit! Er ist der stärkste Kämpfer für den Geist der Wiederverschmelzung vitaler und künstlerischer Interessen, für jenen Geist, der heute einen Jazz 'wichtiger' macht, als eine Sonate- ein Plakat 'wichtiger' als ein Gemälde. Denn Kunst, *lebendige* Kunst ist heute nicht mehr das, was man uns noch in der Schule davon erzählt hat: Nicht mehr eine Flucht aus der Welt in höhere Sphären, sondern ein Hineinsteigen in die Welt und die Verdeutlichung ihres Wesens. *Kunst ist nicht mehr Abstraktion, sondern Stellungnahme!* Kunst, die nicht eine Äußerung enthält, gehört ins Zeughaus. Gleichgülitig natürlich, worüber diese Äußerung geschieht: ob über Frauenschönheit, Sozialismus, Technik oder Natur und ihre Verkettungen. Wichtig nur die Tatsache der menschlichen Stellungnahme." Walter Ruttmann, "Die absolute Mode," in *Walter Ruttmann. Eine Dokumentation,* 82.
60. Sabine Hake, for example, writes: "Yet what does taking a stance mean within the formal and thematic preoccupations of the city symphony? Does it refer to aesthetic or political commitments, a particular attitude or a set of beliefs?"
61. See Corey Ross, "Mass Politics and the Techniques of Leadership," 192.
62. Edward Ross Dickinson, "Biopolitics, Fascism, Democracy: Some Reflections on our Discourse about 'Modernity'," *Central European History* 37:1 (2004): 18-19.
63. This reading marks a shift from former "grand narrative" readings inspired by critical theory and the Frankfurt School. Thus whereas Detlev Peukert once argued that Nazi eugenic policies realized a latent possibility of progressive welfare politics, a more recent study on the German Welfare State by Young-Sun Hong stresses the incompatibility of the two systems (the former based on the primacy of individual rights and the latter on the sacrifice of the individual to the community and the "race"). See Young-Sun Hong, *Welfare Modernity and the Weimar State 1919-1933* (Princeton: Princeton University Press, 1998), 240, 270-276. One can observe a similar transformation in histories of statistics. Whereas previous writers could argue that statistics was an inherently dehumanizing phenomenon characterizing both democratic and totalitarian regimes, a recent study by J. Adam Tooze emphasizes the need to account fort the different political ends to which statistical information was put under Welfare democracies and National Socialism: "The statistical systems developed in Nazi Germany, the Soviet Union, Scandanavia, The Netherlands,

Great Britain and the United States were indeed related. They shared certain common intellectual origins, certain technical preconditions, and they were marked by their simultaneous appearance at a particular moment in time. But they were not identical. They were differentiated in technical terms. But more fundamentally, they were distinguished by their relation to politics. [...] It is this which makes the study of the Third Reich so important. It reveals the potential inherent in common technologies of economic knowledge when combined with a peculiarly racist brand of collectivism." J. Adam Tooze, *Statistics and the German State 1900-1945. The Making of Modern Economic Knowledge* (Cambridge: Cambridge University Press, 2001), 39. Tooze's critique is specifically directed at Götz Aly and Karl-Heinz Roth's *Die restlose Erfassung. Volkszählen, Identifizieren und Aussondern im Nationalsozialismus* (Berlin: Rotbuch-Verlag, 1984).

64. In this sense, I would also agree with Peter Jelavich that we need a concept of intermediality that moves beyond technological or generic analysis in order to attend also to the political circumstances affecting media usage. See Peter Jelavich, *Berlin Alexanderplatz. Radio, Film and the Death of Weimar Culture* (Berkeley: University of California Press, 2009), xiv. Although the "intermedial" dimension I am emphasizing in Ruttmann's work is different from the kind of "intermediality" analyzed by Jelavich (the travel of one story between novel, radio and film), his argument that transformations in politics impinged heavily on the uses of media in the early 1930s goes for my analysis as well.

65. Goergen, in particular, has provided what is still the most informative account of Ruttmann's biography in his essay "Walter Ruttmann – Ein Porträt," *Walter Ruttmann. Eine Dokumentation* 17-57, as well as the chronology he contributed to Quaresima's volume. Both volumes include annotated filmographies.

66. On this aspect, see especially Elsaesser and Hagener, "6. September. Walter Ruttmann: 1929."

67. On Ruttmann's collaboration with Reiniger, see Goergen, "Walter Ruttmann – Ein Porträt," 23-24; on his work for Lang's NIBELUNGEN, see ibid., 106; on the collaboration with Gance, see ibid., 38; Michael Cowan, "Technologies de diffusion simultanée et politique mondiale dans le cinéma de l'entre-deux-guerres," in *Loin des yeux... le cinéma. Imaginaires visuels des technologies de télécommunication* (Lausanne: L'Age d'Homme, forthcoming 2014). On Ruttmann's work for Riefenstahl, see Goergen, "Walter Ruttmann – Ein Porträt," 41; Rainer Rother, *Leni Riefesntahl. The Seduction of Genius* (London: Continuum, 2002), 61-65; Michael Cowan and Kai Sicks, "28 March 1935. Premiere of TRIUMPH DES WILLENS Presents Fascism as Unifier of Communal Will," in *The New History of German Cinema*, ed. Jennifer Kapczynski and Michael Richardson (Rochester: Camden House, 2012), 258. On ACCIAIO, see Paolo Cattelan, "Malipiero et la musica di *Acciaio*," in *Walter Ruttmann. Cinema, pittura, ars acustica*, 192-201; *Schenk*, "Walter Ruttmanns Kultur- und Industriefilme," 111-113.

68. To my knowledge, Bazin only discussed Ruttmann once in his essay "Cinema and Exploration" from *Qu'est-ce que le cinéma?*, in which he mentions MELODIE DER WELT in the context of the history of travel films. But anyone familiar with Bazin's writing can hear the negative overtones in his description of MELODIE DER WELT as "un film de montage du début du parlant où la terre était jetée sur l'écran en un puzzle d'images visuelles et sonores." André Bazin, *Qu'est-ce que le cinéma?* (Paris: Editions du Cerf, 1985), 26.

69. Grierson, "First Principles of Documentary," 150.
70. On this point, see Ross, "Mass Politics," 188-189.

1. Absolute Advertising: Abstraction and Figuration in Ruttmann's Animated Product Advertisements (1922-1927)

1. Important essay collections exist on industrial film and its imbrications with economic management (*Films That Work*) and on educational film and its imbrications with knowledge production (*Learning with the Lights off*). But advertising film has been slower to receive its own extended study. Currently, a volume on the broader history of film advertising is being planned by Patrick Vonderau and Nico de Klerk.
2. See Westbrock, *Der Werbefilm*.
3. One can find parallels in Russia, where artists such as Alexander Rodchenko placed their design skills in the service of poster advertisements and Dziga Vertov proclaimed the power of film advertising within the new state. On Vertov, see Lora Wheeler Mjolsness, "Vertov's Soviet Toys: Commerce, Commercialization and Cartoons," *Studies in Russian and Soviet Cinema* 2 (2008): 247-267.
4. See Westbrock, *Der Werbefilm*, 64-92.
5. In addition to Westbrock, see Hake, "Das Kino, die Werbung und die Avant-Garde"; Hagener, *Moving Forward, Looking Back*, 44-72; Cowan, "Advertising, Rhythm and the Filmic Avant-Garde."
6. This is a frequent explanation of these filmmakers' involvement in advertising. See for example Marion von Hofacker, "Chronology," in *Hans Richter. Activism, Modernism and the Avant-Garde*, ed. Stephen Foster (Cambridge: MIT Press, 2000), 257; Moritz, *Optical Poetry*, 54. Kristin Thompson suggests a similar argument in her review of the Edition Filmmuseum DVD of the restored BERLIN. DIE SINFONIE DER GROSSSTADT (which includes Ruttmann's animated advertisements in the extras) on her and David Bordwell's blog *Observations on Film Art*. Describing Ruttmann's advertisements, she writes: "These [advertisements] tend to be abstract and only bring in the product near the end. In doing the short for Excelsior tires, however, Ruttmann obviously found a round, nearly abstract shape that he could play with." Kristin Thompson, "Preserving Two Masters," in David Bordwell and Kristin Thompson, *Observations on Film Art*, 10 December 2008, http://www.davidbordwell.net/blog/2008/12/10/preserving-two-masters/, accessed 04.01.2013. Ruttmann did indeed privilege the circular form here (as I discuss in more detail below). But the fact that the logo only shows up at the end is hardly evidence that he was only using the commission as an excuse for formal play. This was, on the contrary, standard operating procedure in advertisements of the time.
7. Rancière, *Dissensus*, 121-23; Jacques Rancière, "The Surface of Design," trans. Gregory Elliot, in *The Future of the Image* (London: Verso, 2007), 91-108.
8. See Goergen, "Walter Ruttmann – Ein Porträt," 18-19.
9. The surviving titles include DER SIEGER. EIN FILM IN FARBEN (1922), DAS WUNDER. EIN FILM IN FARBEN (1922), DAS WIEDERGEFUNDENE PARADIES (1925), DER AUFSTIEG (1926), SPIEL DER WELLEN (1926) and DORT WO DER RHEIN (1927). Other surviving advertisements from this period include an experimental sound advertisement for German radio *Tönende Welle* (*Resounding Waves*, 1931) and an extended montage

advertisement for the Hamburg-America Line MELODIE DER WELT (MELODY OF THE WORLD, 1929), which I discuss more fully in chapter 2 below.

10. Ruttmann's assistant Lore Leudesdorff would later recall advertising films they created for grand pianos, sleeping pills and gas factories. See Goergen, "Walter Ruttmann – Ein Porträt," 25.
11. The exhibition title "Gesolei" was an acronym for "Gesundheit" (health), "Sozialfürsorge" (social welfare) and "Leibesübung" (bodily training).
12. "Es ist zweifelsfrei, daß die absolute Kunst, trotz ihrer Ablenhung psychologischer Verständigungsmöglichkeiten, fallweise Wirkungen auf das Publikum ausübt. Nur handelt es sich nicht um einen anschauenden Akt, der die Formen in ihrem Zueinander in aller Reinheit aufnimmt, sondern es findet ein aus der Psychophysik hinreichend bekannter seelischer Vorgang statt: der Zuschauer fühlt sich in die mathematischen Formen ein und erzeugt dadurch antwortende Empfindungen. Der Vorgang vollzieht sich zwangsläufig und unter der Bewußtseinsschwelle; die elementaren Linien und Formenverhältnisse führen das Gefühl ihre Richtungen entlang, mit ihren Bewegungen mit, durch ihre Heiligkeitsabstufungen hindurch, so daß ein seelisches Gegenbild entsteht, daß dem Kampf, der Harmonie, der Versöhnung jener Formverhältnisse entspricht." Kurtz, *Expressionismus und Film*, 93-94.
13. See Charles Féré, *Sensation et mouvement* (Paris: Alcan, 1900), 91: "Le goût des jeux de force, d'adresse et d'agilité: luttes, courses, combats de bêtes, etc. n'a pas d'autre raison. On aime le mouvement sous toutes ses formes, et, dans les arts, sa représentation a la plus grande importance au point de vue de l'esthétique." On the role of sympathetic imitation in telepathy, see p. 16: "Si on peut lire la pensée de son interlocuteur sur son visage, c'est qu'en le regardant on prend inconsciemment son expression, et l'idée se présente en conséquence."
14. This tradition of psychophysics is related to, but also slightly distinct from, the tradition of empathy (Einfühlung) also invoked by Kurtz in the passage above when he describes the process by which spectators "feel their way" (einfühlen) into the forms on the screen. While empathy theorists did describe the spectator's reaction in terms of counter-movements, they tended to insist on the metaphorical quality of such bodily action in an effort to salvage a notion of disinterested aesthetic experience. See Scott Curtis, "Einfühlung und die frühe deutsche Filmtheorie," in *Einfühlung. Zu Geschichte und Gegenwart eines ästhetischen Konzepts*, ed. Robert Curtis and Gertrud Koch (Munich: Fink, 2008), 79-105 (esp. 91-98).
15. "Die gesehene Bewegung ruft in uns ein eigenes Bedürfnis an Bewegung hervor. Richtig hervorgebracht, 'trifft' sie richtig und steckt uns an. [...] Das sind Eigenschaften, die den Menschen zu einem geeigneten und sicheren Objekt der Filmwirkung machen." Leo Witlin, "Von der Psychomechanik des Zuschauers," *Filmtechnik* no. 23 (1927): 407.
16. "Dieser Film hier gibt keine 'Haltepunkte', an denen man in Erinnerungen umkehren könnte, man ist – ausgeliefert – zum 'Fühlen' gezwungen – zum Mitgehen im Rhythmus." Hans Richter, "Die schlecht trainierte Seele," in *G. Material zur elementaren Gestaltung* 3 (1924): 45.
17. See Jonathan Crary, "Spectacle, Attention, Counter-Memory," *October* 50 (Autumn 1989): 96-107; *Techniques of the Observer. On Vision and Modernity in the Nineteenth Century* (Cambridge: MIT Press, 1990), 1-25; *Suspensions of Perception. Attention, Spectacle and Modern Culture* (Cambridge: MIT Press, 1999), 3-4, 73-79.

18. See Friedrich Kittler, *Discourse Networks 1800/1900*, trans. Michael Metteer and Chris Cullens (Stanford: Stanford University Press, 1985), 206-226.
19. An early history of the "form board test" (which was first devised by the French doctor Jean Marc Gaspard Itard in an effort to train a so-called "enfant sauvage," later developed by Séguin and others to test the intelligence of children and the mentally ill, and finally employed by doctors at Ellis Island to test the mental capacity of immigrants) can be found in Reuel Hull Sylvester, *The Form Board Test* (PhD diss., Princeton University, 1913). On the use of the "Farbenkreisel" in 19th-century science and industry, see for example *Das neue Buch der Erfindungen, Gewerbe und Industrien, Zweiter Band: Die Kräfte der Natur und ihre Benutzung*, 6th ed. (Leipzig: Otto Spamer, 1872), 243.
20. The first book in German devoted to advertising psychology was Christof von Hartungen's *Psychologie der Reklame* from 1921. Other titles included Theodor König's *Die Psychologie der Reklame* from 1922, Käthe Kurtzig's *Untersuchung zur Wirkung der Reklame* from 1925, and Karl Marbe's *Psychologie der Werbung* from 1927.
21. For a thorough description of such tests, see König, *Reklame-Psychologie*, 27-101. König cites both Ebbinghaus and Münsterberg throughout his study.
22. As one writer described it: "[Wir haben] außer Straßenbahn-, Autobus- und Untergrundbahnreklame neuerdings auch die fahrbare Postreklame und die Kollektivreklame der beleuchteten Straßenbahn-Haltestellen-Säulen sowei der Glaskästen für 'erste Hilfe', die ebenfalls schon an manchen Straßen und Plätzen zu sehen sind." Max Poculla, "Der Verkehrswart. Eine Neue Strassenreklame in Berlin," *Die Reklame* 15 (1922): 180. For sidewalk advertisements, see Erich Falk, "Bürgersteigreklame," *Die Reklame* 15 (1922): 184; Alexander Fuld, "Wo läßt man den Atrax-Reklame-Projektor wirken?" *Die Reklame* 14 (1921): 334. For streetcar tickets, see W. R. Titz, "Reklame auf Straßenbahnfahrscheinen," *Die Reklame* 15 (1922): 271-272. For advertising on ship exteriors, see Robert Hösel, "Reklamehochflut," *Seidels Reklame* 6 (1921): 146. For construction fences as advertising surfaces, see Rendschmidt, "Der Bauzaun als Reklameträger," *Seidels Reklame* 7 (1922): 257-258. For advertising on the sky (via airplane smoke letters), see "Das Beschreiben des Himmels," *Seidels Reklame* 7 (1922): 207. Even paper money was used for advertising purposes. See Lavoby, "Notgeld mit Reklame," *Seidels Reklame* 6 (1921): 381.
23. See Hösel, "Reklamehochflut"; Pfiffikus, "Spaziergänge im Reklamewald," *Die Reklame* 14 (1921): 253-254. Hösel explicitly attributed the "flood of advertising" to the new laws governing the placement of advertisements: "Ganz besonders die Post und Eisenbahn und sonstige Verkehrsunternehmen kennen keine Grenzen mehr, um ihre Einnahmenquellen durch Zulassung von Reklamen zu vergrößern" (145).
24. Moede, "Psychologie der Reklame," 245. See also König, *Reklame-Psychologie*, 46-47.
25. König, *Reklame-Psychologie*, 40, 52, 78. König insists again and again that the guiding rule for advertising theory is the energetic imperative: i.e. the imperative to achieve a maximum effect on spectators with the most economic means possible.
26. See Adolf Behne, "Deffke," *Seidels Reklame* 8 (1923): 2-6.
27. Although few of Ruttmann's own prewar posters survived, there is reason to believe that his work was influenced by this tendency. Based on a series of Ruttmann paintings shown in Heinz Steike's 1977 documentary *Walter Ruttman 1887-1941. Versuch einer Befreiung*, Goergen describes Ruttmann's increasing "Tendenz zur Abstraktion und Reduktion." Goergen, "Walter Ruttmann – Ein Porträt," 19.

28. "Inserat vom Tage," *Seidels Reklame* 5 (1920): 193.
29. *Die Reklame* published an article by Ostwald summarizing his theories in 1919. See Wilhelm Ostwald, "Farbkunst und Werbekunst," *Die Reklame* 13 (1920): 7-8.
30. On Chevreul, see Kenneth E. Burchett, *A Bibligraphical History of the Study and Use of Color from Aristotle to Kandinsky* (Lewiston: Edwin Mellen Press, 2005), 21-23, 105-112. Chevreul was also a critical source for avant-garde experiments in color. See for example Elder, *Harmony and Dissent*, 41.
31. Moede, "Psychologie der Reklame," 244.
32. See Robert Hösel, "Die Plakatfarben in ihrer Fernwirkung," *Seidels Reklame* 4 (1919): 187-188.
33. König, *Reklame-Psychologie*, 42-43.
34. On advertising at the Bauhaus, see Schwartz, "The Eye of the Expert," 414-415; on experimental film at the Bauhaus, see Leslie, *Hollywood Flatlands*, 38.
35. On Siedhoff-Buscher's blocks and their relation to pedagogical practices stretching back to the early-19th-century work of Friedrich Froebel and Heinrich Pestalozzi, see Christine Mehring, "Alma Buscher: 'Ship' Building Toy. 1923," in *Bauhaus 1919-1933. Workshops in Modernity*, ed. Berry Bergdoll and Leah Dickerman (New York: Museum of Modern Art, 2009), 156-162. On the use of the color top in Bauhaus preliminary courses, see Elder, *Harmony and Dissent*, 68.
36. See Goergen, "Walter Ruttmann – Ein Porträt," 18.
37. On Leudesdorff's collaboration, see Friedrich Zglienicki, *Der Weg des Films. Die Geschichte der Kinematographie und ihrer Vorläufer* (Berlin: Rembrandt, 1956), 597-599; Steike, "Walter Ruttmann," 61; Goergen, "Walter Ruttmann – Ein Porträt," 24-25; Westbrock, *Der Werbefilm*, 48-49.
38. Goergen, "Walter Ruttmann – Ein Porträt," 25.
39. Cited in Steike, "Walter Ruttmann," 61. The entire quote reads: "Da konnte ich alles anwenden, was ich am Bauhaus gelernt hatte. Das Abstrakte, das Hintergründige, das Neue an Farben und Formen, und dazu noch dreidimensional." For more evidence of Ruttmann's interest in the Bauhaus, see Clarus, "Gespräch mit Ruttmann," 79.
40. Schwartz, "The Eye of the Expert." This is precisely the development that Robert Hösel had in mind when he explained in a 1920 article for *Seidels Reklame*: "Der *L'art pour l'art* Standpunkt ist freilich durch die veränderten Zeitverhältnisse heftig erschüttert worden. Man stellte der wirklichen Kunst die Gleichberechtigung der sogenannten Nutzkunst gegenüber, betonte, daß ein wahres Kunstwerk nichts von seinem Wert verliere, wenn es einem Zwecke diene und wies als schlagendes Beweismittel auf die Architektur, als Mutter aller Künste, die immer eine praktische Aufgabe erfüllt." Robert Hösel, "Reklame und Kunst," *Seidels Reklame* 5 (1920): 299.
41. Ross, "Mass Politics and the Techniques of Leadership," 184-193.
42. On the history of advertisig film before 1918, see Westbrock, *Der Werbefilm*, 30-44; Günter Ägde, *Flimmernde Versprechen. Geschichte des deutschen Werbefilms im Kino seit 1897* (Berlin: Verlag das Neue Berlin, 1998), 1-72.
43. Westbrock, *Der Werbefilm*, 62. For a history of two prominent companies, see Forster, *Ufa und Nordmark*. See also Jeanpaul Goergen, "In filmo veritas! Inhaltlich vollkommen wahr. Werbefilme und ihre Produzenten," in *Geschichte des dokumentarischen Films 2*, 348-363.

44. "Nicht jeder Mensch – und wenn er noch so befähigt ist – ist auf diesem Gebiete Fachmann. Nicht jeder Mensch kann das schwierige Instrument der Propaganda meistern, und dies trifft ganz besonders für die Filmpropaganda zu, da diese sehr individuell behandelt werden muß." Fritz Ziege, "Neue Wege der Filmpropaganda," *Die Reklame* 18 (1925): 155. Not surprisingly, Ziege legitimates the importance of propaganda and advertising in film with reference to the war: "Das Ausland hat von der ungeheueren Werbekraft des Films bereits im Kriege in überlegener Weise Gebrauch gemacht. Noch heute haben wir unter den Nachwirkungen des Propagandafeldzuges des Auslandes zu leiden, es ist daher auf das lebhafteste zu begrüßen, wenn im Bund mit der Aufklärung durch Wort und Schrift die deutschfreundliche Filmpropaganda einhergeht" (157).
45. For more on Pinschewer's career, see Jeanpaul Goergen, "Julius Pinschewer: A Trade-mark Cinema," in *A Second Life. German Cinema's First Decades*, ed. Thomas Elsaesser (Amsterdam: Amsterdam University Press, 1996), 168-174; André Amsler, *"Wer dem Werbefilm verfällt, ist verloren für die Welt". Das Werk von Julius Pinschewer 1883-1961* (Zurich: Chronos, 1997), 9-45.
46. See the newspaper advertisements for Pinschewer's company from 1925 and 1926 reproduced in the CD-Rom section of *Julius Pinschewer. Klassiker des Werbefilms*, ed. Martin Loiperdinger, DVD and CD-Rom (Berlin: Absolute Medien, 2010). For Pinschewer's presence at trade fairs, see for example Robert Hösel, "Messe für Reklame und Werbewesen," *Seidels Reklame* 6 (1921): 180. (Hösel mentions a stand dedicated to films by Pinschewer's company Werbefilm G.m.b.H). See also Pinschewer's advertisement for his presence in trade fairs in *Die Reklame* 20, no. 10 (1927): xviii.
47. On the distribution and screening of advertising films in the 1920s, see Forster, *Ufa und Nordmark*, 32-35. As Forster notes, it was precisely during the early 1920s that the placement of advertising films before the main attraction became the norm (32).
48. Béringuier, "An der Peripherie des Reklamefilms," 429.
49. Kurtzig, "Die Arten des Werbefilms," 313.
50. "Der absolute Film [...] bringt in seiner Durchführung keine geschlossene Handlung, sondern versucht, durch das Bewegungsspiel von Ornamenten und Figuren einen gedanklichen Inhalt sichtbar zum Ausdruck zu bringen; er wirkt vor allem durch die rhythmische Kraft der Bewegung, die den Zuschauer zum Mitschwingen bringt und ihn die Vorgänge auf der Leinwand nicht nur sehen und verstehen, sondern erleben läßt." Ibid., 314.
51. On Pauli's impact, as well as his place within the wider interdisciplinary field of rhythm research in the 1920s, see my book *Technology's Pulse. Essays on Rhythm in German Modernism* (London: University of London – IGRS, 2012), 133-138.
52. "Ein solcher Rhythmus wirkt hypnotisierend und hinterläßt einen unauslöschlichen Eindruck ohne üble Begleitempfindungen; denn jeder stimmt sich sofort auf diese Lichter- und Silbenresonanz ab." Fritz Pauli, *Rhythmus und Resonanz als ökonomisches Prinzip in der Reklame* (Berlin: Verband deutscher Reklamefachleute, 1926), 18.
53. Ibid., 22. For Pauli's term "Werbeschwingungen," see p. 39.
54. "...das neuartige Moment der Formen- und Farbenwirkung in deutlich erkennbaren Ansätzen zur rhythmischen Gestaltung." Pauli, "Das Problem des Werbefilms," 617. Pinschewer himself would later celebrate Ruttmann's work in similar

language when he described the latter's "Bestreben, auch die Kunst des 'absoluten Filmes in den Dienst der Werbung zu stellen, das ist diejenige Filmart, die sich auf die Verwendung *filmisch-optischer Mittel* und auf *rhythmisch-dynamische Gestaltung allein beschränkt.*" Julius Pinschewer, "Von den Anfängen des Werbefilms," *Die Reklame* 20 (1927): 410.

55. "Und wenn es mir gelungen ist, die Menschen zum Schwingen zu bringen, sie die Stadt Berlin erleben zu lassen, dann habe ich mein Ziel erreicht." Ruttmann, "Wie ich meinen BERLIN-Film drehte" (1927), in *Walter Ruttmann. Eine Dokumentation,* 80.
56. "Ruttmann versteht sich in der Tat nicht als [...] Reporter. [...] Er will vielmehr eine neue künstlerische Wirklichkeit entstehen lassen; er betrachtet Berlin ästhetisch – es sind seine künstlerischen Empfindungen, die er an den Zuschauer weiterleiten will. Diesen will er berauschen, ihn zum Schwingen bringen, Vibrationen auslösen." Goergen, "Walter Ruttmann – Ein Porträt," 30.
57. Heinrich von Schieferstein, "Die Ausnützung mechanischer Schwingungen im Maschinenbau," *Bayerisches Industrie- und Gewerbeblatt* 111, no. 19 (1925): 117-123, 125-129. For Pauli's citation of Schieferstein, see Pauli, *Rhythmus und Resonanz,* 13.
58. I use the term "dispositif" here and aferwards in the sense outlined by François Albera and Maria Tortajada to designate audio-visual media arrangement that includes the material-technological apparatus (here moving images used for animation), the discursive dimension informing how that technology is conceptualized and put to use (here the discourse on resonance and its uses for advertising), and the disposition of elements that assigns a place to the spectator-subject (here the viewer assumed to resonate with the visual rhythms of advertising film). See François Albera and Maria Tortajada, "The 1900 Episteme," in *Cinema Beyond Film,* ed. François Albera and Maria Tortajada (Amsterdam: Amsterdam University Press, 2010), 25-44.
59. König, *Reklame-Psychologie,* 94-97.
60. "[N]ach einem bekannten psychologischen Gesetz [überträgt sich] die Lust am bloßen Wiedererkennen leicht auf den wiedererkannten Gegenstand." Ibid., 156.
61. Ibid., 48.
62. "[S]tarke Gedächtnisstützen [können und müssen] durch möglichst sinnvolle Bilder oder Zeichnungen, Diagramme u. dgl. von leichter Auffassungs- und Merkfähigkeit gegeben werden." Ibid., 135.
63. "Warenzeichen [sollen] sinnvoll sein, denn solche Figuren, die eine assoziative Vorstellungsanknüpfung, einen Deutvorgang anregen, werden in erster Linie behalten und von anderen unterschieden." Ibid., 117-118. In this call for the reintroduction of meaningful syllables and forms in practical situations, König was hardly alone. Fritz Giese, for example, argued that meaningless syllables, while useful for experimental psychology, were less helpful for advertising because they could not be remembered by lay people: "Die Gedächtnisleistung wird beim Laien erst möglich, indem er sich künstlich zu Dingen wie 'zöf' – 'mik' – 'lur' mnemotechnische Assoziationen künstlicher Art mühsam ermittelt." Fritz Giese, *Methoden der Wirtschaftspsychologie* (Berlin: Urban & Schwarzenberg, 1927), 21.
64. "Die starke Anziehungskraft liegt in den psychologischen Reizen der Ruttmannschen Filme, die ihre Wirkung ununterbrochen ermöglichen. Seine Komposi-

tionen sind dramatisch erlebt und haben als Akteure mathematische Formen, die in reicher Fülle organische Anklänge enthalten." Kurtz, *Expressionismus und Film,* 102.

65. "[W]ie groß die Ausdrucksfülle dieser buntbewegten Formen ist, geht am deutlichsten aus der Tatsache hervor, daß Ruttmann mit einem Industrie-Reklame-Film dieser Art erhebliche Erfolge erzielt hat." Ibid. Kurtz was not the only artistically-minded critic to make this point. After a screening of Ruttmann's second OPUS film in 1922, the critic Bernhard Diebold wrote: "Diese neue Augenmusik [...] wird einen schweren und langsamen Passionsweg zur Gunst des Publikums haben. Beschleunigung wäre höchstens möglich, wenn kluge Geschäftsleute sich den gemalten Film zu einer Reklame modernster Art erwählten." Cited in Goergen, "Walter Ruttmann – Ein Porträt," 23.
66. See George Grosz, "Man muß Kautschukmann sein!" *Neue Jugend* 1.2 (1917): 1: "Wo vordem die gotische Kirche, messelt sich heute das Warenhaus hoch–! / Die Fahrstühle sausen ... Eisenbahnunglücks, Explosionskatastrophen. [...] Wie gesagt, Kautschukmann sein / beweglich in allen Knochen / nicht bloß im Dichter Sessel dösen / oder vor der Staffelei schön getönte Bildchen pinseln."
67. See Ward, *Weimar Surfaces,* 116-128. As I've argued elsewhere, however, the model of rhythmical "resonance" espoused by theorists such as Pauli and Kurtzig was explicitly understood as an alternative to advertising via shocks. See Cowan, "Advertising, Rhythm and the Avant-Garde," 41.
68. See Wilhelm Worringer, *Abstraktion und Einfühlung,* 14th ed. (Munich: Piper, 1987), 49-56. "Während der Einfühlungsdrang ein glückliches pantheistisches Vertraulichkeitsverhältnis zwischen dem Menschen und den Außenwelterscheinungen zur Bedingung hat, ist der Abstraktionsdrang die Folge einer großen inneren Beunruhigung des Menschen durch die Erscheinungen der Außenwelt und korrespondiert in religiöser Beziehung mit einer stark transzendentalen Färbung aller Vorstellungen" (49).
69. Ibid., 49, 57-58. Although Worringer himself never framed his arguments about abstraction in terms of industrial modernity, Anthony Viddler has shown how his recourse to the notion of "agoraphobia" took part in a much broader debate about the experience of modern urban space. See Viddler, *Warped Space. Art, Architecture and Anxiety in Modern Culture* (Cambridge: MIT Press, 2000), 25-50.
70. "Telegraf, Schnellzüge, Stenografie, Fotografie, Schnellpresen usw. [...] haben zur Folge eine früher nie gekannte Geschwindigkeit in der Übermittlung geistiger Resultate. Durch diese Schnelligkeit des Bekanntwerdens ergibt sich für das Einzelindividuum ein fortwährendes Überschwemmtsein mit Material, dem gegenüber die alten Erledigungsmethoden versagen." Walter Ruttmann, "Malerei mit Zeit," *Walter Ruttmann. Eine Dokumentation,* 74.
71. For more on this point, see chapter 2 below.
72. "[I]nfolge der erhöhten Geschwindigkeit, mit der die Einzeldaten gekurbelt werden, [wird] der Blick von den einzelnen Inhalten abgezogen und auf den Gesamtverlauf der aus den verschiedenen Punkten gebildeten Kurve als eines sich zeitlich abwickelnden Phänomens gelenkt. Das Objekt unserer Betrachtung ist also jetzt die zeitliche Entwicklung und die in stetem Werden begriffene Physiognomie einer Kurve und nicht mehr das Starre Nebeneinander einzelner Punkte." Ibid., 74.

73. On this point (with respect to Marey), see Georges Didi-Huberman, "La courbe de toute chose," in Georges Didi-Huberman and Laurent Mannoni, *Mouvements de l'air. Étienne Jules-Marey, photographe des fluides* (Paris: Gallimard, 2004), 191-213.
74. On Fuller's connection to Bergson, see Tom Gunning, "Loïe Fuller and the Art of Motion: Body, Light, Electricity and the Origins of Cinema," in *Camera Obscura. Camera Lucida. Essays in Honor of Annette Michelson*, ed. Richard Allen and Malcolm Turvey (Amsterdam: Amsterdam University Press, 2003), 75-90.
75. See Freud, "Beyond the Pleasure Principle" (1920), in *The Standard Edition of the Complete Psychological Works of Sigmund Freud*, vol. 18, ed. James Strachey (London: The Hogart Press, 1955), 37.
76. "[D]as Publikum *muß* diese Werbung annehmen, ob es will oder nicht. Man kann den Inseratenteil einer Zeitung geflissentlich übersehen, mann kann den Anblick von Verkehrs- oder Lichtreklamen mehr oder weniger meiden, man kann den Hörer bei der Funkwerbung vom Kopf nehmen oder den Empfänger abstellen, aber man kann nicht gut im Lichtspieltheater die Augen schließen." Pauli, "Das Problem des Werbefilms," 616.
77. "Dem Publikum kommt es darauf an, nicht quasi um seine Zeit und sein Eintrittsgeld betrogen zu werden [...] Das Publikum will entweder belustigt, in Spannung versetzt oder interessant belehrt werden. Dann betrachtet es sich als unterhalten und steht der propagierten Sache wohlwollend gegenüber." Ibid.
78. Käthe Kurtzig, for example, in an article on advertising film for *Die Reklame*, wrote: "Der Werbefilm, ob im Lichtspieltheater oder im Vortragssaal, drängt sich dem Beschauer fast unweigerlich auf und muß von ihm beachtet werden, gleichgültig, ob ihn das Dargebotene interessiert oder nicht. [...] [E]s muß [daher] unter allen Umständen vermieden werden, daß der Betrachter von vornherein dem Gebotenen Widerstand entgegensetzt. Bei der Dauer der zwangsweisen Beobachtung müßte eine solche Einstellung des Zuschauers den erstrebten Erfolg der Werbung in das krasseste Gegenteil umkehren." Käthe Kurtzig, "Werbefilm und Volkswirtschaft," *Die Reklame* 20 (1927): 417-418.
79. "Ein besonderer Vorzug der Filmwerbung besteht darin, daß der im verdunkelten Raume sitzende Zuschauer sich dem Film nicht entziehen kann. Gerade deswegen soll der Werbegedanke in gefälliger Form vorgetragen werden. Das ist auch der Grund, weshalb der Werbefilm gern in die Form des Trickfilms gekleidet wird, denn dieser befriedigt das Bedürfnis nach entspannender Unterhaltung." Julius Pinschewer, "Der Trickfilm in der Reklame," Vortrag auf der Kantonalen bernischen Handelskammer (1938), reprinted in *Julius Pinschewer. Klassiker des Werbefilms*, CD-Rom, Teil 1.
80. "Die Note, die das Volk heute haben will, ist der Humor. Der Trickfilm bietet Möglichkeiten, die groteskesten Chaplinaden, die märchenhaftesten Unwahrscheinlichkeiten auf die Bildfläche zu zaubern." "Glasbild und Glasstreifen," *Seidels Reklame* 11 (1927): 163.
81. "[...] hat [zunächst] darauf zu achten, daß er keinen aggressiven Humor entwickelt (Satire), sondern daß seine Typen auf gemütlich humorvoller Charakterisierung beruhen. (Um einen krassen Vergleich zu wählen Wilhelm Buschs Karikaturen dollig gemütlich – George Grosz in jedem Federstrich scharf aggressive)." Lutz Michaelis, "Wie entsteht ein Werbetrickfilm?" *Die Reklame* 20 (1927): 434.
82. Gilles Deleuze, *Cinema 1*, 83-88.

83. Ibid., 88.

2. The Cross-Section: Images of the World and Contingency Management in Ruttmann's Montage Films of the Late 1920s (1927-1929)

1. Although some of Ruttmann's other films would circulate internationally, even winning occasional prizes, BERLIN undoubtedly received the most international recognition. After its initial screening in Berlin's *Tauentzienpalast* on 23 September 1927, it would go on to receive numerous international screenings in 1928 in Austria, England, Tchechoslowakia, France and Japan (see *Walter Ruttmann. Eine Dokumentation,* 114).
2. Cited in Goergen, "Walter Ruttmann – Ein Porträt," 28.
3. Béla Balázs, *Der Geist des Films* [1930] (Frankfurt a. M.: Suhrkamp, 2004), 50.
4. Thus Jeanpaul Goergen describes the film as "*cinéma pur* […], der seinen ganzen Sinn aus seinen Bildern, aus ihrem Rhythmus, ihrer Harmonie und ihrer Montage zieht." Goergen, "Walter Ruttmann – Ein Porträt," 28. More recently, Nora Alter, writes that "*Berlin, Symphony of a Great City* is, to use Béla Balázs's contemporaneous term, a piece of 'optical music.' It is fully conceived of as a synthesized audiovisual production in which a sound score drives the image track." Alter, "Berlin, Symphony of a Great City," 199.
5. "[…] eine genaue graphische Kurve des Tempos und der Bewegung der Szene." Clarus, "Der Schöpfer des abstrakten Films. Walther Ruttmann," *Film-Kurier* 11 September 1926, n.p. Newspaper clipping from Seeber archive, Deutsche Kinemathek, Berlin. Also cited in Goergen, "Walter Ruttmann – Ein Porträt," 27. Ruttmann himself described his goal in editing BERLIN as "die Sichtbarmachung der symphonischen Kurve […], die mir vor Augen stand." Ruttmann, "Wie ich meinen Berlin-Film drehte," in *Walter Ruttmann. Eine Dokumentation,* 80.
6. For more on newspapers and the transformation of reading around 1900, see Peter Fritzsche, *Reading Berlin 1900* (Cambridge: Harvard University Press, 1998). Significantly, Ruttmann would later recycle both the train sequence and the newspaper sequence in *Blut und Boden: Grundlagen zum Neuen Reich* (1933), a propaganda film commissioned by the Stabsamt des Reichsbauernführers to illustrate the dangers of urbanization. See chapter 3 below.
7. "Es ist schon ein Gemeinplatz geworden, wenn man von einem Plakat verlangt, daß es dem im Auto Vorbeifahrenden auf den ersten Blick erkennbar und verständlich sei." Heinrich Inheim, "Messe und Ausstellung," *Das Plakat* 11 (1920): 292-293.
8. Kracauer, "Wir schaffens," 404.
9. Helmut Korte, for example, argues that the films of Cavalcanti, Vertov and Vigo are all more attentive to social disparities than Ruttmann: "Keiner dieser Filme weist die (unmenschliche) formale Strenge von *Berlin* auf oder bleibt bei einer betont sachlich registrierenden Neutralität stehen […]. Mit graduellen Unterschieden in der Deutlichkeit ist an Stelle des beziehungslosen Nebeneinanders eine Stellungnahme erkennbar." Helmut Korte, "Die Welt im Querschnitt: *Berlin – Die Sinfonie der Großstadt* (1927)," in *Fischer Filmgeschichte. Band 2: Der Film als gesellschaftliche Kraft 1925-1944,* ed. Werner Faulstisch and Helmut Korte (Frankfurt am Main:

Fischer, 1991), 84-85. In the North American context, this argument can be found for example in the following reading by Lutz Koepenick: "Although influenced by Dziga Vertov's experiments with the optical rhythms of everyday life, Ruttmann's montage differs vastly from Vertov's own MAN WITH A MOVIE CAMERA (1929). Whereas Ruttmann depicts Berlin life as an aesthetic spectacle seen from the detached vantage point of an auteur director, Vertov engages with the political process of post-revolutionary Moscow. Whereas Ruttmann emphasizes tempo as a formal quality, Vertov praises metropolitan speed as a means to accelerate the construction of the new society." Lutz Koepnick. *Walter Benjamin and the Aesthetics of Power* (Lincoln: University of Nebraska Press, 1999), 133.

10. "Ruttmann will diese Tatsachen des Berliner Lebens nur verwenden, wie der Musiker Töne verwendet, aber eben darin beruht vielleicht ein künstlerischer Irrtum, denn man kann nicht einen Ton gleichsetzen einem dinghaften Eindruck, wie ihn das einzlene Filmbild darstellt." Goergen, "Walter Ruttmann – Ein Porträt," 30.
11. Ellis and McLane, *A New History of Documentary Film,* 53.
12. See Lev Manovich, *The Language of New Media* (Cambridge: MIT Press, 2001), 218-252.
13. This is not to argue that there are no differences between the two projects. For an in-depth discussion, see my article "Rethinking the City Symphony after the Age of Industry," *Intermédialités* 11, special issue on Harun Farocki, ed. Philippe Despoix (2009): 69-86.
14. Christa Blümlinger, *Kino aus zweiter Hand. Zur Ästhetik materieller Aneignung im Film und in der Medienkunst* (Berlin: Vorwerk 8, 2009), 54.
15. See Mathew Rampley, "Archives of Memory: Walter Benjamin's *Arcades Project* and Aby Warburg's *Mnemosyne Atlas,*" in *The Optic of Walter Benjamin,* ed. Alex Coles (London: Black Dog Publishing, 1999), 94-119; Benjamin Buchloh, "Gerhart Richter's *Atlas*: The Anomic Archive," *October* 88 (Spring 1999): 117-145 (esp. 122-134); Philippe-Alain Michaud, *Aby Warburg and the Image in Motion,* trans. Sophie Hawkes (New York: Zone Books, 2004), 37, 39, 261-262, 282-289; Blümlinger, *Kino aus zweiter Hand,* 30-31.
16. On this point, see Antje Ehmann, "Wie Wirklichkeit erzählen? Methoden des Querschnittfilms," in *Geschichte des dokumentarischen Films in Deutschland. Band 2: Weimarer Republik,* ed. Peter Zimmermann (Stuttgart: Reclam, 2005), 588-591.
17. The projected films included *Henny Porten: Leben und Laufbahn einer Filmkünstlerin; Nervosität, Hysterie oder Wahnsinn?* (on G. W. Pabst's *Geheimnisse einer Seele*); *Filmschauspieler und Filmschauspielerin oder Wie werde ich Filmstar?; Achtung! Aufnahme! Los! Moderne Filmregisseure bei der Arbeit; Spuk, Geister und Expressionismus im Film; Von Kindern und Tieren im Film*; and *Erotik und Ästhetik im Film.* See "Das Auge der Welt," *Süddeutsche Filmzeitung* 7, no. 28 (21 September 1928): 10.
18. In one article for *Film-Kurier,* Kalbus himself claimed to have coined a new term: "'Querschnittfilm' ... Schon wieder eine neues Wort! Ein neuer Begriff! Eine ganz neue Sache!" Kalbus, "Querschnitt-Film," *Film-Kurier* 29 September 1928, cited in Ehmann, "Wie Wirklichkeit erzählen?," 587.
19. Blum's film was used by László Moholy-Nagy as a prime example of the "film of the future" in a set of lectures he gave in Berlin. See H. S., "Der Film der Zukunft," *Lichtbild-Bühne* 23, no. 70 (23 March 1929): 20.

20. Boleslas Matuszewski's pamphlet *Une nouvelle source d'histoire* (1898) is generally recognized as the first proposal for a film archive. See Boleslas Matuszewski, *Ecrits cinémathographiques. Une nouvelle source d'histoire,* ed. Magdalena Mazaraki (Paris: Cinémathèque Française, 2006).
21. See Jay Leyda, *Films Beget Films* (New York: Hill and Wang, 1964), 13-49; Hagener, *Moving Forward, Looking Back,* 113-119. In Germany, the first official state archive was founded in 1934 as part of the Reichsfilmkammer, but already in the 1920s there were calls for a state archive. See for example F[ritz] Schimmer, "Zur Frage des Reichsfilmarchivs," *Lichtbild-Bühne* 19:79 (3 April 1926): 11-14.
22. See Béla Balázs, *Theory of the Film* (London: Denis Dobson, 1952), 165-166; see also Leyda, *Films Beget Films,* 29.
23. Thus one reviewer described the Henny Porten film as offering interesting information not only about Porten but also "about the development of *film generally,* [...] about techniques of directing, shooting and recording, as well as sets." "Das Auge der Welt. Der erste Querschnitt-Film 'Henny Porten'," *Lichtbild-Bühne* 21, no. 233 (7 November 1929): n.p. Similar assessments could be found in other reviews. See "Henny Porten" (review), *Der Kinematograph* 22, no. 1162 (1929); "Rund um die Liebe" (review), *Berliner Börsen-Courier* 217 (12 May 1929), reprinted in *Der Film der Weimarer Republik: 1929. Ein Handbuch der zeitgenössischen Kritik,* ed. Gero Gandert (Berlin: De Gruyter, 1997), 560; P. M. "Von der Wundertrommel bis zum Werbe-Tonfilm," *Lichtbild-Bühne* 22, no. 191 (12 August 1929): n.p.
24. Other examples include *Ein Querschnitt durch die deutschen Städteverfassungen* (Albert Meyer-Lülmann, 1925), *Musikdienst am Volk: ein Querschnitt in Dokumenten* (1927), *Jean Arthur Rimbaud: Ein Querschnitt durch sein Leben und Werk* (Paul Zech, 1927), *Russland, Europa, Amerika: ein architektonischer Querschnitt* (Erich Mendelsohn, 1929), *Das proletarische Schicksal: ein Querschnitt durch die Arbeiterdichtung der Gegenwart* (Hans Mühle, 1929), *Der Berater: ein Querschnitt auf dem Gebiet des Laienspiels, des Volkstanzes und der Jugendmusik* (ed. Frieda Cleve, 1929), *Die Welt auf der Waage: ein Querschnitt durch 20 Jahre Weltreise* (Colin Ross, 1930), *Leichte Tanze: ein Querschnitt durch die neuen Tanzrhythmen für instruktive Zwecke* (Matyas Seiber, 1933). To my knowledge, the first use of the term *Querschnitt* to describe an anthology in this sense was Gustav Wyneken's text *Wickersdorf: ein Querschnitt* (1917).
25. Hans Kafka, "Liebe im Querschnitt," *Tempo* 107 (10 May 1929), cited in *Der Film der Weimarer Republik, 1929,* 560. In another review of *Henny Porten* for the British journal *Close-up,* Andor Kraszna-Krausz described the new genre as a means of disseminating knowledge and allowing audiences to take in the essentials of given field in a single glance (or sitting). "Twenty years of film acting. They have never been so tersely put to us as here, netted in the short space of two hours." A[ndor] Kraszna-Krausz, "The Querschnittfilm," *Close-Up* 3, no. 5 (November 1928): 27. The Porten film, he wrote, displays concisely "the acme of what Henny Porten can do" a "summary of the whole" (30). Significantly, this use of the term *Querschnitt* as an "anthology" format would also persist, in both print and film form, well into the Third Reich and beyond. Thus audiences in 1936 could see (two years before Leni Riefenstahl's OLYMPIA film), a reportage on the Olympic games entitled *Olympische Spiele: kurzer Querschnitt,* and interested readers could learn about the German air force in *Vom Werden deutscher Luftgeltung: ein Querschnitt durch die Entwicklung des deutschen Flugwesens* (Berlin, 1937). Postwar readers could learn about recent history in books

such as *Diktatur. Ein Querschnitt* (Westheim, 1947) and *Widerstandsliteratur. Ein Querschnitt durch die Verfolgungen und den Widerstand im Dritten Reich* (Hamburg, 1948).

26. "Es liegt [im Simultaneismus] dieselbe Absicht zugrunde: nämlich die, sich in der Darstellung nicht nur auf ein einziges Bild der großen Welt zu konzentrieren, sondern eine Menge gleichzeitiger Ereignisse zu zeigen, auch wenn diese miteinander und mit der Hauptsache in gar keinem kausalen Zusammenhang stehen. So wollen sie mit einem Querschnitt des ganzen Lebens einen kosmischen Eindruck hervorrufen, eine Totale der Welt, denn nur diese kann ihr wirkliches Bild sein." Béla Balázs, *Der sichtbare Mensch oder die Kultur des Films* [1924] (Frankfurt am Main: Suhrkamp, 2008), 89.
27. Here too, Balázs described his film as an attempt to show a "Querschnitt" of urban life already in 1926, but he did not use the term *Querschnittfilm*. See Balázs, "Der Film sucht seinen Stoff" [1926], *Schriften zum Film II,* ed. Helmut H. Diederichs and Wolfgang Gersch (Berlin: Henschenverlag, 1984), 215.
28. Balázs, *Der Geist des Films,* 71.
29. Grierson, "First Principles of Documentary," 149.
30. See especially Margrit Tröhler, *Offene Welten ohne Helden. Plurale Figurenkonstellationen im Film* (Zürich: Schüren, 2007), 111-166.
31. "Es lässt sich also konstatieren, dass es ein konsistent beschreibbares 'Genre' des Querschnittfilms gar nicht gibt." Ehmann, "Wie Wirklichkeit erzählen," 578.
32. The Grimm Brothers disctionary defines the "Durchschnitt" as "die bildliche Darstellung einer sache, wie sie sich ausnimmt, wenn sie durchschnitten ist oder wie sie als durchschnitten gedacht wird." *Deutsches Wörterbuch von Jacob und Wilhelm Grimm,* http://woerterbuchnetz.de/DWB/?sigle=DWB&mode=Vernetzung&lemid=GD06628, accessed 01.12.2012.
33. See Boehm, "Bilder als Instrumente der Erkenntnis," in *Wie Bilder Sinn erzeugen,* 94-114.
34. See Balázs, *Der sichtbare Mensch,* 73; Walter Benjamin adopted a terminology reminiscent of the cross-section in his surgical analogy of the film operator's ability to cut through the tissue of reality and establish new relations through montage. See Benjamin, "Das Kunstwerk im Zeitalter seiner technischen Reproduzierbarkeit," *Illuminationen* (Frankfurt am Main: Suhrkamp, 1977), 157-158.
35. Not by chance, all of these forms will become important intermedial figures in Ruttmann's subsequent filmmaking. I explore several of them in chapters 3 and 4 below.
36. For a discussion of this process in geology, see Martin Rudwick, "The Emergence of a Visual Language for Geological Science 1760-1840," *History of Science* 14 (1976): 149-195. On the balancing of aesthetic and scientific codes in Leondardo, see Boehm, *Wie Bilder Sinn Erzeugen,* 103-106. One could also consider the history of the cross-section in terms of Lorraine Daston and Peter Galison's history of "objectivity." Whereas earlier scientific cross-sections (such as 17th- and 18th-century anaotomical drawings) offer idealized representations of invisible interiors filtered through artistic subjectivity, many later cross-sections would aspire to mechanical objectivity, either by copying actual specimens (for example dissected organs) with their imperfections or by the use of mechanical media such as the x-ray. Other cross-sections (such as geological and architectural cross-sections) would – as already discussed above – downplay the role of subjective observation by emphasizing *functional* rela-

tions. Although Daston and Gallison's book has little to say about the latter strategy, it does support their observations on the 19th-century's desire to achieve images "untouched by human hands" and "untainted by subjectivity." See Lorraine Daston and Peter Galison, *Objectivity* (New York: Zone Books, 2010), 43.

37. It shared this tendency with scientific illustration generally. See Boehm, *Wie Bilder Sinn erzeugen,* 108.
38. "[Im] Gesicht [des Individuums] ist, wie in einem Querschnitt durch geologische Schichten, die Geschichte seines Lebens und das, was ihr als die zeitlose Mitgift seiner Natur zugrunde liegt, gezeichnet." Georg Simmel, "Soziologie der Sinne," *Aufsätze und Abhandlungen 1901-1908,* vol. 2 (Frankfurt am Main: Suhrkamp, 1993), 285.
39. "Die Geschichte ist der Längeschnitt, die Soziologie der Querschnitt durch das Sein." Rudolf Goldschied, "Soziologie und Geschichtswissenschaft," in *Annalen der Naturphilosophie* vol. 7, ed. Wilhelm Ostwald (Leipzig: Veit and Comp, 1908): 243. Other writers allowed for both historical and cross-sectional analyses within sociology. As one American textbook from 1917 stated: "Sociology has its 'longitudinal' divisions wherein are studied genetic (evolutional) aspects of group life; and its 'latitudinal' or 'cross-section' divisions, in which contemporary society (or that of a given period) is studied in cross-section." David Snedden, *Educational Sociology* (New York: Columbia University Teachers College, 1917), 6.
40. On the transition from deterministic thinking to thinking in terms of probabilities and statistics in the 19th century, see Hacking, *The Taming of Chance,* 1-10. In a discussion with obvious implications for the popularity of the *Querschnitt* model in sociology, Hacking discusses the emergence of "representative sampling" as a key moment in this epistemological transformation (6).
41. See Siegfried Kracauer, "Georg Simmel" (1919), in *The Mass Ornament. Weimar Essays,* ed. and trans. Thomas Y. Levin (Cambridge: Harvard University Press, 1995), 225-259. "[T]he interpretation of historical events is foreign to [Simmel]," Kracauer writes, "and he takes little account of the historical situation in which people find themselves at any given moment" (225).
42. For a broader treatment of this intellectual debate and its relation to Weimar, see David Frisby, *Fragments of Modernity* (Cambridge: MIT Press, 1998).
43. Kracauer, "Georg Simmel," 239.
44. Ibid., 246.
45. Ibid., 250.
46. Ibid., 231-32.
47. Ibid., 242.
48. See Anette Michelson, "On Montage and the Theory of the Interval," *Montage and Modern Life, 1919-1942,* ed. Matthew Teitelbaum. (Cambridge: MIT Press, 1992), 60-82.
49. Buchloh, "Gerhart Richter's *Atlas,*" 131.
50. Hermann von Wedderkop, "Jahresbilanz" [1925], *Der Querschnitt. Das Magazin der aktuellen Ewigkeitswerte 1924-1933,* ed. Christian Ferber (Berlin: Ullstein, 1981), 85-87. The resonance of the journal's title was underscored by a series of annotated lists, placed at the end of each issue, which covered the most significant new releases in various media, including "Sammelquerschnitt" (on artworks), the "Bücherquerschnitt," the "Schallplattenquerschnitt" and, later, the "Radioquerschnitt."

51. See Wedderkop, "Der Siegeszug des 'Querschnitt'" [1924], in *Der Querschnitt. Das Magazin der aktuellen Ewigkeitswerte*, 6.
52. As Kai Sicks has argued, one of the most frequent topics for analogies was the relation between aesthetics and sports. See Sicks, "'Der Querschnitt' oder: Die Kunst des Sporttreibens," in *Leibhaftige Moderne*, ed. Michael Cowan and Kai Sicks (Bielefeld: transcript, 2005), 33-48.
53. The first printed photograph in Germany appeared in the *Illustrierte Zeitung* in 1883. On the emergence of the illustrated press, see Dominique Gaessler, "The Spread of the Photographic Image," *The Abrams Encyclopedia of Photography*, ed. Brigitte Govignon (New York: Harry Abrams, 2004), 90-95 (esp. 92); Rune Hassner, "Photography and the Press," *A History of Photography*, ed. Jean-Claude Lemagny and André Rouillé (Cambridge: Cambridge University Press, 1986), 76-80.
54. "Nein, die Zeiten sind vorbei, da das Bild nur eine museale Angelegenheit war, Augenfutter für die Feiertage, sinniges Zwischenspiel für Familienfeste, Füllung für den Goldrahmen von Liebespaaren. Vorbei. Das Bild, die Photographie, ist in unser täglichstes Leben gedrungen, in jeder Minute, in jeder Sekunde rast es in tausenfacher Gestalt vor unser Auge, noch eins, noch eins, immer wieder ein neues." Erich Bürger, "Bilder-Bilder" in *Film-Photos wie noch nie*, ed. Edmund Bucher and Albrecht Kindt (Frankfurt: Frankfurter Societäts-Druckerei, 1929), 11.
55. Kracauer, "Photography," in *The Mass Ornament*, 57-58.
56. See Doane, *The Emergence of Cinematic Time*, 12-13. For an extended reading of Kracauer's complex understanding of photography both as an agent of "social blinding" (through the sheer accumulation of details in illustrated magazines) and as a medium that could reveal the contingency and arbitrariness of the social order (particularly in the case of aged photographs), see Miriam Bratu Hansen, *Cinema and Experience. Siegfried Kracauer, Walter Benjamin and Theodor W. Adorno* (Berkeley: University of California Press, 2012), 29-35.
57. Warburg scholars have made the point that it was only with the advent of photography that art history could be thought of as a discipline for comparing images by bringing them closer in time and space and reducing them to a similar scale. See Michaud, *Aby Warburg and the Image in Motion*, 102, 278; Georges Didi-Huberman, *L'Image survivante. Histoire de l'art et temps des fantômes selon Warburg* (Paris: Minuit, 2002), 455.
58. Doane, *Emergence of Cinematic Time*, 25.
59. Ibid., 27.
60. Ibid., 13.
61. Ibid., 11, 223.
62. Ibid., 17.
63. Ibid., 28.
64. Ibid., 241-242.
65. See for example Quaresima, "Astrazione e romanticismo," 35-36. Eisenstein first expounded upon the practice of intellectual montage in his 1929 essay, "The Cinematographic Principle and the Ideogram," in *Film Form. Essays in Film Theory*, ed. Jay Leyda (San Diego: Harcourt, 1949), 28-44 (esp. 30). He also discussed the concept in another essay written the same year. See Eisenstein, "The Dialectical Approach to Film Form," in *Film Form*, 45-63 (esp. 61-63).

66. "Der Kinematograph der Begriffe" [1930], in *Der Querschnitt: Das Magazin der aktuellen Ewigkeitswerte*, 369.
67. Mine is not the first reading to point this out. The author of an article on Ruttmann's montage for Quaresima's catalogue, for example, remarks that Ruttmann's montage empties out Eisensteinian montage of its violence and shock. "Ciò che rimane, una volte eliminata la violenza spettacolare, non e altro che una mera analogia." Vicente Sánchez-Biosca, "Tra musica visiva e macchinismo: il montaggio di *Berlin. Die Sinfonie der Großstadt*," in *Walter Ruttmann. Cinema, pittura, ars acustica*, 152. But as should be clear by this point in the discussion, I believe that Ruttmann's "mere" analogies should not be seen an inferior version of Eisenstein, but rather need to be understood in their own right as an expression of a certain statistical epistemology and a key operation of *Querschnitt*-montage.
68. Kracauer, "Georg Simmel," 238.
69. Ibid., 236.
70. On the figure of the "average man," see Hacking, *The Taming of Chance*, 107.
71. "Nur um zu zeigen, daß sie schließen, hätte es genügt, ein oder zwei Schaufenster zu filmen, deren Jalousien heruntergelassen werden, oder ein paar Türen, aus denen die Angestellten ins Freie treten. [...] Ruttmann dagegen läßt über Dutzende von Metern hinweg Dutzende unterschiedlichster Gegenstände in Aktion treten, sie werden wiederholt verschlossen, zugeklappt oder zugeklinkt. [...] Alles geht in einem einheitlichen Tempo und in beinahe einheitlicher Form vor sich." Roland Schacht, "Der BERLIN-Film," *BZ am Mittag*, no. 250, 24 September 1927, cited in Goergen, "Walter Ruttmann – Ein Porträt," 31.
72. On the "law of large numbers," see Hacking, *The Taming of Chance*, 95-104.
73. Ibid., 65-80.
74. Ibid., 177.
75. This was true, of course, not only for suicides, but for all sorts of disruptions such as industrial accidents, which become a central object of statistical research with the rise of social insurance. See Andreas Killen, *Berlin Electropolis. Shock, Nerves and German Modernity* (Berkeley: University of California Press, 2006), 18.
76. Hacking, *The Taming of Chance*, 177.
77. On the suicide scene, see also Kaes, "Leaving Home," 188.
78. See Helmut Lethen, *Cool Conduct. The Culture of Distance in Weimar, Germany*, trans. Don Reneau (Berkeley: University of California Press, 2002).
79. According to Goergen, the Fox Europa company actually commissioned two films, one on Berlin and another one on sports, but only the first film saw the light of day. See Goergen, "Walter Ruttmann – Ein Porträt," 25.
80. Three years later, the poet Erich Kästner would satirize this new vogue for statistics in his poem "Berlin in Zahlen" (1930), clearly a reference to the journal of the same title.
81. See Siegfried Kracauer, *From Caligari to Hitler* (Princeton: Princeton University Press, 1947), 185.
82. Ibid., 187.
83. "Nicht das Radikale der politischen Tendenz gibt den Ausschlag, sondern das Radikale und Konzessionslose der Stellungnahme." Walter Ruttmann, "Die Russen und wir" (1928), in *Walter Ruttmann. Eine Dokumentation*, 83.
84. Ellis and McLane, *A New History of Documentary Film*, 52.

85. "Suppose it be our task to tell of the miserable situation of a starving man; the story will impress the more vividly if associated with mention of the senseless gluttony of a well-to-do man." Vsevelod Pudovkin, *Film Technique and Film Acting* (New York: Grove Press, 1960), 75.
86. On this point, see Kaes, "Leaving Home," 189.
87. This does not mean that *Querschnitt*-montage was – as Kracauer also seems to suggest – *necessarily* apolitical; as a counter-example, one could point to John Heartfield and Kurt Tucholsky's scathing photo-book *Deutschland, Deutschland über alles!* (1929). In the introduction, the authors develop an extended allegory of their satirical book as a "Querschnitt durch Deutschland." John Heartfield and Kurt Tucholsky, *Deutschland, Deutschland über alles. Ein Bilderbuch von Kurt Tucholsky und vielen Fotografen, montiert von John Heartfield,* 15th ed. (Reinbeck bei Hamburg: Rowohlt, 2003), 12. But the authors also oppose their *Querschnitt* to standard less politicized versions in its effort to reveal the rotten elements of modern German society: "Weil aber die offiziellen Bildwerke den Schnitt durch diesen Käse stets so legen, daß sich die Maden nicht getroffen fühlen, wollen wir es einmal anders machen. Was sich beim Schnitt krümmt –: das sind die Maden. Auch sie sind Deutschland." Ibid.
88. See Hagener, *Moving Forward, Looking Back,* 222. For an account of the film's historical context, see Elsaesser and Hagener, "6. September. Walter Ruttmann: 1929." On the different types of advertising film in the 1920s, see Forster, *Ufa und Nordmark,* 27-45 (esp. 35-37, 41-43).
89. "Dem Geiste der Gemeinsamkeit unter den Völkern hat die Hamburg-Amerika-Linie ihr Schifffahrtsnetz zur Verfügung gestellt und eine Filmexpedition um die Erde gesandt, um das Verständnis für die mannigfachen Formen menschlichen Lebens zu vermehren und das Verbindende unter den Menschen zur Darstellung zu bringen."
90. See Balázs, *Der sichtbare Mensch,* 22: "Andererseits scheint uns gerade die Filmkunst eine Erlösung von dem babelschen Fluch zu versprechen. Denn auf der Leinwand der Kinos aller Länder entwickelt sich jetzt die erste internationale Sprache: die der Mienen und Gebärden." Similarly, Fritz Lang could write in 1927: "Werden wir uns doch klar darüber: Der Film ist der Rhapsode des 20. Jahrhunderts. Er kann aber viel mehr noch für die Menschheit werden: Der Wanderprediger, der zu Millionen spricht. Durch die stumme Beredtsamkeit seiner bewegten Bilder, deren Sprache unter allen Breitengraden gleich gut verstanden wird, kann der Film ein redlich Teil dazu beitragen, das Chaos wieder gutzumachen, das seit dem Turmbau zu Babel die Völker daran hindert, sich so zu sehen, wie sie wirklich sind." Fritz Lang, "Ausblick auf Morgen. Zum Pariser Kongress" *Lichtbild-Bühne* 19, no. 229 (September 25, 1926): 1–2.
91. On the gala reception after the premier, see "Hapag Empfang" *Der Kinematograph* 23, no. 61 (13 March 1929): 2; "Melodie der Welt," *Süddeutsche Filmzeitung* 8, no. 12 (22 March 1929): 14.
92. On the reacquisition of the *Resolute* and the recommencement of world tours by HAPAG, see Arnold Kludas, *Geschichte der deutschen Passagierschiffahrt. Band IV: Vernichtung und Widergeburt 1914 bis 1930* (Hambrug: Ernst Kabel Verlag, 1989), 221-223. See also F. W. von der Linde, *Die Hamburg-Amerika Linie* (Berlin: Widder-Verlag, 1930), 80-82.
93. Ibid., 224-225.

94. See Goergen, "Walter Ruttmann – Ein Porträt," 34.
95. In fact, Ruttmann's source material was not limited to the footage shot by the HAPAG crew. He also shot some scenes using the ethnographic exhibitions (so-called "human zoos") then on display at the Berlin Zoo. See Goergen, "Walter Ruttmann – Ein Porträt," 35. In addition, Ruttmann drew on older material in the archives of Emelka-Woche newsreel studio. See "Melodie der Welt," *Süddeutsche Filmzeitung*, 14.
96. Ross's film, as well its illustrated print counterpart from 1926, provides a model for the travel diary film in its forward procession through America, Japan, China, Malaysia (British Malaya), Thailand (Siam), Sumatra, Java, Bali, and back to Germany. See Colin Ross, *Mit dem Kurbelkasten um die Erde* (Berlin: Bild und Buch Verlag, 1926).
97. A more obvious forerunner might be found in projects such as Warburg's or – closer in content to Ruttmann's film – Albert Kahn's *Archives de la planète* (1908-1931), a collection of stereoscopic images, photographs and ethnographic film footage made with the intention of documentating the surface of the globe. In her study on the *Archives de la planète*, Paula Amad mentions MELODIE DER WELT as an obvious successor to Kahn's archival project, but ultimately argues that Ruttmann's tightly controlled montage is antithetical to unfinished and raw quality of Kahn's films. See Paula Amad, *Counter-Archive. Film, the Everyday and Albert Kahn's Archives de la Planète* (New York: Columbia University Press, 2010), 88-89. On Kahn's own relations to French colonialism, see pp. 261-294.
98. "Das wahre Geheimnis der Welt liegt im Sichtbaren, nicht im Unsichtbaren."
99. The film was also received in this sense. As one critic described it, "Auf den geistigen Spuren seines weniger geglückten *Berlin*-Films hat Ruttmann mit dem Objektiv den Planten bereist. Aber das Ergebnis ist kein Reisefilm, sondern etwas tausendmal Stärkeres. Ein Querschnitt durch Kulturen und durch das Menschenwesen. Ruttmann ordnet nicht geographisch und nicht wissenschaftlich. [...] Er gruppiert die Erscheinungen unseres Gestirns nach den Grundreflexen des Lebens." Walther Steinthal, "Melodie der Welt" (review article), *Neue Berliner Zeitung*, no. 61 (13 March 1929), cited in *Der Film der Weimarer Republik: 1929*, 439. Another writer described the film as a "soziologischer Querschnitt durch das Leben der Völker." Heinz Pol, "Die Melodie der Welt" (review), *Vossische Zeitung* 124 (14 March 1929), cited in *Der Film der Weimarer Republik: 1929*, 442. In an obvious reference to Colin Ross's film, a reviewer for *Der Kinematograph* wrote: "Es bleibt der dankenswerte Versuch der Hapag, einmal rund um die Welt mit dem Kurbelkasten zu wandern und so den Film in den Dienst der Werbung und der Kultur zu stellen." But he faulted Ruttmann for not following Ross's model: "Der neue Bearbeiter sah die Dinge nicht mehr ethnographisch, chronologisch oder vom Standpunkt der Orientierung und Belehrung aus, sondern machte daraus eine Photomontage, die technisch nicht uninteressant ist, die aber das Stoffliche vollständig übersah." "Die 'Melodie der Welt.' Grundsätzliches zum ersten großen deutschen Tonfilm," *Der Kinematograph* 23, no. 61 (13 March 1929), 1.
100. See Goergen, "Walter Ruttmann – Ein Porträt," 31.
101. See ibid.; "Neue Tonfilm-Situation" *Lichtbild-Bühne* 22, no. 11 (16 March 1929): 1; "Melodie der Welt," *Süddeutsche Filmzeitung*, 14; "Der erste abendfüllende Tonfilm

im Mozartsaal. Die Melodie der Welt." *Der Film – Wochenausgabe,* no. 11 (16 March 1929): 273.

102. Ruttmann, "Prinzipielles zum Tonfilm" (1928), in *Walter Ruttmann. Eine Dokumentation,* 83. See also Ruttmann, "Tonfilm? – !" *Illustrierter Film-Kurier* 11, no.1115 (1929): n.p. "Man versuche sich klar zu machen, daß Tonfilm seiner Gestaltungsmethode nach nichts anderes sein kann als Kontrapunkt. [...] Tonfilm gestaltender Kontrapunkt aber wäre ein bewußtes Gegeneinanderspielen der beiden Ausdrucksmittel – Bild und Ton in gedanklicher Bindung." MELODIE DER WELT also included several moments of synchronized sound. For a more detailed analysis, see Ulrich Rügner, "Walter Ruttmann pioniere del cinema sonoro," in *Walter Ruttmann. Cinema, pittura, ars acustica,* 172-173.
103. See Goergen, "Walter Ruttmann – Ein Porträt," 33.
104. Eisenstein, "A Dialectical Approach to Film Form," 55.
105. See Elsaesser and Hagener, "6. September, Walter Ruttmann," 317.
106. Ruttmann, "Prinzipielles zum Tonfilm," 83.
107. "Die 'Melodie der Welt'. Grundsätzliches zum ersten großen deutschen Tonfilm," 1.
108. "Die Not der Unterdrückten, die Ausbeutung der farbigen Rassen, diese Melodien fehlten ganz." "Melodien der Welt," *Hamburger Volkszeitung* 70 (23 March 1929), cited in *Der Film der Weimarer Republik,* 442.
109. The passage reads: "Also die Bildeinstellung ist glänzend, nur die Welteinstellung ein wenig schwach. [...] Wenn [...] Chinesenbabys, die auf dem Rücken der arbeitenden Mütter wie eine grimmige Last hängen, unschuldig lächelnd auf der Leinwand erscheinen, so verursacht der Film eine falsche, eine schlechte Heiterkeit. Hier scheint mir Ruttmann der Gefahr, die Welt als Globetrotter zu betrachten, nicht entgangen zu sein." Michael Kurd, "Melodie der Welt" (review article), *Der Welt am Abend* 61 (13 March 1929), cited in *Der Film der Weimarer Republik: 1929,* 440.
110. See Hagener, *Moving Forward, Looking Back,* 227; Elsaesser and Hagener, "6. September," 341.
111. Dziga Vertov, "On Radio Eye," in *Kino Eye. The Writings of Dziga Vertov,* ed. Anette Michelson, trans. Kevin O'Brien (Berkeley: University of California Press, 1984), 91-92, here 91. Although *The Sixth Part of the World* was silent, Vertov saw the film and its titles as a kind of visual analogy to radio, which he understood as a medium capable of inculcating a sense of class-belonging in listeners separated by geographical boundaries (ibid.), and the film also includes several sequences of radio, newspapers and film fulfilling this function.
112. On these and other colonialist films of the 1920s, see Gerlinde Waz, "Heia Safari! Träume von einer verlorenen Welt. Expeditions-, Kolonial- und ethnographische Film," in *Geschichte des dokumentarischen Films in Deutschland. Band 2: Weimarer Republik,* 187-203.
113. In L'Herbier's film, the engineer Einar Norsen builds a device for transporting the concerts of Claire Lescot throughout the entire world – a process we witness in a montage sequence showing audiences in the provinces and the colonies. In Humphrey Jennings's *Listen to Britain,* a sound montage played over an image of radio transistors demonstrates the reach of the BBC radio broadcast to every continent of the earth. Ruttmann himself would engage in a similar colonial vision in his later advertisement for Bayer, *Im Zeichen des Vertrauens* (1937), where Bayer products are presented above all as cures for the tropical illnesses of the world. In one sequence,

an animated map can be seen sending out radio-like waves from Germany to the entire world. Later, as the Bayer planes are sent around the world, we will see the Bayer logo literally illuminating the "dark" regions of Africa and Asia.

114. See Cowan, *Technology's Pulse*, 28-37, 167-171.

115. "Mit bestürzender Sachlichkeit enthüllt Walther Ruttmann die rhythmische Wiederkehr derselben Lebensgewohnheiten im Dasein der Völker: Arbeit, Verkehr, Sport, Krieg, Theater, eine Reihe optisch ineinader fließender Bewegungsmotive, die von New York bis Tokio, von Berlin bis Ceylon über die ganze Erde verfolgt und nach symphonischen Gesetzen komponiert worden sind." Hans Sahl, "Triumph der Photomontage / Melodie der Welt," *Der Montag Morgen* 11 (18 March 1929), cited in *Der Film der Weimarer Republik: 1929*, 442. For more on rhythm in MELODIE DER WELT, see Laurent Guido, "Le film comme 'symphonie du monde': l'universalité des gestes rythmiques dans *Melodie der Welt* (1929) et sa réception française," *Intermédialités* 16 (Fall 2010): 105-128. For more on the rhythm discourse in Germany in the 1920s, see Cowan, *Technology's Pulse*, 15-49.

116. "Sucht man nach einem Bilde für die sich an der Route der 'Resolute' ausbreitende Weltfülle, so liegt es nahe, an eine Symphonie zu denken, in der die Völker der Erde ihre Instrumente spielen. Das amerikanische Girl und die siamesische Tempeltänzerin, der Mann am laufenden Band in einer New Yorker Fabrik und der Rikschkuli in Peking, der Italiener in den Straßen Neapels und der Javaner unter den Palmen seiner Insel, der Jude an der Klagemauer Jerusalems und der Hindu, der in Benares blumengeschmückt in die heiligen Fluten des Ganges steigt, das sind einige Figuren aus dem reichinstrumentierten Orchester, das die Melodie der Welt über alle Stufen des Menschlichen ertönen läßt." *Hapag Weltreise 1933 mit dem Dreischrauben-Luxusdampfer "Resolute" vom Januar bis Mai* (Hamburg: Hamburg-Amerika Linie, 1933), 5.

117. For the emphasis on difference in the HAPAG brochure, see for example p. 24: "Hier [in Kalkutta] wird die ganze Kluft sichtbar, die sich noch heute zwischen Hindu und Europäer auftut." On the staging of authenticity, see Dean MacCannell, *The Ethics of Sightseeing* (Berkeley: University of California Press, 2011), 18.

118. Reports from the *Resolute* cruises emphasized the need to protect passengers from areas of conflict. For example, one report from 1927 explained: "Wegen der politischen Unruhen in China wurde von einem Anlaufen Shanghais abgesehen und als nächster Anlaufhafen gleich Tschingwang-tau gewählt." Cited in Kludas, *Die Geschichte der deutschen Passagierfahrt IV*, 224.

119. "Wir sind plötzlich in fernen Ländern, lernen Sitten und Häuser, Arbeits- und Lebensweise andrer Völker kennen. Die Menschen aller Erdteile ziehen an uns vorbei. Menschenkenntnis erweitert sich und, wie ich glaube, auch Menschenliebe. [...] Wir fühlen, wie alle Menschen aller Erdteile von denselben Motiven geängstigt und beseligt werden; uns kommt zu Bewusstsein, dass wir alle fünf Finger an jeder Hand haben; und irgendwo muß in jeder Frau ein Gefühl der Gemeinschaft erwachen, wenn sie sieht, wie die Indianerin ihr Kind betreut und die Australierin die Kuh melkt." Kurt Pinthus, "Ethische Möglichkeiten im Film," in *Der Film von morgen*, ed. Hugo Zehder (Berlin: Rudolf Kaemmerer Verlag, 1923), 124.

120. Goergen, "Walter Ruttmann – Ein Porträt," 37.

121. Elsaesser and Hagener, "6. September, Walter Ruttmann," 317.

122. On multiple versions and polyglot films, see Abé Mark Nornes, *Translating Global Cinema* (Minneapolis: University of Minnesota Press, 2007), 123-155.

123. See Guido, "Le film comme 'symphonie du monde.'"
124. "Walter Ruttmann, compositeur d'une partition double, pour l'oeil et l'oreille, où les bruits sirènes, machines, cris se conjuguent avec une extraordinaire aisance, a écrit le poème de l'analogie, de la correspondance, le documentaire romancé de l'unité de l'univers humain." Alexandre Arnoux, *Du Muet au parlant. Mémoires d'un témoin* (Paris: La Nouvelle Edition, 1946), 91-92. Cited in Guido, "Le Film comme 'symphonie du monde,' 124-125.
125. For an analysis of the film, see Cowan, "Technologies de diffusion simultanée."
126. See Abel Gance, *LA FIN DU MONDE vue par Abel GANCE. Miracle moderne en 3 parties écrit et exécuté par Abel GANCE* (1929), document held at the Cinémathèque Française, Gance B42, dossier 110.6, p. 54: "Renchaîné sur simultanéisme de croyants: Flash de figures extasiées: Une croix – un chrétien. Un bouddha – un chinois. Un dieu fétiche – un nègre. Races différentes, dieux différents, mais la même foi, montrant que ce qui est encore le plus divin ce n'est pas Dieu, c'est la foi elle-même." For more evidence of Gance's planned segments of world montage, see Abel Gance. *Découpage* for *La fin du monde* (1929), document held at the Cinémathe-que Française, Gance B42, dossier 109.2.
127. On the status of MELODIE DER WELT as a global film, see also Guido, "Le film comme 'symphonie du monde.'"
128. Such cruises cost between $1400 and $9500 per person in 1933 depending on accommodations and extras. For the list of prices, see *Hapag Weltreise 1933*, 73-75.
129. "Der erste abendfüllende deutsche Tonfilm," 273.
130. "Cette recherche des *thèmes* rejoignit la manie catalogueante des universitaires allemands, et devint irritante lorsque *Mélodie du monde* put se diviser en chapitres et paragraphes." Georges Sadoul, *Histoire du cinéma mondiale des origines à nos jours*, 9th ed. (Paris: Flammarion, 1949), 204.
131. "Der erste abendfüllende deutsche Tonfilm," 273.
132. "[...] ein Querschnitt durch eine phantastisch bunte, vielfältige, immer anders schilldernde Welt, der als einheitliches Ganzes dramatisch auf uns wirkt." Rudolf Kurtz, "Die Melodie der Welt," *Lichtbild-Bühne* 22, no. 61 (13 March 1929): n.p.
133. "Das Bedeutende daran ist das geistige Gesicht dieses Querschnitts. Das philosophische Fazit einer Technik, die es nun ermöglicht, so schnell über die Oberfläche eines Weltkörpers zu flitzen, daß das neue Netzhautbild noch auf das vorige trifft, die Erscheinungen einer Welt so aufeinander zu legen, daß ihr Zufälliges sich gegenseitig aufhebt, nur das Wesen bestehen bleibt." Steinthal, "Melodie der Welt," *Der Film der Weimarer Republik. 1929*, 439.
134. See Doane, *The Emergence of Cinematic Time*, 128-129. As Daston and Galison point out, Galton still undersood his efforts to represent the typical within the dictates of objectivity. His method thus stood "poised between [...] two ordinarily disjunct modes of observation: on the one side, it aimed for an ideal type that lay 'behind' any single individual. On the other side, Galton's face-machine proceeded toward that ideal not what he and others had come to see as subjective idealization [...], but with the quasi-automated procedures of mechanical objectivity" (Daston and Galison, *Objectivity*, 169). This was, as Doane has shown, precisely the epistemological balancing act that informed statistics.
135. "Ses images se succèdent à une telle vitesse, elles font sur l'écran une apparition si brève qu'elles semblent superposées, simultanées, placées en regard, perçues en

même temps. C'est l'effet du montage le plus serré qui ait jamais été pratiqué." André Levinson, "Le film sonore. 'La Mélodie du monde' et le miracle du rythme," *Radio Magazine* 9 March 1930, 5. Cited in Guido, "Le film comme 'symphonie du monde,'" 111.

136. "Das Wesen jedes Archivs [...] besteht darin, daß es Gegenstände, die sonst [...] dem Verlust irgendwie preisgegeben wären, die zerstreut und unübersichtlich, im Strom der Zeit vorüberfluten und vergehen, [...] konserviert, ordnet und dadurch auf dem Wege des Vergleichs miteinander zu betrachten, sie voneinander zu unterscheiden ermöglicht." F[ritz] Schimmer, "Zur Frage des Reichsfilmarchivs," 11.
137. According to one reviewer of the Henny Porten film, the new genre constituted "the first living film museum." Hans Feld, cited in Ehmann, "Wie Wirklichkeit erzählen?" 588.
138. Michel Foucault, *The Order of Things. An Archeology of the Human Sciences* (London: Routledge, 1970), xvi.
139. This is, interestingly, the same sequence of themes Ruttmann follows in the newspaper section of BERLIN that I discussed above.
140. The parallel between the cutter and the magician is further underscored by the use a prismatic lens in both instances: the magician's conjuring gesture is followed by a prismatic shot of audience members in kaleidoscopic motion, whereas the cutter's gesture over the image of the thief is followed by a prismatic shot of the illustrated newspaper multiplied and spinning in the same kaleidoscopic motion.

3. Statistics and Biopolitics: Conceiving the National Body in Ruttmann's Hygiene Films (1930-1933)

1. Foucault, *Security, Territory, Population,* 104; ibid., "Governmentality," 99.
2. Foucault, "Governmentality," 100. See also Tooze, *Statistics and the German State,* 21.
3. Ian Hacking, "How Should We Do the History of Statistics?" in *The Foucault Effect,* 181. Cf. Hacking, *The Taming of Chance,* 119: "Functionaries such as [Farr] created the infrastructure of one of the kinds of power by which our society operates. We obtain data about a governed class whose comportment is offensive, and then attempt to alter what we guess are relevant conditions of that class in order to change the law of statistics that the class obeys."
4. See Uli Jung and Wolfgang Mühl-Benninghaus, "Die Kulturfilmdiskussion von 1914 bis 1920. Die politische und ideologische Dynamik der Ufa-Gründung," in *Geschichte des dokumentarischen Films in Deutschland. Band 1: Kaiserreich 1895-1918,* ed. Juli Jung and Martin Loiperdinger (Stuttgart: Reclam, 2005), 480-486.
5. See Klaus Kreimeier, "Komplex-Starr. Semiologie des Kulturfilms," *Geschichte des dokumentarischen Films in Deutschland. Band 2,* 87-119.
6. This is precisely how FEIND IM BLUT was conceived and announced: "Der Film wird als ein teils belehrender, teils als ein bildhaft interessierender Kulturfilm hergestellt, der international Geltung erhalten soll. In der Spielhandlung, die als Träger der Idee dienen muß, sind die medizinisch wissenschaftlichen Teile eingefügt und durch Mediziner bearbeitet worden." "Film ABC," *Der Film* 16, no. 14 (4 April 1931): n.p. Another reviewer praised the film for its combination of education and entertainment: "[Das Manuskript] verbindet nützliche Belehrung mit kultivierter Unterhalt-

samkeit und Spannung." "Feind im Blut," review article, *Der Film* 16, no. 16 (18 April 1931): n.p.

7. According to Heinrich Mutzenbacher, in a short text for the programm that accompanied MELODIE DER WELT, the central operation of the Kulturfilm was to extend the individual drama to the mass: "Das Dramatische, welches der Mensch im Theater, zum Teil aus technischen Gründen, in den Schicksalen von Einzelpersonen sich formte, wird im Kulturfilm, wo die Schranken von Zeit und Ort gefallen sind, auf die gesamte Menschheit projiziert. Es mag sich eine neue Form des Epischen herauskristallisieren, um so mehr, als es unserer Zeit entspricht, das Heldische und das mit ihm verbundene Tragische im Schicksal der Masse zu suchen." Heinrich Mutzenbacher, untitled text, *Illustrierter Film-Kurier* 11, no. 1115 (1929): n.p.
8. Hacking, "How Should We Do a History of Statistics?," 194.
9. I use the term *biopolitics* here in the enlarged sense suggested by Edward Dickinson as "an extensive complex of ideas, practices and institutions focused on the care, regulation, disciplining, improvement and shaping of individual bodies and [...] national populations." Dickinson, "Biopolitics, Fascism, Democracy," 3.
10. Dickinson, "Biopolitics, Fascism, Democracy," 22-23. See also Hong, *Welfare Modernity and the Weimar State*, 270-276.
11. This transformation goes hand in hand with the increasing coercive nature of statistical research under Nazism. As J. Adam Tooze has shown, one of the particularities of National Socialist statistical operations was that they removed the guarantee of confidentiality that had characterized statistical sampling under previous regimes and transformed statistics from a tool of anonymous information gathering into one of totalitarian surveillance. J. Adam Tooze, *Statistics and the German State 1900-1945. The Making of Modern Economic Knowledge* (Cambridge: Cambridge University Press, 2001), 24, 28, 217.
12. Anita Gertiser. "Ekel. Beobachtungen zu einer Strategie im Aufklärungsfilm zur Bekämpfung der Geschlechtskrankheiten der 1920er Jahre," *Figurationen* 1:8 (2008): 63. On the history of the DGBG, see Lutz Sauerteig, *Krankheit, Sexualität, Gesellschaft. Geschlechtskrankheiten und Gesundheitspolitik in Deutschland im 19. und im frühen 20. Jahrhundert* (Stuttgart: Steiner, 1999), 89-126.
13. See Sauerteig *Krankheit, Sexualität, Gesellschaft*, 109-110. The "reformist" groups also enjoyed a much larger membership than their racist counterparts before 1933. See Dickinson, "Biopolitics, Fascism, Democracy," 10-11.
14. Ibid., 64-65; on the French context of anti-syphilis films, see Thierry Lefèbvre, "Représentations cinémagoraphiques de la syphilis entre les deux guerres: séropositivité, traitement et charlatanisme," *Revue historique de la pharmacie* 83 (1995): 267-278.
15. Gertiser, "Ekel," 64.
16. Ruttmann was joined, among other people, by Georg Stilanudis, the cinematographer from Viktor Travas's NIEMANDSLAND (1931), and by Wolfgang Zeller, the composer for Lotte Reiniger's DIE ABENTEUER DES PRINZEN ACHMED (1926), who would go on to collaborate with Ruttmann on many films after 1933 and to work on many of the most notorious propaganda films such as JUD SÜSS (1941).
17. "...die Spitze der Behörden, Vorstände von Versicherungsverbänden, sowie Vertreter der Ärzteschaft." "Praesens startet 'Feind im Blut,'" *Lichtbild-Bühne*, no. 91 (16 April 1931): n.p. The film was also preceded two days earlier by a "press tea" in the Hotel Bristol, in which the head of the DGBG Hermann Roeschmann and represen-

tatives of the medical establishment gave lectures on prostitution and siphylis rates. Ibid. Roeschmann also gave the opening lecture at the gala performance and at least one subsequent performance. See "Feind im Blut. Praesens-Film – Atrium," *Lichtbild-Bühne,* no. 93 (18 April 1931): n.p; "Feind im Blut in veränderter Fassung," *Lichtbild-Bünhne,* no. 102 (29 April 1931): n.p.

18. On account of its sexual subject matter, the film was also received as an "Aufklärungsfilm." See "Feind im Blut," review article, *Süddeutsche Filmzeitung,* no. 22 (29 May 1931): n.p.
19. See FEIND IM BLUT, censor card no. 28713, dated 16 April 1931, Bundesarchiv-Filmarchiv, Berlin, 13. On the function of disgusting images in this film and other medical films, see Gersiner, "Ekel."
20. This might be the connection one reviewer had in mind when he wrote "Man fühlt eine östliche Orientierung Ruttmanns heraus. Er eifert russischen Vorbildern nach. Bleibt dabei aber doch deutsch und gründlich." "Feind im Blut," review article, *Der Film* 16, no. 16 (1931): n.p.
21. On this point, see also Quaresima, "Astrazione e romanticismo," 36. The topos would appear once again in the early Nazi propaganda film HITLERJUNGE QUEX to a very different effect. There, the mother's suicide is what allows Quex's family to dissolve so that he can be adopted by his "rightful" new family: the Hitler youth organization. See Eric Rentschler, "Emotional Engineering: Hitler Youth Quex, *Modernism/Modernity* 2.3 (1995): 27-28.
22. Very little has been published on the film. In addition to Gertiser (64-75), see also Philipp Sarasin, "Feind im Blut: Die Bedeutung des Blutes in der deutschen Bakteriologie, 1870-1900," in *Mythen des Blutes,* ed. Christina von Braun and Christoph Wulf (Frankfurt am Main: Campus, 2007), 296-297. Probably the most important research on the film was presented in June 2010 at a conference in Strasbourg entitled *Tourner autour d'un film sanitaire: regards, lectures, analyse,* which included both medical and film-historical perspectives on FEIND IM BLUT. The papers have not yet been published. For a report of the conference, see Aurore Lüscher, "Tourner autour d'un film sanitaire," http://hsozkult.geschichte.hu-berlin.de/index.asp?id=3699&-view=pdf&pn=tagungsberichte, accessed 01.12.2012.
23. "Unter vielen Tausenden: ein Mechaniker, seine Frau, ein Student, sein Freund."
24. For an analysis of this lack of focus on character in *Menschen am Sonntag,* see Lutz Koepnick, "The Bearable Lightness of Being: *People on Sunday* (1930)," in *Weimar Cinema. An Essential Guide to Classic Films of the Era* (New York: Columbia University Press, 2009), 236-253 (esp. 236-238).
25. This might account for the negative reaction of one critic from the *Süddeutsche Filmzeitung* who complained that Ruttmann's narrative left audiences utterly confused: "Für den Spielfilm, zudem mit mehreren Handlungen, wie sie im zweiten Teil dieses Aufklärungsfilms nebeneinander gelegt sind, ist [Ruttmanns expressionistische Art des Nebeneinander und Durcheinander] kein Segen. […] Der zweite Teil dieses Films, der Spielfilm ist durch Mißachtung der Klarheitsforderung mehr oder minder verkorkst." "Feind im Blut," review article, *Süddeutsche Filmzeitung,* no. 22 (29 May 1931): n.p. Aside from this critique, Ruttmann's critics generally praised the film's use of medical images.
26. I borrow the terms "expository documentary" and "evidentiary editing" from Bill Nichols. See Nichols, *Representing Reality: Issues and Concepts in Documentary* (Bloo-

mington: Indiana University Press, 1991), 34-35; Nichols, *Introduction to Documentary* (Bloomington: Indiana University Press, 2004), 169.

27. Roeschmann's prerecorded lecture was on a separate reel and received a separate censor evaluation on 7 May 1931. See *Walter Ruttmann. Eine Dokumentation,* 134.
28. "Wir haben gesehen, dass die Übertragung der Siphilis in den meisten Fällen durch den Geschlechtsverkehr erfolgt"
29. At least one historian of German film posits the existence of a genre of animated statistics in the "statistical film" of the 1920s. See Frederick W. Ott, *The Great German Films* (Secaucus: Citadel, 1986), 16: "Offshoots of the Lehrfilm [after WWI] included the Werkfilm (industrial film), designed for training employees, the statistische [sic] Film, which presented statistical data in animated graphs and charts, and the Wissenschaftlichen [sic], which described a new apparatus or depicted the performance of a surgical operation."
30. This may well have been the dynamic that one reviewer had in mind when he praised Ruttmann for transforming individual dramas into knowledge: "Hier zeigte sich die Regie ihrer großen Aufgabe, Belehrendes an Ereignissen und Geschicken deutlich werden zu lassen, immer lebendig zu bleiben, doch nie sensationell zu werden, – hier zeigte sich die Regie ihrer ersten Pflicht gewachsen." "Feind im Blut," review article, *Der Film* 16, no. 16 (18 April 1931): n.p.
31. Daston and Galison, *Objectivity,* 43.
32. Ibid., 42.
33. Ibid., 125-138.
34. Ibid., 250.
35. Daston and Galison explore another solution to the problem in the 20th-century paradigm they call "trained judgment," in which scientists relied on intuition to pinpoint the meaningful or the typical in scientific images. Ibid., 309-361. The kind of scientific illustration and animation I discuss here was something different: although not *idealized,* it was an effort to reduce contingent details to arrive at a *typical* or *normal* representation, one I believe to be influenced strongly by 19th-century statistics.
36. Scott Curtis, "Rough and Smooth: Photographic and Animated Images in Scientific and Educational Film," paper delivered at the 29th annual Screen Conference in Glasgow, 30 June 2012. I thank the author for providing me with an unpublished manuscript of his presentation.
37. On the tradition of disgusting images in medical films of the 1920s, see Gertiser, "Ekel."
38. I have focused on the way in which Ruttmann's film highlights the distinction between (animated) filmic images and (still) lantern slides. However, animated images had in fact already existed in scientific lecture halls. As Henning Schmidgen shows, the 19th-century scientific lecture hall or "spectatorium" (whose semi-circular form is still present in Ruttmann's classroom) had already created a "cinematography without film" by means of episcopic projectors designed to project organs and organisms *in movement.* See Henning Schmidgen, "1900 – The Spectatorium: On Biology's Audiovisual Archive," *The Grey Room* 43 (2011), 42-65.
39. As Lisa Cartwright long ago pointed out, scientific film, with its tendency to highlight and even celebrate the apparatus, fits uneasily with Marxist and psychoanaly-

tical theories of the "hidden apparatus." See Cartwright, *Screening the Body. Tracing Medicine's Visual Culture* (Minneapolis: University of Minnesota Press, 1995), 1-17.

40. In invoking the term *dispositif* here, my point is that Ruttmann was not simply showcasing the projector as technology, but a specific model of the cinema for which the *classroom* is paradigmatic: one in which the cinema functions to visualize statistical data and bring spectators to see themselves as part of a biopolitical population. As I discuss in chapter 4, the classroom would reappear in many of Ruttmann's films under National Socialism as a self-reflexive figure for conceptualizing the cinema as a *dispositif* of mass governance.
41. In the United States, although medical films existed before the 1920s, it was not until the late 1920s, that the American College of Surgeons began to collaborate with Eastman Kodak to "place medical motion pictures at the center of surgical training." Kirsten Ostherr, "Medical Education through Film: Animating Anatomy at the American College of Surgeons and Eastman Kodak," in *Learning with the Lights off*, 169. More generally, it was in the late 1920s that film was adopted on a wide scale for the classroom after initial reservations by educators had been overcome. See Jennifer Peterson, "Glimpses of Animal Life: Nature Films and the Emergence of Classroom Cinema," in *Learning with the Lights off*, 145-167.
42. I place the term "predecessor" in quotes here to underscore that the relationship between lantern culture and the cinema is much more complex than accounts of a unidirectional "evolution" could suggest. On this point, see Janelle Blankenship, "To Attract/To Alternate? The Skladanowsky Experiment," *Cinema & Cie: International Film Studies Journal* 9 (2007): 61-79.
43. Anja Laukötter's presentation in the conference mentioned above focused on the presence of the moulages in the film. See Lüscher, "Tourner autour d'un film sanitaire."
44. See Doane, *The Emergence of Cinematic Time*, 128-130; Daston and Galison, *Objectivity*, 169. Closer to Ruttmann's time, one would have to cite August Sander's *Menschen des 20. Jahrhunderts*, which pursued a similar project with individual photographs designed to show "typical" members of a class, a group or a profession.
45. Thomas Schnalke, "Casting Skin: Meanings for Doctors, Artists and Patients, in *Models. The Third Dimension of Science*, ed. Soraya de Chadarevian and Nick Hopwood (Stanford: Stanford University Press, 2004), 220.
46. For an analysis of this discourse, see Jacques Aumont, "The Face in Close-Up," *The Visual Turn. Classical Film Theory and Art History*, ed. Angela Dalle Vacche (New Brunswick: Rutgers University Press, 2003), 127-151, esp. 144-145. For a good analysis of the prehistory of the face on screen, see especially Tom Gunning, "In Your Face: Physiognomy, Photography and the Gnostic Mission of Early Film," *Modernism/Modernity* 4 (1997): 1-29.
47. Thus Lang could write in 1929: "Wenn man von stummen Instrumenten reden kann, so ist im Film das Gesicht des Menschen solch ein stummes Instrument, das deutlich – und vielleicht wegen seiner Stummheit – berufen ist, das stärkste Echo, das vieltönigste Mitklingen in den Herzen derer, die es schauen, zu erwecken. Haben wir vor dem Film gewusst, wieviel das Zucken eines geschlossenen Mundes, das Heben oder Senken eines Augenlids, das leise Sichabwenden eines Kopfes auszudrücken vermögen?" Fritz Lang, "Die mimische Kunst im Lichtspiel" (1929), in

Werkstatt Film. Selbstverständnis und Visionen von Filmleuten der 20er Jahre, ed. Rolf Aurich and Wolfgang Jacobsen (Berlin: Edition Text & Kritik, 1998), 49.

48. On the relation between eugenics, conceived as the means of intervening in populational health, and modern statistics, see Hacking, *The Taming of Chance,* 108.

49. The eugenic dimension to FEIND IM BLUT is perhaps hardly surprising; the film was made during a transitional period on the cusp of a new regime. In the wake of the financial crisis, eugenics was, even before the Nazi seizure of power, beginning to gain serious consideration in government circles as an effective "cost-cutting" strategy. On this point, see Dickinson, "Biopolitics, Fascism, Democracy," 15. See also Hong, *Welfare Modernity and the Weimar State,* 240, 249-250, 263.

50. See Goergen, "Walter Ruttmann – Ein Porträt," 40.

51. Ruttmann had more experience than the other two filmmakers combined. Sonjevski-Jamrowski had only worked on two previous films and Hans von Passavant on four (never as director).

52. Both Uricchio and Loiperdinger suggest that BLUT UND BODEN functioned for Ruttmann as a "Loyalitätsbekundung" (Uriccio, "Ruttmann nach 1933," 60) and a "Bewährungsprobe" (Loiperdinger, "Neue Sachlichkeit und Nationalsozialismus," 45). That the regime still held Ruttmann in suspicion is suggested by the fact that most of the film's initial reviews in the trade journals – now under the control of Goebbels's propaganda ministry – conspicuously avoided mentioning his name in their written reviews. Writers for Lichtbild-Bühne, for example, only mentioned Sonjewski-Jambrowski, Willy Geißler (music) and Karl Motz (script). See "Blut und Boden. Der Bauernfilm," *Lichtbild-Bühne,* no. 260 (3 November 1933): n.p.; "Blut und Boden / Marmorhaus," review article, *Lichtbild-Bühne,* no. 227 (24 November 1933): n.p.

53. On Noldan, see Elsaesser, "Archives and Archeologies," 21-22.

54. On Darré's career, see among others Gesine Gerhard, "Breeding Pigs and People for the Third Reich: Richard Walther Darré's Agrarian Ideology," in *How Green Were the Nazis. Nature, Environment and Nation in the Third Reich,* ed. Franz-Josef Brueggemeier, Mark Cioc and Thomas Zeller (Athens: Ohio University Press, 2005), 129-146.

55. For a presentation of the theme in international art of the 1930s, see *1930s. The Making of the New Man,* ed. Jean Clair, exhibition catalogue (Ottawa: National Gallery of Canada, 2008), 208-219.

56. "Und dieser Staatsgedanke von Blut und Boden unterscheidet sich eben darin grundsätzlich von allen nur nationalistischen Staatsbegriffen, daß er das Blut, d. h. die Rasse, zur Achse seiner Weltanschauung und aller politischen Überlegungen macht, während der rein nationalistische Staatsgedanke auch ohne den Blutsgedanken möglich ist." R. Walther Darré, *Blut und Boden: ein Grundgedanke des Nationalsozialismus. Sonderdruck aus "Odal", Monatsschrift für Blut und Boden.* 21. Bis 25. Tausend (Berlin: Reichsdruckerei, 1938), 12.

57. See Darré, *Blut und Boden,* 7: "Denn es ist damit erstmalig die Folgerung aus der Tatsache gezogen worden, daß in einem Staate germanischer Natur das Blut nur auf dem Lande in Generationen sich erhält und vermehrt, die Abkehr vom ländlichen Leben aber einen starken Verschleiß der Geschlechter bewirkt. Wenn man das Vergleichsbild bringen darf, so kann man sagen, daß das Blut eines Volkes auf seinen Bauernhöfen sozusagen quellenartig emporsprudelt, um in der Stadt über kurz oder lang zu versiegen. Für Völker, deren Grundcharakter nomadischer Art ist, zum Beispiel für das jüdische Volk, gilt dieses Gesetz nicht, dagegen gilt es für

germanisches Blut unbedingt und kann geradezu das eiserne Schicksalsgesetz des germanischen Menschentums genannt werden."

58. Ibid.
59. A general presentation of the film can be fond in Peter Zimmermann, "Landschaft und Bauerntum," in *Geschichte des dokumentarischen Films in Deutschland. Band 3*, 311-312; Jeremiah Garsha, "Dictating the Past: The Capture of Medievalism in Nazi Cinematic Propaganda and the Roots of the Holocaust," *Ex Post Facto: Journal of the History Students at San Francisco State University* 19 (2010): 131-147, http://userwww.sfsu.edu/epf/journal_archive/volume_XIX,_2010/garsha_j.pdf, accessed 15.06.2013.
60. See "Blut und Boden," review article. *Der Kinematograph* 27, no. 228 (24 November 1933): n.p.; "Blut und Boden / Marmorhaus," n.p.
61. An advertisement from the Munich journal *Süddeutsche Filmzeitung* published shortly after the film's Berlin premiere explained that small-gage copies were available for rural screenings: "Es besteht die Möglichkeit, Schmalfilmkopien der Filme 'Blut und Boden' und 'Erntedankfest auf dem Bückeberg' herzustellen, die somit in einem Program vor allem auf dem flachen Lande mit Schmalfilmapparaturen vorgeführt werden können. Die Landesfilmstellen werden aufgefordert, sofort die Anzahl der benötigten Kopien der Reichspropagandaleitung, Hauptabteilung IV (Film) zu melden." "Filme," *Süddeutsche Filmzeitung* 12, no. 49 (10 December 1933): n.p.
62. "In kurzer Zeit wird vom Stabsamt des Reichsbauernführers ein 30 Minuten Film unter obigem Titel [Blut und Boden] herausgebracht, den man wohl den aktuellsten politischen Film nennen kann, der bisher erschienen ist. In einer Zeit, in der die *Sicherung der deutschen Bodenständigkeit* durch das *Erbhofgesetz* und die Ausschaltung der Spekulation im Reichsnähernstandsgesetz das Auge der ganzen Welt auf Deutschland lenkt, wird hier im historischen Zusammenfassung am Beispiel einer Familie all das nochmals an unserem Auge vorbeigeführt, was klar und unzweideutig den Beweis für die Notwendigkeit einer solchen staatspolitischen Linie erbringt." "Blut und Boden. Der Bauernfilm," n.p.
63. "(1) Bauer kann nur sein, wer deutschen oder stammesgleichen Blutes ist. (2) Deutschen oder stammesgleichen Blutes ist nicht, wer unter seinen Vorfahren väterlicher- oder mütterlicherseites jüdisches oder farbiges Blut hat." "Reichserbhofgesetz." *Deutsches Reichsgesetzblatt 1933*, part 1, 686.
64. For more on this point see Wolfgang Benz, *A Concise History of the Third Reich*, trans. Thomas Dunlap (Berkeley: University of California Press, 2006), 102-103.
65. Surviving censor cards from 1936 show that the film was reissued at least twice in 16mm format and classified as a "Lehrfilm" for classroom use. One of those cards stipulates that the film was supposed to follow a public lecture. See *Blut und Boden*, censor card no. 41372, dated 28 January 1936, Bundesarchiv-Filmarchiv, Berlin, 2. Like most of Ruttmann's post-1933 films, BLUT UND BODEN was also approved for special showings on Good Friday, Penance Day and Memorial Day (Heldengedenktag). Ibid., 3.
66. This didactic element was precislely what the film's reviewers touted as its main value. As one reviewer for the *Deutsche Filmzeitung* described it, "Vom Stabsamte des Reichsbauernführers ist ein Film ins Leben gerufen worden, die [...] im Rahmen einer ganz einfachen Spielhandlung die Erkenntnis über die verhängnisvollen Ursachen erschließt, die an der Verarmung und am Rückgange der landwirtschaftli-

chen Betriebe schuld sind." "Blut und Boden," review article, *Deutsche Filmzeitung* Jg 12, no. 47 (26 November 1933): 9.

67. Darré, *Blut und Boden*, 5-6.
68. Darré, *Blut und Boden*, 6.
69. "Fünf hundert sollen es werden, tausend!"
70. For a general presentation of Neurath and the history of Isotype, see for example Frank Hartmann, "Visualizing Social Facts: Otto Neurath's ISOTYPE Project," in *European Moderism and the Information Society*, ed. W. Boyd Rayward (Aldershot: Ashgate, 2008), 279-294.
71. On the relation of Isotype to avant-garde discourse in Constructivism, De Stijl and the Bauhaus, see Ellen Lupton, "Reading Isotype," in *Design Discourse. History, Theory, Criticism*, ed. Victor Margolin (Chicago: University of Chicago Press, 1989), 145-156.
72. "Blut und Boden," *Deutsche Filmzeitung*, 9.
73. "Eine ganz einfache Handlung [...] gibt Gelegenheit, Zahlen einzufügen, die für sich sprechen." "Blut und Boden," review article, *Der Kinematograph* 27, no. 228 (24 November 1933): n.p. As the same reviewer noticed, the "scientificity" of these statistics was underscored by Willi Geißler's musical score, which is most dramatic in the scenes of individual plight but more reserved "wo Statistiken ihre nüchterne Sprache erheben." Ibid.
74. "Wir machen heute Bilanzen und Statistiken über alle Gebiete unseres völkischen Daseins, nur leider noch keine über die biologischen Grundlagen unseres völkischen Lebens. Und noch weiter sind wir davon entfernt, auf Grund einer einwandfreien biologischen Bilanz unseres Volkskörpers auch einmal einen biologischen Haushaltsplan aufzustellen." Darré, *Blut und Boden*, 8. The rhetoric of "Volkstod" had predecessors in the Weimar Republic, where the term begins to be used amid fears of an aging population and above all of women's emancipation. See Detlev Peukert, *The Weimar Republic*, trans. Richard Daveson (New York: Hill and Wang, 1993), 8. But the invocation of "Volkstod" by Weimar authorities (aside from the already existing proponents of "Blut und Boden") did not necessarily assume a racial conception of the population. Under National Socialism, on the other hand, the term was linked to ideas about racial purity. See for example Arthur Gütt, *Bevölkerungs- und Rassenpolitik. Grundlagen, Aufbau und Wirtschaftsordnung des nationalsozialistischen Staates* 12 (Berlin: Industrieverlag Spaeth & Linde, 1936), section 7, "Urscachen des Volksentartung und des Volkstodes," 14-15.
75. See Darré, *Blut und Boden*, 7: "Wir wissen, daß die Geburtenzahl auf dem Lande im Verhältnis zur Zahl der Bevölkerung größer ist als in den Städten. 1927 hatten wir im Reichsdurchschnitt einen Geburtenausfall von 10% gemessen an der für die Bestandserhaltung nötigen Geburtenziffer: das Land stellte dagegen noch einen Geburtenüberschuß von 13%! Im Jahre 1933 betrug die auf 1000 der Wohnbevölkerung berechnete Geburtenziffer in den Gemeinden mit weniger als 2000 Einwohnern, also in den ländlichen Gemeinden, 18 Lebendgeburten auf 1000, in der mittleren Gemeindegruppe von 2000 bis 400.000 Einwohnern nur 14,5 auf 1000 und in den Großstädten nur 11,2 Lebendgeborene auf je 1000 Einwohner. Es geht aber nicht allein um den zahlenmäßigen Bestand unseres Volkes, sondern es geht um die Erhaltung der Erbanlagen, denen wir alle Tüchtigkeit und alle Leistungen in unserem Volke verdanken."

76. "Die Tatsache dieser innerdeutschen Wandering vom Lande in die Stadt hinein bedeutet in der bevölkerungspolitischen Bilanz die Todesgefahr für das ganze Volk." "Blut und Boden, der Bauernfilm," n.p.
77. "Nur ein Bauernwall im Osten rettet und sichert Deutschlands Zukunft vor völkischer Überfremdung." *Blut und Boden,* censor card no. 41372, 4. Some of the film's reviewers also latched onto this point: "Der Schluß des Films zeigt dann die drohende Überfremdungsgefahr im deutschen Osten. [...] Der Osten ist dünn besiedelt. Hier gilt es, ein neues Bauerntum aufzurichten, das gleichzeitig einen Schutzwall bildet gegen jede Überfremdung." "Blut und Boden / Marmorhaus," n.p. The term *Überfremdung* was a Nazi catchword for "racial miscegenation," above all between Germans and Jews. In his *Program der NSDAP* (1936), for example, Hans Fabricus described the phenomenon of intermarriage between Germans and Jews since the 18th century as a "blutmäßige Überfremdung" of the German race. Hans Fabricus, *Das Program der NSDAP. Grundlagen, Aufbau und Wirtschaftsordnung des nationalsozialistischen Staates,* no. 6 (Berlin: Industrieverlag Spaeth & Linde, 1936), 12.
78. On this point, see Garsha, "Dictating the Past,"139.
79. Boaz Neumann, "The Phenomenology of the German People's Body (*Volkskörper*) and the Extermination of the Jewish Body," in *New German Critique* 106 (2009): 156.
80. Hong, *Welfare Modernity and the Weimar State,* 272-273.
81. Neumann, "Phenomenology of the German People's Body," 158, 162.
82. See Cowan, "Advertising, Rhythm and the Filmic Avant-Garde in Weimar."
83. For an analysis, see Sabine Wilke, "'Verrottet, verkommen, von fremder Rasse durchsetzt': The Nazi 'Kulturfilm' 'Ewiger Wald' (1936), *German Studies Review* 24:2 (2001): 353-376. The use the forest as a metaphor for a racially conceived *Volkskörper* was, in fact, a prevalent theme of "Blut und Boden"-inspired discourse, which began in the 1920s and became part of state-sanctioned policy after 1933. See Imort, "'Planting a Forest Tall and Straight Like the German *Volk*,'" 106-107, 110-111, 114.
84. Ruttmann,"Die absolute Mode," 82.
85. Kracauer, *From Caligari to Hitler,* 188.
86. On this point, see Thomas Elsaesser, *Weimar Cinema and After. Germany's Historical Imaginary* (New York: Routledge, 2000), 20-24.
87. Other film historians have commented on the didactic aspects of Ruttmann's later films as compared with his Weimar work. Thus Uricchio writes of BLUT UND BODEN: "Wo z.B. der Film BERLIN von konventiellen Erzählstrukturen, von konventionellen Figuren und Aufnahmestrategien abweicht und eine Fragmentierung bietet, die zur Sinnstiftung auf die Deutung des Publikums angewiesen ist, postuliert BLUT UND BODEN seinen Sinn durch eine erzählende Konstruktion, durch handelnde Figuren und sogar informative Grafiken. Mit BLUT UND BODEN volzieht Ruttmann eine konsequente Abkehr von seiner gewohnten Darstellungsweise einer assoziativen und fragmentierten Filmform mit zuschauerbezogener Sinnstiftung, und greift stattdessen auf ein didaktisches Erzählmodell." Uriccho, "Ruttmann nach 1933," 61. While partly agreeing with Uricchio, I would qualify the notion that Ruttmann's Weimar films leave meaning up to the audience. As I have argued, films like BERLIN and MELODIE DER WELT do suggest all sorts of regularities, assuming a "bureaucratic" quality recognized by many of Ruttmann's critics. But these films do ask spectator's to infer a greater whole inductively from the particular examples

shown, and they do not espouse the kind of prescriptive aesthetics at work in Ruttmann's films for National Socialism.

88. Foucault's "Care of the Self" paradigm, as worked out in the third volume of his *History of Sexuality,* pertains above all to classical and early Christian civilization. However, Foucault also saw it as part of a longer history of techniques of the self, which he defined as follows: "My objective for more than twenty-five years has to sketch out a history of the different ways in our culture that humans develop knowledge about themselves: economics, biology, psychiatry, medicine and penology. The main point is not to accept this knowledge at face value, but to analyze these so-called sciences as very specific 'truth games' related to specific techniques that human beings use to understand themselves." Michel Foucault, "Technologies of the Self," in *Technologies of the Self. A Seminar with Michel Foucault,* ed. Luther Martin, Huck Gutman, Patrick Hutton (Amherst: University of Massachusetts Press, 1988), 17-18.
89. "Bauer ist, wer in erblicher Verwurzelung seines Geschlechtes im Grund und Boden sein Land bestellt und diese Tätigkeit als seine Aufgabe an seinem Geschlecht und seinem Volke betrachtet." *Blut und Boden,* censor card, no. 41373, dated 28 January 1936, Bundesarchiv-Filmarchiv, Berlin, 2.
90. Dickinson, "Biopolitics – Fascism – Democracy," 22-23.

4. "Überall Stahl": Forming the New Nation in Ruttmann's Steel and Armament Films (1934-1940)

1. See "Erstvorführung. 'Altgermanische Bauernkultur,'" *Der Kinematograph* 28, no. 72 (14 April 1934): n.p.
2. On the screenings of ALTGERMANISCHE BAUERNKULTUR, see the review of the film from *Reichsfilmblatt* (19 May 1934) reprinted in *Walter Ruttmann. Eine Dokumentation,* 142.
3. "Schreiben Sie kurz, was Sie Dr. Sandmann zu antworten haben und senden Sie diese Antwort an die Hauptabteilung Werbung im Verwaltungsamt des Reichsbauernführers zu Berlin. Helfen Sie uns durch Ihre Mitwirkung an diesem Preisausschreiben die geschichtliche Lüge von der Barbarei und dem Nomadentum unserer germanischen Vorfahren ein für allemal aus der Welt zu schaffen! Helfen Sie uns, den Stolz des deutschen Volkes auf seine vieltausendjährige bäuerliche Kultur wieder zu wecken." *Altgermanische Bauernkultur,* censor card no. 36148, dated 9 April 1934, Bundesarchiv-Filmarchiv, Berlin.
4. The letter campaign was described by critics as a "Preisausschreiben." See for example "Altgermanische Bauernkultur," review article, *Der Film* 19, no. 20 (19 May 1934): n.p. However, it is unclear whether a "winning" letter was ever chosen or what prize might have been awarded. On prize films, see for example Rudner Canjels, *Distributing Silent Film Serials. Local Practices, Changing Forms, Cultural Transformation* (New York: Routledge, 2011), 27. On *Wo sind die Millionen?,* see the online database of the project StadtFilm Wien, http://www.stadtfilm-wien.at/film/31/, accessed 01.12.2012.
5. See "Aufnahmen zu 'Triumph des Willens,'" *Der Kinematograph* 28, no. 196 (10 October 1934), 3. Ruttmann's prologue appears to have been removed for ideological

reasons having little to do with the filmmaker (i.e. to avoid thematizing the SA leader Ernst Röhm, whom Hitler had just assassinated).

6. On Ufa's conversion to a state-controlled company, see Klaus Kreimeier, *The Ufa Story. A History of Germany's Greatest Film Company, 1918-1945*, trans. Robert Kimber (Berkeley: University of California Press, 1999), 221-229.
7. The relevant films here are KLEINER FILM EINER GROSSEN STADT – DIE STADT DÜSSELDORF AM RHEIN (SMALL FILM FOR A BIG CITY – THE CITY OF DÜSSELDORF ON THE RHINE, 1935), STUTTGART: DIE GROSSSTADT ZWISCHEN WALD UND REBEN – DIE STADT DES AUSLANDDEUTSCHTUMS (STUTTGART: THE CITY BETWEEN FOREST AND VINES – THE CITY OF GERMANY ABROAD, 1935), STADT STUTTGART: 100. CANNSTATTER VOLKSFEST (STUTTGART: THE HUNDREDTH CANNSTATT FESTIVAL, 1935) and WELTSTRASSE SEE, WELTHAFEN HAMBURG (THE OCEAN AS WORLD ROUTE, HAMBURG AS WORLD PORT, 1938).
8. *Stuttgart, die Großstadt zwischen Wald und Reben*, censor card no. 40866, dated 4 December 1935, Bundesarchiv-Filmarchiv, Berlin, 2.
9. See Martin Seckendorf, "Kulturelle Deutschtumspflege im Übergang von Weimar zu Hitler am Beispiel des Deutschen Ausland-Institutes (DAI). Eine Fallstudie," in *Völkische Wissenschaft. Gestalten und Tendenzen der deutschen und österreichischen Volkskunde in der ersten Hälfte des 20. Jahrhunderts*, ed. Wolfgang Jacobeit, Hannjost Lixfeld, Olaf Bochkorn (Wien: Böhlau, 1994): 115–135.
10. "Was unsere Brüder im Ausland geleistet – geistig, organisatorisch, wirtschaftlich – hier wird es gesammelt, bearbeitet und für das ganze deutsche Volk dienstbar gemacht. Eine unendliche Fülle von Beziehungen wird gepflegt, um das Band der Menschen gleichen Blutes zu knüpfen über Berge, Steppen, Ströme und über den Ozean." Ibid., 2.
11. "Mit etwas Bedächtigkeit, Tüchtigkeit und Sinn für Qualität, und so ist's bei uns bis heut' geblieben – im Handwerk wie in der Industrie, und deshalb sind wir auch trotz aller Krisen sicher immer höher gekommen." Ibid.
12. *Deutsche Waffenschmieden*, censor card no. 53178, dated 20 January 1040, Bundesarchiv-Filmarchiv, Berlin, 1.
13. "Die deutsche Seefahrt ist Sache des ganzen Volkes. Rettung aus Seenot ist vaterländische Ehrenpflicht!" *Schiff in Not*, censor card no. 44042, dated 20 November 1936, Bundesarchiv-Filmarchiv, Berlin, 1-2.
14. "…geeignet als Lehrfilm im Unterricht verwendet zu werden." Ibid., 2.
15. This list includes BLUT UND BODEN (1933), ALTGERMANISCHE BAUERNKULTUR (1934), METALL DES HIMMELS (1935), STUTTGART. DIE GROSSSTADT ZWISCHEN WALD UND REBEN (1935), SCHIFF IN NOT (1936), HELDEN DER KÜSTE (1937), MANNESMANN (1937), WELSTRASSE SEE, WELTHAFEN HAMBURG (1938) and DEUTSCHE WAFFENSCHMIEDEN (1940).
16. "Erst der neue Staat hat die psychologischen Hemmungen gegenüber der technischen Errungenschaft des Films völlig überwunden, und er ist gewillt, auch den Film in den Dienst seiner Weltanschauung zu stellen. Das hat besonders in der Schule, und zwar unmittelbar im Klassenunterricht zu geschehen." Cited in Ursula von Keitz, "Die Kinematografie in der Schule. Zur politischen Pädagogik des Unterrichtsfilms von RfdU und RWU," in *Geschichte des dokumentarischen Films in Deutschland 3*, 463.
17. Ibid. 468-470.

18. Hong, *Welfare Modernity and the Weimar State,* 273. For the Nazi discourse on the educational state, see for example Hans von Tschammer und Osten, *Sport und Leibesübungen im nationalsozialistischen Staat. Grundlagen, Aufbau und Wirtschaftsordnung des nationalsozialistischen Staates 10a* (Berlin: Industrieverlag Spaeth & Linde, 1936), 8: "Die höchste aller Staatsaufgaben ist die Erziehung der Volksgenossen. [...] Der Staatsbürger ist in erster Linie Diener der Volksgemeinschaft. Seine Erziehung muß eine umfassende (totale) sein: Nicht nur der Geist, aber auch nicht nur der Leib müssen erzogen werden, sondern der ganze Mensch, in dem die Natur beides untrennbar vereint hat."
19. According to the surviving censor records at the *Filmarchiv-Bundesarchiv,* BLUT UND BODEN (1933) was re-issued in 1936 in two 16mm versions, one with sound (censor card no. 41372) and one with intertitles (censor card no. 41373); ALTGERMANISCHE BAUERNKULTUR (1934) was re-issued in 1937 on 16mm film with intertitles (censor card no. 44493); METALL DES HIMMELS (1935) was re-issued on 16mm film with intertitles in 1935 (censor card no. 39507), 1936 (censor card no. 41309) and 1939 (censor card no. 50296); STUTTGART: DIE GROSSSTADT ZWISCHEN WALD UND REBEN (1935) was re-issued as a 16mm sound film in 1936 (censor card no. 42029) and as a 16mm silent in 1937 (censor card no. 45214); SCHIFF IN NOT (1936) was re-issued as 16mm silent in 1936 (censor card no. 44042) and as 16mm sound in 1936 (censor card no. 43624), 1940 (censor card no. 53132) and 1943 (censor card no. 57945); HELDEN DER KÜSTE (1937), itself a re-release of SCHIFF IN NOT, was re-issued in a 16mm silent version in 1937 (censor card no. 45392); MANNESMANN (1937) was re-issued in 1938 on 16mm with intertitles under the title MANNESMANN. EIN UFA-KULTURFILM NACH DEM INTERNATIONAL PREISGEKRÖNTEN FILM (censor card no. 47900), followed by another silent version in 1939 (censor card no. 52386) and a 16mm spoken version in 1941 (censor card no. 55014); and DEUTSCHE WAFFENSCHMIEDEN (1940) was re-issued in 1940 on 16mm film, once with sound (censor card no. 53753) and once with intertitles (censor card no. 54455).
20. On the use of silent film in the classroom, see Keitz, "Die Kinematografie in der Schule," 472, 475.
21. MANNESMANN (1937)
22. IM ZEICHEN DES VERTRAUENS (1937); IM DIENSTE DER MENSCHHEIT (1938)
23. HENKEL: EIN DEUTSCHES WERK IN SEINER ARBEIT (1938).
24. *Henkel. Ein deutsches Werk in seiner Arbeit,* censor card no. 50137, dated 29 December 1938, Bundesarchiv-Filmarchiv, Berlin, 2-3.
25. "Sie sehen, meine Damen. Werbung ist etwas anderes als Reklame. Die Henkel-Werbung ist in voller Erkenntnis des großen erzieherischen Wertes, den Werbung besitzt, vor allem darauf bedacht, dem Verbraucher zu dienen und ihn in den vollen Genuß aller Vorzüge zu bringen, die ihn unsere Erzeugnisse bieten. Sie verbindet daher mit eigenbetrieblichen Aufgaben zugleich Dienstleistungen für die Allgemeinheit." Ibid., 2.
26. See Imort, "'Planting a Forest Tall and Straight Like the German Volk,'" 104, 115-119. See also Forster, *Ufa und Nordmark,* 21; Ross, "Visions of Prosperity," 68-72. Such a transformation in the understanding of private advertising went hand in hand with the usage of the Germanic term "Werbung" in the place of the Latinate "Reklame" (the journal *Die Reklame* changed its name to *Die Deutsche Werbung* in 1933).

27. See Loiperdinger, "Neue Sachlichkeit und Nationalsozialismus"; Goergen, "Walter Ruttmann – Ein Porträt," 41.
28. See Heinz Heller: "'Stählerne Romantik' und Avantgarde. Beobachtungen und Anmerkungen zu Ruttmanns Industriefilmen," in *Triumph der Bilder*, ed. Peter Zimmermann and Kay Hoffmann (Konstanz, 2003), 105-120; Schenk, "Walter Ruttmanns Kultur- und Industriefilm"; Zimmermann, "Neusachlicher Technikkult und 'stählerne Romantik'"; Quaresima, "Astrazione e romanticismo," 29-45.
29. On the Nazi "male fantasy" of the steel body, see Klaus Theweleit, *Male Fantasies. Volume 2. Male Bodies. Psychoanalyzing the White Terror* (Minneapolis: University of Minnesota Press, 1989), 159-162.
30. Industrial films employed tracking shots at least as early as narrative film and for good reason. As one recent article puts it: "The traveling shot seems to be unavoidable when representing a factory. What could be more natural than having the camera follow the movement of the rolling conveyer belt to suggest the flow of production?" Nicolas Hatzfeld, Gwenaële Rot and Alain P. Michel, "Filming Work on Behalf of the Automobile Firm: The Case of Renault (1950-2002)," in *Films That Work*, 199. On the camera movement in early industrial film (including the Westinghouse films), see *The Encyclopedia of Early Cinema*, ed. Richard Abel (London: Routledge, 2010), 132-135.
31. For the importance of light and abstract composition in early German industrial films, see Frances Guerin, *A Culture of Light. Cinema and Technology in 1920s Germany* (Minneapolis: University of Minnesota Press, 2005), 70-72.
32. In recent decades, research in film and music history has emphasized the fact that popular forms (such as film comedies) dominated the screens and airwaves of the Third Reich, and even modernist forms such as jazz were still practiced within certain limits. See Pamela Potter, "Music in the Third Reich: The Complex Task of 'Germanicization,'" *The Arts in Nazi Germany. Continuity, Conformity, Change*, ed. Jonathan Huener and Francis Nicosia (Burlington: Berghan Books, 2006), 85-110. Siegfried Mattl, "The Ambivalence of Modernism from the Weimar Republic to National Socialism and Red Vienna," *Modern Intellectual History* 6 (2009): 223-234. Nonetheless, in a sector as tightly regulated as advertising and propaganda film, certain practices – such as abstraction – could no longer be espoused in the same form.
33. On this point, see also Schenk, "Walter Ruttmanns Kultur- und Industriefilme," 114.
34. Ruttmann himself described this aspect in abstract terms in an unpublished manuscript from 1940: "Die Vielfalt des psychischen Gehaltes der Maschinenbewegungen setzt sich nämlich aus einer unendlichen Fülle der verschiedensten Formen ihres Ausdrucksvermögens zusammen. So gibt es: unerbittlich zuschlagende, wuchtig stampfende, jauchzend sprühende, sanft gleitende, emsig ineinandergreifende, spielerisch und dennoch sinnvoll umeinander kreisende Bewegungsrhythmen und viele andere mehr." Ruttmann, "Film und Werkfilm," in *Walter Ruttmann. Eine Dokumentation*, 93. Such description of machinic movement are reminiscent of Ruttmann's early descriptions of the action in his OPUS films in terms such as "wellenförmige Bewegung," "schlangenartig schleichende Bewegung," "galoppierende Pferde," tobendes Durcheinander von hellen und dunklen Elementen," and so on. Ruttmann, "Malerei mit Zeit," 74.

35. See also Loiperdinger, "Neue Sachlichkeit und Nationalsozialismus," 48-50; Uricchio, "Ruttmann nach 1933," 62.
36. Cited in Moritz, *Optical Poetry*, 55. See also Leslie, *Hollywood Flatlands*, 189.
37. "Vor Karl dem Großen, dem Bringer des römischen Christentums zu unseren Vorfahren, gab es bei Letzteren überhaupt keine Kultur. Eine mehr als primitive Verzierhungskunst mit einem Hang zur Abstraktion, der ja allen wilden Völkern gemeinsam ist, war alles, was sie hatten." *Altgermanische Bauernkultur* censor card no. 44493, 4.
38. Ibid., 6-8.
39. Heinrich Wölfflin, *Die Kunst der Renaissance. Italien und das deutsche Formgefühl* (Munich: F. Bruckmann, 1931), 6. For Wölfflin, the Italian "feeling for form" valorized self-containment, clarity, harmony and proportion, while the Nordic "feeling for form" longed for limitlessness, intertwined parts and above all a sense of movement. On Wölfflin's racialization of the term "Formgefühl" see Susan Krüger Saß, "'Nordische Kunst'. Die Bedeutung des Begriffes während des Nationalsozialismus," in *Kunstgeschichte im Dritten Reich. Theorien, Methoden, Praktiken*, ed. Ruth Heftrig, Olaf Peters, Barbara Schellewald (Berlin: Akademie-Verlag, 2008), 226.
40. "Unschwer wird das geübte Auge fast geheimnisvoll anmutende Beziehungen zwischen den menschlichen Leibesformen und inneren Wesenseigenheiten von Rassen, Schlägen und Stämmen und den dazugehörigen Gefäßkunstformen feststellen. 'Zackig' ist der nordische Mensch, sein Formgefühl und seine Zierweise. Verschwommen, 'gemütlich' oder kleinlich überfeinert und gespreizt andere." Hans Hahne, *Deutsche Vorzeit* (Bielefeld: Velhagen und Klassing, 1933), 6. Hahne goes on to describe his method of testing such racial characteristics, which was clearly meant to inculcate a sense of racial belonging on the part of spectators: "Auf meine neue Untersuchungsart sei hingedeutet: heutige, noch nach Rassen- oder Stammesartung ausgeprägte Menschen finden immer wieder in unseren Sammlungen diejenigen Gefäßkunstformen schön und ansprechend, die von Vorzeitstämmen hergestellt sind, die ihrer eigenen Rassenart entsprechen oder ihr noch nahestehen." Ibid. Hahne's book would later be reissued under the title *Deutsche Vorzeit. Rassen, Völker und Kulturen* (1937).
41. "Auch der wahre Politiker ist im letzten Sinne des Wortes ein Künstler. So, wie der Bildhauer den rohen Marmor abzirkelt, behaut und meißelt, so formt der Staatsmann aus dem rohen Stoff Masse ein Volk." Joseph Goebbels, Radio address from 18 July 1932, cited in *Goebbels Reden 1932-1945*, ed. Helmut Heiber (Düsseldorf: Droste-Verlag, 1971), 52.
42. See Philippe Lacoue-Labarthe, *Heidegger, Art and Politics*, trans. Chris Turner (Oxford: Basil Blackwell, 1990), 61-76.
43. In his lectures at the Collège de France, Foucault argued that the mechanisms of discipline and biopolitics were not mutually exclusive, but rather co-existed in various configurations in modern states concerned with regulating bodies and life. See Foucault, *Security, Territory, Population*, 6-11; *"Society Must be Defended." Lecture at the College de France 1975-1976*, ed. Mauro Bertani and Alessandro Fontana, trans. David Macey (New York: Picador, 2003), 251-253. The specificity of Nazism resided for Foucault in the way in which it sought to implement both of these modalities of power in their most absolute sense: "[N]o State could have more disciplinary power than the Nazi regime. Nor was there any other State in which the biological was so

tightly, so insistently regulated. Disciplinary power and biopower: all this permeated, underpinned Nazi society (control over the biological, of procreation and of heredity; control over illness and accidents too). No society could be more disciplinary or more concerened with providing insurance than that established, or at least planned, by the Nazis." Ibid., 259. In the same lectures, Foucault argued that the old model of sovereign power, understood as the right to take life, also survives in the modern state in the form of (scientific) racism, which justified the elimination of "biological threats" to populations. Ibid., 256. Here too, Nazism would represent an effort to institute this mode of power absolutely through a politics designed entirely for warfare. Nazism would thus share certain traits with other modern states, but it also constitutes something unique and uniquely totalitarian in its desire to control life absolutely: "We have [...] in Nazi society something that is really quite extraordinary: this is a society which has generalized biopower in an absolute sense, but which has also generalized the sovereign right to kill. [...] Nazism alone took the play between the sovereign right to kill and the mechanisms of biopower to this paroxysmal point." Ibid., 260.

44. On Ruttmann's authorship, see "Metall des Himmels," review article, *Der Film* 20, no. 9 (2 March 1935): n.p.: "Walter Ruttmann, Autor und Spielleiter, hat Wesentliches in guten Bildern festgehalten." On the film's awards, see *Walter Ruttmann. Eine Dokumentation,* 142. The international distribution is also suggested by the fact that Ruttmann published a text on this film in the London journal *Film Art.* See *Walter Ruttmann. Eine Dokumentation,* 143. In contrast to Ruttmann's other films after 1933, this one is also still preserved in international archives (for example the Filmarchiv Austria and the Cinémathèque Française).
45. According to one writer for the *Reichsfilmblatt:* "Ruttmann hat den Film mit jenem Sinn für Rhythmik und Dynamik des Filmgeschehens aufgebaut, die jeden seiner Filme das Gepräge geben." Cited in *Walter Ruttmann. Eine Dokumentation,* 143.
46. "Dem Deutschen warfen die Götter nichts in den Schoß. Aber schon vor mehr als 2000 Jahren brach er im Siegerland Eisenstein, zwang ihn im Schmelzofen sich aufzuschließen und herzugeben den schimmernd-geschmeidigen Schatz: Stahl." *Metall des Himmels,* censor card no. 39507, dated 17 June 1935, Bundesarchiv-Filmarchiv, Berlin, 2.
47. On the resemblance of the figure in METALL DES HIMMELS to the protagonist in Lang's film, see also Loiperdinger, 52; Quaresima, "Astrazione e romanticismo," 43. On the iconography of Siegfried in the 1920s, see Anton Kaes, "Siegfried – A German Film Star. Performing the Nation in Lang's NIBELUNGEN Film," in *The German Cinema Book,* ed. Tim Bergfelder, Erica Carter and Deniz Göktürk (London: British Film Institute, 2002), 63-70.
48. *Metall des Himmels,* censor card no. 39507, 2.
49. "die enge Verbundenheit [des Stahls] mit Volk und Boden." Herbert Dickmann, *Deutscher Stahl. I: Bilder aus der Geschichte der deutschen Eisen- und Stahlerzeugung. Stahl überall 3* (Düsseldorf: Beratungsstelle für Stahlverwendung, 1934), 32.
50. Unlike Ruttmann, the authors of *Stahlfibel* question the legend's veracity: "Es ist nicht sicher, daß die alten Ägypter dem Stahl den Namen 'Metall des Himmels' (benipe) deshalb gegeben haben, weil er ihnen zuerst in Form von Meteoreisen bekanntgeworden ist. Diese Beziechnung kann auch gewählt worden sein, weil die

bläuliche Färbung des erhitzten Stahls an die des Himmels erinnerte." *Stahlfibel* (Düsseldorf: Beratungsstelle für Stahlverwendung, 1935), 2.

51. See *Stahl überall* 1929, no. 11/12: *Beiträge zur Verwendung vom Stahl im Bergbau.*
52. *Stahl überall* 1930, no. 6/7: *Stahlmöbel im Büro.*
53. *Stahl überall* 1930, no. 11/12: *Stahlküchen.*
54. *Stahl überall* 1932, no. 1: *Stahl in der Landwirtschaft.*
55. *Stahl überall* 1934, no. 1: *Gesund sein, gesund werden.*
56. *Stahl überall* 1936, no. 1: *Stahl im Automobilbau.*
57. *Stahl überall* 1936, no. 4: *Stählerne Brücken.*
58. See for example Curt Biging, *Deutsche Vorzeit, Deutsche Gegenwart* (Berlin: Büchergilde Gutenberg, 1933). The notion of a racially grounded *Formgefühl* underlying the change of historical styles clearly played into this effort to insist on the continuity of an essential "Germanness." Biging himself cites the passage from Hans Hahne quoted above (28).
59. Martin Loiperdinger has read the juxtaposition of rural and urban images as evidence of an ideologically inconsistency, ultimately suggesting that Ruttmann was concerned with aesthetics rather than ideology. See Loiperdinger, "Neue Sachlichkeit und Nationalsozialismus," 52. My own reading is closer to that of Quaresima when he argues that the function of the rural images in METAL DES HIMMELS is to *ground* technology – and the "new objective" aesthetics Ruttmann uses to film it – in a tradition associated with *Kultur.* See Quaresima, "Astrazione e romanticismo," 43.
60. This is largely how the montage in the film was read. According to one reviewer in 1935: "Walter Ruttmann hat den Film mit jenem Sinn für Rhythmik und Dynamik des Filmbildes und des Filmgeschehens aufgebaut, die jedem seiner Filme das Gepräge geben." "Industrie- und Kulturfilme," in *Reichsfilmblatt,* no. 9 (2 March 1935), cited in *Walter Ruttmann. Eine Dokumentation,* 143.
61. See Karl Bücher, *Arbeit und Rhythmus. Abhandlungen der philologisch-historischen Classe der königlichen sächsischen Gesellschaft der Wissenschaften* 39:5 (Leipzig: S. Hirzel, 1897), 101. For more on this context, see Cowan, *Technology's Pulse,* 22-25.
62. "Die Kraft des Rhythmus ist erwiesen. Der Takt des Marsches belebt den Schritt. Schiffer erleichtern sich das Rudern durch rhythmischen Gesang. Drescher, Schmiede, Straßenpflasterer vollziehen ihr einförmiges Klopfen im Rhythmus." Hans Richter, *Filmgegner von heute, Filmfreunde von morgen* (Berlin: Reckendorf, 1929), 93.
63. As I discussed in chapter 1, this idea was central to advertising theories such as that of Fritz Pauli, who also drew centrally on Bücher's work. For more on this topic, see Cowan, *Technology's Pulse,* 133-136.
64. See Bücher, *Arbeit und Rhythmus,* 114-115: "[E]s wird eine denkwürdige Tatsache in der Geschichte des Maschinenwesens bilden, dass viele der ältesten Arbeitsmaschinen rhythmischen Gang haben, indem sie [...] die Hand- und Armbewegungen des bisherigen Arbeitsverfahrens bloss nachahmen. [...] Mit der weiteren Entwicklung des Maschinenbaues strebt man darnach, den mit dem rhythmischen Gang des Mechanismus meist verbundenen todten Rückgang zu vermeiden und geht [...] von der wage- oder senkrechten zur gleichförmig rotierenden Bewegung über, die jenen Kraftverlust vermeidet. [...] Damit schwindet die alte Musik der Arbeit, welche die rhythmisch gehenden Maschinen noch deutlich erkennen liessen, aus den Werkstätten."

65. "Der arbeitende Mensch ist nicht mehr Herr seiner Bewegungen, das Werkzeug sein Diener, sein verstärktes Körperglied, sondern das Werkzeug ist Herr über ihn geworden; es diktiert ihm das Mass seiner Bewegungen; das Tempo und die Dauer seiner Arbeit ist seinem Willen entzogen; er ist an den todten und doch so lebendigen Mechanismus gefesselt." Ibid., 115.
66. As we saw in chapter 2, MELODIE DER WELT also refused to differentiate between primitive and modern (or natural and technological) rhythms. But there, Ruttmann's universalism extended to the entire world, which the film sought to represent as an arena for tourism, whereas METALL DES HIMMELS constructs a nationalist argument about the continuity of German production.
67. See Ernst Jünger, *Der Arbeiter. Herrschaft und Gestalt* (Hamburg: Hanseatische Verlagsanstalt, 1932), 21, 138. Ruttmann himself described the relation between people and machines in his film as follows: "Allerdings darf man die Maschinen nicht für den Feind der Menschheit halten. Maschinen sind aus Menschengeist geboren und dazu bestimmt, den Menschen zu dienen. Es wird ferner während ihres Entstehens und im Laufe ihrer Arbeitsleistung eine gewaltige Menge menschlicher Intelligenz, menschlicher Geschicklichkeit und menschlichen Fleißes mobil gemacht." Ruttmann, "Film und Werkfilm," 93.
68. See *Metall des Himmels,* censor card no. 39507, 3. On the Nazi film ratings system, which were carried out centrally in the Berlin censorship office, see Kreimeier, *The Ufa Story,* 257.
69. See David Orgeron, Marsha Orgeron and Dan Streible, "Introduction," in *Learning with the Lights off,* 1-14, esp. 9-10.
70. This is, perhaps, the greatest irony of Ruttmann's film: despite its appeals to German industriousness, the film in fact positions spectators as no less passive recipients than the "thankful" Egyptians and Sumerians of the opening shots.
71. On the premiere of MANNESMANN and its prizes, see S. Jonathan Wiesen, *Creating the Nazi Marketplace. Commerce and Consumption in the Third Reich* (Cambridge: Cambridge University Press, 2011), 77. See also *Walter Ruttmann. Eine Dokumentation,* 148.
72. See *Mannesmann,* censor card no. 47900, dated 17 March 1938, Bundesarchiv-Filmarchiv, Berlin, 3.
73. See the company brochure, *Nahtlose nichtrostende säure- und hitzebeständige Mannesmann-Stahlrohre* (Düsseldorf: Mannesmannröhren-Werke, 1931); *Mannesmann Weldless Steel Tubular Poles* (Düsseldorf: Mannesmannröhren-Werke, 1937).
74. "Remscheid. Dort, wo seit alter Zeit der Schmied das Eisen zum Stahle zwingt, wurzelnd im Boden des Bergischen Landes, gelang die Tat, ein Rohr nahtlos aus einem Block von Stahl zu schmieden." *Mannesmann*, censor card no. 47900, 1-2.
75. "Ich wäre glücklich, wenn diese Idee [...] mir die Gelegenheit geben könnte, das Epos einer deutschen Landschaft zu schaffen, das organisch von der Steinzeit über alle historischen Kämpfe hin zu der Beglückung des wiedererwachten Deutschlands führen würde." "Ruttmann plaudert," unidentified newspaper clipping, reprinted in *Walter Ruttmann. Eine Dokumentation,* 92.
76. Imort, "'Planting a Forest Tall and Straight Like the German Volk,'" 106.
77. "Sehen Sie, es war gar nicht so gefährlich – nur eine leichte Einbeulung – sonst nichts!" *Mannesmann,* censor card no. 47900, 2.
78. See Rancière, "The Surface of Design," 98-99.

79. Quaresima argues that one can see a parallel, in the Third Reich, between the culture of design in visual art and the work of the avant-garde in industrial and cultural film (opposed by academic painting and narrative film). See Quaresima, "Astrazione e romanticismo," 30.
80. DEUTSCHE WAFFENSCHMIEDEN had its premiere in Berlin in March 1940 before being screened in Venice in September. DEUTSCHE PANZER was premiered in Venice. Both films were re-released in shorter 16mm versions, with at least one rerelease (for DEUTSCHE WAFFENSCHMIEDEN) as a silent film.
81. Goergen casts some doubt as to whether this film was actually finished, but it seems likely given that it was included, alongside DEUTSCHE PANZER and ABERGLAUBEN, on a list of Ufa films available for distribution on 31 August 1940. See "Kulturfilme im Verleih der Ufa," insert. *Der Film* 25, no. 35 (31 August 1940): n.p. The list also includes another lost film, GEFAHR!!, which Goergen suggests was probably a working title for EIN FILM GEGEN DIE VOLKSKRANKHEIT KREBS. See *Walter Ruttmann. Eine Dokumentation,* 166, 170.
82. Books such as *Panzer rücken vor!* (Martin Lezius, 1939), *Panzer voran!* (Albert Benary, 1939), *Panzer nach vorn!* (Herbert Reinecker, 1939), *Deutsche Panzer durchbrechen den Korridor* (Dieter Evers, 1940), *Panzer greift an* (Hans Kuersten, 1940), *Panzer packen Polen!* (Kurt Bernhard, 1940), *Ein Zug Panzer in Polen* (Dieter Evers, 1940) all celebrated the feats of German tank divisions, particularly in the East.
83. "Die auf viele tausend Tonnen angewachsenen Metalle kommen in die Hütten- und Schmelzwerke und werden hier von der pulsierenden Kraft der Maschinen und stampfenden Riesenhämmern zu neuer Gestalt geformt. Und plöztlich entsteht aus Onkel Ottos Kegelpreis und der großen alten Kupferschale [...] gänzlich neue und für das deutsche Volk so wichtige Dinge wie zum Beispiel Träger, Granatringe, Kabel, Stahlbänder, Patronen, Gewehrläufe, Torpedos und Kanonen! Das Werk der Nutzbarmachung dieser so unwichtig erscheinenden Metalle ist in vollem Gang. Die kämpfende Front kann sich auf die Heimat verlassen, denn die Heimat hat die 'grosse Reserve'. Ganz Deutschland ist zur großen Waffenschmiede und fest in Stahl gepanzert – so hart wie sein Stahl ist auch der Wille zum Sieg!" "Ein Film von der deutschen Metallspende. Die große Reserve," review article, *Der Film* 25, no. 30 (27 July 1940): n.p.
84. On these and other "homefront films," see Mary Elizabeth O'Brien, *Nazi Cinema as Enchantment. The Politics of Entertainment in the Third Reich* (Rochester: Camden House, 2004), 118-160.
85. "Wir sind jetzt eine verschworene Gemeinschaft! Das hat der Führer gesagt! So gibt es zwei Soldaten heute: den Soldaten an der Waffe und den Soldaten an der Maschine. So arbeiten sie Mann für Mann – auf Zechen – in Gruben – vor den Hochöfen – in Werften und Werken – getreu dem Befehl des Führers!" *Deutsche Waffenschmieden,* censor card no. 53178, 1.
86. "Auch den Männern am Konstruktionstisch und an der Maschine, die in unermüdlichem Einsatz diese Panzerwaffe schufen, gebührt daher die vollste Anerkennung von Front und Heimat." *Deutsche Panzer,* censor card no. 54175, dated 31 August 1940, Bundesarchiv-Filmarchiv, Berlin, 2.
87. For an analysis of workers' faces in these films, see Thomas Mayer, "'Gesichtsverlust' vs. Resemantisierung. Überlegungen zum Gesicht des Arbeiters im National-

sozialismus anhand einiger Filme von Walter Ruttmann," *Montage AV* 13:2 (2004), 75-91.

88. See Walter Ruttmann, "Patentschrift: Verfahen und Vorrichtung zum Herstellen kinematographischer Bilder," in *Walter Ruttmann. Eine Dokumentation*, 75-78.
89. "[...] eine schicksalsverbundene Volksgemeinschaft schaffen und sichtbar machen, wenn zugleich in ganz Deutschlands Gauen die Millionen vor den Lautsprechern aufmarschiert sind." Eugen Hadamovsky, *Der Rundfunk im Dienste der Volksführung. Gestalten und Erscheinungen der politischen Publizistik* 1 (Leipzig: Universitätsverlag von Robert Noske, 1934), 22.
90. See David Bathrick, "Making a National Family with the Radio: The Nazi *Wunschkonzert*," *Modernism/Modernity* 4:1 (1997), 115-127, esp. 119.
91. See Paul Virilio, *War and Cinema*, trans. Patrick Camiller (London: Verso, 1989), 11.
92. Hong, *Welfare Modernity and the Weimar State*, 273.

Afterword: Of Good and Bad Objects

1. Ruttmann, "Die absolute Mode," 82. Goergen notes that Ruttmann's effort to make narrative films such as a version of DON QUICHOTTE in the late 1920s largely fell flat on account of the general perception that Ruttmann was "too abstract" for mainstream film. Goergen, "Walter Ruttmann – Ein Porträt," 39. But this suspicion of Ruttmann as a narrative filmmaker was the pendant to his reputation as a leading expert in "applied" forms from advertising to *Kulturfilm* to industrial film.
2. See for example Fulks, 34; Giorgio Tinazzi, "La città-occhio," in *Walter Ruttmann. Cinema, pittura, ars acustica*, 164. For the argument that Ruttmann's montage functions in the opposite way from that intended by Benjamin, see Koepnick, *Walter Benjamin and the Aesthetics of Power*, 133; Kreimeier, *The Ufa Story*, 272. Sabine Hake offers a more sophisticated version of the aestheticization argument when she reads the cross-sectional montage of Berlin as a means of subordinating "all material to the principles of equivalence, repetition and serialization established by capitalist commodity culture." Hake, *Topographies of Class*, 260. Interestingly, the "aestheticization" argument, while serving as the basis for critiques of Ruttmann, also serves as the basis for the (rarer) attempts to defend his work after 1933. In the most forceful articulation of this argument, Martin Loiperdinger has maintained that Ruttmann retained a formal-aesthetic understanding of film as "rhythmische Organisation der Zeit durch optische Mittel" throughout his life, a fact that relativizes the ideological impact of later industrial films such as *Deutsche Panzer*: "[Ruttmann zeigt] sich nicht an der Tätigkeit der Arbeiter, sondern an der Ästhetik der Maschinen interessiert." Loiperdinger, "Neue Sachlichkeit und Nationalsozialismus," 55.
3. See for example Hans Schoots, "Zooming Out: Walter Ruttmann and Joris Ivens," in *Triumph der Bilder. Kultur- und Dokumentarfilme vor 1945 im internationalen Vergleich*, ed. Peter Zimmermann und Kay Hoffmann (Stuttgart: Haus des Dokumentarfilms, 2003), 235-251.
4. Uricchio, *Ruttmann's Berlin and the City Film to 1930*, 182. Uricchio was in fact critiquing an all too narrow view of Neue Sachlichkeit here.
5. This too is an aspect Ruttmann shared with the constructivist avant-garde. For example, in a published interview from 1933, Werner Graeff and Raoul Hausmann

argued that the expert photographer is characterized precisely by his ability to abstract from the contingent details of the medium to understand and use its formal dimensions for controling perception. "[D]er Zufall im Bilde sollte ausgeschaltet werden. Exakte Führung des Beschauenden, die sorgfältige Wahl oder Heruasschälung der Gegensatzpaare: Form und Formdetail, hell und dunkel, groß und klein, ist allein imstande, die Fotografie aus einer nachahmenden, bestenfalls dokumentierenden Technik zum gestaltenden Ausdrucksmittel zu machen." Werner Graeff and Raoul Hausmann, "Wie siehr der Fotograf" (1933), in *Texte zur Theorie der Fotografie,* ed. Bernd Stiegler (Stuttgart: Reclam, 2010), 185-196, here 194. For Hausmann and Graeff, the model for such a successful "Gestaltung" (constrction) is, once again, the advertising poster: "Das Plakat (sowohl das geschäftliche als auch das politische) ist eine literarische Idee, die aber erst wirken kann, wenn die entsprechende Form-Idee gefunden wird. Die Beherrschung der Form ist für den Fotografen wichtiger als literarische Ideen" (191). Here too, then, "formalism" is hardly opposed to use value; it is, rather, the very mark of the kind of expertise that can make art useful.

6. Susan Sontag, "Fascinating Fascism," in *Under the Sign of Saturn* (New York: Farrar, Strauss and Giroux, 1980), 73-105.
7. "Durch entsprechende Kombination der Darstellungsänderungen mit Beleuchtungsänderungen der Bildplatten, sowie mit den Veränderungen, die durch Verstellen der Bildplatten gegeneinander erzielbar sind, können die mannigfaltigsten, eigenartigsten und stimmungsreichsten kinematographischen Bilderreihen von höchster künstlerisch individueller Beeinflussung erzeugt werden." Walter Ruttmann, "Verfahren und Vorrichtung zum Herstellen kinematographischer Bilder" (1921), in *Walter Ruttmann. Eine Dokumentation,* 76.
8. See also Uriccho, "Ruttmann nach 1933," 61.

Bibliography

1930s. The Making of the New Man. Exhibition catalogue. Ed. Jean Clair. Ottawa: National Gallery of Canada, 2008.

Ägde, Günter. *Flimmernde Versprechen. Geschichte des deutschen Werbefilms im Kino seit 1897.* Berlin: Verlag das Neue Berlin, 1998.

Albera, François and Maria Tortajada. "The 1900 Episteme." In *Cinema Beyond Film.* Ed. François Albera and Maria Tortajada. Amsterdam: Amsterdam University Press, 2010, 25-44.

Alter, Nora. "Berlin, Symphony of a Great City." In *Weimar Cinema. An Essential Guide to Classic Films of the Era.* Ed. Noah Eisenberg. New York: Columbia University Press, 2009, 193-217.

Altgermanische Bauernkultur. Censor card no. 36148. Dated 9 April 1934. Bundesarchiv-Filmarchiv, Berlin.

"Altgermanische Bauernkultur." Review article. *Der Film* 19, no. 20 (19 May 1934): n.p.

Aly, Götz and Karl-Heinz Roth. *Die restlose Erfassung. Volkszählen, Identifizieren und Aussondern im Nationalsozialismus.* Berlin: Rotbuch-Verlag, 1984.

Amad, Paula. *Counter-Archive. Film, the Everyday and Albert Kahn's Archives de la Planète.* New York: Columbia University Press, 2010.

Amsler, André. *"Wer dem Werbefilm verfällt, ist verloren für die Welt". Das Werk von Julius Pinschewer 1883-1961.* Zurich: Chronos, 1997.

Arnoux, Alexandre. *Du Muet au parlant. Mémoires d'un témoin.* Paris: La Nouvelle Edition, 1946.

Aufderheide, Patricia. *Documentary Film. A Very Short Introduction.* Oxford: Oxford University Press, 2007.

"Aufnahmen zu 'Triumph des Willens.'" *Der Kinematograph* 28, no. 196 (10 October 1934).

"Das Auge der Welt." *Süddeutsche Filmzeitung* 7, no. 28 (21 September 1928): 10.

"Das Auge der Welt. Der erste Querschnitt-Film 'Henny Porten.'" *Lichtbild-Bühne* 21, no. 233 (7 November 1929): n.p.

Aumont, Jacques . "The Face in Close-Up." In *The Visual Turn. Classical Film Theory and Art History.* Ed. Angela Dalle Vacche. New Brunswick: Rutgers University Press, 2003, 127-151.

Balázs, Béla. "Der Film sucht seinen Stoff" [1926]. In *Schriften zum Film II.* Ed. Helmut H. Diederichs and Wolfgang Gersch. Berlin: Henschenverlag, 1984, 215.

—. *Der Geist des Films* [1930]. Frankfurt am Main: Suhrkamp, 2004.

—. *Der sichtbare Mensch oder die Kultur des Films* [1924]. Frankfurt am Main: Suhrkamp, 2008.

—. *Theory of the Film.* London: Denis Dobson, 1952.

Bathrick, David. "Making a National Family with the Radio: The Nazi *Wunschkonzert.*" *Modernism/Modernity* 4:1 (1997): 115-127.

Bazin, André. *Qu'est-ce que le cinéma?* Paris: Editions du Cerf, 1985.

Behne, Adolf. "Deffke." *Seidels Reklame* 8 (1923): 2-6.

Behrenbeck, Sabine. "'Der Führer'. Die Einführung eines politischen Markenartikels." In *Propaganda in Deutschland.* Ed. Gerald Diesener, Rainer Gries. Darmstadt: Wissenschaftliche Buchgesellschaft, 1996, 51-78.

Bendersky, Joseph W. *A History of Nazi Germany 1919-1945.* New York: Rowman & Littlefield, 2000.

Benjamin, Walter. "Das Kunstwerk im Zeitalter seiner technischen Reproduzierbarkeit." In *Illuminationen.* Frankfurt am Main: Suhrkamp, 1977, 136-169.

Benz, Wolfgang. *A Concise History of the Third Reich.* Trans. Thomas Dunlap. Berkeley: University of California Press, 2006.

Béringuier, Richard F. C. "An der Peripherie des Reklamefilms." *Die Reklame* 20, no. 12 (1927): 429.

Bernstein, Matthew. "Visual Style and Spatial Articulations in *Berlin, Symphony of a City* (1927)." *Journal of Film and Video* 36:4 (1984): 5-12.

"Das Beschreiben des Himmels." *Seidels Reklame* 7 (1922): 207.

Biging, Curt. *Deutsche Vorzeit, Deutsche Gegenwart.* Berlin: Büchergilde Gutenberg, 1933.

Blankenship, Janelle. "To Attract/To Alternate? The Skladanowsky Experiment," *Cinema & Cie: International Film Studies Journal* 9 (2007): 61-79.

Blümlinger, Christa. *Kino aus zweiter Hand. Zur Ästhetik materieller Aneignung im Film und in der Medienkunst.* Berlin: Vorwerk 8, 2009.

Blut und Boden. Censor card no. 41372. Dated 28 January 1936. Bundesarchiv-Filmarchiv, Berlin.

Blut und Boden. Censor card no. 41373. Dated 28 January 1936. Bundesarchiv-Filmarchiv, Berlin.

"Blut und Boden." Review article. *Deutsche Filmzeitung* 12, no. 47 (26 November 1933): 9.

"Blut und Boden." Review article. *Der Kinematograph* 27, no. 228 (24 November 1933): n.p.

"Blut und Boden. Der Bauernfilm." *Lichtbild-Bühne,* no. 260 (3 November 1933): n.p.

"Blut und Boden / Marmorhaus." Review article, *Lichtbild-Bühne,* no. 227 (24 November 1933): n.p.

Boehm, Gottfried. *Wie Bilder Sinn erzeugen. Die Macht des Zeigens.* Berlin: Berlin University Press, 2008.

Bücher, Karl. *Arbeit und Rhythmus. Abhandlungen der philologisch-historischen Classe der königlichen sächsischen Gesellschaft der Wissenschaften* 39:5. Leipzig: S. Hirzel, 1897.

Buchloh, Benjamin. "Gerhart Richter's *Atlas*: The Anomic Archive." *October* 88 (1999): 117-145.

Burchett, Kenneth E. *A Bibligraphical History of the Study and Use of Color from Aristotle to Kandinsky.* Lewiston: Edwin Mellen Press, 2005.

Canjels, Rudner. *Distributing Silent Film Serials. Local Practices, Changing Forms, Cultural Transformation.* New York: Routledge, 2011.

Cartwright, Lisa. *Screening the Body. Tracing Medicine's Visual Culture.* Minneapolis: University of Minnesota Press, 1995.

Cattelan, Paolo. "Malipiero et la musica di *Acciaio.*" In *Walter Ruttmann. Cinema, pittura, ars acustica,* 192-201.

Clarus. "Gespräch mit Ruttmann." In *Walter Ruttmann. Eine Dokumentation,* 79.

—. "Der Schöpfer des abstrakten Films. Walther Ruttmann." *Film-Kurier* no. 243, 11 September 1926. Archiv Seeber, no. 450, Stiftung Deutsche Kinemathek, Berlin.

Cowan, Michael. "Advertising, Rhythm and the Avant-Garde in Weimar: Guido Seeber and Julius Pinschewer's *Kipho* Film." *October* 131 (2010): 23-50

—. "The Ambivalence of Ornament: Silhouette Advertisements in Print and Film in Early-Twentieth-Century Germany." *Art History*, 36:4 (2013): 784-809.

—. "Rethinking the City Symphony after the Age of Industry." *Intermédialités* 11 (2009): 69-86.

—. "Technologies de diffusion simultanée et politique mondiale dans le cinéma de l'entre-deux-guerres." In *Loin des yeux… le cinéma. Imaginaires visuels des technologies de télécommunication.* Ed. Laurent Guido. Lausanne: L'Age d'Homme, forthcoming 2014.

—. *Technology's Pulse: Essays on Rhythm in German Modernism.* London: University of London, IGRS Books, 2012.

Cowan, Michael and Kai Sicks. "28 March 1935. Premiere of *Triumph des Willens* Presents Fascism as Unifier of Communal Will." In *The New History of German Cinema.* Ed. Jennifer Kapczynski and Michael Richardson. Rochester: Camden House, 2012, 255-261.

Crafton, Donald. *Before Mickey. The Animated Film 1898-1928.* Chicago: University of Chicago Press, 1993.

Crary, Jonathan. "Spectacle, Attention, Counter-Memory." *October* 50 (1989): 96-107.

—. *Suspensions of Perception. Attention, Spectacle and Modern Culture.* Cambridge: MIT Press, 1999.

—. *Techniques of the Observer. On Vision and Modernity in the Nineteenth Century.* Cambridge: MIT Press, 1990.

Curtis, Scott. "Einfühlung und die frühe deutsche Filmtheorie." In *Einfühlung. Zu Geschichte und Gegenwart eines ästhetischen Konzepts.* Ed. Robert Curtis and Gertrud Koch. Munich: Fink, 2008, 79-105.

—. "Rough and Smooth: Photographic and Animated Images in Scientific and Educational Film." Unpublished paper delivered at the 29th annual Screen Conference in Glasgow, 30 June 2012.

Daniels, Dieter. "Sound and Vision in Avantgarde & Mainstream" (2004). *Media Art Net* http://www.medienkunstnetz.de/themes/image-sound_relations/sound_vision/1/. Accessed 10.01.2013.

Darré, R. Walther. *Blut und Boden: ein Grundgedanke des Nationalsozialismus. Sonderdruck aus "Odal", Monatsschrift für Blut und Boden.* 21. bis 25. Tausend. Berlin: Reichsdruckerei, 1938.

Daston, Lorraine and Peter Galison. *Objectivity.* New York: Zone Books, 2007.

Deleuze, Gilles. *Cinema 1: The Movement Image.* Trans. Hugh Tomlinson and Barbara Habberjam. London: Continuum, 2005.

Despoix, Philippe. "La miniature urbaine comme genre. Kracauer entre ethnographie urbaine et heuristique du cinéma." In *Culture de masse et modernité. Siegfried Kracauer sociologue, critique, écrivain.* Paris: Maison des Sciences de l'Homme, 2001, 162-179.

Deutsche Panzer. Censor Card no. 57661. Dated 31 August 1940. Bundesarchiv-Filmarchiv, Berlin.

Deutsche Waffenschmieden. Censor card no. 53178. Dated 20 January 1940. Bundesarchiv-Filmarchiv, Berlin.

Deutsches Wörterbuch von Jacob und Wilhelm Grimm. http://woerterbuchnetz.de/DWB/?sigle=DWB&mode=Vernetzung&lemid=GD06628. Accessed 01.12.2012.

Dickinson, Edward Ross. "Biopolitics, Fascism, Democracy: Some Reflections on our Discourse about 'Modernity.'" *Central European History* 37:1 (2004): 1-48.

Dickmann, Herbert. *Deutscher Stahl. I: Bilder aus der Geschichte der deutschen Eisen- und Stahlerzeugung. Stahl überall 3.* Düsseldorf: Beratungsstelle für Stahlverwendung, 1934.

Didi-Huberman, Georges. "La courbe de toute chose." In *Mouvements de l'air. Étienne Jules-Marey, photographe des fluids.* Ed. Georges Didi-Huberman and Laurent Mannoni. Paris: Gallimard, 2004.
—. *L'Image survivante. Histoire de l'art et temps des fantômes selon Warburg.* Paris: Minuit, 2002.
Doane, Mary Ann. *The Emergence of Cinematic Time.* Cambridge: Harvard University Press, 2002.
Domburg, Adrianus van. *Walter Ruttmann in het beginsel.* Purmerend: Nederlands Filminstituut, 1956.
Ehmann, Antje. "Wie Wirklichkeit erzählen? Methoden des Querschnittfilms." In *Geschichte des dokumentarischen Films in Deutschland. Band 2: Weimarer Republik.* Ed. Peter Zimmermann. Stuttgart: Reclam, 2005, 576-600.
Eisenstein, Sergei. "The Cinematographic Principle and the Ideogram." In *Film Form. Essays in Film Theory.* Ed. Jay Leyda. San Diego: Harcourt, 1949, 28-44.
—. "The Dialectical Approach to Film Form." In *Film Form,* 45-63.
—. "Der Kinematograph der Begriffe." In *Der Querschnitt: Das Magazin der aktuellen Ewigkeitswerte.* Ed. Christian Ferber. Frankfurt am Main: Ullstein, 1981, 367-369.
Elder, Bruce. *Harmony and Dissent.* Waterloo: Wilfrid Laurier Universtiy Press, 2008.
Ellis, Jack, and Betsy McLane. *A New History of Documentary Film.* New York: Continuum, 2006.
Elsaesser, Thomas. "Archives and Archeologies: The Place of Non-Fiction Film in Contemporary Media." In *Films That Work. Industrial Film and the Productivity of Media.* Ed. Vinzenz Hediger and Patrick Vonderau. Amsterdam: Amsterdam University Press, 2009, 19-35.
—. "Die Stadt von morgen. Filme zum Bauen und Wohnen." In *Geschichte des dokumentarischen Films in Deutschland, Band 2. Weimarer Republik 1918-1933.* Ed. Klaus Kreimeier, Antje Ehmann and Jeanpaul Goergen. Stuttgart: Reclam, 2005: 381-409.
—. *Weimar Cinema and After. Germany's Historical Imaginary.* New York: Routledge, 2000.
Elsaesser, Thomas and Malte Hagener, "6. September. Walter Ruttmann: 1929." In *1929. Beiträge zur Archäologie der Medien.* Ed. Stefan Andriopoulos and Bernhard Dotzler. Frankfurt am Main: Suhrkamp, 2002: 317-349.
The Encyclopedia of Early Cinema. Ed. Richard Abel. London: Routledge, 2010.
"Der erste abendfüllende Tonfilm im Mozartsaal: Die Melodie der Welt." Review article. *Der Film – Wochenausgabe.* no. 11 (16 March 1929): 273.
"Erstvorführung. 'Altgermanische Bauernkultur.'" *Der Kinematograph* 28, no. 72 (14 April 1934): n.p.
Fabricus, Hans. *Das Program der NSDAP. Grundlagen, Aufbau und Wirtschaftsordnung des nationalsoyialistischen Staates,* no. 6. Berlin: Industrieverlag Spaeth & Linde, 1936.
Falk, Erich. "Bürgersteigreklame." *Die Reklame* 15 (1922): 184.
Feind im Blut. Censor card no. 28713. Dated 16 April 1931. Bundesarchiv-Filmarchiv, Berlin.
"Feind im Blut." Review article. *Der Film* 16, no. 16 (18 April 1931): n.p.
"Feind im Blut." Review article. *Süddeutsche Filmzeitung,* no. 22 (29 May 1931): n.p.
"'Feind im Blut' im Atrium." *Der Kinematograph* 25, no. 89 (17 April 1931): n.p.
"Feind im Blut in veränderter Fassung." *Lichtbild-Bünhne,* no. 102 (29 April 1931): n.p.
"Feind im Blut. Praesens-Film – Atrium." *Lichtbild-Bühne,* no. 93 (18 April 1931): n.p.
Féré, Charles. *Sensation et mouvement.* Paris: Alcan, 1900.

"Film ABC." *Der Film* 16, no. 14 (4 April 1931): n.p.
Film als Film 1910 bis heute. Ed. Birgit Hein and Wulf Herzogenrath. Cologne: Kölnischer Kunstverein, 1977.
Der Film der Weimarer Republik: 1929. Ein Handbuch der zeitgenössischen Kritik. Ed. Gero Gandert. Berlin: De Gruyter, 1997.
Films That Work. Industrial Film and the Productivity of Media. Ed. Vinzenz Hediger and Patrick Vonderau. Amsterdam: Amsterdam University Press, 2009.
"Ein Film von der deutschen Metallspende. Die große Reserve," review article, *Der Film* 25, no. 30 (27 July 1940): n.p.
Forster, Ralf. *Ufa und Nordmark. Zwei Firmengeschichten und der deutsche Werbefilm 1919-1945. Schriftenreihe der Cinémathèque Municipale de Luxembourg* 17. Trier: WVT, 2005.
Foucault, Michel. "Governmentality." In *The Foucault Effect. Studies in Governmentality.* Ed. Graham Burchell, Colin Gordin and Peter Miller. Chicago: University of Chicago Press, 1991, 87-105.
—. *The Order of Things. An Archeology of the Human Sciences.* London: Routledge, 1970.
—. *Security, Territory, Population. Lectures at the Collège de France 1977-1978.* Ed. Michel Senellart. Trans. Graham Burchell. New York: Picador, 2004.
—. *"Society Must Be Defended". Lecture at the College de France 1975-1976.* Ed. Mauro Bertani and Alessandro Fontana. Trans. David Macey. New York: Picador, 2003.
—. "Technologies of the Self." In *Technologies of the Self. A Seminar with Michel Foucault.* Ed. Luther Martin, Huck Gutman, Patrick Hutton. Amherst: University of Massachusetts Press, 1988, 16-49.
Freibe, Holm. "Branding Germany: Hans Domizlaff's *Markentechnik* and Its Ideological Impact." In *Selling Modernity. Advertising in 20th-Century Germany.* Ed. Pamela Swett, Jonathan Wiesen and Jonathan Zatlin. Durham: Duke University Press, 2007, 78- 101.
Freiere, Sergio. "Early Musical Impressions from Both Sides of the Loudspeaker." *Leonardo* 13 (2003): 67-71.
Freud, Sigmund. "Beyond the Pleasure Principle." In *The Standard Edition of the Complete Psychological Works of Sigmund Freud.* Volume 18. Ed. James Strachey. London: The Hogarth Press, 1955, 7-64.
Frisby, David. *Fragments of Modernity.* Cambridge: MIT Press, 1998.
Fritzsche, Peter. *Reading Berlin 1900.* Cambridge: Harvard University Press, 1998.
Fuld, Alexander. "Wo läßt man den Atrax-Reklame-Projektor wirken?" *Die Reklame* 14 (1921): 334.
Fulks, Barry A. *Film Culture and Kulturfilm. Walter Ruttmann, the Avant-Garde Film, and the Kulturfilm in Weimar Germany and the Third Reich.* PhD dissertation, University of Wisconsin – Madison. Ann Arbor: ProQuest/UMI, 1982, publication no. AAT 8304938.
—. "Walter Ruttmann, the Avant-Garde Film, and Nazi Modernism." *Film and History* 14:2 (1984): 26-35.
Furuhata, Yuriko. "Animating Copies: Japanese Graphic Design, the Xerox Machine, and Walter Benjamin." In *Animating Film Theory.* Ed. Karen Beckman. Durham: Duke University Press, forthcoming 2014.
Gance, Abel. "Découpage for La Fin du monde" (1929). Unpublished document. Cinématheque Française. Gance B42. Dossier 109.2.
—. *LA FIN DU MONDE vue par Abel GANCE. Miracle moderne en 3 parties écrit et exécuté par Abel GANCE* (1929). Document held at the Cinémathèque Française. Gance B42. Dossiers 110.2-110.8.

Ganeva, Mila. *Women in Weimar Fashion. Discourses and Displays in German Culture 1918-1933*. Rochester: Camden House, 2008.

Garsha, Jeremiah. "Dictating the Past: The Capture of Medievalism in Nazi Cinematic Propaganda and the Roots of the Holocaust." *Ex Post Facto: Journal of the History Students at San Francisco State University* 19 (2010): 131-147. http://userwww.sfsu.edu/epf/journal_archive/volume_XIX,_2010/garsha_j.pdf. Accessed 15.06.2013.

Gerhard, Gesine. "Breeding Pigs and People for the Third Reich: Richard Walther Darré's Agrarian Ideology." In *How Green Were the Nazis. Nature, Environment and Nation in the Third Reich*. Ed. Franz-Josef Brueggemeier, Mark Cioc and Thomas Zeller. Athens: Ohio University Press, 2005, 129-146.

Gertiser, Anita. "Ekel. Beobachtungen zu einer Strategie im Aufklärungsfilm zur Bekämpfung der Geschlechtskrankheiten der 1920er Jahre," *Figurationen* 1:8 (2008): 61-77.

Geschichte des dokumentarischen Films in Deutschland. Band 1: Kaiserreich 1895-1918. Ed. Uli Jung and Martin Loiperdinger. Stuttgart: Reclam, 2005.

Geschichte des dokumentarischen Films in Deutschland. Band 2: Weimarer Republik 1918-1933. Ed. Klaus Kreimeier, Antje Ehmann and Jeanpaul Goergen. Stuttgart: Reclam, 2005.

Geschichte des dokumentarischen Films in Deutschland. Band 3: 'Drittes Reich' 1933-1945. Ed. Peter Zimmermann and Kay Hoffmann. Stuttgart: Reclam, 2005.

Giese, Fritz. *Methoden der Wirtschaftspsychologie*. Berlin: Urban & Schwarzenberg, 1927.

"Glasbild und Glasstreifen." *Seidels Reklame* 11 (1927): 163.

Gleber, Anke. "Female Flanerie and the Symphony of the City." In *Women in the Metropolis. Gender and Modernity in Weimar Culture*. Ed. Katharina von Ankum. Berkeley: University of California Press, 1997, 67-88.

Goebbels Reden 1932-1945. Ed. Helmut Heiber. Düsseldorf: Droste-Verlag, 1971.

Goergen, Jeanpaul. "In filmo veritas! Inhaltlich vollkommen wahr. Werbefilme und ihre Produzenten." In *Geschichte des dokumentarischen Films in Deutschland. Band 2*, 348-363.

—. "Julius Pinschewer: A Trade-mark Cinema." In *A Second Life. German Cinema's First Decades*. Ed. Thomas Elsaesser. Amsterdam: Amsterdam University Press, 1996, 168-174.

—. "Il montaggio sonoro come 'ars acustica.'" In *Walter Ruttmann. Cinema, pittura, ars acustica*, 177-192.

—. "Walter Ruttmann – Ein Porträt." In *Walter Ruttmann. Eine Dokumentation*, 17-57.

Graeff, Werner and Raoul Hausmann, "Wie sieht der Fotograf" (1933). In *Texte zur Theorie der Fotografie*. Ed. Bernd Stiegler. Stuttgart: Reclam, 2010, 185-196.

Grierson, John. "First Principles of Documentary" (1932). In *Grierson on Documentary*. Berkeley: University of California Press, 1966, 145-156.

Grosz, George. "Man muß Kautschukmann sein!" *Neue Jugend* 1:2 (1917): 1.

Guerin, Frances. *A Culture of Light. Cinema and Technology in 1920s Germany*. Minneapolis: University of Minnesota Press, 2005.

Guido, Laurent. *L'Age du rythme. Cinéma, musicalité et culture du corps dans les theories françaises des années 1910-1930*. Lausanne: Payot, 2007.

—. "Le film comme 'symphonie du monde': l'universalité des gestes rythmiques dans *Melodie der Welt* (1929) et sa réception française." *Intermédialités* 16 (Fall 2010): 105-128.

Gunning, Tom. "In Your Face: Physiognomy, Photography and the Gnostic Mission of Early Film." *Modernism/Modernity* 4 (1997): 1-29.

—. "Loïe Fuller and the Art of Motion: Body, Light, Electricity and the Origins of Cinema." In *Camera Obscura. Camera Lucida. Essays in Honor of Annette Michelson*, ed. Richard Allen and Malcolm Turvey (Amsterdam: Amsterdam University Press, 2003), 75-90.

Gütt, Arthur. *Bevölkerungs- und Rassenpolitik. Grundlagen, Aufbau und Wirtschaftsordnung des nationalsozialistischen Staates 12*. Berlin: Industrieverlag Spaeth & Linde, 1936.

Hacking, Ian. "How Should We Do the History of Statistics?" In *The Foucault Effect*, 181-197.

—. *The Taming of Chance*. Cambridge University Press, 1990.

Hadamovsky, Eugen. *Der Rundfunk im dienste der Volksführung. Gestalten und Erscheinungen der politischen Publizistik 1*. Leipzig: Universitätsverlag von Robert Noske, 1934.

Hagener, Malte. *Moving Forward, Looking Back. The European Avant-Garde and the Invention of Film Culture 1919-1939*. Amsterdam: Amsterdam University Press, 2007.

Hahne, Hans. *Deutsche Vorzeit*. Bielefeld: Velhagen und Klassing, 1933.

Hake, Sabine. *German National Cinema*. London: Routledge, 2007.

—. "Das Kino, die Werbung und die Avantgarde." In *Die Spur durch den Spiegel. Der Film in der Kultur der Moderne*. Ed. Malte Hagener, Johann Schmidt and Michael Wedel. Berlin: Bertz, 2004, 193-206

—. *Topographies of Class. Modern Architecture and Mass Society in Weimar Berlin*. Ann Arbor: University of Michigan Press, 2008.

—. "Urban Spectacle in Walter Ruttmann's *Berlin, Symphony of the Big City*." In *Dancing on the Volcano. Essays on the Culture of the Weimar Republic*. Ed. Thomas W. Kniesche and Stephen Brockmann. Columbia: Camden House, 1994, 127-142.

Hans Richter. Activism, Modernism and the Avant-Garde. Ed. Stephen Forster. Cambridge: MIT Press, 2000.

Hansen, Miriam Bratu. *Cinema and Experience. Siegfried Kracauer, Walter Benjamin and Theodor W. Adorno*. Berkeley: University of California Press, 2012.

"Hapag Empfang," *Der Kinematograph* 23, no. 61 (13 March 1929): 2.

Hapag Weltreise 1933 mit dem Dreischrauben-Luxusdampfer "Resolute". Vom Januar bis Mai. Hamburg: Hamburg-Amerika Linie, 1933.

Hartmann, Frank. "Visualizing Social Facts: Otto Neurath's ISOTYPE Project." In *European Moderism and the Information Society*. Ed. W. Boyd Rayward. Aldershot: Ashgate, 2008, 279-294.

Hartungen, Christoph von. *Psychologie der Reklame*. Stuttgart: Poeschel, 1921.

Hatzfeld, Nicolas, Gwenaële Rot and Alain P. Michel. "Filming Work on Behalf of the Automobile Firm: The Case of Renault (1950-2002)." In *Films That Work*, 187-211.

Heartfield, John, and Kurt Tucholsky. *Deutschland, Deutschland über alles. Ein Bilderbuch von Kurt Tucholsky und vielen Fotografen, montiert von John Heartfield*. 15th ed. Reinbeck bei Hamburg: Rowohlt, 2003.

Hediger, Vinzenz. "Introduction." In *Films That Work*, 8-16.

—. "Record, Rhetoric and Rationalization." In *Films That Work*, 35-51.

Hein, Birgit. *Film im Underground*. Berlin: Ullstein, 1971.

Heller, Heinz. "`Stählerne Romantik´ und Avantgarde. Beobachtungen und Anmerkungen zu Ruttmanns Industriefilmen." In *Triumph der Bilder*. Ed. Peter Zimmermann and Kay Hoffmann. Konstanz, 2003, 105-120.

Henkel. Ein deutsches Werk in seiner Arbeit. Censor card no. 50137. Dated 9 December 1938.

Henkel. Ein deutsches Werk in seiner Arbeit. Censor Card, Filmarchiv-Bundesarchiv. Card no. 50137. Dated 29 December 1938.

"Henny Porten." Review article. *Der Kinematograph* 22, no. 1162 (1929): n.p.

Herf, Jeffrey. *Reactionary Modernism. Technology, Culture and Politics in Weimar and the Third Reich.* Cambridge: Cambridge University Press, 1984.

Herzogenrath, Wulf. "Wer war der Erste?" In *Film als Film,* 8-13.

Hoesel, Robert. "Die Plakatfarben in ihrer Fernwirkung." *Seidels Reklame* 4 (1919): 187-188.

—. "Reklame und Kunst." *Seidels Reklame* 5 (1920): 299.

Hösel, Robert. "Expressionistische Reklameentwürfe." *Seidels Reklame* 6 (1921): 37-40.

—. "Messe für Reklame und Werbewesen." *Seidels Reklame* 6 (1921): 177-180.

—. "Reklame und Kunst." *Seidels Reklame* 5 (1920): 299-300.

—. "Reklamehochflut." *Seidels Reklame* 6 (1921): 145-146.

Huyssen, Andreas. *After the Great Divide. Modernism, Mass Culture, Postmodernism.* Bloomington: Indiana University Press, 1986.

Imort, Michael. "'Planting a Forest Tall and Straight Like the German *Volk*': Visualizing the *Volksgemeinschaft* through Advertising in German Forestry Journals, 1933-1945." In *Selling Modernity. Advertising in 20th-Century Germany.* Ed. Pamela Swett, Jonathan Wiesen and Jonathan Zatlin. Durham: Duke University Press, 2007: 102-126.

"Inserat vom Tage." *Seidels Reklame* 5 (1920): 193.

Jelavich, Peter. *Berlin Alexanderplatz. Radio, Film and the Death of Weimar Culture.* Berkeley: University of California Press, 2009.

Julius Pinschewer. Klassiker des Werbefilms. DVD and CD-Rom. Ed. Martin Loiperdinger. Berlin: Absolute Medien, 2010.

Junge, Uli, and Wolfgang Mühl-Benninghaus. "Die Kulturfilmdiskussion von 1914 bis 1920. Die politische und ideologische Dynamik der Ufa-Gründung." In *Geschichte des dokumentarischen Films in Deutschland. Band 1,* 480-486.

Jünger, Ernst. *Der Arbeiter. Herrschaft und Gestalt.* Hamburg: Hanseatische Verlagsanstalt, 1932.

Kaes, Anton. "Leaving Home: Film, Migration, and the Urban Experience." *New German Critique* 74 (1998): 179-92.

—. *Shell-Shock Cinema. Weimar Culture and the Wounds of War.* Princeton: Princeton University Press, 2009.

—. "Siegfried – A German Film Star. Performing the Nation in Lang's *Nibelungen* Film." In *The German Cinema Book.* Ed. Tim Bergfelder, Erica Carter and Deniz Göktürk. London: British Film Institute, 2002, 63-70.

Kafka, Hans. "Liebe im Querschnitt" (1929). In *Der Film der Weimarer Republik, 1929,* 560.

Keitz, Ursula von. "Die Kinematografie in der Schule. Zur politischen Pädagogik des Unterrichtsfilms von RfdU und RWU." In *Geschichte des dokumentarischen Films in Deutschland. Band 3,* 463-488.

Killen, Andreas. *Berlin Electropolis. Shock, Nerves and German Modernity.* Berkeley: University of California Press, 2006.

Kittler, Friedrich. *Discourse Networks 1800/1900.* Trans. Michael Metteer and Chris Cullens. Stanford: Stanford University Press, 1985.

Kludas, Arnold. *Geschichte der deutschen Passagierschiffahrt. Band IV: Vernichtung und Widergeburt 1914 bis 1930.* Hambrug: Ernst Kabel Verlag, 1989.

Kolaja, Jiri, and Arnold Foster. "*Berlin, the Symphony of a City* as a Theme of Visual Rhythm." *The Journal of Aesthetics and Art Criticism* 23:3 (1965): 353-358.

König, Theodor. *Reklame-Psychologie, ihr gegenwärtiger Stand – ihre praktische Bedeutung,* 2nd ed. Munich and Berlin: R. Oldenbourg, 1924.

Koepnick, Lutz. "The Bearable Lightness of Being: *People on Sunday* (1930)." In *Weimar Cinema. An Essential Guide to Classic Films of the Era.* New York: Columbia University Press, 2009, 236-253.

—. *Walter Benjamin and the Aesthetics of Power.* Lincoln: University of Nebraska Press, 1999.

Korte, Helmut. "Die Welt im Querschnitt: *Berlin – Die Sinfonie der Großstadt* (1927)." In *Fischer Filmgeschichte. Band 2: Der Film als gesellschaftliche Kraft 1925-1944.* Ed. Werner Faulstisch and Helmut Korte. Frankfurt am Main: Fischer, 1991, 75-91.

Kracauer, Siegfried. *From Caligari to Hitler.* Princeton: Princeton University Press, 1947.

—. "Georg Simmel" (1919). In *The Mass Ornament. Weimar Essays.* Ed. and trans. Thomas Y. Levin. Cambridge: Harvard University Press, 1995, 225-259.

—. *Werke 6.1. Kleine Schriften zum Film 1921-1927.* Ed. Inke Müller-Bach. Frankfurt am Main: Suhrkamp, 2004.

Kraszna-Krausz, Andor. "The Querschnittfilm." *Close-Up* 3:5 (November 1928): 25-34.

Kreimeier, Klaus. "Komplex-starr. Semiologie des Kulturfilms." In *Geschichte des dokumentarischen Films in Deutschland. Band 2,* 87-119.

—. *The Ufa Story. A History of Germany's Greatest Film Company 1918-1945.* Trans. Robert Kimber. Berkeley: University of California Press, 1999.

Kurd, Michael. "Melodie der Welt." Review article (1929). In *Der Film der Weimarer Republik: 1929,* 440.

Kurtz, Rudolf. *Expressionismus und Film.* Ed. Christian Kleining and Ulrich Johannes Bell. Berlin: Chronos, 1997.

—. "Die Melodie der Welt." *Lichtbild-Bühne* 22, no. 61 (13 March 1929): n.p.

Kurtzig, Käthe. "Die Arten des Werbefilms." *Industrielle Psychotechnik* 3 (1926): 311-314.

—. "Werbefilm und Volkswirtschaft." *Die Reklame* 20 (1927): 417-418.

Lacoue-Labarthe, Philippe. *Heidegger, Art and Politics.* Trans. Chris Turner. Oxford: Basil Blackwell, 1990.

Lang, Fritz. "Die mimische Kunst im Lichtspiel" (1929). In *Werkstatt Film. Selbstverständnis und Visionen von Filmleuten der 20er Jahre.* Ed. Rolf Aurich and Wolfgang Jacobsen. Berlin: Edition Text & Kritik, 1998, 48-49.

Lavoby. "Notgeld mit Reklame." *Seidels Reklame* 6 (1921): 381.

Lawder, Standish. *The Cubist Cinema.* New York: New York University Press, 1975.

Learning with the Lights off. Educational Film in the United States. Ed. Devin Orgeron, Marsha Orgeron and Dan Streible. Oxford: Oxford University Press, 2012.

Lefèbvre, Thierry. "Représentations cinémagoraphiques de la syphilis entre les deux guerres: séropositivité, traitement et charlatanisme." *Revue historique de la pharmacie* 83 (1995): 267-278.

LeGrice, Malcolm. *Abstract Film and Beyond.* Cambridge: MIT Press, 1977.

Leslie, Esther. *Hollywood Flatlands. Animation, Critical Theory and the Avant-Garde.* London: Verso, 2002.

Lethen, Helmut. *Cool Conduct. The Culture of Distance in Weimar, Germany.* Trans. Don Reneau. Berkeley: University of California Press, 2002.

Leyda, Jay. *Films Beget Films.* New York: Hill and Wang, 1964.

Linde, F. W. von der. *Die Hamburg-Amerika Linie.* Berlin: Widder-Verlag, 1930.

Loiperdinger, Martin. "Neue Sachlichkeit und Nationalsozialismus. Zur Ambivalenz von Walter Ruttmanns Filmen für das Dritte Reich." In *Perspektive des Dokumentarfilms.* Ed. Manfred Hattendorf. Munich: diskurs film Verlag, 1995, 43-56.

Lupton, Ellen. "Reading Isotype." In *Design Discourse. History, Theory, Criticism.* Ed. Victor Margolin. Chicago: University of Chicago Press, 1989, 145-156.

Lüscher, Aurore. "Tourner autour d'un film sanitaire." Conference report. http://hsozkult.geschichte.hu-berlin.de/index.asp?id=3699&view=pdf&pn=tagungsberichte. Accessed 15.06.2013.

M., P. "Von der Wundertrommel bis zum Werbe-Tonfilm." *Lichtbild-Bühne* 22, no. 191 (12 August 1929): n.p.

MacCannell, Dean. *The Ethics of Sightseeing.* Berkeley: University of California Press, 2011.

Macrae, David. "Ruttmann, Rhythm, and 'Reality': A Response to Siegfried Kracauer's Interpretation of *Berlin. The Symphony of a Great City.*" In *Expressionist Film – New Perspectives.* Ed. Dietrich Scheunemann. Rochester: Camden House, 2003, 251-271.

Mannesmann. Censor card no. 47900. Dated 17 March 1938. Bundesarchiv-Filmarchiv, Berlin.

Mannesmann Weldless Steel Tubular Poles. Düsseldorf: Mannesmannröhren-Werke, 1937.

Manovich, Lev. *The Language of New Media.* Cambridge: MIT Press, 2001.

Mattl, Siegfried. "The Ambivalence of Modernism from the Weimar Republic to National Socialism and Red Vienna." *Modern Intellectual History* 6 (2009): 223-234.

Matuszewski, Boleslas. *Ecrits cinémathographiques. Une nouvelle source d'histoire.* Ed. Magdalena Mazaraki. Paris: Cinémathèque Française, 2006.

Mayer, Thomas. "'Gesichtsverlust' vs. Resemantisierung. Überlegungen zum Gesicht des Arbeiters im Nationalsozialismus anhand einiger Filme von Walter Ruttmann." *Montage AV* 13:2 (2004): 75-91.

Mehring, Christine. "Alma Buscher: 'Ship' Building Toy. 1923." In *Bauhaus 1919-1933. Workshops in Modernity.* Ed. Berry Bergdoll and Leah Dickerman. New York: Museum of Modern Art, 2009, 156-162.

"Melodie der Welt." *Süddeutsche Filmzeitung* 8, no. 12 (22 March 1929): 14.

"Die 'Melodie der Welt.' Grundsätzliches zum ersten großen deutschen Tonfilm." *Der Kinematograph* 23, no. 61 (13 March 1929): 1-2.

"Melodien der Welt." Review article (1929). In *Der Film der Weimarer Republik,* 442-443.

Metall des Himmels. Censor card no. 39507. Dated 17 June 1935. Bundesarchiv-Filmarchiv, Berlin.

Metall des Himmels. Censor card no. 41390. Dated 29 January 1936. Filmarchiv-Bundesarchiv, Berlin.

"Metall des Himmels." Review article. *Der Film* 20, no. 9 (2 March 1935): n.p.

Michaelis, Lutz. "Wie entsteht ein Werbetrickfilm?" *Die Reklame* 20 (1927): 434.

Michaud, Philippe-Alain. *Aby Warburg and the Image in Motion.* Trans. Sophie Hawkes. New York: Zone Books, 2004.

Michelson, Anette. "On Montage and the Theory of the Interval." In *Montage and Modern Life, 1919-1942.* Ed. Matthew Teitelbaum. Cambridge: MIT Press, 1992, 60-82.

Minden, Michael. "The City in Early Cinema: *Metropolis, Berlin* and *October.*" In *Unreal City. Urban Experience in Modern European Literature and Art.* Ed. Edward Timms and David Kelley. Manchester: Manchester University Press, 1985, 193-213.

Mitry, Jean. *Le cinéma expérimental.* Paris: Seghers, 1974.

Mjolsness, Lora Wheeler. "Vertov's Soviet Toys: Commerce, Commercialization and Cartoons." *Studies in Russian and Soviet Cinema* 2 (2008): 247-267.

Moede, Walther. "Psychologie der Reklame." *Die Reklame* 13 (1920): 244-245.

Moritz, William. *Optical Poetry. The Life and Work of Oskar Fischinger.* Bloomington: Indiana University Press, 2004.

—. "Resistance and Subversion in Animated Films of the Nazi Era: The Case of Hans Fischerkoesen." In *A Reader in Animation Studies.* Ed. Jayne Pilling. Sydney: John Libbey, 1997, 228-240.

Mutzenbacher, Heinrich. Untitled text on *Melodie der Welt. Illustrierter Film-Kurier* 11, no. 1115 (1929): n.p.

Nahtlose nichtrostende säure- und hitzbeständige Mannesmann-Stahlröhre. Düsseldorf: Mannesmann-Verlag, 1931.

Das neue Buch der Erfindungen, Gewerbe und Industrien, Zweiter Band: Die Kräfte der Natur und ihre Benutzung. 6th ed. Leipzig: Otto Spamer, 1872.

"Neue Tonfilm-Situation." *Lichtbild-Bühne* 22, no. 11 (16 March 1929): 1.

Neumann, Boaz. "The Phenomenology of the German People's Body (*Volkskörper*) and the Extermination of the Jewish Body." *New German Critique* 106 (2009): 149-181.

Nichols, Bill. *Introduction to Documentary.* Bloomington: Indiana University Press, 2004.

—. *Representing Reality. Issues and Concepts in Documentary.* Bloomington: Indiana University Press, 1991.

Nornes, Abé Mark. *Translating Global Cinema.* Minneapolis: University of Minnesota Press, 2007, 123-155.

O'Brien, Mary Elizabeth. *Nazi Cinema as Enchantment. The Politics of Entertainment in the Third Reich.* Rochester: Camden House, 2004.

O'Pray, Michael. *Avant-Garde Film. Forms, Themes and Passions.* New York: Columbia University Press, 2003.

Orgeron, David, Marsha Orgeron and Dan Streible. "Introduction." In *Learning with the Lights off,* 1-14.

Ostherr, Kirsten. "Medical Education through Film: Animating Anatomy at the American College of Surgeons and Eastman Kodak." In *Learning with the Lights off,* 168-192.

Ostwald, Wilhelm. "Farbkunst und Werbekunst." *Die Reklame* 13 (1920): 7-8.

Ott, Frederick W. *The Great German Films.* Secaucus: Citadel, 1986.

Pauli, Fritz. "Das Problem des Werbefilms." *Die Reklame* 19 (1926): 617.

—. *Rhythmus und Resonanz als ökonomisches Prinzip in der Reklame.* Berlin: Verband deutscher Reklamefachleute, 1926.

Peterson, Jennifer. "Glimpses of Animal Life: Nature Films and the Emergence of Classroom Cinema." In *Learning with the Lights off,* 145-167.

Peukert, Detlev. *The Weimar Republic.* Trans. Richard Daveson. New York: Hill and Wang, 1993.

Pfiffikus. "Spaziergänge im Reklamewald." *Die Reklame* 14 (1921): 253-254.

Piccardi, Carlo. "Rapporti tra suono e vision nel cinema di Ruttmann." In *Walter Ruttmann. Cinema, pittura, ars acustica,* 93-136.

Pinschewer, Julius. "Der Trickfilm in der Reklame" (1938). *Julius Pinschewer. Klassiker des Werbefilms.* CD-Rom Teil 1. Extras.

—. "Von den Anfängen des Werbefilms," *Die Reklame* 20 (1927): 408-411.

Pinthus, Kurt. "Ethische Möglichkeiten im Film." In *Der Film von morgen.* Ed. Hugo Zehder. Berlin: Rudolf Kaemmerer Verlag, 1923, 117-129.

Poculla, Max. "Der Verkehrswart. Eine Neue Strassenreklame in Berlin." *Die Reklame* 15 (1922): 180-182.

Pol, Heinz. "Die Melodie der Welt." Review article (1929). In *Der Film der Weimarer Republik: 1929*, 441-442.

Potter, Pamela. "Music in the Third Reich: The Complex Task of 'Germanicization.'" In *The Arts in Nazi Germany. Continuity, Conformity, Change.* Ed. Jonathan Huener and Francis Nicosia. Burlington: Berghan Books, 2006, 85-110.

Pudovkin, Vsevelod. *Film Technique and Film Acting.* New York: Grove Press, 1960.

"Praesens startet 'Feind im Blut.'" *Lichtbild-Bühne*, no. 91 (16 April 1931): n.p.

Quaresima, Leonardo. "Astrazione e romanticismo. Walter Ruttmann e la mobilità del moderno." In *Walter Ruttmann. Cinema, pittura, ars acustica*, 15-50.

Der Querschnitt. Das Magazin der aktuellen Ewigkeitswerte 1924-1933. Ed. Christian Ferber. Berlin: Ullstein, 1981.

Rampley, Mathew. "Archives of Memory: Walter Benjamin's *Arcades Project* and Aby Warburg's *Mnemosyne Atlas*." In *The Optic of Walter Benjamin*. Ed. Alex Coles. London: Black Dog Publishing, 1999, 94-119.

Rancière, Jacques. *Dissensus. On Politics and Aesthetics.* Ed. and trans. Steven Corcoran. London: Continuum, 2010.

—. "The Surface of Design." Trans. Gregory Elliot. In *The Future of the Image.* London: Verso, 2007, 91-108.

Rees, A. L. "Frames and Windows: Visual Space in Abstract Cinema." In *Avant-Garde Film.* Ed. Alexander Graf and Dietrich Scheunemann. Amsterdam: Rodolpi, 2007, 55-77.

"Reichserbhofgesetz." *Deutsches Reichsgesetzblatt 1933*. Part 1, 685-692.

Rendschmidt. "Der Bauzaun als Reklameträger." *Seidels Reklame* 7 (1922): 257-258.

Rentschler, Eric. "Emotional Engineering: Hitler Youth Quex. *Modernism/Modernity* 2:3 (1995): 23-44.

Richter, Hans. *Filmgegner von heute, Filmfreunde von morgen.* Berlin: Reckendorf, 1929.

—. "Die schlecht trainierte Seele." In *G. Material zur elementaren Gestaltung* 3 (1924): 44-47.

Rogers, Holly. "The Unification of the Senses: Intermediality in Video Art-Music." *Journal of the Royal Musical Association* 136:2 (2011): 399-428.

Ross, Colin. *Mit dem Kurbelkasten um die Erde*. Berlin: Bild und Buch Verlag, 1926.

Ross, Corey. "Mass Politics and the Techniques of Leadership: The Promise and Perils of Propaganda in Weimar Germany." *German History* 24:2 (2006): 184-193.

—. "La professionalisation de la publicité et de la propagande dans l'Allemagne de Weimar." *Vingtième Siècle* 101 (2009): 2-26.

—. "Visions of Prosperity: The Americanization of Advertising in Interwar Germany." In *Selling Modernity. Advertising in 20th-Century Germany.* Ed. Pamela Swett, Jonathan Wiesen and Jonathan Zatlin. Durham: Duke University Press, 2007, 52-77.

Rother, Rainer. *Leni Riefesntahl. The Seduction of Genius.* Trans. Martin Bott. London: Continuum, 2002.

Rudwick, Martin. "The Emergence of a Visual Language for Geological Science 1760-1840." *History of Science* 14 (1976): 149-195.

Rügner, Ulrich. "Walter Ruttmann pioniere del cinema sonoro." In *Walter Ruttmann. Cinema, pittura, ars acustica*, 166-176.

"Rund um die Liebe." Review article (1929). In *Der Film der Weimarer Republik: 1929*, 560.

Ruttmann, Walter. "Die absolute Mode" (1928). In *Walter Ruttmann. Eine Dokumentation*, 82

—. "Berlin? – Berlin!" (1927). In *Walter Ruttmann. Eine Dokumentation*, 79.

—. "Film und Werkfilm." Unpublished manuscript (1940). In *Walter Ruttmann. Eine Dokumentation,* 93.
—. "Der isolierte Künstler" (1929). In *Walter Ruttmann. Eine Dokumentation,* 85-86.
—. "Kino als Kunst" (1925). In *Walter Ruttmann. Eine Dokumentation,* 78.
—. "Kunst und Kino." Undated manuscript. In *Walter Ruttmann. Eine Dokumentation,* 73.
—. "Malerei mit Zeit." Undated manuscript. In *Walter Ruttmann. Eine Dokumentation,* 73-75.
—. "Mein neuer Film" (1926). In *Walter Ruttmann. Eine Dokumentation,* 78-79.
—. "Moderne Werbung im Film" (1929). In *Walter Ruttmann. Eine Dokumentation,* 86.
—. "Der neue Film" (1927). In *Walter Ruttmann. Eine Dokumentation,* 80.
—. Patentschrift: Verfahen und Vorrichtung zum Herstellen kinematographischer Bilder" (1920). In *Walter Ruttmann. Eine Dokumentation,* 75-78.
—. "Prinzipielles zum Tonfilm" (1929). In *Walter Ruttmann. Eine Dokumentation,* 83.
—. "Die Russen und wir" (1928). In *Walter Ruttmann. Eine Dokumentation,* 83.
—. "Technik und Film" (1930). In *Walter Ruttmann. Eine Dokumentation,* 87-89.
—. "Tonfilm? – !" *Illustrierter Film-Kurier* 11, no 1115 (1929): n.p.
—. "Wie ich meinen BERLIN-Film drehte" (1927). In *Walter Ruttmann. Eine Dokumentation,* 80.
"Ruttmann plaudert" (1935). In *Walter Ruttmann. Eine Dokumentation,* 92.
S., H. "Der Film der Zukunft." *Lichtbild-Bühne* 23, no.70 (23 March 1929): 20.
Sadoul, Georges. *Histoire du cinéma mondiale des origines à nos jours.* 9th ed. Paris: Flammarion, 1949.
Sahl, Hans. "Triumph der Photomontage / Melodie der Welt." Review article (1929). In *Der Film der Weimarer Republik: 1929,* 442.
Sánchez-Biosca, Vicente. "Tra musica visiva e macchinismo: il montaggio di *Berlin. Die Sinfonie der Großstadt.*" In *Walter Ruttmann. Cinema, pittura, ars acustica,* 145-153.
Sarasin, Philipp. "Feind im Blut: Die Bedeutung des Blutes in der deutschen Bakteriologie, 1870-1900." In *Mythen des Blutes.* Ed. Christina von Braun and Christoph Wulf. Frankfurt am Main: Campus, 2007, 296-310.
Saß, Susan Krüger. "'Nordische Kunst'. Die Bedeutung des Begriffes während des Nationalsozialismus." In *Kunstgeschichte im Dritten Reich. Theorien, Methoden, Praktiken.* Ed. Ruth Heftrig, Olaf Peters, Barbara Schellewald. Berlin: Akademie-Verlag, 2008, 224-245.
Sauerteig, Lutz. *Krankheit, Sexualität, Gesellschaft. Geschlechtskrankheiten und Gesundheitspolitik in Deutschland im 19. und im frühen 20. Jahrhundert.* Stuttgart: Steiner, 1999.
Schenk, Imbert. "Walter Ruttmanns Kultur- und Industriefilme." In *Mediale Mobilmachung I. Das Dritte Reich und der Film.* Ed. Harro Segeberg. Munich: Wilhelm Fink, 2005, 103-128.
Schieferstein, Heinrich von. "Die Ausnützung mechanischer Schwingungen im Maschinenbau." *Bayerisches Industrie- und Gewerbeblatt* 111, no. 19 (1 October 1925): 117-123, 125-129.
Schiff in Not. Censor card no. 44042. Dated 20 November 1936.
Schimmer, Fritz. "Zur Frage des Reichsfilmarchivs." *Lichtbild-Bühne* 19, no. 79 (3 April 1926): 11-14.
Schleugl, Hans, and Ernst Schmidt, Jr. *Eine Subgeschichte des Films. Lexikon des Avantgarde-, Experimental- und Undergroundfilms.* 2 vols. Frankfurt am Main: Surhkamp, 1974.

Schnalke, Thomas. "Casting Skin: Meanings for Doctors, Artists and Patients." In *Models. The Third Dimension of Science.* Ed. Soraya de Chadarevian and Nick Hopwood. Stanford: Stanford University Press, 2004, 207-241.

Schobert, Robert. "'Painting in Time' and 'Visual Music': On German Avant-garde Films of the 1920s." In *Expressionist Film. New Perspectives.* Ed. Dietrich Scheunemann. New York: Camden House, 2003.

Schönemann, Anika. *Der deutsche Animationsfilm von den Anfängen bis zur Gegenwart, 1909-2001.* Sankt Augustin: Gardez!, 2003.

Schoots, Hans. "Zooming Out: Walter Ruttmann and Joris Ivens." In *Triumph der Bilder. Kultur- und Dokumentarfilme vor 1945 im internationalen Vergleich.* Ed. Peter Zimmermann und Kay Hoffmann. Stuttgart: Haus des Dokumentarfilms, 2003, 235-251.

Schwartz, Frederic J. "The Eye of the Expert: Walter Benjamin and the Avant Garde." *Art History* 24:3 (2001): 401-444.

Seckendorf, Martin. "Kulturelle Deutschtumspflege im Übergang von Weimar zu Hitler am Beispiel des deutschen Ausland-Institutes (DAI). Eine Fallstudie." In *Völkische Wissenschaft. Gestalten und Tendenzen der deutschen und österreichischen Volkskunde in der ersten Hälfte des 20. Jahrhunderts.* Ed. Wolfgang Jacobeit, Hannjost Lixfeld, Olaf Bochkorn. Wien: Böhlau, 1994, 115–135.

Selling Modernity. Advertising in Twentieth-Century Germany. Ed. Pamela Swett, Jonathan Wiesen, Jonathan Zatlin. Durham: Duke University Press, 2007.

Sicks, Kai. "'Der Querschnitt' oder: Die Kunst des Sporttreibens." In *Leibhaftige Moderne. Körper in Kunst und Massenmedien 1918-1933.* Ed. Michael Cowan and Kai Sicks. Bielefeld: transcript, 2005, 33-48.

Simmel, Georg. "Soziologie der Sinne." In *Aufsätze und Abhandlungen 1901-1908,* vol. 2. Frankfurt am Main: Suhrkamp, 1993, 276-292.

Snedden, David. *Educational Sociology.* New York: Columbia University Teachers College, 1917.

Sontag, Susan. "Fascinating Fascism." In *Under the Sign of Saturn.* New York: Farrar, Strauss and Giroux, 1980, 73-105.

Stahlfibel. Düsseldorf: Beratungsstelle für Stahlverwendung, 1935.

Steinthal, Walther. "Melodie der Welt." Review article (1929), In *Der Film der Weimarer Republik: 1929,* 439-440.

Strathausen, Carsten. "Uncanny Spaces: The City in Ruttmann and Vertov." In *Screening the City.* Ed. Mark Shiel and Tony Fitzmaurice. London and New York: Verso, 2003, 15-40.

Stuttgart, die Großstadt zwischen Wald und Reben. Censor card no. 40688. Dated 4 December 1935. Bundesarchiv-Filmarchiv, Berlin.

Sylvester, Reuel Hull. *The Form Board Test.* PhD dissertation. Princeton University, 1913.

Theweleit, Klaus. *Male Fantasies. Volume 2. Male Bodies. Psychoanalyzing the White Terror.* Minneapolis: University of Minnesota Press, 1989.

Thompson, Kristin. "Preserving Two Masters." In David Bordwell and Kristin Thompson, *Observations on Film Art* (blog). 10 December 2008. http://www.davidbordwell.net/blog/2008/12/10/preserving-two-masters/. Accessed 10.01.2013.

Titz, W. R. "Reklame auf Straßenbahnfahrscheinen." *Die Reklame* 15 (1922): 271-272.

Tooze, J. Adam. *Statistics and the German State 1900-1945. The Making of Modern Economic Knowledge.* Cambridge: Cambridge University Press, 2001.

Tröhler, Margrit. *Offene Welten ohne Helden. Plurale Figurenkonstellationen im Film.* Zürich: Schüren, 2007.

Tschammer und Osten, Hans von. *Sport und Leibesübungen im nationalsozialistischen Staat. Grundlagen, Aufbau und Wirtschaftsordnung des nationalsozialistischen Staates 10a.* Berlin: Industrieverlag Spaeth & Linde, 1936.

Uricchio, William. "Ruttmann nach 1933." In *Walter Ruttmann. Eine Dokumentation,* 59-65.

—. *Ruttmann's "Berlin" and the City Film to 1930.* PhD dissertation. New York University, 1981.

Useful Cinema. Ed. Charles Acland and Haidee Wasson. Durham: Duke University Press, 2006.

Vertov, Dziga. *Kino-Eye. The Writings of Dziga Vertov,* ed. Anette Michelson, trans. Kevin O'Brien. Berkeley: University of California Press, 1984.

Viddler, Anthony. *Warped Space. Art, Architecture and Anxiety in Modern Culture.* Cambridge: MIT Press, 2000.

Virilio, Paul. *War and Cinema.* Trans. Patrick Camiller. London: Verso, 1989.

Walter Ruttmann. Cinema, pittura, ars acustica. Ed. Leonardo Quaresima. Trento: Manfrini, 1994.

Walter Ruttmann. Eine Dokumentation. Ed. Jeanpaul Goergen. Berlin: Freunde der Deutschen Kinemathek, 1989.

Ward, Janet. *Weimar Surfaces. Urban Visual Culture in 1920s Germany.* Berkeley: California University Press, 2001.

Waz, Gerlinde. "Heia Safari! Träume von einer verlorenen Welt. Expeditions-, Kolonial- und ethnographische Film." In *Geschichte des dokumentarischen Films in Deutschland. Band 2,* 187-203.

Wedderkop, Hermann von. "Jahresbilanz" (1925). In *Der Querschnitt. Das Magazin der aktuellen Ewigkeitswerte,* 85-87.

—. "Der Siegeszug des 'Querschnitt'" (1924). In *Der Querschnitt. Das Magazin der aktuellen Ewigkeitswerte,* 6.

Weitz, Eric. *Weimar Germany. Promise and Tragedy.* Princeton: Princeton University Press, 2007.

Westbrock, Ingrid. *Der Werbefilm. Ein Beitrag zur Entwicklungsgeschichte des Genres vom Stummfilm zum frühen Tonfilm.* Hildesheim: Georg Olms, 1983.

Westerdale, Joel. "The Musical Pomise of Abstract Film." In *The Many Faces of Weimar Cinema. Rediscovering Germany's Filmic Legacy.* Ed. Christian Rogowski. Rochester: Camden House, 2010, 153-167.

Wiesen, S. Jonathan. *Creating the Nazi Marketplace. Commerce and Consumption in the Third Reich.* Cambridge: Cambridge University Press, 2011.

Wilke, Sabine. "'Verrottet, verkommen, von fremder Rasse durchsetzt': The Nazi 'Kulturfilm' 'Ewiger Wald' (1936)." *German Studies Review* 24:2 (2001): 353-376.

Windisch, Albert. "Gebrauchsgraphik in Frankfurt am Main." *Die Reklame* 16 (1923): 84-85.

Witlin, Leo. "Von der Psychomechanik des Zuschauers." *Filmtechnik,* no. 23 (1927): 407.

Wölfflin, Heinrich. *Die Kunst der Renaissance. Italien und das deutsche Formgefühl.* Munich: Brückmann, 1931.

Worringer, Wilhelm. *Abstraktion und Einfühlung.* 14th ed. Munich: Piper, 1987.

Zglienicki, Friederich. *Der Weg des Films. Die Geschichte der Kinematographie und ihrer Vorläufer.* Berlin: Rembrandt, 1956.

Ziege, Fritz. "Neue Wege der Filmpropaganada." *Die Reklame* 18 (1925): 155.
Zimmermann, Peter. "Filmpropaganda und Warenästhetik." In *Geschichte des dokumentarischen Films in Deutschland. Band 3*, 505-510.
—. "Landschaft und Bauerntum." In *Geschichte des dokumentarischen Films in Deutschland. Band 3*, 309-319.
—. "Neusachlicher Technikkult und 'stählerne Romantik'. Walter Ruttmanns Symphonien der Industriearbeit." In *Geschichte des dokumentarischen Films in Deutschland. Band 3*, 231-241.
Zimmermann, Yvonne. "A Missing Chapter: The Swiss Films and Richter's Documentary Practice," in *Hans Richter: Encounters*. Exhibition catalogue. Ed. Timothy O. Benson. Los Angeles: Los Angeles County Museum of Art, 2013: 108-119.
Zinman, Gregory. "Analog Circuit Palettes, Cathode Ray Canvases: Digital Analog, Experimental Past." *Film History* 24:2 (2012): 135-157.
Zryd, Michael. "Experimental Film as Useless Cinema." In *Useful Cinema*, 315-336.

Filmography

The following list includes films mentioned or analyzed in the present book. For a complete and annotated list, readers may consult Jeanpaul Goergen's *Walter Ruttmann. Eine Dokumentation.*

ABERGLAUBE (SUPERSTITION, GER 1940).
ACCIAIO (STEEL, IT 1933).
ALTGERMANISCHE BAUERNKULTUR (ANCIENT GERMAN AGRARIAN CULTURE, GER 1934).
DER AUFSTIEG (THE ASCENT, GER 1926).
BERLIN. DIE SINFONIE DER GROSSSTADT (BERLIN. THE SYMPHONY OF A GREAT CITY, GER 1927).
BLUT UND BODEN. GRUNDLAGEN ZUM NEUEN REICH (BLOOD AND SOIL. FOUNDATIONS OF THE NEW REICH, GER 1933). Co-directed with Rolf von Sonjevski-Jamrowski, Hans von Passavant, and Ernst Th. Bruger.
DEUTSCHE PANZER (GERMAN TANKS, GER 1940).
DEUTSCHE WAFFENSCHMIEDEN (GERMAN WEAPONS MANUFACTURERS, GER 1939).
DORT WO DER RHEIN (THERE WHERE THE RHINE, GER 1927).
FEIND IM BLUT (ENEMY IN THE BLOOD, CH/GER 1931).
EIN FILM GEGEN DIE VOLKSKRANKHEIT KREBS
LA FIN DU MONDE (THE END OF THE WORLD, FR 1931). Directed by Abel Gance.
LA GUERRE ENTRE LE FILM INDEPÉNDANT ET LE FILM INDUSTRIEL / TEMPÊTE SUR LA SARRAZ (STORMING OF LA SARRAZ, CH 1929). Directed by Sergei Eisenstein and Hans Richter.
DES HAARES UND DER LIEBE WELLEN (WAVES OF HAIR AND LOVE, GER 1929).
HELDEN DER KÜSTE (HEROES OF THE COAST, GER 1937).
HENKEL. EIN DEUTSCHES WERK IN SEINER ARBEIT (HENKEL. A GERMAN FACTORY AT WORK, GER 1938).
IM DIENSTE DER MENSCHHEIT (IN THE SERVICE OF HUMANITY, GER 1938).
IM ZEICHEN DES VERTRAUENS (UNDER THE SIGN OF TRUST, GER 1937).
IN DER NACHT. EINE MUSIKALISCHE BILDPHANTASIE (IN THE NIGHT: A MUSICAL VISUAL FANTASY, GER 1931).
KLEINER FILM EINER GROSSEN STADT ... DIE STADT DÜSSELDORF AM RHEIN (LITTLE FILM OF A BIG CITY ... THE CITY OF DÜSSELDORF ON THE RHINE, GER 1935).
LICHTSPIEL OPUS I (LIGHTPLAY OPUS I, GER 1921).
LICHTSPIEL OPUS II (LIGHTPLAY OPUS II, GER 1922).
MANNESMANN. EIN FILM DER MANNESMANN RÖHREN-WERKE (MANNESMANN. A FILM OF THE MANNESMANN PIPE INDUSTRY, GER 1937).
MANNESMANN. EIN UFA KULTUFILM NACH DEM INTERNATIONAL PREISGEKRÖNTEN FILM (MANNESMANN. AN UFA KULTURFILM ADAPTED FROM THE INTERNATIONAL AWARD-WINNING FILM, GER 1938).

Melodie der Welt (Melody of the World, GER 1929).

Metall des Himmels (Metal from the Sky, GER 1935).

Die Nibelungen (GER 1924). Directed by Fritz Lang.

Ruttmann Opus III (GER 1925).

Ruttmann Opus IV (GER 1925).

Schiff in Not (Ship in Distress, GER 1936).

Der Sieger. Ein Film in Farben (The Victor. A Film in Colors, GER 1922).

Spiel der Wellen (Play of the Waves, GER 1926).

Stadt Stuttgart. 100. Cannstatter Volksfest (Stuttgart. The Hundredth Cannstatt Festival, GER 1935).

Stuttgart, die Grossstadt zwischen Wald und Reben – die Stadt des Auslanddeutschtums (Stuttgart, the City between Forest and Vines. The City of Germany Abroad, GER 1935).

Tönende Welle (Resounding Waves, GER 1931).

Der Warthegau (The Warthe District, GER 1940).

Weekend (GER 1930).

Weltstrasse See – Welthafen Hamburg (The Ocean as World Route – Hamburg as World Port, GER 1938).

Das wiedergefundene Paradies (Paradise Regained, GER 1925).

Das Wunder. Ein Film in Farben (The Miracle. A Film in Colors, GER 1922).

Index of Names

Index of Film Titles

Index of Subjects

Film Culture in Transition

General Editor: *Thomas Elsaesser*

Thomas Elsaesser, Robert Kievit and Jan Simons (eds.)
Double Trouble: Chiem van Houweninge on Writing and Filming, 1994
ISBN paperback 978 90 5356 025 9

Thomas Elsaesser, Jan Simons and Lucette Bronk (eds.)
Writing for the Medium: Television in Transition, 1994
ISBN paperback 978 90 5356 054 9

Karel Dibbets and Bert Hogenkamp (eds.)
Film and the First World War, 1994
ISBN paperback 978 90 5356 064 8

Warren Buckland (ed.)
The Film Spectator: From Sign to Mind, 1995
ISBN paperback 978 90 5356 131 7; ISBN hardcover 978 90 5356 170 6

Egil Törnqvist
Between Stage and Screen: Ingmar Bergman Directs, 1996
ISBN paperback 978 90 5356 137 9; ISBN hardcover 978 90 5356 171 3

Thomas Elsaesser (ed.)
A Second Life: German Cinema's First Decades, 1996
ISBN paperback 978 90 5356 172 0; ISBN hardcover 978 90 5356 183 6

Thomas Elsaesser
Fassbinder's Germany: History Identity Subject, 1996
ISBN paperback 978 90 5356 059 4; ISBN hardcover 978 90 5356 184 3

Thomas Elsaesser and Kay Hoffmann (eds.)
Cinema Futures: Cain, Abel or Cable? The Screen Arts in the Digital Age, 1998
ISBN paperback 978 90 5356 282 6; ISBN hardcover 978 90 5356 312 0

Siegfried Zielinski
Audiovisions: Cinema and Television as Entr'Actes in History, 1999
ISBN paperback 978 90 5356 313 7; ISBN hardcover 978 90 5356 303 8

Kees Bakker (ed.)
Joris Ivens and the Documentary Context, 1999
ISBN paperback 978 90 5356 389 2; ISBN hardcover 978 90 5356 425 7

Egil Törnqvist
Ibsen, Strindberg and the Intimate Theatre: Studies in TV Presentation, 1999
ISBN paperback 978 90 5356 350 2; ISBN hardcover 978 90 5356 371 7

Michael Temple and James S. Williams (eds.)
The Cinema Alone: Essays on the Work of Jean-Luc Godard 1985-2000, 2000
ISBN paperback 978 90 5356 455 4; ISBN hardcover 978 90 5356 456 1

Patricia Pisters and Catherine M. Lord (eds.)
Micropolitics of Media Culture: Reading the Rhizomes of Deleuze and Guattari, 2001
ISBN paperback 978 90 5356 472 1; ISBN hardcover 978 90 5356 473 8

William van der Heide
Malaysian Cinema, Asian Film: Border Crossings and National Cultures, 2002
ISBN paperback 978 90 5356 519 3; ISBN hardcover 978 90 5356 580 3

Bernadette Kester
Film Front Weimar: Representations of the First World War in German Films of the Weimar Period (1919-1933), 2002
ISBN paperback 978 90 5356 597 1; ISBN hardcover 978 90 5356 598 8

Richard Allen and Malcolm Turvey (eds.)
Camera Obscura, Camera Lucida: Essays in Honor of Annette Michelson, 2003
ISBN paperback 978 90 5356 494 3

Ivo Blom
Jean Desmet and the Early Dutch Film Trade, 2003
ISBN paperback 978 90 5356 463 9; ISBN hardcover 978 90 5356 570 4

Alastair Phillips
City of Darkness, City of Light: Émigré Filmmakers in Paris 1929-1939, 2003
ISBN paperback 978 90 5356 634 3; ISBN hardcover 978 90 5356 633 6

Thomas Elsaesser, Alexander Horwath and Noel King (eds.)
The Last Great American Picture Show: New Hollywood Cinema in the 1970s, 2004
ISBN paperback 978 90 5356 631 2; ISBN hardcover 978 905356 493 6

Thomas Elsaesser (ed.)
Harun Farocki: Working on the Sight-Lines, 2004
ISBN paperback 978 90 5356 635 0; ISBN hardcover 978 90 5356 636 7

Kristin Thompson
Herr Lubitsch Goes to Hollywood: German and American Film after World War I, 2005
ISBN paperback 978 90 5356 708 1; ISBN hardcover 978 90 5356 709 8

Marijke de Valck and Malte Hagener (eds.)
Cinephilia: Movies, Love and Memory, 2005
ISBN paperback 978 90 5356 768 5; ISBN hardcover 978 90 5356 769 2

Thomas Elsaesser
European Cinema: Face to Face with Hollywood, 2005
ISBN paperback 978 90 5356 594 0; ISBN hardcover 978 90 5356 602 2

Michael Walker
Hitchcock's Motifs, 2005
ISBN paperback 978 90 5356 772 2; ISBN hardcover 978 90 5356 773 9

Nanna Verhoeff
The West in Early Cinema: After the Beginning, 2006
ISBN paperback 978 90 5356 831 6; ISBN hardcover 978 90 5356 832 3

Anat Zanger
Film Remakes as Ritual and Disguise: From Carmen to Ripley, 2006
ISBN paperback 978 90 5356 784 5; ISBN hardcover 978 90 5356 785 2

Wanda Strauven
The Cinema of Attractions Reloaded, 2006
ISBN paperback 978 90 5356 944 3; ISBN hardcover 978 90 5356 945 0

Malte Hagener
Moving Forward, Looking Back: The European Avant-garde and the Invention of Film Culture, 1919-1939, 2007
ISBN paperback 978 90 5356 960 3; ISBN hardcover 978 90 5356 961 0

Tim Bergfelder, Sue Harris and Sarah Street
Film Architecture and the Transnational Imagination: Set Design in 1930s European Cinema, 2007
ISBN paperback 978 90 5356 984 9; ISBN hardcover 978 90 5356 980 1

Jan Simons
Playing the Waves: Lars von Trier's Game Cinema, 2007
ISBN paperback 978 90 5356 991 7; ISBN hardcover 978 90 5356 979 5

Marijke de Valck
Film Festivals: From European Geopolitics to Global Cinephilia, 2007
ISBN paperback 978 90 5356 192 8; ISBN hardcover 978 90 5356 216 1

Asbjørn Grønstad
Transfigurations: Violence, Death, and Masculinity in American Cinema, 2008
ISBN paperback 978 90 8964 010 9; ISBN hardcover 978 90 8964 030 7

Vinzenz Hediger and Patrick Vonderau (eds.)
Films that Work: Industrial Film and the Productivity of Media, 2009
ISBN paperback 978 90 8964 013 0; ISBN hardcover 978 90 8964 012 3

François Albera and Maria Tortajada (eds.)
Cinema beyond Film: Media Epistemology in the Modern Era, 2010
ISBN paperback 978 90 8964 083 3; ISBN hardcover 978 90 8964 084 0

Pasi Väliaho
Mapping the Moving Image: Gesture, Thought and Cinema circa 1900, 2010
ISBN paperback 978 90 8964 140 3; ISBN hardcover 978 90 8964 141 0

Pietsie Feenstra
New Mythological Figures in Spanish Cinema: Dissident Bodies under Franco, 2011
ISBN paperback 978 90 8964 304 9; ISBN hardcover 978 90 8964 303 2

Eivind Røssaak (ed.)
Between Stillness and Motion: Film, Photography, Algorithms, 2011
ISBN paperback 978 90 8964 212 7; ISBN hardcover 978 90 8964 213 4

Tara Forrest
Alexander Kluge: Raw Materials for the Imagination, 2011
ISBN paperback 978 90 8964 272 1; ISBN hardcover 978 90 8964 273 8

Belén Vidal
Figuring the Past: Period Film and the Mannerist Aesthetic, 2012
ISBN 978 90 8964 282 0

Bo Florin
Transition and Transformation: Victor Sjöström in Hollywood 1923-1930, 2012
ISBN 978 90 8964 504 3

Erika Balsom
Exhibiting Cinema in Contemporary Art, 2013
ISBN 978 90 8964 471 8

Christian Jungen
Hollywood in Canne$: The History of a Love-Hate Relationship, 2014
ISBN 978 90 8964 566 1

Michael Cowan
Walter Ruttmann and the Cinema of Multiplicity: Avant-Garde Film – Advertising – Modernity, 2014
ISBN 978 90 8964 585 2

Temenuga Trifonova
Warped Minds: Cinema and Psychopathology, 2014
ISBN 978 90 8964 632 3

Christine N. Brinckmann
Color and Empathy: Essays on Two Aspects of Film, 2014
ISBN 978 90 8964 656 9

François Albera and Maria Tortajada (eds.)
Cine-Dispositives: Essays in Epistemology Across Media, 2015
ISBN 978 90 8964 666 8

Volker Pantenburg
Farocki/Godard: Film as Theory, 2015
ISBN 978 90 8964 891 4

Paul Cuff
A Revolution for the Screen: Abel Gance's NAPOLÉON, 2015
ISBN 978 90 8964 734 4